A CRITIQUE ON ŚABDA

Sri Garib Dass Oriental Series No. 112

A CRITIQUE ON ŚABDA

(Based on Viśvanātha's Bhāṣāpariccheda)

Ashok Kumar Goswami

Sri Satguru Publications
A Division of
Indian Books Centre
Delhi - India.

Published by :

SRI SATGURU PUBLICATIONS
Indological and Oriental Publishers
A Division of
INDIAN BOOKS CENTRE
40/5, Shakti Nagar,
Delhi-110007
(INDIA)

First Edition : Delhi. 1991

ISBN 81-7030-247-1

PRINTED IN INDIA

DEDICATED
TO THE SACRED MEMORY OF
MY MOTHER

CONTENTS

PREFACE

I had the pleasure and privilege of studying the *Bhāṣāpariccheda* as a text book in the M.A. Class of the Gauhati University during the years 1959-1961. During that period I developed a keen interest in epistemological studies. Later on I had the scope to teach the second chapter of the *Sāhityadarpaṇa* in the M.A. classes of the Gauhati Univeristy.

In respect of the contents of the Śabdakhaṇḍa of the *Bhāṣā pariccheda* and the second chapter of the *Darpaṇa*, there are a number of points of agreement and disagreement. As I explained things to my students and tried to reconcile the trends of these two different texts, I came to realise that the Śabdakhaṇḍa itself requires a more comprehensive exposition. Thus, I had been toying with the idea of studying the said Śabdakhaṇḍa more seriously as a research project for over a decade or so. But the idea could not be more promptly translated into action mainly because of physical disabilities.

The present work is an abridged form of my Ph.D. thesis 'THE ŚABDA KHAṆḌA OF THE BHĀṢĀPARICCHEDA'.

The scheme of the present work is somewhat unusual inas much as it is in the form of a running commentary written in English. It is divided into two broad parts. The first part comprises of the Introduction which again consists of three subsections A.B. & C. The section A is devoted to a general survey of Indian Philosophy with special reference to the Nyāya-vaiśeṣika school. The section B is devoted to the details about the *Bhāṣā pariccheda* and the section C is concerned with the Pramāṇas and the various aspects of the concepts of Śabda and Śābdabodha.

The second part of the present work is an exposition of the text of the Śabdakhaṇḍa. Here the Kārikā is given first, then it is followed by a translation and a general exposition. Then the relevant Vṛtti is presented piecemeal. Each piece of the Vṛtti is followed by critical and comparative exposition word for word.

I have no words to express my deep sense of gratitude to my preceptor Professor Dr. Mukunda Madhava Sharma, M.A., Ph.D., D. Litt., Kāvyatīrtha, for his ungrudging guidance and untiring help offered to me during the preparation of my disertatation. I must put on record that the present work is entirely an outcome of his constant guidance, pressure and inspiration.

I have been suffering from an obstinate type of eye-disease since childhood. Ever since the days of my preparation for the Matriculation Examination the books had to be read out to me by my friends and relatives. In case of the present work also I received the help of a host of students, of whom I must never fail to name with a deep sense of gratitude, a few such as Dr. Rajendra Nath Sharma, now an esteemed colleague and Shri Dipak Kumar Sharma, A.C.S.

I remain extremely thankful to my wife Smt. Beena Devi Goswami, M.A. LL.B for relieving me of all the domestic responsibilities during the period of my more serious studies.

Sincere thanks are also due to Messrs Indian Books Centre, Delhi for kindly accepting the work for publication.

I shall feel myself amply rewarded if the works comes to serve the purpose of readers in the field. Let me now conclude with the select saying of the great poet Kālidāsa,—

'ā paritoṣād viduṣāṁ na sādhu manye prayogavijñām'.

1.5.1990

Gauhati University **A.K. Goswami**

ABBREVIATIONS

AK	Amarakoṣa
APTE	The Student's Sanskrit English Dictionary
BHC	Bhāṭṭacintāmaṇi
BM	Bālamanoramā
BP	Bhāṣāpariccheda
BPM	Bhāṣāpariccheda, tranaslated by Swami Madhavananda
BPS	Bhāṣāpariccheda, edited by Pañcānana Śāstrī
BPV	Bhāṣāpariccheda, edited by Gurunath Vidyanidhi
BR	Bṛhatī
BS	Brahmasūtra
BSB	Brahmasūtraśānkarabhāṣya
CIT	Citsukhī (Tattvapradīpikā)
DK	Dinakarī
DL	Dhvanyāloka
GITA	Śrīmadbhagavadgītā
HIL	History of Indian Literature (Winternitz)
HSL	A History of Sanskrit Literature (Keith)
IP	Indian Philosphy (Radhakrishnan)
ITM	Indian Theories of Meaning (Raja)
JNV	Jaiminīyanyāyamālāvistara
K	Kārikāvalī of Viśvanātha
k	Kārikā
KD	Kāvyādarśa
KIR	Kiraṇāvali (Udayanācārya)
KI	Kiraṇāvalī (commentary on BP)
KKT	Kṛṣṇakāntī
KL	Kāvyālaṅkāra
KLSV	Kavyālaṅkārasūtravṛtti
KM	Kāvyamīmāṁsā
KP	Kāvyaprakāśa
KTS	Kāvyatattvasamīkṣā
LCAI	Literary Criticism in Ancient India (Mukherjee)
M	Muktāvalī

Manu	Manusmṛti
MBH	Mahābhāṣya
MD	Mānameyodaya
MS	Mīmāṁsāsūtra
MUS	Muktāvalīsaṁgraha
ND	Nyāya-darśana
NIR	Nirukta
NK	Nyāyakośa
NKU	Nyāyakusumāñjali
NM	Nyāyamañjarī
NRM	Nyāyaratnamālā
NS	Nyāyasūtra
NSM	Nyāyasiddhāntamuktāvalī (with Dinakarī and Rāmarudrī)
NSM(2)	Nyāyasiddhāntamuktāvalī (with the commentary Kiraṇāvalī)
NSMR	Nyāyasiddhāntamñjarī
NSV	Nyāyasūtravṛtti
NTK	Nyāya Theory of Knowledge
NV	Nyāyavārtika
NVTT	Nyāyavārtikatātparyaṭīkā
PLM	Paramalaghumañjuṣā
PMS	Pūrvamīmāṁsā in its sources
PP	Prakaraṇapañcikā
PPB	Praśastapādabhāṣya
PWM	Philosophy of Word and Meaning
RG	Rasagaṅgādhara
RR	Rāmarudrī
RSL	Some Remarks on Similies in Sanskrit Literature
RV	Ṛgveda
SB	Śābarabhāṣya
Sb	Sārabodhinī
SBH	Śāṅkarabhāṣya
SD	Sāhityadarpaṇa
SDK	Sāhityadarpaṇa (Kane)
SIK	Siddāntakaumudī

SK	Sāṁkhyakārikā
SAKV	Śaktivāda
SM	Śikhāmaṇi
SP	Saptapadārthi
SPB	Sāṁkhyapravacanabhāṣya
SRP	Śṛṅgāraprakāśa
SSP	Śabdaśaktiprakāśikā
STK	Sāṁkhyatattvakaumudī
SV	Ślokavārtika
TBR	Tāṇḍyabrāhmaṇa
TC	Tattvacintāmaṇi
TC(2)	Tattvacintāmaṇi (Pratyakṣakhaṇḍa, Delhi reprint)
TD	Tarkadīpikā
TP	tarkapāda (of Bhāṭṭacintāmaṇi)
TR	Tantrarahasya
TRK	Tārkikarakṣā
TS	Tarkasaṁgraha (Chowkhamba)
TS(MB)	Tarkasaṁgraha (Motilal)
TU	Taittiriyopaniṣad
V	Kātyāyana's vārtikas
VB	Vātsyāyana's Bhāṣya (on the Nyāyasūtras)
VM	Vākyārthamātṛkā
VMB	Vaiyākaraṇamahābhāṣya
VP	Vākyapadīya
VPB	Vedāntaparibhāṣā
VPB(2)	Vedāntaparibhāṣā (with the commentary Śikhā maṇi)
VS	Vedāntasāra
VSS	Vaiśeṣikasūtra
YS	Yogasūtra

PART I
INTRODUCTION
A

India inherits from her past a very great treasure of philosophical wisdom. Ancient India is known all over the world for her rich philosophical speculations. The philosophical thinking began with the *Ṛgveda* itself, prominently revealed in the hymns like the Devīsūkta, Puruṣasūkta and the Sūktas ascribed to Dīrghatamas. The Puruṣasūkta and the Devīsūkta show the germs of monistic idealism and the sūktas of Dīrghatamas contain the germs of the dualistic realism. Thus, as a result of this nucleus, there arose six philosophical systems in India, based on either monistic idealism or dualistic realism. These six systems are namely the Pūrvamīmāṁsā or the Mīmāṁsā school of Jaimini, the Uttaramīmāṁsā or the Vedānta school of Bādarāyaṇa, the Sāṁkhya system of Kapila, the Yoga school of Patañjali, the Nyāya system of Gotama and the Vaiseṣika school of Kaṇāda. These six schools of Indian thought are known as 'āstika' (orthodox) or 'vaidika' (Vedic) on account of their recognising Vedic authority as well as the existence of God. Side by side with these orthodox schools, there developed three 'nāstika' (non-orthodox or heterodox) or 'avaidika' (non-Vedic) schools of philosophy as they came to defy the authority of the Veda and the existence of God. Those are the Bauddha, Jaina and Cārvāka darśanas.

The Vedic schools can again be found in two divisions. Mīmāṁsā and Vedānta accept only the Vedas as the authority. But the other four schools, in the matter of recognising the authority, unhesitatingly combine the Vedic knowledge with the worldly logic. The trend is so conspicuous in the Nyāya system that Tarka (Logic) comes to be a synonymn for the Nyāya school.

We have to add here that other minor systems also cropped up in support of the main trends in the arena of Indian philosophy.

The relative chronology of these Darśanas still remains a guess work. Despite serious efforts of scholars in the field, we are still in the dark as to the exact dates of these systems of thought for lack of adequate materials.

Now to suit our proposed subject of investigation we have to deal, in particular, with the two systems known as Nyāya and Vaiśeṣika. It is because the *Bhāṣāpariccheda* of Viśvanātha, the work in our hand for an intensive study, belongs to the Nyāyavaiśeṣika system, the syncratised form of thought of the Naiyāyikas and Vaiśeṣikas.

THE NYĀYA, THE VAIŚEṢIKA AND THE SYNTHESIS:

Scholars feel that the history of Nyāya and Vaiśeṣika is still clouded in mystery. The vedic literature itself bears an obscure stamp of these philosophical trends. The study of certain upaniṣads like the *Bṛhadāraṇyakopaniṣad* and the *Kāṭhakopaniṣad* gives strong impression that these logical thoughts occurred to the minds of the Vedic seers also. It is believed that the Sāṁkhya and the Vaiśeṣika emerged in Pre-Buddhistic periods.[1] From the prevalence of philosophical debates and symposia in the courts of king Ajātaśatru and Janaka, it is gathered that Nyāya and Tarka very much occupied the scholars of the day. During the days of propagation of Buddhism in the 5th century B.C., the champions of Vedic religion also tried to meet the challange as far as practicable by taking the aid of logic and reasonings. In the 4th century B.C., it is surmised, the Nyāya and Vaiśeṣika speculations assumed the final shape although the extant Nyāya and Vaiśeṣika sūtras ascribed to Gautama and Kaṇāda may reasonably be accepted as having been composed in later times.

The utility of the Nyāya philosophy amongst the branches of knowledge is sought to the brought out in a traditional verse which is seen oft-quoted even by the modern scholars.[2] Regarding the importance of the Nyāya and the Vaiśeṣika schools of philosophy, we must bear in mind that these two systems come to us as an analytic type of philosophy and as Dr. Radhakrishnan puts it, 'uphold common sense and science.'[3] The Naiyāyika trend of accepting something as true only when it is proved by reason makes it more acceptable even to the moderners with a bias for science. The critical treatment of metaphysical problems and the examinations of objects of knowledge with the aid of the logical canons is the distinctive features of the school of Nyāya. Hence the study of the Nyāya system comes to be essential as an introduction to other systems also.[4] The Vaiśeṣikas also earned distinction by their recognition of the atomic constitution of things.

Gautama, known also as Gotama and Akṣapāda, is by tradition, the founder of the Nyāya school of thought. Whatever be the origin of this school, the first systematic extant work of this school of philosophy is the *Nyāyasūtra* of Gautama, divided into five 'adhyāyas' or books. The system is mainly occupied with the problem of determining the conditions of correct thinking and the means of acquiring the true knowledge of the reality. This school of thought comes to be very much useful in developing the powers of logical thinking for the scholars of the succeeding periods. This is what had warranted the new names for the system such as Nyā yavidyā, Tarkaśāstra (logic or the science of reasoning) and Ānvī kṣikī (the science of critical study). It must, however, be added in this context that like other orthodox systems, Nyāya also has 'mokṣa' (liberation) as its ultimate goal.

Subsequently there developed a huge corpus of literature on the system. The notable works thereof are namely *Nyāyabhāṣya* of *Vātsyāyana*, the *Nyāyavārtika* of Uddyotakara, the *Nyāyavā rtikatātparyaṭīkā* of *Vācaspatimiśra*, the *Nyayavārtikatātparyaṭī kāpariśuddhi* and the Nyāyakusumāñjali of Udayana, and the *Nyāyamañ*jarī[5] of Jayanta. Mention may also be made of the

Pramāṇasamuccaya and the *Nyāyapraveśa* of Diṅnāga, the *Nyā yabindu* of Dharmakīrti, the *Nyāyasāra of Bhāsarvajña*, the Nyā yāvatāra of *Siddhasenadivākara* and the *Pramāṇamīmāṁsā* of Hemacandra. These works explain, defend and develop the ideas contained in the *Nyāyasūtra*. The said treatises, by way of maintaining the spirit of the sūtras of Gautama, represent the Prācī nanyāya or the old school of Nyāya; it is because, the later Naiyā yikas develop new trends in their thoughts and approaches in the context of different issues and come to form a somewhat separate school of thought that has passed as the Navyanyāya or the modern school of Nyāya. The Navyanyāya keeps its difference from the prācīnanyāya with the conspicuity of employing a peculiar argumentative process. Some of the later Naiyāyikas again combine their thoughts with those of the Vaiśeṣikas. As a result of this amalgamation, there arose a series of works of syncretic character belonging to the so called Nyāyavaiśeṣika school.

Udayana was the last Prācīnanaiyāyika after whom there flourished the Navya school of Nyāya. Scholars feel that it was Udayana who paved the way for the emergence of the Navyanyā ya trends of thought which came to be in full form at the hands of Gaṅgeśa. Dr. Gaurinath Śāstrī is of the opinion that it was Udayana who, for the first time, made an effort to effect a synthesis of the two systems of Nyāya and Vaiśeṣika[6]. Now, to pursue our present issue of the division of the Nyāya into two schools, we find Dr. Śāstrī maintaining that as the seed of Navyanyāya was actually sown in the works of Udayana, he is to be recognised as the Ādipuruṣa of the Navyanyāya school; it is because the analytical approach peculiar to the Navyanyāya logic was conspicuously evident in Udayana's works.[7] In this context we simply feel that Gaṅgeśopādhyāya, the author of the *Tattvacintāmaṇi*, deserves the highest credit as the founder of the Navyanyāya as a distinct school. Though amongst the Naiyāyikas, Udayana made a departure from the common trend of thought initiated by Gautama, it was only Gaṅgeśa who fully broke away from the Prācīnanyāya and came to be the chief champion of the Navyanyāya. It is why the modern scholars accept the history of Navyanyāya as beginning with the Tattvacintāmaṇi, the magnum-opus of Gaṅgeśa. This Navya school first arose in Mithilā and later came to be privilege of Bengal with Navadvīpa as the main centre of these trends of thought. After Gaṅgeśa, there followed a large galaxy of illustrious scholars in the line. The chief amongst them were Jayadeva, Raghunātha Śiromaṇi, Mathurānātha Tarkavāgīśa, Jagadīśa Tarkālaṅkāra, Gadādhara Bhaṭṭacārya etc. Their immortal works are Āloka, (a commentary on the *Tattvacintāmaṇi*), *Tattvacintāmaṇidīdhiti, Tattvacintāmaṇidihitirahasya, Śabdaśaktiprakāśikā, Śaktivāda* etc.

The first systematic work of the Vaiśeṣikas is the *sūtra* of Kaṇāda. Kaṇāda came to be named so for his reputation of living on 'grains of corn gleaned from the field.' His other names are Kaṇabhuk, Kaṇabhakṣa, Yogī, Ulūka and Kāśyapa. The system is also known as the Kāṇāda system or the Aulūka system. This system is called Vaiśeṣika because of its attitude towards 'Viśeṣa' as one of the categories.[8] Praśastapāda's commentary on Kaṇāda's sū tras, viz. *Padārthadharmasaṁgraha,* which is celebrated as *Praśastapādabhāṣya,* reads rather like an independent exposition of the philosophy. The well-known commentaries on the Bhāṣya are the *Vyomavatī* of Vyomaśiva, the *Kiraṇāvalī* of Udayana, the *Nyāyakandalī* of Śrīdhara, the *Setu* of Padmanābha, and the Sū kti of Jagadīśa.[9] Vallabhācārya's *Nyāyalīlāvatī* Udayana's *Lakṣaṇāvalī,* and Saṅkaramiśra's *Upaskāra* are also valuable works in this line of thought.

Here it is relevant on our part to make a brief reference to the common characteristics and differences between the Naiyāyikas and the Vaiśeṣikas. The two schools of the Naiyāyikas and the Vaiśeṣikas are basically so akin that Dr. Radhakrishnan even opines that they might have branched off from a hypothetical common original system.[10] It is also observed that both systems supplement each other and finally merge into a single system.[11]

Both the systems believe in the realisation of bliss ('niḥśreyasā dhigama') from the knowledge of the true nature ('tattvajñāna') of the categories (padārthas).[12]

Both the systems establish the existence of Ātmā with the help of Inference (anumāna).[13] Both came to be recognised as systems of the same status ('samānatantra').[14] Yet the two schools of thought reveal distinctive features of their own to deserve separate identities. The Naiyayikas recognise sixteen categories while the Vaiśeṣikas only seven.[15] Though Kaṇāda does not mention Abhā va along with the six Padārthas yet from VSS 1.2.1 and 9.1.1 it may be gathered that Kaṇāda takes due cognigence of Abhāva also as a Padārtha. It is not mentioned because the idea of Abhāva invariably depends on the idea of 'bhāva-padārthas' and because the idea of 'bhāvapadārthas' should automatically lead to the idea of the relative category of Abhāva.[16] Viśvanātha in his *Bhāṣā pariccheda* says that the Naiyāyikas are also not opposed to the recognition of the seven categories of the Vaiśeṣikas.[17] Vātsyāana clearly admits that the six Padārthas viz. Dravya, Guṇa, Karma, Sāmānya, Viśeṣa and Samavāya are to be recognised under the purview of what is metnioned as prameya in the list of the sixteen categories of Gotama.[18] The list of six Padārthas given by the Bhā ṣyakāra should drag in Abhāva also on the strength of the arguments given earlier. But even if we take these seven Padārthas as common to both the schools, the Naiyāyikas' recognition of nine other 'Padārthas' serves as a differentiating point. Another distinguishing feature is the Vaiśeṣikas' recognition of Viseṣa as a separate category. Moreover, the Naiyāyikas recognise four 'Pramāṇas' namely Pratyakṣa, Anumāna, Upamāna and Śabda, while the Vaiśeṣikas admit only Pratyakṣa and Anumāna.

As shown earlier, the amalgamation of the Nyāya and the Vaiśeṣika systems took place at a later stage[19] and hence, we find only such later works like Śivāditya's *Saptapadārthī*, Laugākṣi Bhāskara's *Tarkakaumudī*, *Viśvanātha's Bhāṣāpariccheda* with the *Siddhāntamuktāvalī*, Jagadīśa's *Tarkāmṛta*, Annaṁbhaṭṭa's

Tarkasaṁgraha with the commentary *Dīpikā* and Keśavamiśra's *Tarkabhāṣā* as the representative works of the syncretic system of Nyāyavaiśeṣika.

In the opinion of some scholars, Śivāditya's *Saptapadārthī* appears to be the earliest work of the syncretic school of Nyā yavaiśeṣikas. It may, however, be observed that the *Saptapadārthī* is not completely identical in respect of its scope and pattern with a typical Nyāyavaiśeṣika work like the *Bhāṣāpariccheda*. For instance, it does not recognise the Śabdapramāṇa.

THE IMPORTANCE OF NAVYANYĀYA

The Bhāṣāpariccheda of Viśvanātha, the work in hand for a specific examination, is undoubtedly of a syncretic nature as a treatise belonging to the Nyāyavaiśeṣika group. But we have to note that the Vaiśeṣikas do not believe in the Śabdapramāṇa. So, Viśvanātha, as a prominent exponent of Śabda, comes to us only as a Naiyāyika. As a Naiyāyika also, his approach to issues and techniques employed in the treatment of problems bears clear testimony to his identity as a Navyanaiyāyika. Hence, in our present study on the Śabdakhaṇḍa of the *Bhāṣāpariccheda* we are chiefly concerned with the trends of thought of the Navyanyā ya.

In direct contrast with the Prācinanaiyāyikas, the Navyaniyāyikas are known for their exclusive stress on logical aspects of the Nyā ya. Navyanyāya develops its theory of knowledge into a formal logic of relations between concepts, terms and propositions. Navyanyāya scholars present their own ways of interpretation with the help of numerous abstracts. Wonderfully enough, the highest possible perfection and extreme thoroughness in analysis come to be an outstanding feature of Navyanyāya. Navyanyāya is a vast mass of literature which comprises of not only Logic but also Epistemology, Physics, Grammar and many other incidental topics of interest. The techniques and methods of navyanyāya are so thorough and subtle that they can only be compared with those of highly advanced Mathematics. The Navyanyāya techniques, because of their super-excellence are accepted in the whole of India in the matter of giving expression to any subtle idea that might have occurred in the mind of a scholar of any branch of Sanskrit study. Navyanyāya has, as a result, an overwhelming influence on modern students of Mīmāṁsā, Vedānta, Vyākaraṇa, law and theology and even literature and rhetorics. Without a thorough grounding in Navyanyāya dialectics and techniques, no one, however, intelligent, will ever be competent to understand different schools of Indian Philosophy with accuracy.[20] The study of Navyanyāya itself goes a long way in sharpening one's faculty of understanding and makes it thorough and incisive. But it must be admitted that comparatively very little has so far been done in the matter of interpreting Navyanyāya according to modern methods of critical research.

COMPARATIVE CHRONOLOGY OF PRINCIPAL WORKS IN NYĀYA, VAIŚEṢIKA AND NYĀYAVAIŚEṢIKA:

(The bracketed numbers shown with dates signify various opinions. The sources of such opinions are mentioned in the foot note)

1. *Nyāyasūtra* of Gautama - (1) C 500 B.C.; (4) between 300 A.D. - 500 B.C.; (5) 2nd century B.C.
2. *Vaiśeṣikasūtra* of Kaṇāda - (2) C 300 A.D.; Kaṇāda may have been contemporary to Buddha (C. 567 B.C.); (4) Uncertain but surely before 80 A.D.; (5) 3rd century B.C.
3. *Nyāyasūtrabhāṣya* of Vātsyāyana- (3) 4th century A.D.; (4) 300 A.D.; (5) 4th century A.D.
4. *Vaiśeṣikasūtrabhāṣya* of Praśastapādācārya - (3) 5th century A.D.; (4) 4th century A.D.; (5) 5th century A.D.
5. *Nyāyavārtika* of Udyotakara - (1) C 620 A.D.; (4) last part of the 6th century A.D.; (5) 6th century A.D.

B

BHĀṢĀPARICCHEDA:KĀRIKĀVALĪ AND MUKTĀVALĪ

The *Bhāṣāpariccheda* is the name of a work consisting of kārikās (technical verses) written vy Viśvanāthanyāyapañcānana. The name *Bhāṣāpariccheda* occurs in the colophon.[21] Viśvanātha himself is the author also of a running prose commentary (vṛtti) of the aforesaid Kārikās, which is called the *Siddhāntamuktāvalī*. At the beginning of this *Muktāvalī*, the core treatise is referred to as Kārikāvalī by Viśvanātha himself.[22] In the traditional commentaries also, the word *Bhāṣāpariccheda* is used in the sense of the *Kārikāvalī*, i.e., the cluster of the basic Kārikās.[23] Some modern scholars also take the term *Bhāṣāpariccheda* only in the sense of the Kārikās.[24] Yet the fact remains that the word *Bhāṣāpariccheda* has now come to be used to cover the cluster of the Kārikās and the *Muktāvalī* as well. It is because, the verse work and the prose commentary on it are so closely related in respect of the philosophical ideas presented therein that they cannot be thought of as distinct works. In the present dissertation the proposed exposition will be with reference to both the works treated as one organic whole. Hence, the word *Bhāṣāpariccheda* is used in the present work to cover both the so-called *Kārikāvalī* and the *Muktāvalī*.

SIGNIFICANCE OF THE TITLE 'BHĀṢĀPARICCHEDA':

Nowhere in the existing literature, old or modern, we have come across an attempt at interpretating the title '*Bhāṣāpariccheda*.' The title word comprises of two parts, 'bhāṣā' and 'pariccheda' and may be analysed as 'bhaṣāyāḥ paricchedaḥ'. The word 'bhāṣā' is derived from the root 'bhāṣ' with the addition of suffix 'a' together with 'ṭāp'. The word 'pariccheda' is the resultant of pari-$\sqrt{}$chid + ghañ. With this in mind, an attempt may be made to interpret the title in two ways.

(i) One of the several meanings of the root 'chid' preceded by 'pari' is 'to fix accurately or ascertain'. From this the word 'pariccheda' may be taken to mean 'an accurate fixation or ascertainment'.[25] The word 'bhāṣā' means definition or description.[26] The word 'bhāṣāpariccheda' comes to mean 'an accurate fixation of definitions.' In this way the treatise is supposed to contain the most accurate analysis of the problems of the domain of Indian Philosophy, in general, and of the school of Nyāya-Vaiśeṣika, in particular.

(ii) The word 'bhāṣā' may be taken to stand for 'paribhāṣā' according to the maxim 'Nāmaikadeśagrahaṇe nāmamātragrahaṇam'. On the strength of this maxim, a part of a name may be taken to mean the corresponding whole word. Paribhāṣā means terminology or technical terms also.[27] In consonance with this meaning of the first part of the word, i.e., 'bhāṣā', the word 'pariccheda' may be taken in its sense of 'a definition'.[28] Viewed thus, the title '*Bhāṣā pariccheda*' means 'definitions of the technical terms'. As a matter of fact, this work contains the most useful explanations of the technical terms of the sphere of Nyāya-Vaiśeṣika, which are almost invariably come across also in the other schools of Indian Philosophy.

THE AUTHOR OF THE BHĀṢĀPARICCHEDA :

The authorship of the *Bhāṣāpariccheda* has been ascribed to Viśvanāthanyāyapañcānana who is the author of the *Nyāyasūtravṛtti*. Pañcānana Śāstrī, however, has recorded in the preface to his own edition of the *Bhāṣāpariccheda* a difference of opinion in this context. As referred to by him, Dinesh Ch. Bhattacharyya is of the opinion that the author of the *Siddhāntamuktāvali* is one Kṛṣṇadāsa Sārvabhauma and not Viśvanāthanyāya-pañcānana. Bhattacharyya deduces his conclusion on the following grounds.

(i) There is the mention of Kṛṣṇadāsa Sārvabhauma as the author in some of the manuscripts of the book;

(ii) The *Muktāvalyullāsa* of one Viśvanātha, an exposition of the

Muktāvalī , has been composed prior to Viśvanāthanyāyapañcā nana, the author of the *Nyāyasūtravṛtti.*

(iii) Another exposition of the *Muktāvalī* namely *Raudrī* has come to us as a work of Rudratarkavāgiśa who happens to be only a contemporary of Viśvanāthanyāyapañcānana.

(iv) The example of Upamānapramāṇa given in the *Nyāyasū travṛtti,* decidedly a work of Viśvanāthanyāyapañcānana, is different from that in the *Muktāvalī* .

(v) The date of the Maithili MSS of the *Muktāvalī* is given as only 205 Śaka year. But the accepted date of Viśvanātha's *Nyāyasū travṛtti,* i.e., the *Gautamasūtravṛtti* is 1556 śakābda.

Pañcānana Śāstrī rejects the view of Dinesh Chandra Bhattacharyya and argues as follows:

(1) The mention of Kṛṣṇadāsa Sārvabhauma by name in a few manuscripts of the book can never be a strong ground to prove the authorship of the work otherwise. In a large number of manuscripts of the work available in different parts of India, the name of Viśvanātha also has been mentioned and scholars in general have no contention in respect of the authorship of Viśvanātha. The tradition is very strong in this respect ever since the very date of the composition of the book.

(2) There is nothing to prove that the *Muktāvalyullāsa* has been composed before the life of the Viśvanāthanyāyapañcanana. As we cannot claim fullscale knowledge regarding the identity of Viśvanātha, the author of the *Ullāsa,* we cannot contradict the probability that Viśvanātha, the author of *Muktāvalyullāsa* is a person other than and posterior to Viśvanāthanyāyapañcā nana.

Bhattacharyya wants to create an impression that as one Viśvanā tha was to have composed the *Muktāvalyullāsa* (a commentary on the *Muktāvalī*), there cannot be another Viśvanātha. It is, however, not warranted by facts that there can be only one person bearing a particular name. There is no harm if two or more persons bearing the same name came to be associated with a work and its commentary.

(3) It is quite possible that notwithstanding his being a contemporary of Viśvanāthanyāyapañcānana, Rudratarkavāgīśa composed *Raudrīṭīkā* which came as a sub-commentary on the *Muktāvalī*. There is nothing to prevent the composition of a commentary and a sub-commentary on it by two contemporaries. Sometimes necessity demands even a contemporary to write a commentary or a sub-commentary on some particular work. So there is no point ion arguing that the *Muktāvalī* must have been composed earlier than Viśvanāthanyāyapañcānana as one of his contemporaries is found to have composed a commentary on the *Muktāvalī*.

(4) The difference in the illustrations of the Upamānapramāṇa in the *Nyāyasūtravṛtti* and the *Muktāvalī* does not carry weight in the matter of deciding the authorship of the *Muktāvalī*. The same author may give two different examples in his two different books even with regard to the same context. An author may sometimes correct himself in a later work regarding a mistake done in an earlier one. So even though the examples of Upamāna-pramāṇa are different in the two books, the books could have been composed by the same author. It may be that his illustration of Upamāna in the *Muktāvalī* was under the influence of the Maithilī logician Śaṅkaramiśra and his fresh illustration in the *Nyāyasūtravṛtti* was out of his anxiety to correct himself at a mature age.

(5) The word 'śaka' indicative of time as appearing in the last part of the *Muktāvalī* in Maithilī script might have been used in the sense of a local year. The Maithilī scholars are found using the word 'śaka' in their language in the sense of a 'samvat' (a year in general). Thus there should be no difficulty in placing the Maithili MSS near about the *Nyāyasūtravṛtti*, the date of which is undoubtedly the 1556 śakābda. No proot has been there as yet to

show that the *Muktāvalī* had been composed at least one hundred years earlier than the *Nyāyasūtravṛtti* which has undoubtedly passed as Viśvanāthanyāyapañcānana's work. If it were otherwise, there would have been obvious scope of doubting Viśvanātha's authorship of the *Muktāvalī*.[29]

Dr. Dayānanda Bhārgava also refers to this difference of opinion with late D.C. Bhattācharyya. As Dr. Bhārgava informs us, MM Haraprasād Śāstrī also believes that Kṛṣṇadāsa Sārvabhauma was the author of the *Bhāṣāpariccheda* with the *Siddhāntamuktāvalī* and that Viśvanātha wrote only the commentary *Ullāsa* on it.[30] Pending discovery of stronger evidences, we may conclude, that there is no point in doubting Viśvanāthanyāyapañcānana as the author of the *Bhāṣāpariccheda*.

VIŚVANĀTHA -- A PERSONAL INTRODUCTION

Viśvanātha makes a very brief reference to his family. He introduces himself simply as the son of Śrīmadvidyānivāsa Bhattācāryya.[31] Hence, it becomes difficult to determine the time and place of this great scholar. In the *Bhāṣāpariccheda* there is only one more personal reference made by Viśvanātha as he discloses that he composed the work in the interest of some one, Rājīva by name.[32] A section of the scholars conjecture Viśvanātha to be a Bengali on the ground that BP is most popular as a text in Bengal and that the name Rājīva appears to be a typical Bengali name. Another section suppose Viśvanātha to be a Maharastrian on the ground that the authors of both *Dīnakarī* and *Rāmarudrī, the celebrated principal commentaries on the Muktāvalī*, hail from Maharastra.[33] It is, however, useless to indulge in such conjectures. Regarding the identity of Rājīva, *Dinkarī feels that he was a disciple of Viśvanātha.*[34] *Some others hold him to be a grandson of Viśvanātha on the strength of a colophon in certain MSS of the Bp.*[35] *About Viśvanātha's geneology, Dr. Satkari Mookerjee and pt Pañcānana* Śāstrī have referred the readers to a valuable book in Bengali, the *Nyāyaparicaya* by MM Phaṇibhūṣaṇa Tarkavāgīśa. As the said book is not available to us, we reproduce here an account of Viśvanātha's family as detailed by Pañcānana Śāstrī on the strength of the findings of the Tarkavāgīśa.

Ratnākara Vācaspati was the youngest brother of Vāsudeva Sārvabhauma, the eminent Naiyāyika and founder of Navyanyāya studies in Navadvīpa. This Sārvabhauma was the first teacher of Raghunāthaśiromaṇi. Ratnākara, the brother of Sārvabhauma, became celebrated as Vidyāvācaspati. Kaśinātha Vidyāvāgīśa was the son of that Vidyāvacaspati. Kaśīnātha was reknowned as Vidyānivāsa Bhaṭṭācārya. Viśvanāthanyāyapañcānana was the son of this Vidyanivāsa Bhaṭṭācārya. Viśvanātha had a brother of his own, Rudranātha by name. As Dr. Mookerjee informs us,[36] Viśvanātha's grandfather Ratnākara, together with his illustrious brother Sārvabhauma were the sons of Maheswara Viśārada, celebrated for his scholarship and piety, whose father Narahari of the Vandopādhyāya family settled at Navavīpa in the 14th century A.D.

DATE OF THE *BHĀṢĀPARICCHEDA*

If Viśvanāthanyāyapañcānana is the author of the *Siddhāntamuktāvalī*, then he is automatically the author of the whole BP as warranted by the expressions 'nijanirmitakārikāvalim' etc. Viśvanātha is undisputedly accepted as the author of *Nyāyasūtravṛtti*, the date of which is given by himself as 1556 śakābda.[37] Now we can fix the date of BP (the *Kārikāvalī* with the *Muktāvalī*) around the date of *Nyāyasūtravṛtti*. Pañcānana Śāstri takes the example of Upamānapramāṇa given in the *Nyāyasūtravṛtti* as an evidence of maturity, while the example given in the *Muktāvalī* appears to be the act of an earlier age. Thus the *Muktāvalī* seems to have been composed earlier than the *Nyāyasūtravṛtti*. The date of *Muktāvalī* being fixed, it is not difficult to fix the date of the *Kārikāvalī* slightly prior to that of the *Muktāvalī* and to place the BP as a whole some time earlier than 1556 śaka. This date is equivalent to 1634 A.D. The *Nyāyasūtravṛtti* was composed by

Viśvanātha at the fag end of his life at Vṛndāvana.[38]

OTHER LITERARY CONTRIBUTIONS OF THE AUTHOR

In addition to the *Kārikāvalī*, the *Siddhāntamuktāvalī*, and the *Nyāyasūtravṛtti*, Viśvanātha is credited with the authorship also of three more works viz. *Nyāyatantrabodhinī*, *Padārthatattvā valoka* and *Suvarṇatattvāvaloka*.[39] Dr. Satkari Mookerjee refers to a work called *Māṁsatattvaviveka* as to have been composed by Viśvanātha. Dr. Mookerjee describes it as an interesting smṛti treatise in which Viśvanātha advocates the custom of meat-eating amongst the brāhmins in northern India and ridicules the South-Indian scholars for deprecating the custom.[40]

OTHER AUTHORS OF THE SAME NAME

In the domain of Nyāya philosophy itself there are three more Viśvanāthas. One is the author of the *Muktāvalyullāsa*, the second one is the author of the *Tattvacintāmaṇi*, the *Tarkataraṅgiṇī* and the *Tarkasaṁgraha*, which are all commentaries and the third one is Viśvanāthabhaṭṭa, the author of the *Nyāyavilāsa*, a work on Gaṅgeśa's *Tattvaprabodhinī*.[41] *To avoid confusion, it should be noted that Viśvanātha Kavirāja, author of the Sāhityadarpaṇa*, is altogether different from all the aforesaid Viśvanātha's of the domain of Nyāya.

BHĀṢĀPARICCHEDA — A NYĀYA-VAIŚEṢIKA WORK

In view of the contents the *BP* (i.e. *Kārikāvalī* of Viśvanātha with the *Muktāvalī*) belongs to the syncretic school of Nyā yavaiśeṣikas. Viśvanātha gives his own elucidation of the concept of the seven categories (Saptapadārtha) recognised by the earlier Vaiśeṣikas and agin deals with four sources of valid knowledge (pramāṇas) as enunciated by the earlier Naiyāyikas. The pure Nyā ya tradition believes in sixteen categories. By ways of admitting seven categories Viśvanātha behaves like a Vaiśeṣika. Vaiśeṣikas again believe in only two Pramāṇas, namely Pratyakṣa and Anumāna. They do not recognise Upamāna and Śabda. Because of recognising all the four Pramāṇas admitted by the Nyāyasūtrakāra Gotama, Viśvanātha emerges out as a Naiyāyika. Under this circumstance, it will be wrong to characterise Viśvanātha exclusively as a Naiyāyika or a Vaiśeṣika. In the matter of methods and technicalities he is out and out a Navyanaiyāyika.

DIVISION OF THE *BHĀṢĀPARICCHEDA* -- *MAIN CONTENTS*

The BP is broadly divided into two parts, viz., the *Kārikāvalī* and the *Muktāvalī*. The *Kārikāvalī* consists of 168 Kārikās (verses).[42] The Kārikās are mostly in the Anuṣṭubh metre. A few of them, however, appear in Āryā and Upajāti also. The *Muktāvalī*, the prose vṛtti on *Kārikāvalī*, proceeds in accordance with the relevant Kārikās. The *Muktāvalī* consists of five divisions (Khaṇḍas) namely Pratyakṣakhaṇḍa, Anumānakhaṇḍa, Upamānakhaṇḍa, Śabdakhaṇḍa and Guṇanirūpaṇa khaṇḍa.

Both the *Kārikāvalī* and the *Muktāvalī* are begun with separate 'maṅgala' -- verses (i.e. bendictory verses). Immediately after the 'maṅgalācaraṇa' of the *Muktāvalī*, Viśvanātha discusses the utility of the 'maṅgalācaraṇa' (benediction) by way of explaining the 'maṅgala' verse of the *Kārikāvalī*. Thereafter, he informs that he has written the *Muktāvalī* for the sake of easy understanding of the Kārīkās by some Rājīva. Then he poceeds to the treatment of the issues in the following order -- categories (padārtha), Substances (Dravya), Perception (pratyakṣa), Inference (Anumāna), Comparison (Upamāna), Verbal comprehension (śābdabodha) Recollection (smṛti), mind (Manas) and Qualities (Guṇas).

Following the Vaiseṣika trend initiated by Kaṇāda, Viśvanātha deals with the seven categories namely, Dravya (substance), Guṇa (quality), Karma (action) Jāti (universality), Viśeṣa (particularity) *Samavāya* (inherence) and Abhāva (negation or non-existence).

Following Kaṇāda and his successors Viśvanātha discusses the nine types of Dravya, twenty-four types og Guṇa, five types of Karman, two types of Sāmānya, then Viśeṣa, Samavāya and Abhāva in great detail.

Viśvanātha's treatment of Vyāpti, Hetvābhāsa, Pakṣatā, Upādhi, Upamāna and Śabda is in the line of the Naiyāyikas. Thus Viśvanātha's *BP* comes to cover physics and psycophysics of the Vaiśeṣikas and logic and metaphysics of the Naiyāyikas. While following the traditions of Nyāya and Vaiśeṣika, Viśvanātha naturally happened to be influenced by the earlier authorities of these two schools of thought. But even then Viśvanātha exhibits a lot of originality in his treatment of the various traditional concepts. It is rightly pointed out by Dr. Satkari Mookerjee that "Viśvanātha follows the plan of Praśastapāda in his treatment of the Vaiśeṣika categories and their relations, although his exposition embodies new contributions."[43] Viśvanātha's originality even in the face of his indebtedness to Praśastapāda is acknowledged by Gurunātha Vidyānidhi also.[44]

THE IMPORTANCE OF THE *BHĀṢĀPARICCHEDA* IN THE HISTORY OF NAVYANYĀYA

The *Bhāṣāpariccheda* may be reckoned as the foremost of the standard and comprehensive Navyanyāya works suited to the beginners. The work seems to have been composed on the basis of the *Vaiśeṣikabhāṣya* of Praśastapāda; yet the Nyāya doctrines also have been suitably incorporated into it. The *Muktāvalī* brings into its fold all the important conclusions and thoughts of the Nyāya school. It bears testimony to Viśvanātha's knowledge of methods, techniques and findings of the Navyanyāya school. As Dr. Satkari Mookerjee opines, of all the Nyāyavaiśeṣika works the *BP* is "most popular and most extensively studies in India."[45] In the considered opinion of Dr. Mookerjee, the popularity of the work lies in "its comprehensive treatment of most of the important topics and problems that exercise the minds of the exponents of the Navyanyāya school for several centuries."[46] It is said to have summed up the latest results of thinking in the Nyāya line of thought. Dr. Mookerji highly advocates the study of the book by the advanced students to get acquainted with the Navyanyāya dialectics.[47]

TRADITIONAL COMMENTARIES, TRANSLATIONS AND MODERN EDITIONS OF THE *BP*

Of the commentaries the *Dinakarī* is the main and the most celebrated one. The *Dinakarī* was begun by Mahādevabhaṭṭa and completed by Dinkarabhaṭṭa. The original name of the commentary was *Prakāśa* but it passes as the *Dinakarī* through its association with Dinakara. The *Rāmarudrī* is a commentary on the *Dinakarī* and it is equally celebrated. The composition of the *Rāmarudrī* was started by Rāmarudra Bhaṭṭācārya and completed by Paṇḍitarāja Rājeśvara Śāstrī. The actual name of the work is *Taraṅgiṇī*, but the sub-commentary passes as the *Rāmarudrī* through its association with Rāmarudra. Other commentaries on the *BP* as far as we know are the following - the *Muktāvalyullāsa* of one Viśvanātha, the *Raudrī* by Rudratarkavāgīsa, the *Muktāvalīsaṁgraha* of Pañcānana Śāstrī, the *Prācīna Prabhā* of Drāviḍanṛsiṁha Śāstrī, the *Mañjuṣā* of Pattābhirāmaśāstrī, the *Mayukha* of Śuryanārāyaṇaśuktā, the Nyāyacandrikā, the Abhinavaprabhā by Mukundaśarmā and a commentary by Gaṅgārāma yati.

The *Bhāṣāpariccheda* was first printed in India in 1827.[48] Then it came to have a rendering in Bengali.[49] In 1850 Dr. E. Roer published in the Bibiotheca Indica series an English edition of the *Bhāṣāpariccheda* with extracts from the *Muktāvalī*. The book, however, is now out of print.[50] the *Bhāṣpariccheda with the Siddhāntamuktāvalī* is a very valuable translation by Swami Madhavananda, published by Advaita Ashrama in 1940. Of various subsequent editions of BP, we can make mention of the *Bhāṣāpariccheda* by Śri Pañcānana Śāstrī with his expositions in Sanskrit and Bengali, the *Bhāṣāpariccheda* by Sri Gurunā thavidyānidhibhaṭṭācāryya with translation and exposition in Bengali, the *Nyāyasiddhāntamuktāvali* along with the commentaries, *Dinakarī* and *Rāmarudrī*, and *Nyāyasiddhāntamuktāvali* with the commentary, *Kiraṇāvalī*, both published from the Chowkhamba Sanskrit Series Office, Varanasi.

SCOPE AND UTILITY OF THE PRESENT WORK

The problem of word-meaning and its communication as presented in different schools of Indian Philosophy has arrested the attention of many a modern scholar. The Nyāya concept of Śabda in this context demands a serious study as it contributes largely to the Indian theory of meaning. But because of its abstruse nature, the Nyāya thought is yet to be fully explored. The Śabdakhaṇḍa of the *Bhāṣāpariccheda* sums-up the latest thinking of Nyāya scholars, in the matter of the concept of Śabda. Hence it is deemed necessary to make a critical exposition of the śabdakhaṇḍa of the *Bhāṣāpariccheda*. The exposition is expected to assume the form of a critique on Śabda from the Nyāya point of view.

The text of the *Bhāṣāpariccheda* itself is a knotty one as it is written in the style of Navyanyāya terminology. Hence an exposition is necessary to facilitate the study of the work as a text book also. The contents require an elucidation, also because of embodying certain highly controvertial issues.

The chapter under consideration has many technical terms and issues in common with Mīmāṁsā, Vyākaraṇa, Alaṅkāraśāstra etc. To illustrate the point, we can name Karaṇa, Vyāpāra, Śakti etc. as common technical terms and as for common issues we may consider the cases like those of Vṛtti, Lakṣaṇa, Sphoṭa Śaktigraha, Āsatti etc. In order to bring out the real implications of these terms and issues a fuller exposition of the Śabdakhaṇḍa of the *Bhāṣāpariccheda* is highly desirable. Moreover, we find that these common terms and issues do not necessarily show affinity in thought, rather sometimes they reveal marked differences.

It may be humbly pointed out that the traditional as well as the modern commentaries on the *Bhāṣāpariccheda* still leave scope for such an expositon. DK and RR, the celebrated traditional commentaries are really helpful in following the *Bhāṣā pariccheda* text. The traditional commentators, as is usual, do not deal with the issues in their historical perspective nor in the critical and comparative lines. This is equally true of other commentaries including the *Muktāvalīsaṁgraha* of Pañcānana Bhaṭṭācā rya, comparatively a modern scholar. The English editor of the *Bhāṣāpariccheda* of Dr. Roer is no longer available to us. The English translation of the *Bhāṣāpariccheda* by Svāmī Mādhavā nanda (abbr. BPM) is only a helpful English rendering of the work. *The Philosophy of word and meaning* by Dr. Gaurinātha Śāstrī, otherwise a very important work, is concerned mainly with the doctrine of Bhartṛhari, the grammarian. *The Indian theories of meaning* by K. Kunjanni Raja, which is no doubt comprehensive and thematic, has not dealt elaborately with the Śabdakhaṇḍa of the *Bhāṣāpariccheda.* The treatment of Śabda in the *Nyāya theory of knowledge* by S.C. Chatterjee also is not adequate so far as the *BP* is concerned. We, therefore, feel that a fuller treatment of Śabdakhaṇḍa of the *Bhāṣāpariccheda* is a desideratum in the domain of the Nyāya concept of Śabda which forms a very important part of Indian epistemology.

C

THE GENESIS OF THE CONCEPT OF ŚĀBDABODHA: THE ORIGIN OF THE VARIOUS THEORIES OF MEANING:

The proposed critical exposition of the Śabdakhaṇḍa of the *Bhāṣā pariccheda* is expected to be a review of the problem of Śābdabodha as dealt with by Viśvanātha Nyāyapañcānana.

The problem of Śābdabodha is the issue of the total meaning conveyed by the corresponding words as parts of a sentence. It is the issue of the relational thought to be gathered from a sentence. The problem of meaning has arrested, though in different ways, the attention of scholars almost in all parts of the world. The various systems of thought even in Ancient India came to present vast and variegated discussion on the problem. Those very discussions may be said to have formed the Philosophy of language in Ancient India. Even from the days of the Ṛgveda, probably the earliest document of mankind, language or speech has been viewed with all importance. We come across innumerable passages in the Saṁhitās, Brāhmaṇas and Upaniṣads in reverential praise of speech or language. In order to avoid much digression from our main theme we have to resist the temptation of reproducing them in full. Only for illustration, we may refer to *Ṛgveda* X.125.3[51] and X.114.8[52]. The Vedic passages testify to the fact that the speech or language as the Vehicle of communication amongst the members of society was duly valued. Insistence also on correct use of language was seen in India since very early time. According to a Vedic seer, those who cannot use the language correctly are fools. The speech of the learned is beautiful as it is free from blemishes.[53] The stress on the meaningful statements was duly given by the Vedic scholars.[54] Vedic passages are eloquent even in respect of the advantages that can be derived from the proper understanding of the speech.[55]

The trend of thought regarding language continues to acquire new dimensions with the various schools of thought in Vedic and Post-Vedic periods. The speculations on the nature of speech, i.e., the problem of word and its meaning also began with the Ṛgvedic thinkers. The four-fold division[56] of words (Padas) into Nāma, Ākhyāta, Upasarga and Nipāta by Yāska and endorsed by Patañjali is originally found in a Ṛgvedic verse[57] which is quoted in the *Mahābhāṣya*. We meet with attempts at etymological analysis of different words like Indra, Agni etc., in the Brāhmaṇas (namely *Śatapatha, Tāṇḍya* etc.), Āraṇyakas and the Upaniṣadas. With the increasing importance of ritualistic part of the Vedas, there grew up some sort of a science of language or word meanings also out of an anxiety to check the distortion of the Vedic meanings. This anxiety is best revealed in the Pūrvamīmāṁsā school of Jaimini. We find the Prātiśākhyas and Yāska's *Nirukta* attempting metaphysical and syntatical speculations on language. Yāska refers to several earlier authorities like Audumbarāyaṇa, Vārṣyāyaṇi, Śākaṭāyana and Gārgya who are said to have speculated on the problem of meaning.[58] Yāska's treatment may be said to have served as the basis for further speculations in later schools of Indian Philosophy.

Pāṇini came to be concerned more with the form of language than with its meanings. He made elaborate speculations on the nature of the parts of speech and etymological derivations of words. But he did not make any attempt at metaphysical explanation of language. It was Patañjali who dealt with the syntatical problems with due elaboration. He also supplied the metaphysical explanation of the Sūtras of Pāṇini. Bhartṛhari, the author of the *Vākyapadīya* was responsible for the continuation and elaboration of the Philosophy of word-absolute as begun in the Upaniṣads. As claimed also by Bhartṛhari, this absolutistic Philosophy is based on the Vedas.[59] The process of the spiritualisation of the word became too obvious in the tantras.

An objective analysis, however, shows that pure grammar and logic make the twin that serve as unavoidable aids in presenting meaningful language. In India, there came to take place an increasing and systematic growth of these two disciplines in subsequent periods. A form of a language expressing a proposition is called a sentence. Pending further discussion on the nature of a sentence in subsequent pages in the present work, we may say this much at this stage that a sentence has a definite form and it also expresses a definite meaning, true or false. The probability of truth or falsehood involved in this context leads to the problem of validity (prāmāṇya) of a Vākyārthajñāna (the knowledge of the meaning of a sentence). Here again we have to remember that the Śābdabodha, the subject under investigation, is nothing but this Vākyārthjñāna. Śabda by way of serving as the principal instrument for giving such a Śābdabodha (verbal cognition) comes to get later on the status of a Pramāṇa. In this context Śābdabodha as the valid verbal knowledge is the Pramā (valid knowledge) and the Śabda is the Pramāṇa (the chief instrument for the attainment of the valid knowledge). This history of Śabda as Pramāṇa can be easily traced back to the time of Pūrvamīmāṁsā. The Mīmāṁsā sūtras commenced with a discussion on the nature of human duty. It is stated there that which gives one some urge is the very duty.[60] Now Pratyakṣa or perception as a source of knowledge depends on the contact of sense organs with objects. So, such a Pramāṇa can guide us only in case of contemporaneous duties, in which objects are physically present. But it cannot guide us in the context of past or future duties. Inference, itself being based on perception can also be of no help. Hence the Mīmāṁsakas resort to Śabda as the pramāṇa to guide us in respect of past and future acts. It is possible, because, according to the Mīmāṁsakas, the words have a perpetual and eternal capacity to signify things. The knowledge from the use of words proceeds without any other aid.[61]

THE CONCEPT OF ŚABDA WITH SPECIAL REFERENCE TO VIŚVANĀTHA NYĀYAPAÑCĀNANA:

Śabda basically means sound (dhvani)[62] and the organ of hearing (śravaṇendriya) is the sense-organ responsible for perceiving it. In this basic point, there is agreement amongst all thinkers.[63] The trouble arises when the Mīmāṁsakas conceive it as an eternal substance (nitya dravya) while in contrast, the Naiyāyikas describe it as an attribute of Ākāśa and understand it as 'anitya' (impermanant).[64] In the domain of linguistics again, the word 'śabda' is found to be used to signify a Pada (word). A Pada, however, consists of certain letter or letter (varṇas).[65] A letter is undoubtedly a special kind of sound. So even in linguistics Śabda keeps in tact its basic character of being a sound. We find Viśvanātha dividing Śabda into two types, viz., Sound and Letter.[66] In view of the difference that a letter maintains from an ordinary sound, this division of Viśvanātha is justified. A 'dhvani' (ordinary sound) is an inarticulate sound, e.g., the sound of a drum (paṭaha). This sound is a confused mass of sound sensations without any order or arrangement of its parts. It does not possess any fixed relation with other similar sounds. A Varṇa (vocal sound) is produced by the action of the vocal organ of the human beings. It is characterised by a fixed nature which enables it to occupy a place in a particular language. Thus letters happen to constitute the human speech and appear in two forms, spoken and written. Spoken letters are directly the auditory sensations of certain significant sounds. The written are the representation of the former by the medium of some script. This basic division of Śabda by Viśvanātha is in conformity with the position of the Naiyāyikas earlier to him.[67] In the matter of such a division of Śabda (dhvani), the Mīmāṁsakas also do not differ.[68]

The word Śabda' again is technically used in the school of Nyāya in the sense of a Pramāṇavākya. A sentence is undoubtedly a specific collection of words. So, a sentence is inevitably a special collection of sounds, i.e., mutually related articulate sounds. This Śabda in its basic character of dhvani is a Guṇa (quality) and not a Dravya (substance). Being a Guṇa it must belong to a substratum. The substratum to which Śabda belongs is the Ākāśa. This is the position of the Nyāya-Vaiśeṣikas including Viśvanātha. Śabda,[69] the sound, according to them, is the specific or differentiating quality (Vaiśeṣika Guṇa) of Ākāśa. Here the Naiyāyikas differ from the Mīmāṁsakas, who understand Śabda as a Dravya.[70] The approach of the Naiyāyikas including Viśvanātha to the problem of eternity (nityatva) of Śabda (both as mere 'dhvani' and 'articulate' varṇa) is being discussed seperately.

We are convinced of the Naiyāyikas, using the word 'śabda' in the sense of Vākya on the strength of the following impressions.

Gautama himself defines Śabdapramāṇa as 'Āptopadeśa'.[71] This Āptopadeśa means a communication from or assertion of a trustworthy person. Manu understands Upadeśa only in the sense of an instructive statement or assertion.[72] We have reasons to believe that at least the Prācīna Naiyāyikas understood this 'upadeśa' only in the sense of such an instructive assertion. Such an idea can be gathered from the *Bhāṣya* of Vātsyāyana.[73] But if we understand Gautama's Upadeśa only in the sense of an instruction, all non-instructive statements or assertions emanating even from the Āptas (trusted persons) will not obtain the status of the Śabdapramāṇa. It will limit the scope of Sabda very much. Presumably on this account, some Navyanaiyāyikas came to replace the word Upadeśa by the word 'vākya' in the context of defining Śabda.[74] They did it perhaps in order to widen the scope of Śabdapramāṇa. But still upto this stage there remains in tact the basic character of Śabdapramāṇa in its being a sentence (vākya), instructive or non-intructive, uttered or used by an Āptapuruṣa (trustworthy persons). Here we simply note that in the context of Viśvanātha's kārikās on Śabda we shall have to discuss the issue of the acceptability of Śabda in the sense of a Pada or Vākya as a Pramāṇa, i.e., Śābdabodhakaraṇa.

With regard to the term 'upadeśa', we may further add that the grammarians understand the term Upadeśa in the sense of 'the first utterance.'[75] We cannot understand Gautama's Upadeśa in the sense of 'the first utterence' as in that case the subsequent utterences of the trustworthy persons will not get the status of Śabdapramāṇa. The Mīmāṁsakas understand 'Upadeśa' in the sense of a context of a work that comes to convey a series of desired meanings.[76] We shall have to conclude here by simply reiterating that the Upadeśa, taken in any of the above senses, shall have to come to us in the form of a sentence. The very etymology of the word comes in support of this position.[77] In view of this, there must be a sentence to carry out the Upadeśa. The position of those Navyanaiyāyikas who replaced the term 'Upadeśa' by the word 'Vākya' comes to be more acceptable both for the sake of simplification and the avoidance of ambiguity. As gatherede from the analysis of the later Naiyāyikas, Śābdabodha, which may be described as Śābdajñāna also came to be universally understood as the Vākyārthajñāna.[78] The knowledge pertaining to Śabda came to be deemed as the knowledge of the meaning of a Vākya. From this it may be deduced that with the Naiyāyikas, a Śabda stands for a Vākya in the matter of getting the status of a Pramāṇa. But to be a Pramāṇa, however, that Vākya must belong to an Āpta (trustworthy person) by way of being uttered or used by him.

A note is here imperative on the term 'Āpta' also. While Gautama defines Śabdapramāṇa as 'Āptopadeśa', he personally gives no explanation as to who is an Āpta'. But the Bhāṣyakāra explains the term at length. According to him Āpta is one who has directly perceived the true nature of things and who is prompted to communicate the properly experienced ideas. Perception of objects may be termed 'āpti'. As he is prompted to communicate by that very 'āpti', he is called an Āpta. According to the context or the object perceived, anybody irrespective of caste or status, may emerge out as an Āpta or authority. Thus this definition of the term Āpta holds good equally with seers, Āryas (guileless or innocent people) and even Mlecchas (low or uncultured people).[79] Sometimes even thieves and dacoits may speak the truth. According to one opinion, an Āpta is one who possesses true knowledge that comes to serve as the ground for further application, or engagement.[80] Viśvanātha's own idea is that the Āpta is one who possesses a perfect knowledge in respect of the meaning of the sentence of the context.[81] Annaṁbhaṭṭa more precisely explains the term Āpta as a truthful speaker, i.e., who speaks about the things as they really are.[82] In other schools of Indian Philosophy also, almost a Similar view is maintained. Nāgeśa in his *Paramalaghumañ*juṣā refers to Patañjali, the author of the *Carakasaṁhitā*, according to whom an Āpta is one who comes to be fully aware of something through experience and who does not make false or distorted version of own experience even out of any passion.[83] If we take into consideration the aforesaid ideas regarding an Āpta, the point comes to be certain that for all, the Āpta is a truthful speaker as he does not falsify his experience. In the present work hereafter, we shall use only 'the statement of a trustworthy person' to mean an 'Āptavākya'.

Here we want to point out that the Naiyāyikas strictly wanted Śabda to be the statement of an Āpta in order to give it the status of a Pramāṇa. By Śabda in the sense of Āptavākya, they covered both Vedic and non-Vedic statements.

In case of Viśvanātha, we may say that though he does not directly define Śabda as Āptavākya, we have internal textual evidences in the *Muktāvali* itself to conclude that he also accepts an Āptavākya as the Śabda.

It is interesting to note that Īśvarakṛṣṇa in his *Sāṁkhyakārikā* refers to the verbal testimony not as Śabda but directly as the Āptavacana (the statement of a trustworthy person).[84] He explains his Āptavacana as Āptaśruti. Later writers of Sāṁkhya freely understand this Śruti here in the sense of a Vākya.[85]

These Āptavākyas, we may add, are seen divided into two groups (i) Dṛṣṭārtha, i.e., those relating to perceptible objects and (ii) Adṛṣṭārtha,i.e., those relating to non-preceptible objects. The Nyāyabhāṣyakāra feels that hereby the Sūtrakāra intends a division of sentences uttered by ordinary trustworthy persons and extra-ordinary ones like the seers.[86]

Annaṁbhaṭṭa, a later Naiyāyika, first divides sentences into worldly and Vedic and maintains that all the Vedic sentences are valid because of being uttered by God. But of the wordly, i.e., non-Vedic sentences, only those which are the versions of trustworthy persons, are to be treated as valid, otherwise not.[87]

ŚABDĀNITYATVAVĀDA :

The Mīmāṁsakas, Naiyāyikas and Vaiyākarṇas have a discord among themselves regarding the basic nature of Śabda. The Mīmāṁsakas were very much careful in asserting the eternity (nityatva) of Śabda inasmuch as the admission of the non-eternality of Śabda would mean non-eternality of the Vedas too.[88] As Dr. Radjakrishnan sums-up, according to the Mīmāṁsakas, "the Vedas are eternal, since the words of which they are composed are eternal. The relationship between the word and its meaning is natural--------- words and objects denoted by them are both eternal."[89] As Dr. Ganganath Jha points out, in the view of the Mīmāṁsakas, the meaning of the word cannot be comprehended 'except on the hypothesis of its eternality.'[90] Jaimini contends that the utterance only helps to make the already existing word perceptible.[91] He is of the opinion that the volume of the word does not undergo increase or decrease, though the sound proceeding from men increases or decreases.[92] The Bhāṭṭas also unhesitatingly accept Śabda as nitya. Kumārila recognises Śabda as an eternal and all-pervading substance (Dravya).[93] His followers also subscribe to this very opinion.[94] The Prābhākaras also advocate the eternality of Śabda.[95] They hold that there is no such thing as mere dhvani or indistinct sound. All sounds come to be heard in the shape of some letters only.[96] Some letters compose a word (śabda). Though the Bhāṭṭas admit the existence of indistinct sounds,[97] yet, they seem to be concerned with the issue of the eternality of only the distinct sounds, i.e., letters which come to constitute a word. The letters being admitted as eternal, the word comprising of it is obviously recognised as such. The Mīmāṁsakas' admission of eternality of Varṇātmakaśabda is due to their recognition of it as a Dravya on a par with Ākāśa.[98] They, however, dont recognise the sounds that manifest the letters as eternal.[99]

Despite differences in opinion amongst themselves, Grammarians may be generally described as the Śabdanityatvavādins. The Grammarians assert the eternality of Śabda primarily in a different way. According to them, a word is a series of successive sounds called letters. A series of such letter-sounds manifests one inarticulate sound-essence called Sphoṭa. This Sphoṭa is an eternal essence that exists corresponding to every word. The Mīmāṁsakas and the Naiyāyikas join hands in opposing vehemently this Sphoṭa theory of Grammarians. We shall have the scope to discuss the issue in the context of our exposition of the *Muktāvalī* where we have a direct reference to the view of the Naiyāyikas in this regard. Regarding the issue of 'nityatva' of a 'Varṇātmakaśabda' Patañjali introduces the query in his *Bhāṣya* and seems to offer a balanced view.[100] It is opined that Patañjali tries to take a non-partisan attitude in this context.[101] But Patañjali hastens to add that his distinguished predecessor Pāṇini recognised the eternality of word, meaning and the relation between the two.[102] That both Mīmāṁsakas and Vaiyākaraṇs recognise the term 'akṣara' as a synoymn of varṇa is also very significant.[103]

The Naiyāyikas as against the Mīmāṁsakas and the Vaiyākaraṇas in particular are known very much for their concept of non-eternality of Śabda. The Naiyāyikas controvert the position of Mīmāṁsakas asserting that Śabda is 'anitya.'[104] But even amongst the Naiyāyikas, we come to observe differences in handling of the issue.

Viśvanātha asserts that though all sounds (Śabda in all forms) remain inherent as quality in a substratum, namely, Ākāśa, they come to be objects of perception only when they are produced in the ear.[105] As we have the notion that a particular sound, say 'ka' is produced and that it is destroyed, the conviction that sound (Śabda) is transitory is quite obvious.[106] That which originates and gets destroyed is what is known as anitya. Viśvanātha then replies to those who accept the eternality of sounds on account of what is called Pratyabhijñā (recognition). When we recognise that "this is the same 'ka'," the object of that very recognition is the fact of (the present sound 'ka') belonging to the same class as that of the first 'sound ka' and not that of its identity with the first 'sound ka'.[107] Such a position justifies both the notions of origination and recognition. Viśvanātha clarifies his concept of the Pratyabhijñā na by way of giving a popular illustration. When some person says 'The very medicine I made comes to be made by another person also', we understand the two medicines as being similar and not as identical.[108] As Mīmāṁsakas were very much insistent on the notion of Pratyabhijñāna for proving the 'nityatva' of Śabda,-[109] the Naiyāyikas like Jayantabhaṭṭa are found giving lengthy rejoinders in the context.[110]

Viśvanātha concludes that all Varṇas (letters) are transitory.[111] The conclusion is quite logical. As sound is proved to be basically 'anitya' in the sense of being produced and destroyed, the Varṇa also obviously comes to be 'anitya'. Though Viśvanātha does not proceed further to add that Padas and Vākyas are 'anitya', the conclusion is implied. A Vākya is a collection of Padas, a Pada is a Varṇa or a collection of Varṇas. A Varṇa being proved 'anitya', a Pada or a Vākya will obviously be 'anitya'.

As against the above notion of the Naiyāyikas, the Mīmāṁsakas contend that the Śabda standing for the Vedas is eternal and impersonal and that the Vedas are without any author.[112] The Mīmāṁsakas are not prepared to accept the Vedas as revelations and they assert that the Vedas need nothing external for their validity. Thus in the context of Śabdapramāṇa also, there ensues the two notion of intrinsic validity (Svataḥ prāmāṇyavāda) (of the Mīmāṁsakas) and extrinisic validity (parataḥ prāmāṇyavāda) (of the Naiyāyikas). The Naiyāyikas give extra-ordinary stress on Śabdapramāṇa being accepted as extrinsically valid (Parataḥ-pramāṇa) as demanded by their own concept of Śabda as 'anitya' and 'kārya'.[113]

Here we may note that the Vedas or the Vedic utterances being but Collections of Words are naturally viewed as non-eternal by the Naiyāyikas. But yet the earlier Naiyāyikas were ready to declare the Vedas as 'nitya', probably in somewhat a secondary sense, only on the plea of its traditional continuity, which is categorically rejected in later times.[114] Udayana who is known for initiating new ideas, thereby helping in the emergence of the Navyanyāya, points to the deluge and other factors which do not allow such a traditional continuity of the Vedas.[115] Here we feel like this. The Vedas have two aspects, -(i) linguistic and (ii) essential (tāttvika). In the linguistic aspect, even the old logicians thought of the Vedic sentences as they did of the non-Vedic ones. By speaking of 'nityatva' of Vedas, they were anxious, we may presume, to stress on the permanent character of the essentials taught in the Vedas. But in the matter of validity of knowledge produced, they placed the 'vedavākya's on a par with the 'laukika' Vākyas. The Naiyāyikas treated the 'vedavākya's as Āptopadeśa or Āptavākya as they did in case of non-vedic sentences in the context of producing valid verbal knowledge (Śābdapramā). The Āpta in connection with the Vedas was no other than God.[116] The validity of the Vedas is derived from the trustworthiness of God, the Āptapuruṣa.

ŚĀBDABODHA : AN EPISTEMOLOGICAL ISSUE :

The concept of Śābdabodha, with which we are primarily concerned in the present work, with special reference to its treatment in Viśvanātha's *Bhāṣāpariccheda*, is obviously an epistemological issue. Śābdabodha means the knowledge of the meaning of a sentence, i.e., the total relational idea converyed by a proposition, as distingusihed from the expression 'śabdabodha', which simply signifies the knowledge of a particular word. As we shall see by and by, śābdabodha is the valid knowledge (Pramā) coming from Śabda as its source or means (Pramāṇa). In the very first Kārikā in the chapter on Śabda in his *Bhāṣāpariccheda*, Viśvanātha introduces Śābdabodha as the 'phala' of the 'padajñāna' which is the Karaṇa. The term Karaṇa here means Pramākaraṇa, as it does so in other works and other systems also.[117] Pramākaraṇa means Pramāṇa (i.e., a source of valid knowledge) and the 'phala' of a Karaṇa (i.e., Pramākaraṇa) is the Pramā (i.e., valid knowledge).[118] As the concept of śābdabodha is related with the concept of a valid knowledge, it will be pertinent to preface a more detailed study of the theory of Śābdabodha with an account of the Indian Epistemology or the Indian theory of knowledge in brief outlines.

As is usual with all times and climes, Indian philosophical schools also sprang up out of an urge for enquiry into the real state of things and beings (tattvajijñāsā). Different schools of Indian philosophy came to be busy not only in deducing conclusions but also in determining the methods of arriving at them. The thinkers were interested not merely in knowing things but also were heavily occupied with the task of sorting out the means for ascertaining the knowledge of objects. Because of such an approach, the Indian Epistemology comes to involve four basic factors.[119]

(1) The Pramātā — the knower, the cognizer of valid knowledge.

(2) The Prameya — the knowable : the object known, the object of valid knowledge.

(3) The Pramāṇa — the chief instrument or organ of knowing : the source of valid knowledge.

(4) The Pramā or Pramiti — the valid knowledge (of the object).[120]

But here we must be cautious to note that in the context of the concept of the aforesaid factors, there are marked and delicate differences amongst the different schools. As for instance, some understand the Pramāṇa as the source of valid knowledge and the others as the valid knowledge itself. As a result in the case of the latter, the Pramā and the Pramāṇa come to be identified. Hence, our interpretation of the four factors here is from a general point of view especially from the stand point of the Naiyāyikas. Naiyāyikas have objected to attempting at identification between Pramā ṇa and Pramā.[121]

Notwithstanding the difference maintained by the various schools regarding the number and nature of the knowable entities (prameyas),[122] the thinkers belonging to different schools behaved as one in their strong common anxiety for realising only the valid knowledge (Pramā). Hence in order to ascertain the validity of their knowledge, the scholars paid serious attention to those so-called Pramāṇas.

Before we discuss the Prāmaṇas, we shall have to take a note of the very validity ('prāmāṇya') of knowledge. Why the knowledge is to be valid ? Why again a Pramāṇa is necessary ?

Almost all the principal schools of Indian Philosophy have commenced with a reply to such an anticipated question. As Gautama puts it, the very aim of philosophical speculations is Niḥśreyasa (final Beatitude or Supreme Bliss). The different schools ofcourse understand this Niḥśreyasa in their own ways. As for illustration, the Sāṁkhya aims at Kaivalya, the Vedānta at the oneness with the Brahman and the Yoga speaks of an union in the state of Samādhi. But how to realise this Niḥśreyasa ? Gautama asserts that the Tattvajñāna (the ascertainment of reality) serves as the means towards this end. Niḥśreyasa, according to Gautama, follows only when one gets rid of Mithyājñāna (false knowledge) which is the root cause of one's getting involved in the worldly process.[123] Our knowledge of objects is not automatically valid or real. There is, therefore, the scope of 'Mithyājñāna'. As tattvajñāna, i.e., lack of Mithyājñāna is the means for the realisation of Niḥśreyasa,[124] our knowledge demands a serious scrutiny. Thus the problem of tattvajñāna obviously leads to the relevant issues of Pramā, Pramātā, Prameya and Pramāṇa. Insistence is naturally laid on the validity of knowledge by way of wanting it to be free from doubt, uncertainity and contradiction and to be different from remembrance.[125] For the sake of obtaining the valid knowledge of such a description, there followed a serious search for the so called Pramāṇas (the means of the valid knowledge) in different schools of philosophy in ancient India.

In the context of the importance of the Pramāṇas, we can take a special note of the Naiyāyikas' approach in the matter. As we can gather an idea from the Bhāṣya of Vātsyāyana, the Naiyāyikas believe that the Pramāṇas lead to the cognition of objects and hence result in some physical or mental action or activity of the cogniser (the Pramātā).[126] Vātsyāyana points out the basic relation between the aforesaid four epistemological factors. Only when the Pramāṇas are 'meaningful', the other three factors, Pramātā, Prameya and Pramiti come to be 'useful'.[127] Hence the insistence on the validity of Pramāṇas stands justified. A controversial issue exists insofar as whether it is activity which preceds knowledge or vice-versa. Again there is the much debated problem of simultenaity of Pramā and Pramāṇa.

Opinions differ as to the nature of Pramā and Pramāṇa. As for instance, while the Mīmāṁsakas and the Naiyāyikas agree in respect of the concept of Pramāṇa, they differ in the case of Pramā. Again with regard to the Pramāṇas, the Naiyāyikas basically differ from the Buddhas.[128] The various schools of Ancient Indian philosophy are again not unanimous in their choice of the Pramāṇas. There is marked difference in opinion again in the context of the validity (prāmāṇya) of knowledge. We propose to make a brief discussion on the said issue of the validity of knowledge.

SVATAḤPRĀMĀṆYAVĀDA AND PARATAḤ PRĀMĀṆYAVĀDA

Ancient Indian Philosophers distinctively differ from each other on the question ofthe vaidity and invalidity of knowledge.[129] In this regard, two rival theories come to our notice - (i) The theory of self validity of knowledge and (ii) The theory of external validity of knowledge.

According to the Bhāṭṭa Mīmāṁsakas, the validity of knowledge is self-evident. They advocate that truth is self-validating, requiring no extraneous evidence. To the Prābhākaras, the valid knowledge is the direct and immediate apprehension. Recollection or Smṛti, they say, is invalid as it depends on the impression left by some past experience. While the Bhāṭṭas also accept the view of the Prābhākaras that the valid knowledge is an apprehension, they maintain that the invalidity of knowledge is only inferred from the knowledge of imperfections in its causes and the knowledge of its disagrement with its object. The Advaita Vedāntins agree with the Mīmāṁsakas that the validity of knowledge is its inherent character and that the knowledge of invalidity proceeds only from extraneous circumstances. The Sāṁkhyaits beleive in knowledge as the consciousness of the self and regard validity and invalidity of knowledge as the inherent characteristics of knowledge. As opposed to such treds of thought. the Nyāya-vaiseṣikas assert that there is a correspondence between knowledge and its object. That knowledge is valid which represents the real nature of its object. When there is a disagreement between the two it (i.e., the knowledge) is invlid. Thus, the Nyāya realists reject the theory of self-validity of knowledge. In this context, the Naiyāyikas get full support from the Jainas. To the Jainas also, the validity of knowledge lies in its agreement with the object cognized and the invalidity in its disagreement with the object cognized. According to the Naiyāyikas, both validity and invalidity of knowledge are inferred from fruitful and fruitless results respectively.But, the Bauddhas differ from the Naiyāyikas only in this point that according to the former, only the validity of knowledge is known through fruitful activity, but the invalidity of knowledge is inherent in itself and does not depend on any other circumstances.

Viśvanātha as a Naiyāyika is strictly opposed to the concept of self-validity or self-invalidity of knowledge. He refers to the divergent views[130] of his predecessors belonging to different schools of thought, rejects them and finally asserts that the theory of self-validity of knowledge is not acceptable as it will leave no scope for any doubt whatsoever.[131] But the occurrence of doubt here is a matter of experience. Hence it is not a desirable position. As a matter of fact, the knowledge is valid when there is agreement or correspondence between knowledge and its object. Similarly the knowledge is invalid where there is no such agreement or correspondence between the two.[132]

To take an idea regarding the Naiyāyikas' view of Pramā, we place below the basic classification of knowledge by the Naiyāyikas in a tabular form.

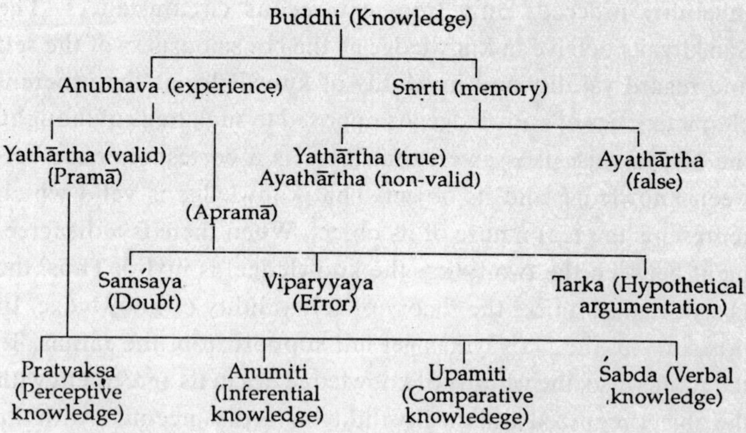

THE PRAMĀṆAS :

In the matter of recognising different Pramāṇas, the various schools of Indian philosophy may be conveniently referred to as follows:[133] The cārvākas or the materialists recognised only perception. The Vaiśeṣikas and Bauddhas add Inference to that (Perception). The Sāṁkhyāits accept Verbal Testimony also with the earlier two. Some of the Naiyāyikas add comparision to the earlier three, namely Perception. Inference and Verbal Testimony. The Prābhākaras admit all these four Pramāṇas along with Arthā patti, the Bhāṭṭa Mīmāṁsakas recognise six sources of knowledge as they add Abhāva to the above. Paurāṇikas add two other Pramā ṇas to the earlier list, namely Saṁbhava and Aitihya. Here we may add that in Yogadarśana three Pramāṇas are admitted namely, Perception, Inference and Scriptural knowledge.[134] But these three sources are supposed as not competant to give an absolutely valid knowledge. In addition to Perception and Inference, the Vaiśeṣikas appear to admit as Pramāṇas corresponding to Remembrance (Smṛti) and Intuitive knowledge (Ārṣajñāna) which are also recognised by them as kinds of valid knowledge.[135]

In various treatises, these problems Pramā, Prameya and Pramāṇa have been extensively dealt with. Jayanta Bhaṭṭa has alluded to all these rival views on a preamble to his opinion.[136]

In the school of Nyāya, four Pramāṇas have been admitted. They are namely, Pratyakṣa Anumāna, Upamāna and Śabda.[137] Vātsyāyana points out the necessity of admitting more than one Pramāṇa. In the matter of acquiring knowledge, only Perception would not help. It gives us the knowledge of an object only when somebody is near it to have the object within the reach of his sense organs. While one can have the visual perception of fire only when one is near it, the same knowledge can be gathered even from a short distance through an Inference by seeing the smoke. The very knowledge of the presence of fire at the same place can be gathered also by means of a Verbal Testimony, i.e., on the strength of the assertion of a trustworthy person in the form of 'There is fire'. Moreover in the context of proving the validity of vedic sentences regarding unperceptible objects like heaven,

Śabda, the Verbal Testimony comes to be the only aid.[138] Yet the Naiyāyikas as realists contend that pratyakṣa should be deemed the best of the four as only through Pratyakṣa the desire of one to know something can be finally set at rest.[139] Interestingly a basic difference is sought to be maintained between Pratyakṣa on one hand and other three Pramāṇas on the other hand. In Anumāna, Upamāna and Śabda, the knowledge respectively of premise, similarity and word serves as the data or source or what is technically called Karaṇa for corresponding Pramās. But in the matter of Pratyaksa, no knowledge what-soever comes to serve as the instrumental cause.[140] As defined by Gaṅgeśa, Pratyakṣa is a direct apprehension.[141] Here the contact of senses with objects serves as the data.[142] Hence the Naiyāyikas as the realists show an obvious preference for Pratyakṣa. The Naiyāyikas differ from both the sections of the Mīmāṁsakas as they do not admit Arthāpatti or Presumption as a source of knowledge. The Naiyāyikas differ from the Bhāṭṭa Mīmāṁsakas further on the ground of not recognising Abhāva as a Pramāṇa. Unlike the paurāṇikas, the Naiyāyikas do not accept Aitihya and sambhava as separate Pramāṇas. According to them Arthāpatti, Abhāva, Aitihya and Sambhava are not separate Pramāṇas as they can easily be included within the scope of the four Pramāṇas accepted in the Nyāya school.[143]

THE ORDER IN THE LIST OF PRAMĀṆAS:

Now it is desirable on our part to examine if there is any significance in the order of counting or naming the Pramāṇas. We are to find out if there be any criterion followed in this regard.

In all schools, Pratyakṣa or Perception is placed first. It is obvious and logical as Perception forms the basis of all other Pramāṇas. In the view of Naiyāyikas, Perception is the chief of the sources of knowledge (pramitiḥ pratyakṣaparā). But the question arises as to why Śabda is not placed just after Pratyakṣa and before Anumāna. It may be argued the the scope of Śabda is as large or wide as that of Pratyakṣa and that Anumāna is of lesser scope in comparision to Śābda. But it is a common fact that Śabda is placed not after Pratyakṣa but only after Anumāna. It has been replied in this context that the Śabdapramāṇa necessitates the prior involvement not only of Pratyakṣa but also of Anumāna. In the context of Śādabodha, in the first stage words are heard. Here is the admission of auditory Perception (Śrauta pratyakṣa). Then comes the problem of knowing the meanings of words. One can know the meaning of word only after knowing the significative power (Śakti) of the word concerned. Now in the process of learning the significative power of words by observing Vṛddhavyavahāra (behaviour of the elderly people),a process of Anumāna is obviously involved. We shall discuss the involvement of Anumāna in the context of Vṛddhavyavahāra in connection with our exposition of the relevant Muktāvalī text. Here we are to note that some authorities like Viśvanātha describe Vṛddhavyavahāra as only one of the Śaktigrāhakas (factors which serve as aids in one's knowing the significative power of a word). Others like Nāgeśa admit Vṛddhavyavahāra as the chief or the first of all Śaktigrāhakas. The scholars belonging to the second group believe that in case of new words, the first Śaktigraha is possible only through Vṛddhavyavahāra. Pending our elaborate discussions on Vṛddhavyavahāra, we reiterate the agreed opinion of scholars including Viśvanātha that because of the Śaktigraha, through Vṛddhavyavahāra, involving an Anumā na, Śabda is justifiably placed after Anumāna.[144] In the list of Pramāṇas maintained by the two schools of Mīmāṁsakas, Śabda is placed third.[145] In view of the aforesaid argument, this can be appreciated. But how is it that the Vedāntins and the Naiyāyikas have come to place Śabda fourth and Upamāna third in the list of Pramāṇas maintained by them.[146] The Vedāntins have clarified their position with the aid of the maxim 'A needle and a frying pan.'[147] The maxim may be amplified as follows : In response to two orders placed by a customer at the same time for a frying pan and a needle, a blacksmith shows his practical wisdom by supplying the needle first. There can be no denying of the fact that a frying pan has more importance to a household in comparision to a needle. But the needle is supplied first as it can be manufactured more easily and hence earlier. Similarly not withstanding the relatively greater importance of Śabda, the Vedāntins name and explain Upamāna first as its concept comes to be easier for clarification. It cannot be argued that on the same ground Upamā na could be dispensed with even before Pratyakṣa.[148]

Unlike Śabda, Upamāna is saught by a large number of schools to be included in Pratyakṣa and Anumāna. To arrest such wrong notions, the concepts of Pratyakṣa and Anumāna are required to be brought to focus earlier. That Naiyāyikas and others place Śabda only after Upamāna has been noticed by the Mīmāṁsakas. But yet they justify their own stand of placing Śabda immediately after Pratyakṣa and Anumāna by maintaining that Śabda is admitted by a larger number of theorists in comparison to Upamāna.[149] Now Naiyāyikas also might have utilized the Sūcīkaṭāhanyāya in placing Śabda after Upamāna although we do not find them being vocal about it. But there is a practical difficulty forthe Naiyāyikas to behave like Vedāntins in this matter since their concept of Upamāna is basically different from that of the Vedāntins. According to the Vedāntins, both Upamāna and Śabda should be preceded by Pratyakṣa and Anumāna and there is no muutal dependence between Śabda and Upamāna. What concerns them is the importance of Śabda because of its wider scope in comparision to Upamāna. Yet they can dispense with Upamāna earlier as a matter of practical wisdom in the manner of a blacksmith giving delivery of the needle prior to a frying pan. But in view of the Naiyāyikas, every case of Upamāna necessitates the prior involvement of Śabda. So is it not necessary to elucidate the concept of Śabda earlier to that of Upamāna ? Hence let us add a few more lines on the issue.

The Vedāntins' idea of the Upamānapramāṇa runs thus: One

who has seen an individual cow in one's own homeyard comes to have the visual perception of an individual 'gavaya'. He understands that this individual creature is like a cow. Thereafter he comes to conclude that his cow is like this creature. Here the knowledge of similarity with 'go' in 'gavaya' serves as the data or Karaṇa to give the knower the final knowledge of similarity of his 'go' with the 'gavaya' he has just seen. The final knowledge, i.e., the conclusion is the sādṛśyapramā i.e. Upamiti and the earlier knowledge of similarity of 'gavaaya' with a 'go' i.e. the Karaṇa is the Upamāna. The final knowledge here can not be called perceptive as the 'go' is not being perceived by the owner now. It cannot be inferencial also because of the involvement of the knowledge of similarity therein.[150] Of course, both Perception and Inference serve as the basis of the conclusion. Thus the Sādṛśyapramā or Upamiti of Vedāntins is purely a personal affair without allowing any scope for participation of another person. As the knower does not need to hear from someone earlier, regarding the 'gavaya' being similar to a 'go' the question of prior involvement of Śabda does not arise. Hence, the Vedāntins are not required to clear the concept of Śabda before that of Upamāna. It may be mentioned that the Mīmāṁsakas' concept of Upamāna also does not give scope for the involvement of Śabda in it. But the position of the Naiyāyikas is to be viewed with caution. Despite some difference[151] in approach between the earlier and the later Naiyāyikas the concept of Upamāna of the Naiyāyikas requires that the knower is to hear ealier from someone else (a forester who has the perceptive knowledge of 'gavaya') that the 'gavaya' is like a 'go'. This earlier statement (say of the forester in case of comparative knowledge regarding 'go' and 'gavaya') is technically known as Atideśavākya. This Atideśavākya admitted by the Naiyāyikas must be regarded as an Āptavākya to safeguard the validity of Upamiti itself inasmuch as in the Nyāya view it forms the basis for the functioning of Upamāna. An outsider goes to a forest, sees a 'gavaya', observes its similarity with a 'go', remembers the earlier statement of the forester and concludes that this creature 'gavaya' is what the 'gavaya' stands for. Hence the prior involvement of Śabda in the concept of Upamāna of the Naiyāyikas in the form of Atideśavākya cannot be ruled out. It is therefore, essential for a Naiyāyika to elucidate the concept of Śabda before he comes to ascertain the nature of Upamāna.

As the four Kārikās of Viśvanātha on Śabda in his *Bhāṣāpariccheda* come after his two Kārikās on Upamāna, we have to add a few more lines on the issue in the context of our present work. As Viśvanātha himself puts it,[152] the result of an Upamāna is the ascertaining of the significative power (śakti) of words like 'gavaya'. In the process of production of the Śābdabodha (verbal comprehension), according to Viśvanātha, the knowledge of Padas (padajñāna) serves as the Karaṇa (instrumental cause) being possessed of the functional intermediary (Vyāpāra) in the form of knowledge of the meanings of Padas (Padārthajñāna). But the knowledge (i.e., ascertaining) of the very signifcative power of words, i.e., Śaktidhīḥ is the way or course by which the Karaṇa in Śābdabodha comes to give rise to the Vyāpāra. Thus Upamiti (i.e., the result produced by an Upamāna Pramāṇa) coms to serve as an aid in case of Śābdabodha. Judged from this point of view, the precedence of the discussion of Upamāna to that on Śabda comes to be justified. But here we face the following problem. Upamāna as Śaktigrāhaka comes to help us not in all but a few cases of Śābdabodha. It is why like others Viśvanātha also has referred to Upamāna as only one of the Śaktigrāhakas (i.e., the factors responsible for ascertaining the denotative power of words). We shall have to discuss in appropriate time the service that can be rendered by Upamāna as one of the Śaktigrāhakas. But here we again come back to the point of prior involvement of Śabdapramāṇa in the concept of Upamāna. Viśvanātha also does not differ from other Naiyāyikas in this regard.

As we learn from Viśvanātha's own exposition in the *Muktāvalī* of his Kārikās on Upamāna, the process of an Upamāna, may be briefly stated as follows : A villager who has never seen a 'gavaya' learns from a forester that a 'gavaya' is like a 'go' (cow). When the villager sees a 'gavaya', he first observes the similarity of the creature with a cow. This knowledge of similarity comes to serve as the instrumental cause for an Upamāna (UpamānaKaraṇaṁ). Then the villager remembers the statement of the forester that a 'gavaya' is like a cow. This remembrance of the statement of the forester serves as the operative cause (Vyāpāra) for an Upamāna. Then the villager comes to have the final knowledge that the creature 'gavaya' is what is denoted by the word 'gavaya'. This is the 'Upamiti' which is undoubtedly the knowledge of the significative power of the word 'gavaya'[153]

The statement of forester, the remembrance of which is regarded as the Vyāpāra of an Upamāna in a particular context, is the Atideśavākya. An Atideśavākya is nothing but an instructive statement (somewhat like Upadeśa). The very etymology of the word (i.e. atidiśyate iti) also confirms it. Nevertheless, as we have already pointed out earlier, it is not different from an Āptavākya as the statement comes from one who speaks with knowledge. Āpta is defined as one who speaks with knowledge, i.e., points out what is what. If the Atideśavākya is nothing other than Āptavākya, it is then no other than a Śabdapramāṇa itself. Here in the illustration of Upamāna by Viśvanātha, the forester is to be regarded as an Āpta (trustworthy) as his version tallys undoubtedly with facts. Hence the Atideśavākya, i.e., the Vākya of forester here is to be recognised as Śabdapramāṇa for its being an Āptavākya. We have already discussed the Naiyāyikas' appraoch to Śabdapramāṇa as an Āptopadeśa or an Āptavākya. Thus Śabda comes to be involved as a precondition in the process of an Upamāna. But we find that Upamāna comes to serve as an aid of Śabda only in certain specific cases and not in all cases. Simply speaking, Upamāna is not the only Śaktigrāhaka but is one of the Śaktigrāhakas. All cases of Śābdabodha are not the result of Upamānas. But every case of Upamāna implies prior invovement of Śabda as there can be no Upamāna without an Atideśavākya.

Thus there can be no Upamāna without a prior Śabda though there can be Śabda leading to a Śābdabodha without a prior Upamāna.

In view of above observation, we can not argue that the service of Upamāna as an aid of Śabda in the production of Śābdabodha should be treated as the ground for the order of presentation of Pramāṇa followed by Viśvanātha and other Naiyāyikas. Hence atleast upto this stage, we form an impression that the treatment of Śabda in case of Naiyāyikas should have preceded that of the Upamānapramāṇa. But we can also argue otherwise. Granting that a Naiyāyika comes to discuss Śabda Prior to Upamāna because of the argument that the concept of Upamāna necessitates a prior clarification of the concept of Śabda, he would still come to be in an awkward position at the time of discussing the Śaktigrāhakas which include Upamāna also. Should he break-away to discuss the concept of Upamāṇa while he is in the mid stream of discussion of the process of Śābdabodha ? It will in no way be justified on his part again to refer to Upamāna as a Śaktigrāhaka without having a prior analysis of the technical and hence not immediately understandable term Upamāna. Viewed thus, the dependence of Śabda on Upamāna, however partial, stands admitted. Again between the two terms, Atideśavā kya and Upamāna, the latter comes to be less immediately understandable. Because of such a position, they had to dispense with Upamāna earlier. Or if we simply realise the fact of both the Pramāṇas being inter-dependent, one fully and other partially, in that case, we can utilize the sūcīkaṭāhanyāya as the Vedāntins did.

ŚABDAPRAMĀṆA : A SPECIAL NOTE

As we have already mentioned, Śabda has been recognised as a separate Pramāṇa by almost all the important schools of Indian Philosophy except Jaina, Bauddha, Cārvāka and Vaiśeṣika. The Mīmāṁsakas and Vedāntins give the status of this Pramāṇa primarily[154] to the Vedas. Hence, in these schools, Śabda pramāṇa is known as Śāstra, Śruti and Āgama also [155] The Sāṁkhyas also understand the Verbal testimony in the sense of scripture. Yet with some of the Sāṁkhyas, we directly find Śabdapramāṇa being named as Āptavacana.[156] But in the Nyāya school althroughout, this Pramāṇa is named as Śabda only. Mīmāṁsakas differ amongst themselves in the matter of determining as to what is to be the Śābdabodhakaraṇa. Whether it should be Pada, Padārtha, Vākya, Vākyārtha or the knowledge of any one of these ? We shall have to discuss various views on Śābdabodhakaraṇa elsewhere in the context of the examination of Viśvanātha's concept of Karaṇa. Here we may simply note that Śabda as Pramāṇa is understood in the sense of a Vākya almost by all the Naiyāyikas. A sentence (Vā kya) (Of course, uttered by a trustworthy person) comes to be later on directly given the name 'Śabda' and the status of a Pramāṇa. This position is agreed to by some Vedāntins also.[157] We are to note that the Ārṣajñāna admitted by the Jainas as a Pramāṇa is not to be mistaken as Śabda.

Śabda as a Pramāṇa means the source of the knowledge that we get about things, (which are not otherwise directly perceived at the same moment) from relevant sentences by understanding the meanings of the words which they are composed of.[158] We have two types of sentences, 'Vaidika' or Vedic and 'Laukika' or non-Vedic. Only certain schools recognise all sentences as capable of being Śabdapramāṇa under permissible conditions. As for instance, while the Bhāṭṭas accept both Vedic and non-Vedic Verbal cognitions as based on Śabdapramāṇa, the Prābhākaras understand the non-Vedic Verbal Cognitions only as acts of inference. In other words, with the Bhāṭṭas[159] all the Vākyas, Vedic or non-Vedic can get the status of ŚabdaPramāṇa while according to the Prābhākaras[160] the Verbal knowledge obtained from the human words, i.e., Laukika Vākyas, is actually derived from an act of Inference (Anumāna). The Naiyāyikas, maintain a difference with the Prābhākars in so far as they define the

ŚabdaPramāṇa as the Āptopadeśa, i.e., Āptavākya meaning both Vedic and non-Vedic utterences.[161] We shall discuss this view point of Prābhākaras in course of our examining Vṛddhavyavahā ra as a 'śaktigrahopāya', which obviously involves the inferential process in it. But a point of agreement between the two schools of Mīmāṁsā comes to our notice. Both the set of thinkers regard the relationship between the word and its meaning as natural and never conventional. We shall discuss in an appropriate stage that as opposed to the Mīmāṁsakas, the Naiyāyikas regarded this relationship as strictly acquired or conventional. In the case of proper names, however, the Prābhākaras admitt convention as the basis of the relationship between the word and its meaning.

ŚABDA-PRAMĀṆA OPPOSED :

The Mīmāṁsakas who are great votaries of Śabda-Pramāṇa themselves raised doubts regarding the acceptability of Śabda as a Pramāṇa.[162] This they did only in order to establish their arguments in favour of the Śabda-Pramāṇa.[163] They anxiously tried to meet the possible objections against the eternal character of words in general and the Veda in particular. But in subsequent times all the orthodox Philosophers had to join hands against the Buddhists in the matter of non-acceptability of Śabda in the sense of Veda. They had to argue also against the Buddhists' concept that even an ordinary word cannot signify anything positive.

The non-recognition of Śabda as Pramāṇa by the Materialists (cārvākas), the Buddhists and Vaiśeṣikas is also a known fact. Of the schools accepting ŚabdoPramāṇa, the Nyāya is very much alive to this opposition. Gautama, himself raises the doubts of the opponents against the Śabda-Pramāṇa and elaborately argues in this context. Gautama makes the examination separately of (i) Śabda-Sāmānya and (ii) Śabda-Viśeṣa. By the Śabda-Sāmānya, Gautama means the word in general and by the Śabda-Viśeṣa, he means the Veda,i.e., the Vedic sentences.

(i) Some scholars, particularly the Vaiśeṣikas, want to cover 'śabda' by the Anumāṇa (Pramāṇa).[164] It is argued that the Verbal testimony is nothing but an Inference in so far as the meanings of words can be known only through an inferential process. Just as in a pure Inference, from an already known premise ('mitena liṅgena') some other object (i.e., the Liṅgī) comes to be subsequently known, in the so-called 'śabda' also, from the already known word, the meaning comes to be known afterwords.[165] In both Śabda and Anumāṇa, the same is the process of experience. The two do not differ in the process of giving us to know something new.[166]

Further more, just as the relation between a Liṅga (Premise) and a corresponding Liṅgī (Conclusion) is the basis of an Anumā na, the relation between a word and its meaning is also the basis of Verbal testimony.[167] Only because of the existence of such a relation between the two, a meaning comes to be known from an already known word. Thus it is argued that the so-called Śabda-Pramāṇa does not differ from an Anumāṇna. Gautama replies that the Verbal testimony can by no means be included in or equated with an inferential process. It is mainly because the apprehension of meanings from words takes place only on the strength of Āptopadeśa.[168] In his enunciation of the relevant Sūtra, Vātsyāyana points out that the apprehension of even unperceptible object takes place from words like heaven, nymphs etc. only because of the acceptability of the Āptopadeśa.[169] This very factor that Śabda to get the status of a Pramāṇa is to be an Āptopadeśa differentiates it from an Anumān.[170] Though the verbal knowledge presupposes the knowedge of a relation between words and their meanings, yet this fact does not present any affinity between Śabda and Anumāṇna. The sambandha between a Śabda and its Artha cannot be cognised by Pratyakṣa as its knowledge is purely suprasensuous. This sambandha is a peculiar one and that cannot be covered by Samavāya or Saṁyoga.[171] Or as Gautama and his Bhāṣyakāra put it, the apprehension of meanings from words, is not due to any so-called relation but because of the corresponding conventions.[172] This convention is of the form that from such and such a word, such and such a meaning is to be understood."[173] In the context of the exposition of Viśvanātha's *Muktāvalī* we shall again have to elaborately discuss this peculiar concept of the Naiyāyikas regarding the relation in the shape of a convention or the conventional relation between a word and its meaning.[174] Simply we add here that the Naiyāyikas' idea of conventional relation between a Śabda and its Artha comes in sharp contrast with the Mīmāṁsakas' notion of inherent (Autpattika or Svābhāvika) relation between the two. Later Naiyāyikas including Jayantabhaṭṭa have very elaborately discussed the issue and have strongly advocated the acceptability of Śabda as a separate Pramāṇa. Viśvanātha makes a direct reference to the Vaiśeṣikas' attempt to explain away Śabda and Upamāna as mere Anumānas and strongly refuses the arguments forwarded by the opponents on that account.[176] The Vaiśeṣikas see the operation of a pure inferential process in both Verbal Comprehension (Śābdabodha) and comparative knowledge (Upamiti). Viśvanātha fully opposes such a notion inasmuch as even without the involvement of the knowledge of Vyāpti Śābdabodha and Upamiti are found to take place.[177] Viśvanātha elucidates the point in the *Muktāvalīī*.[178] Now the Vyāpti (the law of invariable concommittance) which forms the basis of the Anumāna Pramāṇa is virtually a natural or inherent relation[179] which actually does not exist between a word and its meaning. It is why the same word may be found to convey different meanings in different countries or in different parts of the same country.[180]

Yet, if it is insisted that Śabda falls within Anumāna because of involving a relation, then it could also be claimed with equal force that Anumāna should be included in Śabda in so far as at least involves the use of Vākyas.

(ii) Gautama again tries to justify the validity of Śabda-Viśeṣa' i.e. the Vedic utterences (Vedavākyas).

The opponents argue that the Śabda in the sense of Veda-Vākya cannot be treated as valid due to various reasons, like falsehood, contradictions and repetitions.[181] The Bhāṣyakāra amplifies the arguments. The birth of a son is not seen even to him who performe the ritual called 'Putreṣṭi' out of belief in the Vedic injunction 'Putrakāmaḥ putreṣṭyā yajet'. This śrutivākya enjoins that one desirous of a son should perform the putreṣṭiyāga. If a Vedic sentence regarding a perceptible object like the birth of a son could thus be false, then there can be no guarantee, it is argued, regarding the truth of Vedic sentences like 'Agnihotraṁ juhyāt etc.' which enjoin the performance of Agnihotra sacrifice for one desiring a place in the heaven which is obviously not perceptible.[182] Again the Vedic sentences clash with each other by coveying contradictory meanings. As for illustration, at one place one is enjoined to perform a sacrificial rite only when the sun rises and at another place it is given to understand that the performance of the sacrificial rite at the rise of the sun does not bear any fruit.[183] Moreover, repetitions of Vedic mantras are enjoined in the injunctions like 'triḥ prathamāmanvāha' etc. occuring in the context of the Sāmidheni sacrifice, which speaks of the recitation of the same 'mantra' thrice at the beginning and thrice at the end.[184] But any such repetition is natural only forthe lunatics. Thus the opponents challenge the validity of the Śabdaviśeṣa (Vedavākya). Here we refer to Gautama's rejoinder in brief. The charge of falsehood against the Veda-Vākyas is not tenable inasmuch as the VedaVākyas regarding even some perceptible objects may not bear fruit because of some other reasons like defects in agents, actions and the materials employed.[185] In the context of the performance of the Putreṣṭi, the performers (Kartā) i.e. the parents may have defects like ignorance or misconduct. Their union representing the action (Karma) may also be defective. The materials (Sādhana) also may have defects. The ghee may be impure or the 'mantras' may be wrongly uttered.[186] There are also no contradictions in Vedavākyas if properly understood. The Śrutivākayas like 'Yo' bhyupagataṁ' etc. pinpointing the possibility of loss of fruit of a ritual is meant for those who donot honour the stipulated time.[187] The defect of repetition also does not ensue in the context of enjoining 'abhyāsa' when it goes to be useful. An useless repetition is to be discarded as 'punarukta' while an useful one should be accepted in the name of Anuvāda.[188] Śabdaviśeṣa is to be accepted as Pramāṇa even because of there being the division of Veda-Vākya into Vidhi, Arthavāda and anuvādavacana.[189] Gautama asserts that the validity of the Veda-Vākyas may be established on the strength of their being on a par with the magic charms and the prescriptions of the Āyurvedic Physicians, which come to us in the form of Āptavākyas.[190] The point comes to be more understandable from the *Bhāṣya.*[191] One comes to get advice from the *Āyurveda* thus - 'Doing this, one can maintain health' or 'by way of not doing that, one comes to be ill'. Now it is a matter of experience that such Āyurvedic statements are warranted by facts. By employing the 'mantras' (charms or magic words) also people surely get rid of poison, ghost etc. But the cause of the validity of both above lies in their being the assertions or statements of certain trusted people (Āpta). The Veda-Vā kyas are also certain Āptavākyas. So there is every reason to believe that the Vaidika Āptavākyas are also by all means valid (Pramāṇa). We have already pointed out that the Naiyāyikas understand Āptopadeśa or Āptavākya to cover both vedic and non-vedic utterances. Later Naiyākyas like Jayantabhaṭṭa also strongly and elaborately advocate the validity of Vedavākyas. But so far as Viśvanātha is concerned, he makes no special treatment of the Vedavākyas. He is also not found giving any special recognition to Vedavākyas by way of using terms like Śabdaviśeṣa. As we find him in the BP, he seems to treat Śabda in general and is more occupied with the logical problem involved in the process of words conveying the relational thought in a sentence or briefly speaking the Vākyārtha. We shall elucidate our point by and by.

PART II
TEXT

K. (1) PADAJÑĀNTU KARAṆAṀ DVĀRAṀ TATRA PADĀRTHADHĪḤ/ŚĀBDABODHAḤ PHALAM TATRA ŚAKTIDHĪḤ SAHAKĀRIṆĪ.//

With the above Kārikjā, Viśvanātha initiates his treatment of the problem of Śābdabodha (Verbal Comprehension).

This Kārikā involves certain technical terms which we propose to discuss in two series. The terms, Pada, Padārtha, Śakti and Śābdabodha, because of their inherent mutual relation are discussed in the first series, and the terms, Karaṇa, Dvāra, Sahakāri (-Kāraṇa) and Phala in the second, because of all of them being concerned with the concepts of cause and effect.

Pada : As to the basic constitution of Pada by Varṇa or Varṇas (letters), there is no difference of opinion amongst the scholars of different schools of Philosophy, Grammar and Rhetorics.[1] What goes by the name of Pada in the domain of Linguistics and Logic basically comprises of varnas which we have discussed earlier. Now we are simply to examine what differentiates a Pada from a Varṇa. Pāṇini defines Pada as that which contains as its end either an inflectional (sup) or a conjugational (tin) suffix (vibhakti).[2] Gautama accepts this grammatical notion of Pada. He defines Pada as those (letters) which end in suffixes.[3] The Bhāṣyakāra clarifies that the term 'te' (those) of Gautama referring to the constituents of a Pada, actually means letters.[4] Vātsyāyana appears to have accepted the Grammarian's division of the words into 'suvanta' and 'tiṅanta' varieties by way of classifying and illustrating Vibhakti as Nāmikī and Ākhyātikī.[5] Thus in early Nyāya, there did not exist any basic difference from Vyākaraṇa with regard to the concept of Pada. It may be added here that the Prācīna Nyāya fully acknowledged the utility of Grammar in the matter of representation of linguistic symbols, Pada and Vākya.[6] But with the passage of time, the Naiyāyikas came to be gradually liberal in their concept of Pada and Vākya. The later Naiyāyikas including Viśvanātha understand as Pada whatever letter or cluster of letters is found to be significant.[7] In other words, what is endowed with the significative power (Śakti) is a Pada. The concept of this significative power is also controversial. In this regard, the Naiyāyikas as we shall see in the succeeding pages differ from the Mīmāṁsakas, Vaiyākaraṇas and others. There remains a difference also between the older and the later Naiyāyikas. It cannot be said again that there is complete agreement in their notion in this context even amongst the Navyanaiyāyikas themselves. Pending our discussion on the issue for the time being, we may say that this significative power is the power of primary signification. On the strength of the knowledge of current convention (Samaya or Saṁketa) people come to understand a single meaning being primarily signified by a letter or cluster of letters. The unit formed by that letter or letters in primarily signifying a single meaning is the Pada in the view of the later Naiyāyikas. For the later Naiyāyikas, to be a Pada, a letter or letters donot end in any suffix. The suffixes occurring in what are recognised as words by the Grammarians, are independent Padas by virtue of their having own independent significances.Thus the Ghaṭapada of the Vaiyākaraṇas is a 'padasamūha' for the Naiyāyikas. The expression 'ghaṭaḥ' consists of two parts, the Prātipadika and the suffix sup. Both the parts being significative (śakta) by themselves, can be Padas for the Naiyāyikas.The Vākya for the Naiyāyikas is the collection of more than one such Padas.[8] Thus a Pada of the Vaiyā karaṇa is treated as a Vākya by the Naiyāyika for the logical purposes.[9] Viśvanātha himself introduces the terms 'khaṇḍavākya' and 'mahāvākya' in the Muktāvalī. The expression 'khaṇḍavākya' there stands for smaller Vākyas like 'ghaṭaḥ' and the other term 'mahāvākya' for bigger sentences starting from 'bhūtale ghaṭo'sti' to even a long treatise. The use of the terms is to be understood as relative. Under the circumstances, in handling Navya Nyāya texts on Śabda, it requires us to be vigilent about the intended meaning of the terms concerned.

Padārtha : The term 'Padārtha' here stands for 'the meaning of a word'.[10] We shall see in due course that this 'padārtha' is viewed by Viśvanātha to be usually a denoted (Śakya) and only casually an indicated (Lakṣya) one.

Śakti : Here in the Kārikā, Viśvanātha uses the term in the sense of the denotative power or the power of primary signification of a word. Ālaṁkārikas use the term Śakti in a broad sense to cover all the three significative powers of a word, namely Abhidhā (Denotation), Lakṣaṇā (Indication) and Vyañjanā (Suggestion). But as with other Naiyāyikas, Viśvanātha's Śakti is here to mean only Abhidhā (the Denotation or the Primary power of Signification). Viśvanātha is found to use the word 'Vṛtti' in place of Śakti in the same context in the *Muktāvalī*. Scholars are there to opine that Viśvanātha uses the word Śakti in the aforesaid Kārikā in the sense of a Vṛtti to cover both Lakṣaṇā and Śakti or Abhidhā. Here we donot agree and our arguments will be presented under the relevant *Muktāvalī* text. Mīmāṁsakas also understand this Śakti in the sense of primary signification that works on the strength of a relation between the word and its meaning. But the Naiyāyikas including Viśvanātha conceive this Śakti directly as a particular relation that exists between a Pada and a Padārtha. The *Muktā valī* bears testimony to this effect. We may note further that while the Mīmāṁsakas recognise the relation existing between a Pada and the Padārtha as natural and eternal, the Naiyāyikas recognise the same as mere conventional.

Śābdabodha : The term 'Śābdabodha' may be derived thus : Śabdasya ayaṁ śābdaḥ, śābdaḥ (śabdasambandhī yaḥ) bodhaḥ śā bdabodhaḥ. Or it may be presented thus : śabdādāgataḥ śābdaḥ śā bdaścāsau bodhaśca śābdabodhaḥ. It means the knowledge pertaining to or coming from a 'Śabda'. As the Naiyāyikas understand the word Śabda technically as a Pramāṇavākya. Śabda here in the context of the term śābdabodha as intended by Viśvanātha undoubtedly means a Vākya and Śabda stands for a Vākyārtha. The expressions 'śābdabodha' and 'śābdajñāna' are understood universally in the circle of Naiyāyikas as the Vākyārthajñāna, the knowledge of the total meaning of a sentence. Pending our discussion on the process involved in the understanding of that very Vākyārtha, we can sum up here with this much that this Śābdabodha in the sense of Vākyārthajñāna is the valid verbal knowledge (Śābdapramā) to which Śabda in the form of Āptavākya serves as the Pramāṇa, i.e., śabdapramā karaṇa. Or even without going to the technical use of the word Śabda, we may argue that there can be no doubt as to Viśvanātha's presenting the term Śābdabodha in the sense of Vākyārthajñāna. This is warranted by his naming Proximity etc. as the auxiliary cause of Śābdabodha in a later Kārikā. It is obvious that Proximity etc. may pertain only to a sentence and not to a single word. As we shall see in the succeeding pages, the knowledge of Āsatti etc. has no scope in the production of the meaning of an individual word. Āsatti, Yogyatā etc. are essential only in effecting the logical relation between the meanings of different words in a sentence in order to bring out a total meaning, i.e., a Vākyārtha. We can explain the Śābdabodha as the Vākyārthajñāna from a general point of view also. It is a fact, no doubt, that we do not find Śābda directly understood as a Pramāṇavākya in all systems of thought other than Nyāya. It is understood in the sense of Vedic word or words in general even when viewed by the Mīmāṁsakas as the Pramāṇa. But yet there is no difference with regard to the opinion that the result of Śābdapramāṇa, whether it is a Pada or Vākya, is a Vākyārthajñāna.[11] All universally understand Śābdabodha as the Vākyārthajñāna which is not different from the 'anvayabodha'.

Now we come to the second series -

Karaṇa : The word Karaṇa is used in a variety of senses.[12] Here, however, Karaṇa is a technical term used in the sense of a specific cause (Kāraṇa) of an effect (Phala). In the sphere of Nyāya we come across two different concepts of Karaṇa.

According to an earlier opinion, 'Karaṇa' is an extra-ordinary cause possessed of an operation (Vyāpāra).[13] But as per a later definition, Karaṇa is simply an extra-ordinary cause.[14] In the former difinition a cause of an effect is viewed as extra-ordinary (asādhāraṇa) when it is found not to be common; in the later, this extra-ordinary cause is one that is immediately antecedent[15] to an effect in the sense that the delay in its occurrence results in the non-occurrence of the effect.[16]

In view of the earlier definition, the Karaṇasaṁjñā can be given to an extra-ordinary, i.e., uncommon cause provided that it is possessed of an operation (Vyāpāra) of its own. In view ofthe latter, the said Karaṇa - Saṁjñā would go to any immediately antecendent cause. From the later stand-point, the Vyāpāra itself would come to be admitted as a Karaṇa since it precedes the effect more immediately than anything else. Such an admission would lead to an undesirable position.[17] As is evident from the above Kārikā, of the *BP*, Viśvanātha leaves no room for confusing Vyāpāra for Karaṇa. In the context of Śābdabodha as a Phala (effect), the element which is given the status of Vyāpāra is undoubtedly an immediately antecedent cause (asādhāraṇaṁ kāraṇam) which most immediately precedes the effect. But he gives the status of Karaṇa to another element which of course is possessed of an operation. So in the case of Viśvanātha's Karaṇa, only the earlier definition fits in. It may be pointed out again that the commentator, Govardhanamiśra in course of his exposition of Annaṁbhaṭṭa's definition of Karaṇa, comments that the qualification 'Vyāpāravat' (Possessed of an operation) should also be added.[18] Some editions of Annaṁbhaṭṭa's work show the reading 'vyāpāravat' also along with 'asādhāraṇa.'[19] If we accept this reading in case of the *Tarkasaṁgraha*, we may safely conclude that there is no general difference between the earlier and the later Nyāya-scholars regarding the concept of the Karaṇa.

Here we may bring the analogy of the Grammarian's Karaṇa not without an advantage. The Karaṇa (the instrumental case) in

Grammer is defined as a 'sādhakatama' Kāraka.[20] All the six types of cases (Kārakas), namely Kartā (Nominative), Karma (Accusative), Karaṇa (Instrumental), Sampradāna (Dative), Apā dāna (Ablative) and Adhikaraṇa (Locative) come to be beneficial (sādhaka) to i.e. give their own service to the Kriyā (the contexual verb) by being syntactically related to it[21] (Kriyānvayin) in their respective way. But the Karaṇa Kāraka comes to be most beneficial (sādhakatama) to Kriyā by way of giving the best or greatest service (Prakṛṣṭopakāraka) in the matter of the completion of the action (Kriyāniṣpatti).[22] The explanation of the qualification 'sādhakatama' as 'prakṛṣṭopakāraka' is further elucidated thus[23]: Instrumentality (Karaṇatva) is recognised with regard to that thing just after the operation of which there emerges the completion of an action. In other words, a Karaṇa is that which operates to bring in a result in immediate succession. As for illustration in the proposition, 'Hari cuts the wood with an axe' we understand Hari as Karta, the wood as Karma and an axe as Karaṇa; all the three, come to contribute towards the act of cutting. But the presence of Hari and the wood would be of no avail unless the axe comes to operate. The operation of the axe in the form of contact with the wood (Kāṣṭhasaṁyoga) would immediately bring about the result of cutting the wood.

The analogy between Karaṇa of Grammarians and that of logicians may not be drawn too far. The Naiyāyikas conceive Karaṇa basically as a Kāraṇa; while the Vaiyākaraṇas draw a line of demarcation between a Kāraṇa and a Karaṇa. But here we want to point out only the affinity of the two schools in the matter of the concept of Karaṇa. The affinity lies in the insistence on Vyāpā ravattva (the state of possessing a Vyāpāra) of the element to be regarded as a Karaṇa. We have reasons to believe that the Naiyā yikas' concept of Karaṇa developed under the influence of that of the Vaiyākaraṇas.[24]

Of the Naiyāyikas, however, Jayantabhaṭṭa wants to give the status of Karaṇa only to the sum-total of the causes responsible for the production of an effect as he feels that it is not possible to regard a particular cause as the most instrumental (Sā dhakatama) in the matter.[25] The other Naiyāyikas reject his view as they accept as Karaṇa only a single cause possessed of an 'operation' (Vyāpāra). The widely accepted view is that this Karaṇa is in 'asādhāraṇa kāraṇa' in the sense of being 'Vyāpāravat' and not in the sense of being 'phalayogavyavacchinnaam'. Hence in the matter of cutting some wood by an axe, the axe (and not the contact of the axe with the wood) comes to be the Karaṇa. Only with this concept of Vyāpāra, the position of Viśvanātha tallys.

Dvāra : Dvāra in the above Kārikā is used in the sense of Vyāpā ra. The word Dvāra is found traditionally used as a synonym of Vyāpāra.[26] Viśvanātha himself replaces the word Dvāra by the word 'vyāpāra' in the relevant *Muktāvalī* text. The word 'Dvāra' also means a way or medium or means.[27] Hence the term is used in the sense of Vyāpāra which stands as a medium in between the effect and the principal cause.

In the process of causation, Vyāpāra occupies an intermediate position. It is the immediate cause of the effect, itself being the effect of the chief cause (Karaṇa) of the final effect it (Vyāpāra) produces.[28] In traditionally handed down definition of Vyāpāra, i.e., 'tajjanyatve sati tajjanyajanakatvaṁ nāma vyāpāratvaṁ'; 'tat' stands for 'Karaṇa'. Hence 'tajjanyatve' means karaṇajanyatve;. Vyāpāra itself is the effect of the Karaṇa, the principal cause of an effect. We have already stated that Karaṇa comes to distinguish itself from other causes of the effect by being 'vyāpāravat' i.e. by virtue of the possession of an operation. Now the final effect to be produced by Karaṇa immediately follows the Vyāpāra. Thus Vyāpāra comes to be immediately responsible for production of the (final) effect of which Karaṇa is the chief cause. Hence in the above definition, the second 'tajjanya' also stands for 'karaṇajanya', meaning the final effect of which Vyāpāra comes to be a 'janaka'. As for illustration, in the matter of cutting of some wood with an axe by someone, say Hari, the actual cutting of the wood (Vṛkṣachedana) immediately follows the contact (of the axe) with the wood (Kāṣṭhasaṁyoga). This 'saṁyoga' is the immediate cause of the result, the cutting (chedana). This Saṁyoga occurs because of the 'kuthāra' which is the Samavāyikāraṇa for it. Here 'kuthāra' is the Karaṇa and "Kāṣṭhasaṁyoga" is the Vyāpāra. Now in the context of the verbal cognition, the final effect, i.e., the Śā-bdabodha immediately follows the knowledge of the meanings of words (Padārthajñāna). But this knowledge of meanings of words is caused by the knowledge of corresponding words (Padajñāna) which is the main cause in producing the Śābdabodha. Thus while Padajñāna serves as the Karaṇa of a Śābdabodha, the padā rthajñāna comes to be the Vyāpāra as it is itself Karaṇajanya, i.e., Padajñānajanya and yet is the Karaṇajanyaphalajanaka, i.e., the immediate cause of the verbal cognition which is the final effect of the knowledge of words. We here do not discuss two other characteristics of Vyāpāra, i.e., 'dravyānyatva' (the state of being other than the Dravya) and 'bhāvatva' (the state of being bhāva) as the part of the definition of Vyāpāra containing these two characteristics does not have relevance to the context of verbal cognition as viewed by Viśvanātha. In the view of Viśvanātha, all the causes of Śābdabodha, i.e., Karaṇa Vyāpāra and Sahakārikā raṇas are finally some knowledge (jñāna) of this or that sort. Here, in the context of Śābdabodha, the Vyāpāra distinguishes itself from other Kāraṇas only by being Karaṇajanya and Karaṇajanyajanaka.

Sahakāri (Kāraṇa)

The word 'Sahakāriṇī' is used in the Kārikā under discussion to mean a 'Sahakāri-Kāraṇa'.

Viśvanātha himself has defined a Kāraṇa (cause) as an invariable antecedent failing which there is no occurrence of the effect.[29] The Kāraṇa is basically divided into three types, viz., samavāyi, asamavāyi and Nimitta Kāraṇa. It is apparently needless on our part to go for a discussion on the earlier two varieties as all the causes (Kāraṇa) responsible for the effect in the form of Verbal Knowledge (Śābdabodhaphala) belong to the third category. In the context of Śābdabodha, we have three Nimitta Kāraṇas, namely, Karaṇa, Vyāpāra and Sahakāri Kāraṇa. But a Nimitta Kāraṇa is described as neither Samavāyi nor Asamavāyi. Hence, we shall have to take note also of samavāyi and Asamavāyi Kāraṇas. A Samavāyi Kāraṇa is that cause in which an effect (Kārya) exists through the relation of Samavāya (Inherence).[30] The cause which remain in the Samavāyi cause of an effect by the relation of inherence is an Asamavāyi Kāraṇa.[31] Of the three Nimitta Kāraṇas responsible for a Śābdabodha, Karaṇa is the chief one. This is because it is an extra-ordinary cause possessed of a Vyāpāra. Vyāpāra again is different from the other two causes as it is an effect of the Karaṇa and at the same time a cause of the effect of that very Karaṇa. The Sahakārikāraṇa is neither a Vyāpāra nor a Vyāpāravat (Kāraṇa). For the convenience of understanding, we can describe the three Kāraṇas respectively as the instrumental, operative and auxiliary causes of an effect.

'Phala', as we usually understand, is a result or effect.[32] But we are to note here that this Phala or result in the context of a 'Pramāṇa, the (Principal) cause of conveying a knowledge, is the very Pramā or Valid knowledge.[33] So, appropriately in the context of Śabdapramāṇa, the Śābdabodha or valid verbal knowledge is viewed as the Phala or result.

Viśvantha's description of the Śābdabodha with Padajñāna as its Karaṇa is in consonance with his earlier statement, 'Padajñānakaraṇakam jñānam śābdabodah' which we come across in the chapter on Perception (Pratyakṣakhaṇḍa) of the Bhāṣāpariccheda. In course of the examination of the sources of valid knowledge Viśvanātha divides knowledge basically into two types, Anubhava and Smṛti. Anubhava is again divided into four types, namely, Perceptual, Inferential, Comparative and Verbal.[34] Thereafter he determines them by showing their chief or extra-ordinary causes technically known as the Karaṇa.[35] He is found in that context to state that the Śābdabodha.

is the knowledge which has the knowledge of a Pada as its

Karaṇa. Thus we find that Viśvanātha's description of Śābdabodha as having Padajñāna as its Karaṇa above is not abrupt.

Now we shall have to note that the 'tu' in the expression 'Padajñānantu' in the Kārikā under discussion is obviously significant as it suggests an already existing controversy on the issue. The indeclinable 'tu' is used to give the idea that the author's present view is a departure from earlier ones.

In this context we have to remember that prior to Viśvanātha, there existed several notions regarding the Śabdapramāṇa, i.e., the Karaṇa of Śābdabodha. Kumārila himself, under the Jaimini *Śutra* 1.1.2 introduces the alternatives in the context of the Śābdabodhakaraṇa.[36] The problem is, which of these, namely, the word, its knowledge, the meaning or its knowledge, or even the knowledge of the sentence meaning be regarded as the Pramāṇa, i.e., Pramā-Karaṇa. Animated discussions on the issue are conspicuously present in all the important philosophical treatises. Śālikanātha also refers to such divergent views on the subject.[37]

We find in fine that while the Prābhākaras regard Pada as the Śābdabodha-Karaṇa,[38] the Bhāṭṭas accept Padārtha as such.[39] In the school of Nyāya, Gautama and some of his followers admit Śabda as the Karaṇa under discussion.[40] We have earlier shown that the term 'Śabda' carries the sense of a Vākya. The later Naiyāyikas directly use this Śabda in the sense of a Vākya.[41] Some Naiyāyikas proceed further even to regard Vākyajñāna or even Vākyārthajñāna[42] as the Śābdabodhakaraṇa. Hence, Viśvanātha had to include 'tu' in his Kārikā quite significantly to assert his own position. Regarding the question as to whether the Padas or Padārthas are the causes of Verbal Knowledge, the Prābhākaras hold that the Vākyārtha in the form of an Anvaya is expressed by the Padas themselves. If it could be understood from the Padārthas directly, then there should have been a Śābdabodha even on the basis of ideas of an object comprehended by other means of valid knowledge. This is out of experience.[43] Prābhākaras hold that the words do have isolated meanings but they do not stop at that. They proceed further to give the related sense, the Vākyāratha.[44] Thus the Prābhākaras' approach to Śābdabodhakaraṇa is from their bias for Anvitābhidhānavāda. Similarly the Bhāṭṭas, the Abhihitānvayavādins, true to their spirit as such, maintain that words denote unrelated meanings, and these meanings aided by Ākāṁkṣā, Yogyatā and Sanniddhi come factually to give rise to the Vākyarthajñāna, i.e., the Śābdabodha.[45]

In view of such an already existing controversy on the issue, the use of 'tu' by a later writer in the context of ascertaining the Śābdabodhakaraṇa, comes to be quite natural. But Viśvanātha, as is apparent from the relevant *Muktāvalī* text, seems to be interested only in refuting the logic that the Pada is the Karaṇa of Śābdabodha. He does not discuss or refer to the claims of factors like Padārtha, Vākya and Vākyārtha in the context.

Now we propose to examine Viśvanātha's position regarding the Karaṇa of Śābdabodha in the light of his assertion 'Padajñānantu' etc. If we explain the term 'padajñānaṁ' in the expression 'Padajñānatu Karaṇaṁ as 'Padasya jñānaṁ' and understand thereby that Viśvanātha conceives the knowledge of a Pada (a single word) as the Karaṇa of Śābdabodha it will give rise to some difficulties as detailed below.

(1) The generally accepted position in the entire school of Nyāya is that Śabda as Pramāṇa, i.e., a Pramā-Karaṇa is a 'Vākya' (a sentence). Gautama defines Śabda as 'Āptopadeśa' and the later Naiyāyikas, as already pointed out have in their analysis shown clear indications of understanding this 'upadeśa' in the sense of Vākya. As we have already observed, presumably for both perspicuity and simplification, the Navya Naiyāyikas like Annaṁbhaṭṭa have directly declared Āptavākya as the Śabda. Keeping apart the issue of requiring an Āpta for its utterance or use to validate itself, it is in structure a Vākya or sentence which stands already accepted as the Karaṇa for Śābdabodha. Under the circumstances is it possible for Viśvanātha to deviate so much

from the stand taken by all his predecessors including Gautam a in order to make the knowledge of even a single pada accepted as Ś ābdabodhakaraṇa ?

(2) Such a position is not logically tenable for Viśvanātha himself, in view of his own concept of Ś ābdabodha. If the knowledge of a single word be the Karaṇa, the knowledge of its meaning will be the Vyāpāra of the contextual Ś ābdabodha. The Ś ābdabodha as the effect (Phala) must immediately follow the knowledge of the meaning of that word as demanded by the definitions of Vyā pāra and Karaṇa. But it does not take place as it is not possible. Ś ā bdabodha is universally accepted as the Vākyārthajñ āna, i.e., the knowledge of the total meaning of sentence brought about by the syntactical connection amongst different meanings of different words in it. Viśvanātha himself envisiages such a position as he accepts the knowledge of proximity, compatibility, expectancy and the speaker's intention (Āsattiyogyatākāṁksātātparyajñā nam) as an auxiliary cause in the matter of Ś ābdabodha. He uses the word Ś abdabodha and not Ś ābdabodha, and there is nothing to prove that he does not understand the Ś ābdabodha in the universally accepted sense of 'Vākyārthajñāna'. There is again no scope for the knowledge of Āsatti, etc., to enter in between a single word and its meaning. Ś ābdabodha or 'Vākyārthajñāna', i.e., the 'Ś abdapramāṇaphala' is universally understood as brought about by the knowledge of the relation of a meaning of a word with regard to that of another in a sentence and so forth (ekapadārthe aparapadārthasaṁsargaviṣayakaṁ jnānam). So it is not possible for Viśvanātha to make a big departure by not admitting Vākya as the Ś ābdabodhakaraṇa.

It will be reasonable, therefore, on our part, to understand the term 'Padajñānam' as 'Padānāṁ jñānam'. In that case, 'Padajñāna' would amount to mean 'Padasamūhajñ āna' and the stand taken by Viśvanātha would be neither off the track nor out of logic. Here we note that there is no difficulty on our part to understand a 'Padasamūha' (read from the expression Padānām) in the sense of a Vākya, as in the concept of Naiyāyikas, any collection of words possessed of a syntactical connection amongst themselves because of satisfying the necessary conditions, Āsattijñāna etc., can be regarded as a Vākya.[46] Instead of explaining the Padajñānam of Viśvanātha as 'Padānāṁ jñānam' we can also interpret the single word 'Padam' to carry the sense of plurality to mean a collection of words and finally a Vākya. We can do it on the strength of a grammatical rule which enjoins that a word may be used optionally in the singular number to mean an entire class.[47]

If we understand, however, the word 'Pada' in Viśvanātha's expression 'Padajñāna' in its grammatical sense supported by the definition 'Suptiṅantaṁ padam', we may not find any difference between Viśvanātha and other Naiyāyikas like Annaṁbhaṭṭa, even in case of recognising a single Pada as the Śābdabodhakaraṇa. This is because a Pada of the Vaiyākaraṇas is a Vākya for the Naiyāyikas. We have already pointed out that according to the later Naiyāyikas including Viśvanātha, anything that can signify a meaning is a Pada. We may recapitulate the idea again. A 'Pada' of the Vaiyākaraṇas has two parts, namely a 'Prātipadika' or a 'dhātu' and a suffix. Whichever group here we choose for examination, the parts by themselves are siginificant (Śakta, i.e., Śaktimat) and hence are 'padas' in view of the Naiyāyikas. We shall find in the exposition of the *Muktāvalī* hereafter that Viśvanātha himself admits 'dhātu', 'prakṛti', etc. as significative as he maintains that one can learn the significative power of 'dhātu', 'prakriti' etc. with the aid of Grammar. And by being significative a letter or letters in any combination may be a Pada. So when judged from the standpoint of the Naiyāyikas, the difference between a grammatical pada and a grammatical Vākya comes to be almost nil. A grammatical pada is a logical vākya which allows scope between its parts for functioning of Āsttijñāna etc. In order to produce a total meaning in the shape of a relational thought. Thus Śābdabodha is possible even in the context of the so-called grammatically single expression 'ghaṭaḥ'. The expression 'ghaṭaḥ', a Vākya for the Naiyāyikas, comes to give its own Śābdabodha which is the knowledge of the relation that exists between the meanings of the Prātipadika ghaṭa and the suffix 'su' in the sense of Kartā. Under the circumstances the term Pada in the expression Padajñānantu may be taken to mean a Vākya for the Naiyāyika Viśvanatha.

It may be noticed that Viśvanātha makes an improvement in Naiyāyikas' concept of Śābdabodhakaraṇa. Gautama, maintains that Āptopadeśa is the Śabdapramāṇa, i.e., Śābdabodhakaraṇa. Now if we understand 'upadeśa' only in the sense of instruction, the non-instructive sentences consequently would loose the status of the Pramāṇa even when they are Āptokta (i.e., uttered by Āptas). Hence, to accept Āptavākya (and not Āpta-upadeśa), as the Pramāṇa covering thereby all reliable statements, instructive or otherwise, is an improvement no doubt. But there still remains a lacuna. When the emphasis is laid on a Vākya being directly recognised as the Śabdapramāṇa, it carries the impression that words involved in the sentence shall have to be audibly uttered. But the Śābdabodha is found to take place even when the Vākya or the collection of words physically stands unheard for not being uttered. So Gautama's concept of Śabda leaves a loophole to catch the notice of his successors like Viśvanātha.[48] So Viśvanātha maintains in his *Muktāvalī* that in order to give due recognition to the Śābdabodhas occurring as they do in case of writings by a silent person etc., the knowledge of a Pada (samūha) (i.e. Vākya) and not directly the Pada (samūha) should be treated as the Karaṇa of Śābdabodha. It cannot be said that prior to Viśvanātha. none did try to improve upon the earlier concept of Śābdabodhakaraṇa. Vācaspatimiśra in his *Tātparyaṭīkā* counts the knowledge of the meaning of a Vākya along with that of a Vākya as the Śābdabodhakaraṇa.[49] Viśvanātha might have been influenced by Vācaspati to make a further improvement. The admission of mere Vākya, as the Karaṇa of Śābdabodha does not cover all cases of Śābdabodha. But the admission of the knowledge of Vākya even in the form of Padasamūha as such would cover all cases. Hence, Viśvanātha as a matter of simplification comes to admit only the Vākyajñāna as the Śā bdabodhakaraṇa. He has reasonably done so. The knowledge of a Vākya presupposes the existence of a Vākya. Can there be the knowledge of a Vākya without a Vākya, uttered or otherwise? So the admission of the knowledge of a Vākya as the Karaṇa in question amounts to the basic admission of Vākya as such.

A very pertinent question arises here. If Viśvanātha did accept Vākyajñāna as the Śābdabodhakaraṇa, he should have directly used the expression 'vākyajñāna' instead of 'padajñāna' to mean the former in a round about way. Yes, Viśvanātha avoids the use of the word Vākya in the concept of Śābdabodhakaraṇa deliberately to arrest misgivings that may arise as a result.

As far as we can gather the idea from Viśvanātha and other Naiyāyikas, the process through which Śābdabodha is produced is as follows:

(1) At first the words (padas) in a sentence come to be heard or understood as heard. In the sentence 'ghaṭo'sti', the words will be 'ghaṭa', 'ḥ', 'as' and 'ti'. Thus the knowledge of all the words in the sentence form 'one and the first unit' as a factor responsible for a Śābdabodha. Now just as there is difficulty in admitting a single Pada as the Śābdabodhakaraṇa, there is similarly a difficulty in naming directly a Vākya as such. The necessity of all the individual words being known shall not be duly recognised in that case, and the role that the individual words play in bringing about their respective individual meanings by virtue of their own significative power will stand unadmitted. But the admission of Padasamūha which virtually means a Vākya, in the concept Śā-bdabodhakaraṇa is the most possible ideal position in the context.

(2) Next to the knowledge of Padas in a Vākya, in the context of a Śābdabodha, there comes the recollection of the meaning of the words (Padārthasmaraṇaṁ). This Padārthasmaraṇa is actually the knowledge of the things signified by the words. Now if Vākya

is directly named as Śābdabodhakaraṇa, it will be utterly confusing and misleading to say that by the knowledge of a Vākya, one comes to recollect the meanings of the individual words. And there must be the recollection of the individual words to serve as Vyāpāra in the process of Śābdabodha. Moreover, only individual words are significant (Śakta) to convey their individual meanings. Naiyāyikas are clear in this regard that the Vākya or sentence as a whole does not possess the primary power of signification. The knowledge of the Vākyārtha again can never be Vyāpāra as it is itself the effect (Phala). Under the circumstances it is not possible to speak of Vākya directly as the Śābdabodhakaraṇa in the interest of the recognition of the intermediate stages involved. As a matter of fact, the knowledge of the meanings of all the words in a sentence forms the second unit as a factor responsible for production of a Śābdabodha.

(3) Then comes the knowledge of the mutual connection (saṁsargajñāna) of things already recollected. This saṁsargajñāna is virtually the Śābdabodha.

We may conclude that by admitting Pada (samūha) jñāna as the Karaṇa Viśvanātha not only simplifies the issue, but presents also the concept of the Śabdapramāṇa in a clear way so as to cover all cases of Śābdabodha, but at the same time he does not make any basic departure from the stand taken by the earlier Naiyāyikas including Gautama.

M(1). Śābdabodhaprakāraṁ darśayati padajñānantviti:

As is observed in the *Muktāvalī* above, Viśvanātha has shown the process of Śābdabodha in his *Kārikā* 'padajñānantu' etc. The term Śābdabodha is already explained. 'Śābdabodhasya prakāraḥ, taṁ'. 'Prakāra' here means the process of the involvement of causes leading to an effect. Viśvanātha's intention is to show how the Śābdabodha as an effect results from the operation of some principal cause along with certain auxiliary ones. That Viśvanātha comes to deal with the 'śābdabodha' a bit elaborately may be the result of a direct influence over him of his celebrated predecessor, Gaṅgeśa, the author of the *Tattvacintāmaṇi.* Though Śabda has been accepted by all the Naiyāyikas, their treatment of Śābdabodha is not found to be so much elaborate as that of Gaṅgeśa. Gaṅgeśa for the first time deals with the topic in a very detailed manner in the fourth section of his work *Tattvacintāmaṇi.* Thereafter Jānakīnātha Bhaṭṭācarya, though less extensively, follows Gaṅgeśa's pattern of exposition of Śabda. Hence the work that has influenced the *Bhāṣāpariccheda* in the context of such treatment of Śabda may also be the *Nyāyasiddhāntamañjarī* of Jānakīnātha Bhaṭṭācārya. In comparison to Gaṅgeśa, however, Viśvanātha is less elaborate, much simpler and even less cryptic in his language. Nevertheless, the pattern of the treatment as well as the approach to the topic along with the illustrations in Viśvanātha's work immediately remind the reader of the earlier Nyāya treatise, Tattvacintāmaṇi. While Gaṅgeśa presents the older views exhaustively some time even with categorical references to the sources of the views discussed, Viśvanātha's references to the earlier views are casual, concise and sometimes even not immediately discernible.

It is interesting to note that unlike some other Naiyāyikas such as Annaṁbhaṭṭa, Viśvanātha does not proceed in his treatment of Śābdabodha with a definition of Śabda. We do not come across any specific definition of Śabda in Viśvanātha s work. We simply find Viśvanātha describing Śabda as a specific attribute of Ākāśa[50] and dividing it into Dhvani and Varṇa.[51]

As we have already observed, a Śābdabodha as a 'vākyārthajñāna' involves certain Padas constituting a Vākya. But Viśvanātha is not found defining the technical terms, Pada and Vākya also. It may be guessed that Viśvanātha is bent on making a treatment in his work of only those topics and issues which stand hitherto undiscussed or not yet wellchalked out or which still remain controversial. In the context of problems and issues, therefore, except those which are found to be treated independently or atleast found to be contradicted, we may have to accept the position that Viśvanātha believes in definitions and ideas as given by his predecessors in the school of Nyāya.

M(2). na tu jñāyamānaṁ padaṁ karaṇam, padābhāve'pi mauniślokādau śābdabodhāt.

The text of the *Muktāvalī* above is obviously with reference to the kārikā text, 'padajñānantu'. As we have already pointed out, the particle 'tu' in the Kārikā is significant. Viśvanātha here in the *Muktāvalī*, as we have observed earlier, explains in his own way the significance of 'tu' he uses in the Kārikā.

In the light of our earlier arguments, the word 'pada' used by Viśvanātha in the context of the concept of Śābdabodhakaraṇa is to be understood as 'padasamūha' if and when Pada is taken from the stand-point of the Naiyāyikas. If, however, it is understood in the sense accepted by the Vaiyākaraṇas, it would, of its own course, come to be a 'padasamūha' of the Naiyāyikas.

Viśvanātha describes the knowledge of the Pada as the Karaṇa of Śābdabodha. He thereby means that the Pada in question is not necessarily to be uttered (uccāryamāṇa). This very idea is sought to be brought home by the use of the particle 'tu' in the Kā rikā. There the particle is being used in the sense of 'eva' (only). Thereby a stress is given on the very knowledge of a word instead of on a word as being known, i.e., uttered. This idea as is rightly pointed out in DK,[52] has been sought to be brought out in the *Muktāvalī* above 'na tu jñāyamānam', etc. The idea may be otherwise presented thus : even if there is no utterance of a Pada, the very knowledge of it will be entitled to be the Karaṇa of the corresponding Śābdabodha. If only a Pada known by virtue of being uttered is allowed the status of a Śābdabodhakaraṇa, it would lead us to an annomalous position; because one comes to have Śā bdabodha even from the writings of a silent person like some one under a vow of silence. On the strength of the word 'etc.' (ādi) in the expression 'mauniślokādau', the physical movements by hand etc. indicative of number etc. are also to be understood.[53] Here we are to note that the expression 'jñāyamāna' in the *Muktāvalī* above is to be understood as 'uccāryamāṇa' and the expression 'padābhāve'pi' should stand for 'uccāryamānapadābhāve'pi'.[54] Thus a Pada can safely remain 'unknown' (na jñāyamānam) in the sense of being unuttered (na uccāryamānam), while its mere knowledge comes to be a Śābdabodhakaraṇa. In the light of such a position, the concept of Karaṇa would justifiably cover all cases including those which involve even the writings of a silent person, mere movement of two hands or fingers etc. In addition to Viśvanātha's own explanation in the *Muktāvalī* , we can also recapitualate our earlier discussion on the issue here. In addition to what we have already stated, we like to add that even the earlier Naiyāyikas were seized of this controversial issue of Śābdabodhakaraṇa. We already referred to Vācaspati Miśra having admitted both Vākyajñāna and Vākyārthajñāna as the Karaṇa of a Śābdabodha.

Udayaṇācārya, as is understood by the scholars, was also alive to the rival views of the two schools of Mīmāṁsākas in this regard. The Bhāṭṭas insisted that the Padārtha directly serves as the Karaṇa of a Śābdabodha in the shape of a Vākyārthajñāna. The Prābhākaras, to the contrary, asserts that the Pada and not the Padārtha should be given the status of Karaṇa. They contend that Padas appear earlier to Padārthas; the former signify the latter and come to be the determinent of the purport in the sentence. Hence Padas deserve to be admitted as being possessed of the basic capacity in producing a Verbal knowledge. The author of the *Nyāyakusumāñ*jali, as we can understand him, tried to strike a balance by maintaining that neither Pada nor Padārtha, but the Padajñāna be accepted as Śābdabodhakaraṇa.[55]

We find that Gaṅgeśopādhyāya, names 'Śabda' as Śābdabodhakaraṇa. Annaṁbhaṭṭa also admits 'Śabda' as Śābdajñānakaraṇa.[56] In view of the Naiyāyikas' general acceptance of Āptavākya as the Śabdapramāṇa, it follows that this word 'Śabda' which is given the status of Śābdabodhakaraṇa is afterall a Vākya. But in veiw of the Naiyāyikas' notion of Śābdabodha in the shape of Vākyārthajñāna involving a process of syntactical relation between the Padārthas conveyed by the Padas with the aid of Āsatti, Yogyatā etc., it is very difficult to understand the Śābdabodhakaraṇa directly as a Vākya. So we tend to understand even the word 'Śabda' used by Gaṅgeśa and Annaṁbhaṭṭa in the sense of 'padasmūha' or loosely the speech. As against this amount of ambiguity Viśvanātha's description of Karaṇa as Padajñāna is quite clear and precise.

M(3). padārthadhīriti. padajanyapadārthasmaraṇaṁ vyāpāraḥ anyathā padajñānavataḥ pratyakṣādinā padārthopasthitavāpi śābdabodhāpatteḥ.

Here in the *Muktāvalī* , Viśvanātha elucidates the expression 'padārthadhīḥ' occurring in the Kārikā, 'padajñānantu' etc.

After the 'padajñāna' being ascertained as the Karaṇa for a Śābdabodha 'padārthadhī' is named here as the Vyāpāra of that Karaṇa. The word Dvāra in the Kārikā is obviously used in the sense of this Vyāpāra. We have already discussed the concept of Vyāpāra and the use of the word Dvāra in the sense of Vyāpāra.

Viśvanātha, as he explains in the *Muktāvalī* above, understands the word 'dhīḥ' in the sense of smaraṇa (recollection) and replaces Padārthadīḥ as 'padārthasmaraṇam'.

Now the Padārthadhīḥ, i.e., 'padārthasmaraṇaṁ' (the knowledge of the meaning of a word) must be 'Padajñānajanya' i.e., is to be invariably generated or produced by the knowledge of the corresponding Pada in order to quality itself as the Vyāpāra of a corresponding Śābdabodha. As is rightly pointed out by Pañcānana Śastrī,[57] the expression 'Padajanya' in 'Padajanyapadārthasmaraṇaṁ' etc. of the *Muktāvalī* is to be understood as 'Padajñānajanya' in the light of Viśvanātha's own stand that only 'Padajñāna' is to be admitted as Śābdabodhakaraṇa. If the mere knowledge of on object (Padārthasmaraṇa) without any reference to its being produced by the knowledge of the corresponding Pada is allowed to be a Vyāpāra of a Śābdabodhakaraṇa, it would lead to serious irregularities. In such a case, a person with the knowledge of a Pada would be supposed to have the Śābdabodha even where the knowledge of the object (padārtha) occurs to him through Perception etc. (pratyakṣādi) and not as 'padajñānajanya'. This is not a desirable position as other Pramāṇas should find no place in the domain of Śabdapramāṇa, at its own cost. We have to concede that 'pratyakṣapramāṇa' is involved in the auditory perception of individual words, in the very initial stage. Anumānapramāṇa is also involved in one's learning the significtive power (Śaktigraha) of a word by observing the usage of the elderly persons. After ascertaining the significative power of the Padas one comes from the knowledge of the Padas to the knowledge of the objects signified by the Padas. Thus the process leads to what is called Śābdabodha. But if the knowledge of the Padas is deprived of or disallowed the function of signifying the objects, the knowledge of Padas no longer remains a Karaṇa in true sense of the term. As a matter of fact, the domain of Śabdapramāṇa stands disrupted thereby. Hence the need to restrict the status of a Vyāpāra of a Śābdabodhakaraṇa only to Padajñānajanyapadārthasmaraṇa, i.e., the knowledge of an object only as generated by the knowledge of the corresponding Pada. The idea can be put like this. If a person knows the word 'Ganges' and at the same time he has a visual perception of the current of water of the river Ganges and yet does not have any knowledge of necessary connection between his knowledge of the 'Gaṅgāpada' and that of a 'jalapravāhaviśeṣa', the object perceived, he may be said to have a 'pratyakṣajñāna' and never a Śābdabodha. This is because his knowledge of the object (Padārthasmaraṇa) here results not from any knowledge of the corresponding Pada although it may be that he knows the Pada.

M(4). tatrāpi vṛttyā padajanyatvaṁ bodhyaṁ. anyathā ghaṭādipadāt samavāyasambandhenākāśasmaraṇe jāte ākāśasyāpi śābdabodhāpatteḥ.

'Tatrāpi' in the *Muktāvalī* above refers to the preceding text 'padajanyapadārthasmaraṇaṁ'. By virtue of its locative sense, 'tatrāpi' means 'padajanyapadārthasmaraṇaṁ'. In the earlier *Muktāvalī* 'padajanyapadārthasmaraṇaṁ' etc., Viśvanātha asserts that in order to generate the Śābdabodha in a particular context, the knowledge of the meaning of a word (Padārthasmaraṇa) must be due to the knowledge of the corresponding word (Padajñāna) and not because of any other factor. Here he observes further that the generation of the Padārthajñāna by the Padajñāna must be specifically by means of Vṛttijñāna (the knowledge of the significative power of the word in the cotext). In the exposition of the immediately preceding *Muktāvalī* , we observed that even if a person possesses both 'Padajñāna' and 'Padārthajñāna', he cannot be said to have obtained the contextual Śābdabodha unless his 'Padārthajñāna' is due to his knowledge of some sort of connection between the Pada and the padārtha. This connection hinted earlier must not be other than Vṛtti. Viśvanātha will assert hereafter that this Vṛtti is nothing but a specific relation that exists between Pada and Padārtha. In 'anyathā' etc. of the *Muktāvalī*, Viśvanātha points out the serious irregularity that may result in the event of not admitting the knowledge of Vṛtti in the matter of producing the Padārthasmaraṇa by the relevant Padajñāna. If the Padajñāna is allowed to give rise to the 'Padārthasmaraṇa' by means of the knowledge of any sort of sambandha (relation), then one will obviously have the Śābdabodha with reference to Ether (ākāsā) from any word like 'jar' (ghaṭa) inasmuch as the relation of Inherence (samavāya) exists between Ākāsa and any Pada that is basically a sound-unit or a collection of it. Viśvanātha earlier maintains that Śabda (sound unit) is a specific quality[58] (Vaiśeṣika guṇa) of Ākāsā (ether), one of the nine Dravyas. A quality exists only being inherent in i.e. not being separable from the qualified (guṇī). Hence the knowledge of the qualified object will lead to that of the quality, vice versa. As a result, the knowledge of the Śabda in the form 'ghaṭa' etc. will automatically bring about the knowledge of the Ākāsa (Ether) also. It will not be a desirable position to admit Śābdabodha in case the knowledge of a sound resulting from hearing of any word brings about the knowledge of Ether. In order to avoid such a difficulty, Viśvanātha demands the knowledge of Vṛtti in the matter of giving rise to the knowledge of a meaning by the knowledge of a word.

Thus, Viśvanātha, in full agreement[59] with his predecessors recognises the 'Vṛttidhīḥ' (the Knowledge of Vṛtti) as responsible in the matter of a 'Padajñāna' giving rise to corresponding 'Padārthajñāna', which leads to the corresponding Śābdabodha. But here is a problem. Viśvanātha, in the Kārikā above, refers only to the 'Śaktidhīḥ' (the knowledge of Śakti) as an aid in the matter. Śakti therein cannot be taken to stand for Vṛtti as Viśvanātha himself in the *Muktāvalī* text hereafter describes Śakti as one of the two kinds of Vṛtti. A particular variety cannot be taken to mean the whole class it belongs to. Had there been two authors, separately for the K and the M, there would have been, however, no problem. But as we have not objected to the single authorship for both the works, we are to see if the author is not involved in a self-contradiction. We are here to read the mind of Viśvanātha for not using 'Vṛttidhīḥ' directly in place of Śaktidhīḥ in the Kārikā. We also can not argue the case as a metrical necessity for lack of any difference in structure of both the expressions.

On the strength of the following calculations, we feel that Viśvanātha's reference to 'Śaktidhī' instead of Vṛttidhī is neither arbitary nor without motive.

(1) Viśvanātha, recognises only two significative powers of a word, namely Śakti and Lakṣaṇā. There is nothing to prove Viśvanātha's admission of Vyāñjanā and Tātparya. The two

'Padavṛttis' admitted by him, Śakti and lakṣaṇā, respectively stand for primary and secondary powers of verbal signification. He uses the word Vṛtti widely in the sense of any significative verbal function in order to cover both Śakti and Lakṣaṇā. Unlike an Ālaṁkārika or Vaiyākaraṇa, he does not make indiscriminate use of the word Śakti as a synonymn of Vṛtti. The Śakti of Viśvanātha undoubtedly stands for Abhidhā function as admitted in other schools of thought. Hence there arises the possibility of Viśvanātha being involved in a case of self contradiction as the knowledge of both Śakti and Vṛtti has been held as auxiliary cause in the matter of Śābdabodha in two separate observations. It stands admitted that in the matter of Śābdabodha, the Padajñāna as 'Śābdabodhakaraṇa' comes to give rise to the 'padārthadhīḥ', the 'śābdabodhavyāpāra' on the strength of a significative power, sometimes Śakti and sometimes Lakṣaṇā. So our immediate impression is quite likely that Viśvanātha should have directly used 'Vṛttidhīḥ' in the concerned Kārikā.

But compared to the scope of Śakti, that of Lakṣaṇā is very much limited. In our day to-day life, only a few cases of Śābdabodha are covered by Lakṣaṇā in comparison to Śakti or Abhidhā. Lakṣaṇā operates in the matter of production of a Śābdodha only when Śakti fails to cover it for whichever reason it may be.

(2) It is Śakti that may be called a relation between a Pada and Padārtha (padapadārthasambandha) in true sense of the term. Because according to Viśvanātha himself, Lakṣaṇā is a relation only between śakyārtha and another meaning (that comes to be later designated as Lakṣyārtha). We can call Lakṣaṇā a relation between a Pada and Padārtha only directly. Hence Viśvanātha might have felt the necessity to bring Śakti to lime-light which it deserves by mentioning it at the earliest opportunity.

(3) So we feel that by giving the expression 'Śaktidhīḥ, Viśvanātha wants to pinpoint the importance of Śakti (or the primary power) and in doing so, he commits no crime. It is because every

case of Lakṣaṇā presupposes an earlier Śakti. Without a preceding Sakti for conveying a śakyārtha, there can be no Lakṣaṇā in the form of 'śakyasambandha'. We shall elucidate the concept in the succeeding pages in the context of the exposition of the relevant BP text dealing with Lakṣaṇā. Though Vṛtti is subsequently divided into Śakti and Lakṣaṇā Viśvanātha's presentation of Śakti to stand for both itself and Lakṣaṇā is quite logical in view of Śakti being the very basis of Lakṣaṇā.

Now Viśvanātha comes to deal with the significative power of a word. The general name given by him to it is Vṛtti. He understands this power to be of two kinds, Śakti, the power of primary signification and Lakṣaṇā, the power of secondary signification. Here we must be careful to note that the general name for the significative power of a word is also not always the same with all the systems of thought and thinkers as well. As for illustration, the Ālaṁkārikas use the terms Śakti, Vṛtti and Vyāpā ra indiscriminately to mean any one of the three significative powers of a word admitted by them.[60] The individual names of those three powers of a word as admitted by the Ālaṁkārikas are Abhidhā, Lakṣaṇā and Vyañjanā. Viśvanātha uses only the term Vṛtti to mean any kind of significative power of a word. Here we may fruitfully examine the Nyāya tradition. In the early stage of Nyāya the picture of Lakṣaṇā does not seem to be clear. Śakti is virtually the only significative power of a word admitted at that stage. Even at the stage when Lakṣaṇā comes to be admitted the Naiyāyikas' concept of Lakṣaṇā stands in the way of placing it on par with Śakti. Śakti is understood by the Naiyāyikas as the relation of a Pada with a Padārtha. Lakṣaṇā is again thought of in the form of a relation between a Śakyārtha with another 'artha'. As every case of Lakṣaṇā presupposes a case of Śakti, some of the Naiyāyikas seem not to have reckoned Lakṣaṇā as very much distinguished from Śakti. So they might not have felt the necessity of maintaining a general name to cover Lakṣaṇā also along with

Abhidhā. Such an impression we may gather from Annaṁbhaṭṭa, a later Naiyāyika of the Navya group. Apparently he admits only Śakti as we find him in his *Tarkasaṁgraha*. But he clearly adds Lakṣaṇā as Śabdavṛtti (significative function of a word) in his *Tarkadīpikā*.[61] Yet we find some eminent Naiyāyikas like Gadā dhara and Gaṅgeśa who have unhestitatingly given the general name Vṛtti in order to include Lakṣāṇā along with Śakti.[62] The Vaiyākaraṇas also use the term Vṛtti only to mean all the three kinds of significative powers admitted by them.[63] We find other Naiyāyikas using the term Saṁketa also along with Śakti in the same sense.[64] This Śakti or Saṁketa of the Naiyāyikas goes by the name of Abhidhā in other circles as amongst the Mīmāṁsakas, Vaiyākaraṇas and the Ālaṁkārikas.[65]

Now to persue our examination of the *Muktāvalī* above, we have to remember that the essential nature of a word lies in its significative power. Hence the relation between a word and its meaning stands undeniable. So Viśvanātha understands his Vṛtti, the significative power of a word in the form of either of the two relations, Śakti and Lakṣaṇā. An examination of this relation between a word and meaning demands a discussion of the views on the issue prevailing in other circles.

The Mimāṁsakas have admitted two functions of a word to convey a meaning. Abhidhā is the name for the primary function and Lakṣaṇā is that for the secondary one.[66] The Vedāntins and the Naiyāyikas have done the same. But they have generally used the term Śakti to mean Abhidhā. The Vaiyākaraṇas have admitted three functions, namely, Abhidhā or Śakti, Lakṣaṇā and Vyā ñjanā.[68] The Ālaṁkārikas have generally recognised three functions, Abhidhā, Lakṣaṇā and Vyāñjanā.[69] Some Ālaṁkarikas have come to recognise Tātparya as another function.[70] As a matter of fact, it is the function not of an individual word, but of a whole sentence. By means of this function, according to a section of scholars, the unrelated meanings of the individual words come to be syntactically connected with each other. As a result, the meaning of the sentence is conveyed. If this Tātparya Vṛtti is admitted as a function pertaining to a word as some critics have done,[71] the number of functions of a word for conveying meanings comes to be four in the scheme of certain Ālaṁkārikas. Mahimabhaṭṭa stands as a striking exception as he admits only one function of a word to convey its meaning. That is Abhidhā. According to him, the so-called Lakṣyārthas and Vyaṅgyārthas can be apprehended through Anumāna.[72]

M(6). atraiva śaktijñānasyopayogaḥ, pūrvaṁ śaktigrahābhāve padajñāne'pi tatsambandhena tatsmaraṇānutpatteḥ. padajñānasya hyekasambandhijñānavidhayā padārthopasthāpakatvaṁ.

In the *Muktāvalī* above, Viśvanātha proceeds to point out the necessity of admitting 'śaktidhī' in the Kārikā text as an auxiliary cause in the matter of production of Śābdabodha. Here the author of the *Muktāvalī*, by way of an illustration, wants to show the serious anamoly that may crop-up if Śakti be not given the singular privilege of helping the 'padajñāna' in producing a 'padārthasmaraṇa'. Now before we move further with the explanation of Viśvanātha in the context, we shall have to answer a very pertinent question.

In the earlier *Muktāvalī*, 'tatra'pi vṛttyā padajanyatvaṁ' etc, Viśvanātha asserted that the recollection of padārthas by the knowledge of Padas must be understood as being due to the operation of Vṛtti, the significative power of words in general covering both Abhidhā and Lakṣaṇā. But he comes to speak of the utility only of śakti in the very same matter. Is he not involved in a self-contradiction? It is why, to arrest such a notion, a modern commentator hastens to replace in his own explanation, Viśvanātha's above expression 'Śaktijñānasya' by 'Vṛttijñānasya'.[73] In this regard, we are promoted to observe as follows.

In 'tatrā'pi vṛttijñānasya' etc. Viśvanātha already pointed out the irregularities that might take place in the event of not admitting the assistance of a word's significative power in general in the matter of producing the knowledge of the meaning by that of a word. But his intention here is solely to draw the attention to the peculiar relation that exists between a Pada and a Padārtha and to the process by which one can convey the other. Here we reiterate our earlier point that as Viśvanātha wants to refer to the 'padapadārthasambandha', he must refer to Śakti alone. It is because Śakti is the direct relation between a Pada and a Padārtha. It is the 'padapadārthasambandha' worth the name. Lakṣaṇā is only an indirect relation between a Pada and Padārtha since it is only a relation of the denoted sense (śakyārtha) with another sense. In other words, it is a direct relation between two meanings and not between a word and its meaning. Hence Viśvanātha's expression 'śaktijñānasya' in 'atraiva' etc. above seems to be significant.

Viśvanātha's idea as expressed in the *Muktāvalī* above is this: In the case of a Śābdabodha, the knowledge of words in the sentence occurs first, then follows the stage of ascertaining the significative power of these words leading to the knowledge of the meanings of those words. Then follows the knowledge of the syntactical connection in shape of the total meaning of the sentence with the aid of some other factors involved in the process. Now in all cases, Śakti, the primary power of signification, of the words involved must get ascertained. There can be no case of Lakṣaṇā also, without a prior knowledge of Śakti. Śakti being a 'sambandha' between a Pada and its 'artha', without the knowledge of this Śakti, the Padārtha cannot be known even where, the corresponding Pada stands known. This is obvious as the very concept of 'sambandha' demands it. A relation presupposes two related things on two sides. The relation being known, the knowledge of one would lead to that of the other. This is what Viśvanātha wants to mean by the 'ekasambandhijñānavidhā' i.e., the process (of the knowing the other related factor or object) by the knowledge of one related factor or object. By this very process, the Śakti (i.e., the Padapadārthasambandha) being earlier known, the knowledge of

Pada, one related factor automatically leads to that of the Padārtha, the other related factor.

M(7). śaktiśca padena saha padārthasya sambandhaḥ.

Viśvanātha here introduces Śakti as the relation between a word (Pada) and its meaning (Padārtha). In the succeeding *Muktāvalī* text he would further divulge the nature of this relation in order to reject the notion in this regard of the Mīmāṁsakas and the Vaiyākaraṇas. Pañcānana Śāstri explains the significance of the particle 'ca' in the expression 'śaktiśca' as 'api' so as to cover Lakṣaṇā also as a relation between a Pada and Padārtha.[74] But this explanation seems to be untenable. It will be seen hereafter that Lakṣaṇā is defined as the relation of the śakyārtha (with another meaning i.e., the Lakṣayārtha). As such, in Lakṣaṇā, the relation between Śakyārtha and Lakṣyārtha is immediate and direct and that between the Pada and Lakṣyārtha is remote and indirect. Hence Lakṣaṇā cannot be tagged together with Śakti as 'padapadārthasambandha'. If Viśvanātha would have understood Lakṣaṇā as 'padapadārthasambandha' on a par with Śakti, he would have justifiably used Vṛtti in place of Śakti in the above context. To understand the aforesaid 'ca-kara' of Viśvanātha in the sense of 'api' is to delegate the Śakti itself to a secondary position in relation to Lakṣaṇā. In that case, it would mean 'śakti also' (śaktirapi) along with Lakṣaṇā. If we accept Pañcānana Śāstri's interpretation, Lakṣaṇā would come to be of primary consideration as the 'padapadārthasambandha'. This is not a desirable position. So we understand the 'ca-kara' in Śaktiśca above in the sense of an emphatic 'again'.

In the context of our examination of the Kārikā 'padajñānantu' etc., we have already discussed how the term Śakti is used variously in different schools of thought even in the sense of a significative power of a word. Simply to recapitulate the idea here, we may mention that the Ālaṁkārikas make indiscriminate use of the words, Śakti, Vṛtti and Vyāpāra in the sense of any of the three or four significative powers of words admitted by them. But the

Naiyāyikas like Viśvanātha and the Vaiyākaraṇas like Nageśa use[75] the term Vṛtti alone in such a broad sense to cover any of the significative powers admitted by them. They use the term Śakti only in the sense of the primary power of signification. Viśvanātha's Śakti in the context of Śābdabodha stands for Śruti or Abhidhāna or Abhidhā of the Mīmāṁsakas, and only Abhidhā of the Ālankārikas. Like the Naiyāyikas and Vaiyākaraṇas, the Vedāntins also use Śakti in the sense of only the primary significative power of a word.

But yet amongst the Naiyāyikas, themselves, we notice a difference.[76] Old Naiyāyikas are found using the term Saṁketa in a broader sense to cover within its fold 'īśvarasaṅketa' and 'ādhunikasaṁketa'. They give the name Śakti only to 'īśvarasaṁketa' and 'paribhāṣā to the 'ādhunikasaṁketa'. This is because, they understood Śakti as only the divine will (īśvarecchā). But as the Navyanaiyāyikas came to be liberal in their concept of Śakti in order to understand it in the sense of any will, divine or non-divine, they understand the terms Śakti and Saṁketa as synonymous. Though Viśvanātha is not vocal on this point, we have nothing to doubt that he can be an exception as a Navyanaiyāyika in this regard. He presents the Navyanaiyāyikas' concept of Śakti as mere Icchā in the manner of a conclusive proposition (siddhāntipakṣa).

The problem of the nature of this primary significative power of the word, i.e., the issue of the relation between a word and its meaning leads to the emergence of two theories. The Mīmāṁsakas and the Vaiyākaraṇas advocate the 'natural' or 'inherent' theory while the Naiyāyikas advocate the 'conventional' theory.

According to the Mīmāṁsakas, the relationship between a word and its meaning is eternal in the sense that it stands everfixed by nature without a beginning or end.[77] There is inherent capacity of words to convey instantaneously the ideas of objects invariably associated with them.[78] The relation is not manmade.[79]

This significative power of a word is, according to the Mīmāṁsakas, as eternal as the property of burning in fire. In the context of such an opinion of the Mīmāṁsakas, two questions are very much pertinent. (1) Firstly, if it is so natural, then why the meanings of words are not grasped by all people as soon as they are heard? Kumārila replies that the understanding of meanings from words is restricted to one with prior knowledge of the same eternal relation.[80] (2) Secondly, if it is as inherent as the burning capacity of fire, then why the utterance of the word 'kṣura' does not result in cutting of the mouth of the utterer? The reply of this question is that the word conveys the idea of the object and does not present the object itself.[81] The Mīmāṁsakas have described this denotative capacity of a word as an uncommon power like the extra-ordinary power of a visual organ to reveal the coloured shapes.[82]

The Naiyāyikas fully oppose such a view. The Nyāya philosophers do not recognise 'śakti' as a different category (Padā rtha) and do not accept it as 'natural'. According to them, an object is apprehended from the relevant word due to 'convention' (samaya or saṁketa).[83] As Śakti of Naiyāyikas is entirely dependant on Saṁketa, some Naiyāyikas like Gadādhara and Gaṅgeśa as we have already seen, unhesitatingly use Saṁketa as a synonym of the term, 'Śakti'. We find Vātysāyana mentioning in his *Bhāṣya* the possible sources from which the common people acquire the knowledge of the same convention.[84] The Naiyāyikas, unlike the Mīmāṁsakas, donot accept the significative power of a word on a par with the burning capacity of fire.[85] As the utterence of words like 'udaka', 'agni' etc. does not result in filling up and burning the mouth etc., the author of the *Nyāyasūtra* does not believe in any 'natural' relation that may exist between a word and its meaning. Gautama points out that there is no fixed law for the use of the same set of words amongst the different groups of people. He categorically assets that the apprehension of an object from a word is 'Conventional' (Sāmayika).[86] Vātsyāyana expounds this 'convention' of Gautama and maintains that the object is known from a word through 'Convention' and not because of any natural relation. According to him, the words are used to signify specific objects according to the arbitrary wishes of the sages, nobles and the mlecchas. If the relation between the word and its meaning would have been fixed, this much of latitude would not have been possible.[87] This 'Convention', Vātsyā yana observes, is known to the common people by observing the use by the olders of specific words to denote specific objects. If there be no knowledge of this 'Convention', the comprehension of the object is not likely to occur even in the event of the relevant word being heard.[88] It is seen further that 'groups of people' come to use the same word to mean different objects.[89] This fact all the more confirms the notion that the relation between a Pada and Padārtha is rather 'Conventional' (Sāmayika) and never natural (autpattika). Sometimes even amongst people belonging to different groups in a country, a word is found to carry the same meaning. Hence, Uddyotakara hastens[90] to explain Gautama's expression, 'group of people' as 'different group of people belonging to different countries.'

In the *Muktāvalī* hereafter, we shall find Viśvanātha recording the notion of Śakti, as maintained in both Prācīna and Navya schools of Nyāya. In Prācīna Nyāya, Śakti is understood as the will of God and in Navya Nyāya as the will of anybody. Either case carries a sense of arbitrariness. Thus, being conceived as an 'icchā', Śakti, the relation between a word and its meaning is regarded by the Naiyāyikas obviously as conventional and never natural.

It will not be out of context to record here the views of the Vaiśeṣikas in this regard. The Vaiśeṣikas as we have already stated, admit only two Pramāṇas, namely Pratyakṣa and Anumāna. Kaṇāda describes Śabda as the perception of the ear.[91] The Vaiśeṣikas hold that the verbal cognition can be included within the sphere of Inference (Anumāna) because of its similar activity.

A word in fact, according to them, leads to the knowledge of an object through Inference.[92] Yet in the context of the concept of relation between a word and its meaning the Vaiśesikas think like the Naiyāyikas. The Vaiśeṣikas donot believe that a 'Śabda' can possess conjugation (saṁyoga) with its Artha. Saṁyoga is a quality. Śabda also is a quality of Ākāśa (Ether). How can it be possible for a quality to possess another quality? So they cannot accept the position that there is a natural relation between the word and its meaning. On the other hand, the Vaiśeṣikas assert, the relation between the word and its concept owes its existence to the 'Convention' of a particular community. Hence, the relation under discussion, according to the Vaiśeṣikas, is conventional.

The Vaiyākaraṇas, again, rally behind the Mīmāṁsakas. According to them, the relation between the word and its meaning is eternal.[93] Bhartṛhari understands this relation as fixed and permanent. According to him the essential nature of this relation lies in an endless potentiality (anādiyogyatā) of a word to convey its meaning. It is like the capacity of the sense-organs to reveal their respective objects.[94] In the opinion of the Vaiyākaraṇas, this Śakti is other than the generally accepted 'sambandhas' like Saṁyoga, Samavāya etc. It is a phenomenon producing conceptual cognition only when the relation between the object and the word is ascertained. Just as the illuminative capacity of a lamp, though inherent in it, can illumine an object only when the object comes into the contact of the light, similarly the Śakti of a word can give rise to an idea of an object to a listener only when the relation of the word and the object is already known to him.[95] Nāgeśa, however, conceives this Śakti as a different type of relation that may be called Vācyavācakabhāvasaṁbandhaḥ.[96] To elucidate the point further, the relation between a Pada and a Padārtha, as viewed by Nāgeśa, rests not on saṁketa or convention (as the Naiyāyikas including Viśvanātha put it); but the said relation is apprehended through an identity (tādātmya) between the word and the object signified by it. This notion of Tādātmya is again realized on the strength of what may be called mutual illusory attribution (itaretarādhyāsa).[97] The idea can be explained thus : In the process of Itaretarādhyāsa, the 'artha' is superimposed upon the Śabda and the Śabda is superimposed upon the 'artha'. Now they come to be identical like Guṇa and Guṇin. This is not possible in 'ghaṭaḥ paṭaḥ' but is possible in 'Nīlo ghaṭaḥ. It is because we can think as follows - 'Nīla is (the) ghaṭa' and '(the) ghaṭa is Nīla'. Thus without superimposition the notion of identity is not possible and without the notion of identity, the words donot denote and the meanings also do not get denoted. Thus the 'Padapadārthasaṁbandha' viewed by Nāgeśa as the 'Vācyavācakasaṁbandha' is virtually a tādātmyasaṁbandha' of which 'itaretarādhyāsa' is the source. As is admitted by Nāgeśa himself, he is influenced some way in this concept of 'Padapadārthasaṁbandha' by Patañjali's idea of Saṁketa in the shape of 'itaretarādhyāsa'.[98] We shall discuss Nāgeśa's view again in succeeding pages in the context of our examining the Naiyāyikas' concept of Śakti as 'icchā'.

As for Ālaṁkārikas, they regard convention as the basis for the primary relation between the word and its meaning. A word is 'Vā caka' (expressive), as Mammaṭa points out, only when it conveys a meaning through direct convention.[99] But they treat Abhidhā as different from the conventional relation. Jagannātha, author of the *Rasagaṇgādhara*, however, follows the Naiyāyikas fully in thisregard. He maintains that Abhidhā is same with the conventional relation.[100] The attitude of the Naiyāyikas revealed in their anxiety to equate both 'Īśvarasaṁketa' and Śakti is opposed by the Grammarian Nāgeśa by way of showing difference between the two.[101] This is because, being inspired by Patañjali, Nāgeśa also understands that the general relation between words and meanings is eternal in the sense that all words are related to all meanings. The convention in the form of mutual illusory superimposition (itaretarādhyāsarūpasaṁketa) helps in ascertaining the Śakti, the relation of identity on the strength of which words come to denote and meanings come to be denoted.[102]

M(8). sā cāsmācchabdādayamartho boddhavya itīśvarecchārū pā. ādhunike nāmni śaktirastyeva, "ekādaśe'hani pitā nāma kuryā di" tīśvarecchāyāḥ sattvāt. ādhunikasaṁketite tu na śaktiriti sampradāyaḥ. navyāstveśvarecchā na śaktiḥ, kintvicchaiva. tenādhunikasaṁketite'pi śaktirastyevetyāhuḥ.

Here Viśvanātha presents the peculiar Naiyāyikas' concept of the 'Padapadārthasaṁbandha' in clear contrast with that of the Mīmāṁsakas. Before we proceed to examine the Naiyāyika view, we have to note that Mīmāṁsakas do not understand the significative power of a word (Padaśakti) separately from the power in general like the burning capacity of fire. They conceive even Śakti in general as a separate category (Padārthāntara). The Naiyāyikas including Viśvanātha donot subscribe to that view also. For fear of digression, we may avoid a discussion on that issue here. Mīmāṁsakas divide their Śakti as 'Sahajā' (natural) and ādheyā' (produced).[103] They regard the power pertaining to a word (padaniṣṭhaśakti) also as 'Sahaja-śakti' of the 'nitya' (Permanent or eternal) type. Some later Mīmāṁsakas, however, are found to admit Padaśakti differently as the third type of Śakti in addition to the already accepted 'sahajā' and 'ādheyā' types.[104] In view of this, the Naiyāyikas' concept of Śakti as 'Īsvarecchā' or mere 'icchā' comes to strike a contrast. We have already stated that the Naiyāyikas donot believe that there is any eternal, natural or permanent relation between a word and its meaning. They conceive this relation in the form of some Samaya or Saṁketa. But what is the true nature of this Samaya or Saṁketa ? Here the Prācīna and Navya school of Nyāya maintain a difference. Viśvanātha alludes to that difference here. In 'sā ca ------ īśvarecchārūpā', Viśvanātha refers to the view of the older Naiyāyikas that the Śakti i.e. Padaśakti is nothing but the will of God in the form of 'this meaning be understood from this word.' In other words, the samaya or saṁketa established by God Himself with regard to a word in the matter of conveying a meaning is the very primary power of signification. The Nyāyasūtrakāra asserted first that the understanding of meanings from words is due to some 'samaya' (convention).[105] In explaining the position of the Sūtrakāra, the Bhāṣyakāra interpreted this 'samaya' as the application of the regulations in the matter of denoting the denoted senses in the shape of 'these meanings stand as denotable by this word.'[106] Whose is this first application which comes as the source of such permanent regulations regarding the denotative capacity of words ? The picture in this regard comes to be clear a bit later. Vācaspati Miśra, in course of his examination of the position of the Sūtrakā ra and the Bhāṣyakāra in the *Nyāyavārtikatātparyaṭīkā*, points out that the object possessing dewlap etc. (sāsnādimānevārtha) is what is denoted by the word 'cow'[107] and thus again the object possessing manes etc. (keśarādimān) is what is denoted by the word 'horse'. Now, as to the source of this regulation regarding such denotativeness of such words, the Samaya (convention) established by the almighty God before the creation by making the use of such and such words with reference to such and such meanings is to be understood.

Vātsyāyana himself pointed out the utility of Vyākaraṇa in preserving the Samayas (conventions) regarding the words siginifying the meanings.[108] As Vācaspati explains,[109] the words with regard to which Divine convention exists are correct and those without the same are corrupt. And in maintaining the correct words apart from the corrupt ones, the competance of Grammar is to be admitted. Now a pertinent question arises. If only the Divine will be admitted as the real nature of the primary power of signification, what will be the fate of modern or non-Vedic words. The Prācīna Naiyāyikas donot find any difficulty in replying to this query. Viśvanātha refers to this in the *Mūktāvalī* above, i.e. "ādhunikanāmni śaktirastyeva ------- sattvāt." : When a son is born, he is named by the father as 'Devadatta'. The word 'Devadatta' signifies the boy apparently on the strength of the will of an individual other than God. But, we must not forget that the father of 'Devadatta' is empowered to exercise the will of God by the Divine Will standing in the form of an injunction : 'the father should name (his child) on the 11th day (since birth)'.[110] In other words, the Divine Will is revealed here in the form of the will of the father. The author of the *Tattvacintāmaṇi* also refers to such a logic of the Prācīna Naiyāyikas by illustrating the naming of a boy as Maitra by his father on the strength of such an injunction.[111] Thus, in case of non-Vedic or modern names, the Prācīna Naiyāyikas accept the existence of a Divine Will as determining the convention, in the shape of such general divine statements. At this stage we may remember that the Vedas according to the Naiyāyikas, are created by Īśwara, while the Mīmā ṁsakas accept the Vedas as being eternal and self-existant. Here we may record the dissent of a modern Naiyāyika, Jagadiśa.[112] As new names are ever in the process of being coined by the moderners, Jagadisa is not happy with such a weak argument in admitting Śakti in modern names on the strength of such general scriptural propositions. He maintains that in the case under discussion, the shastric injunction in the context prescribes the duty of the father in the matter of naming the son and it has nothing to do with the significative power of the word Caitra etc. Thus he does not accept the presence of Śakti in modern words, Caitra etc. on the presumption of the presence of 'īśvarasaṁketa' in their regard. In the context of purely modern names in respect of which such divine sanctions cannot be traced-out, the Prācīna Naiyā yikas are not prepared to admit any Śakti.

This idea of the Prācīna Naiyāyikas is referred to by Viśvanā tha in the *Muktāvalī* above in 'ādhunikasaṁketite tu na śaktiriti saṁpradāyaḥ'. As a matter of fact, we find that with the Prācīna Naiyāyikas, the convention (Saṁketa) as the relation between Pada and Padārtha is of two types. (1) one is permanent and is known as Śakti. This Śakti depends upon the will of God manifesting itself in the form of 'let such and such a thing be understood by such and such a word.' (2) The other type of

Saṁketa is occasional and is called Paribhāṣā (technicality). Technical terms of Vyākaraṇa like Nadī and Vṛdhī are examples of this sort.[113] The Prācīna Naiyāyikas feel that the Saṁketa of the words 'go' etc. with regard to certain meanings stand determined, as of God, at the very beginning of the creation. That very Saṁketa comes to be learnt in subsequent times, even today, by children also, without any knowledge of relevance, merely by observing the use of the words by elderly people. The children finally understand the meanings which they infer as the cause of the reactions of the elderly people who hear the more elderly ones. Thus for the moderners Vṛddhavyāvahāra comes to be the ascertainer of this Saṁketa made by God himself.[114]

The Navya Naiyāyikas do not endorse the view of thier predecessors in this regard. They simplify the idea and accept mere will, to whomsoever it may belong, as the Śakti or Significative Power of a word. Viśvanātha refers to this view of the Navya Naiyā yikas in the *Muktāvalī* above, 'navyāstu ---- etc. In this context, we may speak of Gaṅgeśopādhyāya who elaborately examines the position of the Prācīna Naiyāyikas and tends towards evolving a new formula. He questions the propriety of accepting as correct only the words in case of which the Saṁketa stands fixed by God. It is risky to presume that only the 'īśvarasaṁketita' words (with regard to which the convention stands set by God) are 'sādhu' (correct). It may lead us to accept at one stage that all possible words are correct as īśvarasaṁketa' is found with regard to all. Or it may so happen that all the secondary uses are to be admitted as corrupt for lack of 'īśvarasaṁketa'. Again it is found that even without the knowledge of 'īśvarasaṁketa', one comes to make a correct use. Sometimes even the reverse is seen. Thus Gaṅgeśa[115] appears to be reasonably aware of the loopholes in the older concept of Padaśakti. As evidenced by the observation of Viśvanātha, the Navya Naiyāyikas gradually come to accept the liberal view that any will and not merely God's will is the Śakti or Saṁketa of a word. But, we cannot offhand declare it as the only opinion of the Navya Naiyāyikas since the weakness to regard only 'Ī-śvarasaṁketa' as Śakti is seen in case of certain Navya Naiyāyikas also. Jagadiśa, for instance, refuses to recognise Śakti in modern names like Caitra and enlists them as technical (Pāribhāṣika)[116] since such words with what are connotated by them now could not have existed in the very beginning of the creation. Annaṁbhṭṭa records only the old views in his *Saṁgraha*.[117] But Dr. Dayānanda Bhārgava presumes that Annaṁbhaṭṭa was aware of the weakness of the arguments to cover the modern names by 'Ī śvarasaṁketa' and wanted also to present a more ideal notion in the context. So he defines Śakti in his *Dīpikā* as a relation between a Pada and a Padārtha[118] which conditions the recollection of meanings. Annaṁbhaṭṭa is understood by Dr. Bhārgava to have made hereby an attempt to bring about a compromise between the Naiyāyikas and the Mīmāṁsakas.[119] Dr. Bhārgava's impression is based on the relevant portion of the commentary *Nī laakanthaprakāśikā*.[120] To the Mīmāṁsakas, Śakti is a separate category and a Dravya. To the Naiyāyikas, it is an 'icchā' and as such is a Guṇa. We for ourselves, on verification of the concerned texts in the *Tarkadīpikā* and the *Nīlakanthaprakāśikā* on it, could not be so convinced. The text of the *Dīpikā*., "arthasmṛtyanukūla" etc comes as an explanatory note of the word Śakti. This is not at all different from Viśvanātha's earlier *Muktāvalī* text 'śaktiśca padena saha padārthasya sambandhaḥ'. Here also there is no difference, rather a conformity between Naiyāyikas and Mīmāṁsakas. Difference lies in the fact that while the Mīmāṁsakas treat the 'śabdārthasambandha' as eternal or natural (autpattika or sahaja), the Naiyāyikas treat it as (merely) conventional or artificial (sāmayika). To bring about this difference only, the Naiyāyikas proceed to divulge the real nature of the samaya or saṁketa as 'Īśvarecchā' or mere 'icchā'. Only to confirm the position that they do not believe in Śakti as an additional category (padārthāntara), both Viśvanātha and Annaṁbhaṭṭa proceed to add 'asmācchabdadayamartho' etc. in the *Muktāvalī* and 'asmātpadādayamartho etc.' in the *Saṁgraha*.

In Annaṁbhaṭṭa's case, this is clear from the relevant *Dīpikā* and Nīlakantha-*prakāsīkā* texts. But we do not find Annaṁbhaṭṭa giving any evidence of his accepting or introducing any newer formula in respect of the concept of Śakti. Here we may add that Nāgeśa objects to the Naiyāyikas' conceiving of Śakti simultaneously as both 'saṁbandha' and 'icchā'. By way of quoting the definition of 'saṁbandha' by some unnamed learned people, Nāgeśa says that a 'saṁbandha' or relation belongs to both the 'saṁbandhins' (related objects) and yet remains different from both the related objects. The 'saṁbandha' leads to the recognition of one of the related objects to be qualified (Viśiṣṭa) in terms of the other related object. Under the circumstances, 'icchā' and 'saṁbandha' can not be equivalent inasmuch as 'icchā' unlike 'saṁbandha' here can not pertain to both Pada and Padārtha, the 'saṁbandhins'. Icchā being an 'ātmaguṅa' in the view of Naiyā yikas themselves, it will be an unsound proposition to talk of it as beloning to Pada and Padārtha.[121]

But in the view of the Naiyāyikas' peculiar concept of the 'padapadārthasaṁbandha', we do not feel that the Naiyāyikas are out of their way in conceiving the 'saṁbandha' under discussion as the very 'icchā'. Naiyāyikas have admitted 'icchā' undoubtedly as an attribute of the self, either an individual self or the supreme self.[122] But the 'saṁbandha' they conceive between Pada and Padā rtha is peculiar to themselves. It does not belong to known types of relations like inherence (samavāya), contact (saṁyoga) etc. But then what it is? The relation between a word and its meaning as conceived by the Naiyāyikas, unlike the Mīmāṁsakas and the Vaiyākaraṇas is nothing eternal, natural or real. It is superimposed on Pada and Padārtha by the will of a self. Thus it is artificial and unreal. In essence, it is a result of the functioning of a conscious factor. So virtually there stands no difference between a 'padapadārthasaṁbandha' and the 'icchā' of the original speaker or employer of the Pada or Padas. Nāgeśa's objection would have carried any meaning if the Naiyāyikas would have understood the 'saṁbandha' as natural or eternally existing in Pada and Padārtha. The 'saṁbandha' as conceived by the Naiyāyikas virtually and originally does not pertain either to a Pada or a Padārtha but to a conscious self. It comes to be understood as belonging to a pair of Pada and Padārtha only subsequently, after the Saṁketa, in form of the will of someone, stands ascertained.

Now by way of examining the earlier *Muktāvalī* , 'śaktiśca padena saha padārthasya sambandhaḥ' along with the subsequent one 'sā ca --- icchaiva', we can conclude, as Nāgeśa notices it,[123] that for the Naiyāyikas, the Saṁketa and 'padapadārthasambandha' are identical. But a difference between the two sections of the Naiyāyikas is here noticed. While the Navya Naiyāyikas deem Saṁketa and Śakti as equivalent, to the Prācīna Naiyāyikas, all Saṁketas cannot get the status of Śakti.

M(9). śaktigrahastu vyākaraṇāditaḥ tathā hi --

"śaktigrahaṁ vyākaraṇopamānakoṣāptavākyād vyavahārataśca/ vākyasya śeṣād vivṛtervadanti sānnidhyataḥ siddhapadasya vṛddhāḥ" //

Now that the Śakti is understood as a specific relation between a word and its meaning, there is the subsequent problem as to how one can have the knowledge of this denotative power of a word or as to how some one understands this relation between a word and its meaning: This is the problem known in the circles of Grammarians, Logicians and Rhetoricians as the problem of Śaktigraha, Śaktijñāna or Saṁketagraha. We have already seen in the context of our discussion on Kārikā I and the relevant text of the *Muktāvalī* that the Padārthadhī is the immediate cause of a Śābdabodha. But the Padārthadhī must be however, produced by the corresponding 'Padajñāna'. But the 'Padajñāna' may lead to corresponding 'Padārthajñāna' only throughg the relevant 'Śaktijñāna' (the knowledge of Śakti). This Śakti is nothing but a specific relation of a word with its meaning. This specific relation in its essence is the Saṁketa or Samaya that stands already set by the God or by society. Hence, in all the appropriate circles, the very ways of understanding this relation between a Pada and its 'artha' have been discussed. The aforesaid ways may otherwise be described as the means of ascertaining Saṁketa. It is suggested that there are as many as eight ways for learning a new word or Vocabulary. These ways have been summarily recorded in the aforequoted verse 'śaktigrahaṁ' etc. The verse comes to be oft-quoted in later circles of scholars belonging to various schools.[124] This is a summarising verse (saṁgrahaśloka) based on the crystalised opinion of the earlier scholars. For instance, we find that Jagadīśācārya recognises all the said Śaktigrāhakas without literally quoting the verse and that Gaṅgeśa who preceded Jagadīśa refers to the said 'śaktigrāhakas', except Vivṛti or Vivaraṇa, though not in a verse.[125]

We may, however, mention that the number of ways prescribed for learning the meaning of a new word i.e. for obtaining the knowledge of Śakti in particular context is not always the same with all scholars. Of the Grammarians, Nāgeśa quotes this list 'śaktigrahaṁ' etc. entirely. In Sāṁkhya only three ways have been admitted for learning the meanings of words.[126] They are, namely Āptopadeśa, Vṛddhavyāvahāra and Prasiddhapadasannidhi. Of the Ālaṁkārikas, Vāmana recognises only Koṣa (Lexicon) in this context.[127] Modern Ālaṁkārikas have come to admit ways more than one. As for instance, Viśvanātha Kavirāja deals with Vṛddhavyavahāra primarily and elaborately and adds two others, namely 'prasiddhapadasamabhivyāhāra' (simultaneous utterance of a famous or known word) and Āptopadeśa (statement of a trustworthy person).[128] Even amongst the Naiyāyikas, Annaṁbhaṭṭa recognises only the Vyavahāra as the 'śaktigrāhaka'. He maintains that to say that the Śakti of an unknown word can be ascertained from the knowledge of an already known word uttered along with the earlier one is not finally acceptable. It is because even in that case, the Śakti of the very known word is to be understood as originally ascertained through Vṛddhavyavahāra.[129]

Though the number of ways suggested for acquiring the knowledge of new words varies in different treatises, it is interesting to find that Vṛddhavyavahāra is invariably recognised by almost all the scholars of various schools and hence it deserves to be admitted as the most important of the ways suggested in this regard. It is why we find Nāgeśa referring to (Vṛddha) Vyavahāra as Śaktigrāhakaśiromaṇi, the chief (lit. the crest jewel) of the factors determining the denotative power (of words).[130] This singular position is given to Vṛddhavyavahāra in all the chief schools including Mīmāṁsā.[131]

In the circle of Naiyāyikas also, generally speaking, Vṛddhavyavahāra gets due recognition. Of the predecessors ofViśvanātha, Gaṅgeśa comes to admit that the knowledge of all words primarily results from Vṛddhavyavahāra i.e. the observations of usage of elderly persons. He understands the other ways to be dependant on the basic knowledge of meaning of words derived through Vṛddhavyavahāra.[132] Jagadīśā categorically asserts that the knowledge of Saṁketa first takes place in all cases through Vṛddhavyavahāra and only thereafter, scope arises for the knowledge of Śakti through other factors like Upamāna.[133] Viśvanātha Nyāya Pañcānana, however, quotes the aforesaid verse 'śaktigrahaṁ' etc. and explains each of the eight 'śaktigrā hakas' in the same order as is given in the verse. He seems to place all the 'śaktigrāhakas' on a par. He cannot be said to have attached any special importance to any one of them.

Now 'tu' in the expression 'śaktigrahastu' in the text of the *Muktāvalī* above seems to carry some significance. Śaktijñāna being admitted as essential for bringing about the knowledge of the meaning of a word concerned, the author of the *Bhāṣāpariccheda* cautions that the very knowledge of Śakti of words is to be gathered only from recognised sources as enlisted in the quoted verse. Otherwise there is the risk of the resulting verbal knowledge being invalid. We shall see in our discussion later on that all the 'śaktigrāhakas' mentioned in the kārikā are in consonance with the Naiyāyikas' understanding of the Śabda Pramāṇa, in the sense of Āpta-vākya. As we shall find that these 'śaktigrāhakas' are only certain sepcific Āptavākyas, we can interpret Viśvanātha's 'tu' as carrying a sense of caution not to violate the sanction made in the list. Or we may say that in presenting the list of 'śaktigrāhakas', he is influenced by his predecessor Gaṅgeśa who raises the doubt, on behalf of a Pūrvapakṣa, that as there are no means of ascertaining Śaktigraha, the Śābdabodha for whicdh Śaktigraha stands admitted as a pre-requisite is not possible.[134]

M(10) dhātu-prakṛti-pratyayādīnāṁ śaktigraho vyākaraṇād bhavati. kvacit tu sati bādhake tyajyate. yathā-vaiyākaranairā khyātasya karttari śaktirucyate. caitraḥ pacatītyādau kartrā saha caitrasyā'bhedānvayaḥ. tacca gauravāt tyajyate. kintu kṛtau śaktirlāghavāt. kṛtiścaitrādau prakārībhūya bhāsate.

In the *Muktāvalī* above, Viśvanātha begins his exposition and illustration of these 'śaktigrāhakas' or 'śaktigrahopāyas' (the methods or means for acquiring the knowledge of the primary meaning of words). At the first instance, Viśvanātha admits Grammar as a means of learning the meaning of Prakṛtis (in the form of Dhātus), Pratyayas (suffixes), etc. As such he appears to echo an earlier opinion. Even according to Patañjali we can learn the meanings of the radicals, verbal roots, suffixes etc. of a language easily with the aid of Grammar. It is a fact that in the view of Patañjali, the words stand in a fixed relationship with their respective meanings. Yet, according to him, the help of Grammar is indispensable for learning the meanings of words used in a sentence. Whatever may be the basic difference between Naiyāyikas and others in the approach to the relation between a word and its meanig or, in other words, to the nature of Śakti, the importance of Grammar in the matter of learning language is widely admitted. Of the Naiyāyikas, the older theorists stressed the utility of Grammar for distinguishing between correct and corrupt uses or words on the strength of corresponding convention.

This we may gather from Vātsyāyana's *Nyāyabhāṣya*[135] and Vācaspati Miśra's *Tātparyaṭīkā.*[136] Vācaspati explicitly puts that Grammar is essential for distinguishing between the correct and corrupt forms even in case of learning a language through Vṛddhavyavahāra.[137]

Now to resume our exposition of the text of the *Muktāvalī* above, we find the expression Dhātuprakṛti quite interesting. As accepted in the circle of the Naiyāyikas, Prakṛti stands for Dhātu also. Jagadīśa directly divides Prakṛti into Nāmapadas and Dhātus.[138] By Nāmapadas he covers the Prātipadikas of Pāṇini. Now the question arises as to why Viśvanātha makes a separate mention of Dhātu in addition to Prakṛti which covers the former. Hence Rāmarudrabhaṭṭa explains Viśvanātha's *Muktāvalī* text 'dhātuprakṛti' as 'dhāturūpapṛakrti'.[139] This may be that hereby Viśvanātha wants to exclude the Nāmapadas from the scope of Vyākaraṇa as a śaktigrāhaka. If Viśvanātha would have wanted to include the Nāmapadas, he could and should have used only the word Prakṛti. So in the commentary *Rāmarudrī*, it is opined that actually the Śaktigraha in case of Prātipadikas, e.g. Garga, etc. takes place from Koṣa.[140] Now Dhātu stands for the roots 'bhū', 'pac' etc.[141] The word 'ādi' in the *Muktāvalī* text above is there to cover Samāsa as well, since the Vaiyākaraṇas admit Śakti in Samāsa also.[142] The term Pratyaya stands for Subādi (inflexional suffices), tibādi (conjugational suffixes) taddhita and kṛt (primary and secondary suffixes)[143]

Now it is found that Grammar fixes the meanings of Dhātuprakṛti etc. mentioned above. As for instance, the Dhātu (root) 'bhū' is read in the sense of 'being' (Sattā),[144] the pratyayas (suffixes) 'tip' etc. in the sense of present tense (vartamāna)[145] or the pratyayas (suffixes) 'sup' etc. are read in the sense of number one etc.[146] The Navya Naiyāyikas like Viśvanātha also accept these meanings as determined by Grammar. It is, however, not that the Naiyāyikas do accept all the meanings as fixed by Grammar. When there is a chance of their fundamental principles being contradicted, they do not agree with the Grammarians. An instance of difference of idea between the Grammarians and the Naiyāyikas is provided by the denotation of the term Ākhyāta. While the Naiyāyikas understand the 'tiṅ' suffixes by the term Ākhyāta, the Grammarians understan the tinantas, i.e. the verbs comprising of roots, tiṅ suffixes and also other arguments.[147] In the sentence 'Caitraḥ pacati', for example, the Ākhyāta 'pacati', according to the Grammarians, means 'Kartā' (the agent).[148] So the entire Verbal form stands for 'Pākakartā'. Caitra as the proper name standing for the actual agent of cooking in the context comes to be syntactically connected by the relation of identity (abheda) with the verbal form 'pacati' which means nothing but the 'pākakartā' (the agent of cooking) himself. So the Śābdabodha in the context comes in the form of 'Caitrābhinnaḥ pākakartā' giving the idea of Caitra as (not different from i.e. identified as) the agent of cooking. The Navya-Naiyāyikas come to reject this position. As Viśvanātha points out, they understand 'an effort' (Kṛti) and not the 'agent' (Kartā) as the meaning of a verbal suffix (Ākhyāta). It requires to be noted here that, as shown under footnote (no. 147) above, the Naiyāyikas and the Grammarians differ in respect of the very concept of Ākhyāta. The Naiyāyikas discard the view of the Grammarians as the stand taken by the latter leads to a fallacy of complexity (Gaurava). For the sake of the merit of simplicity (Lāghava), the Naiyāyikas assert that it is wiser to understand the Śakti of Ākhyāta with regard to Kṛti. The Naiyā yikas understand 'effort' (Yatna) by the word Kṛti.[149] In the matter of recognising the signification of effort (Yatnavācyatvaṁ) from Ākhyāta, the Naiyāyikas clash also with the Mīmāṁsakas. Udayanācārya points out this difference of opinion amongst the Mīmāṁsakas and the Naiyāyikas. The Mīmāṁsakas who understand Vyāpāra as the Śakyārtha are not prepared to accept Kṛti (Yatna) as denoted by an Ākhyāta.[150] They of couse understand a sense of 'Yatna' or Kṛti corresponding to an Ākhyāta only by 'ā kṣepa' (i.e. by Anumāna). The process of Anumāna involved therein according to the Mīmāṁsakas takes such a form : 'Caitraḥ pākānukūla kṛtimān pākānukūlavyāpāravattvāt.' They do not pretend not to know that a sense of effort comes to be conveyed in case of every Ākhyāta, though they do not understand it by the very Ākhyātaśakti. Without going to the detailed arguments, we can conclude that even at the stage of Udayanācārya,[151] the Naiyā yikas have asserted that the 'Kṛtyartha' (Yatnārtha) cannot be had through an inferential process but by the Śakti only of Ākhyātārtha itself. Jagadīśa also confirms Kṛti as Ākhyātārtha.[152] In consonance with this earlier position, Viśvanātha now points out the Śakti of an Ākhyāta with regard to Kṛti in the sense of effort. As a result, 'Pacati' means 'Pākakṛti' and the total meaning of the sentence comes to be 'Pākakṛtimān caitraḥ'. The (pāka) kṛti as the Śakyārtha of the Ākhyāta in 'Pacati' stands' as Prakāra of Viśeṣṇa (qualification) of the agent Caitra here. Such is the way of explaining other Ākhyātas also.

Now the notion of Gaurava and Lāghava, involved in the context as being thought of by Viśvanātha may be explained thus: All Śakyārthas must have their Śakyatāvacchedakas (i.e., the exclusive factor which restricts the state of being Śakyārtha to the Śakyārtha alone). All the Śakyatāvacchedakas again except Jāti must be understood along with their own Śakyatāvacchedakas. The Śakyatāvacchedaka is the 'dharma' (qualification) or attribute and the Śakyārtha is the 'dharmī (qualified or that which is possessed of an attribute). Without the knowledge of 'dharma', that of 'dharmī' cannot follow. Whenever there is 'Padārthajñāna', through 'śaktijñāna', the śakyārtha comes to be understood along with its śakyatāvacchedaka.

Now, if Kartā is the Śakyārtha of an Ākhyāta, the Kartā or agent comes to be Kṛtimān, i.e., one that possesses the effort. Hence Kṛti is obviously the Śakyatāvacchedaka here. Now Kṛti being a meaning other than a Jāti, it must also have a Śakyatā vaccedaka for its own in the form of 'Kṛtitva'. Thus it will lead to a 'Kalpanā-gaurava' (complexity in imagination, i.e., a complex imagination). Moreover as even the Kṛti can be innumerable, one is to admit innumerable denotative powers (anantaśakti) again to have the knowledge of Kṛti. In this way also, a scope for another 'Kalpanāgaurava' arises. But if the Kṛti is directly understood as the Śakyārtha of an Ākhyāta, the 'Kṛtitva' will be the Śakyatā vacchedaka. The Kṛtitva standing for a Jāti and being one in number, no scope for 'Kalpanāgaurava' will arise in either way. Thus, for sake of simplicity (Lāghava), the Naiyāyikas come to reject the view of Vaiyākaraṇas in the matter of understanding the meaning of an Ākhyāta.

Thus in a sentence like 'Caitraḥ pacati', the Naiyāyikas understand only Kṛti as Śakyārtha from the Ākhyāta in 'Pacati' and have the Śābdabodha as 'Pākakṛtimān Caitraḥ' But they are silent as to how they come to get the meaning 'Kṛtimān' from Kṛti, which is necessary to effect the syntactical relation between Caitraḥ and Kṛti. In our opinion here also an involvement of Lakṣaṇā is to be admitted. While Śakti gives the sense of Kṛti, it must be none other than Lakṣaṇā to convey the sense of the Kṛtimān. But Viśvanātha maintains an enigmatic silence about the possibility of the involvement of a Lakṣaṇā here.

Here we may note that Nāgeśa as a Grammarian could not appreciate the view of the Naiyāyikas in this regard. He refers to the grammatical view of recognising Śakti of suffixes[153] (that is tiṅ) with regard to Kartā and Karma. He in that context refers to the Naiyāyikas who accept Śakti of 'lakāras' with regard to Kṛti and not Kartā for sake of a Lāghava[154] (Simplicity). He opposes the Nyāya view as inaccurate.[155]

M(11). na ca kartturanabhidhānāc caitrādipadottaraṁ tṛtīyā syāditi vācyam, karttṛsaṁkhyānabhidhānasya tatra tantratvāt. Saṁkhyābhidhānayogyaśca karmatvādyanavaruddhaḥ prathamāntapadopasthāpyaḥ. karmatvādityasyetaraviśeṣaṇatvena tātparyaviṣayatvamarthaḥ. tena caitra iva maitro gacchatītyādau na caitre saṁkhyānvayaḥ. yatra karmādau na viśeṣaṇatve tātparyam, tadvāraṇāya prathamānteti. yadvā dhā tvarthātiriktaviśeṣaṇatvaṁ prathamadalārthaḥ. tena caitra iva maitro gacchatītyādau caitrādervāraṇam. stokaṁ pacatītyādau stokādervāraṇāya dvitīyadalam. tasya dvitīyāntapadopasthāpyatvādvāraṇamiti.

In the foregoing passage, it has been established that the Ākhyāta does not have a Śakti in respect of the Kartā. This amounts to saying that the Kartā is not denoted (i.e., not 'abhihita') by the Ākhyāta. This position ushers in a problem. According to the Grammarians' rule 'kartṛkaraṇayostṛtīyā' (P 2.3.18), a Kartā which is not 'abhihita' (i.e., not denoted by the Ākhyāta) should occur in the third case-ending. Hence in the expression, 'Caitraḥ pacati', Caitra being not denoted by the Ākhyāta in 'pacati', the word 'caitra' should have occurred in the third case-ending. Viśvanātha says that such an objection is not tenable, because, when it is said that a certain Kartā is not 'abhihita' by the Ākhyāta, what is meant is that the number of the Kartā is not denoted by the number of the Ākhyāta. In other words, the state of the number of the Karta, being not denoted by the Ākhyata is the governing factor for the Kartā having the third case-ending. In this connection, it is further pointed out that the Kartā or the Karma which deserves to have its number being denoted by the Ākhyāta must be 'karmatvādyanavaruddha' and at the same time 'prathamāntapadopasthāpya'. The plain meaning of the clause 'karmatvādyanavaruddha' is that it should not be fettered by the state of being Karma etc; but the actual purport of the clause is that the meaning of the word should not occur as an attribute of some other meaning. For example, in the expression. 'Caitra iva Maitro gacchati', the number of the word 'Caitra' is not denoted by the Ākhyāta in 'gacchati' or in other words, there need not necessarily be a syntactical conformity between 'Caitra' and 'gacchati' in respect of their number. This is because, Caitra occurs here as an attribute of the idea of 'sādṛśya' (i.e., similarity) conveyed by the word 'iva'. Because from the expression 'Caitra iva', what we understand is 'caitraviṣayakasādṛśya' where the idea of 'sādṛśya' is qualified by the idea of 'Caitra'. Hence there need not be a conformity between 'Caitra' and 'gacchati' and we can also have an expression like 'Caitra iva Maitro gacchati' without affecting the denotation of the Ākhyāta. Our author further says that the clause 'prathamāntapadopasthāpya' is given to make sure the elimination of a situation where the purport is not in respect of the state of being an attribute for the Karma etc. For example, in the expression, 'taṇḍulaṁ pacati', the Śābdabodha occurs in the form of 'taṇḍulakarmakapākānukūlakṛtiḥ' where 'taṇḍula' is a Viśeṣaṇa of the meaning of the root no doubt but it is not the attribute of anything else. Hence the number in 'Taṇḍula' should have been in conformity with the number of the Ākhyāta. But it is not so since we can have the expression 'taṇḍulān pacati' also. Now 'taṇḍula' cannot claim this conformity only because of not occurring in the first case ending. In the expression, 'taṇḍulaṁ pacyate', where the Śābdabodha is in the form of 'pākānukūlakṛtikarmatvavat taṇḍulaṁ', 'taṇḍulam' occurs only as a Viśeṣya and not as a Viśeṣaṇa and hence there is full conformity between 'taṇḍula' and the Ākhyāta in respect of the number. In the example, 'taṇḍulaṁ pacati', 'taṇḍulaṁ' is a Viśeṣana only of the meaning of the Dhātu and not of anything else. When anything occurs as the attribute of the meaning of a Dhātu and not of anything else, that is taken to be as good as being not the attribute of anything at all. Hence, there was the doubt that the word 'taṇḍulaṁ' of the expression, 'taṇḍulaṁ pacati' should have been covered by the purport of the clause 'karmatvādyanavarūddha' or by that of 'itaraviśeṣaṇatvena tātparyaviṣayatvaṁ'. We do not have the number in the word 'taṇḍulaṁ' denoted by the Ākhyāta only because it occurs in the first case-ending. To make it clear that being an attribute of the meaning of a root is not taken to be the state of being an attribute, the author improves upon his position by saying that the earlier clause (i.e., Karmatvādyanavarūddha) should mean that the particular object is not an attribute of anything other than the meaning of a root. Hence the word 'Caitra' in the expression 'Caitra iva maitro gacchati', even though it is 'Prathamāntapadopasthāpya', does not have its number denoted by the number of the Ākhyāta, because of being the attribute of something other than the meaning of a root. In the expression. 'stokaṁpacati' (Cooks slightly) the word 'stokaṁ' is an attribute of the meaning of the concerned root. As such it is not an attribute of anything else and hence it should have had its number denoted by the number of the Ākhyāta. But the scope for such a denotation is not there and we can have an expression like 'stokaṁ pacati' because the word 'stokaṁ', as desired by the grammatical injunctions, occurs in the second case-ending and is thus debarred by the clause 'Prathamāntapadopasthāpya'.

Now coming back to the original position of Viśvanātha that the Kṛti and not the Kartā is the meaning of the Akhyāta, we have to face the question as to how the idea of the Kartā comes to be understood at all. Viśvanātha is himself silent on this point. But we find that the question in the context has been replied as early as in Udayana's *Nyāyakusumāñ*jali. According to Udayana the sense of a Kartā can be had through an 'ākṣepa' (an inferential process) from the number (saṁkhyā) of a Kartā, which stands undoubtedly denoted by an Ākhyāta. Such an 'ākṣepa' is possible as because, a Kartā is the substratum of its own saṁkhyā which is a quality. Hence according to Udayana, there is no necessity of imagining the Śakti of an Ākhyāta with regard to a Kartā.[156]

Nāgeśa also makes a reference to Naiyāyikas' admitting Kartā as known by its being presented only in the first case-ending and that to the meaning of a word ending only in the first case-ending, the meaning of an Ākhyāta also comes to be an attribute. In a sentence like 'Caitraḥ pacati' the Śābdabodha as a result will take the shape of 'pākānukūlavyāpārānukūlakṛtimāṁścaitraḥ.'[157]

In summing-up this context of Śaktigraha from Vyākāraṇa we may add that Gaṅgeśa recognised but did not illustrate it. Gaṇgeśa, of course illustrated the utility of Grammar in distinguishing between corrupt and correct words.[158] Jagadīśa very briefly refers to it by way of illustrating the Śaktigraha of Pratyayas from it (Vyākaraṇa).[159]

M(12). evaṁ vyāpāre'pi na śaktirgavrauāt. ratho gacchatītyādau tu vyāpāre āśrayatve vā lakṣaṇā. jānātītyādau tvāśrayatve, naśyatītyādau tu pratiyogitve nirūḍhalakṣaṇā.

Viśvanātha now proceeds to explain cases where it is not possible to understand Kṛti as Śakyārtha of the conerned Ākhyāta.

Viśvanātha first takes up the expression 'ratho gacchati' to bring home the idea that in certain cases where Kṛti cannot be had as a denoted sense of an Ākhyāta, the idea of a Vyāpāra is conveyed by the same Ākhyāta to give the contextual Śābdabodha. But in any case, a Vyāpāra can at best be a Lakṣyārtha of the Ākhyāta. Here it may be useful to make a reference to the Mīmāṁsakas' assertion that only a Vyāpāra can be the Śakyārtha of an Ākhyāta.[160]

The Mīmāṁsakas, particularly the Prābhākaras took great pain in maintaining that neither Kartā nor Kṛti can be the denoted sense of an Ākhyāta. We come across lengthy discussions on the issue in works like the *Prakaraṇapañcikā*.[161] Nāgeśa also refers to Mīmaṁsakas' admission of Vyāpāra as the Śakyārtha of the Ākhyāta and disapproves of the same.[162]

Viśvanātha has already voiced his opposition to the Kartā being a śakyārtha of an Ākhyāta. Presumably to show his disagreement with also the Mīmāṁsakas as with the Vaiyākaraṇas, Viśvanātha discusses the position of Vyāpāra in the context. Normally when both Kṛti and Vyāpāra are there to put their claims to be an 'ākhyātaśakya' (i.e., a meaning denoted by ākhyāta), the choice would naturally fall on Kṛti. If Vyāpāra be admitted as a Śakyārtha, then the Śakyatāvacchedaka Vyāpāratva, as demanded by the definition of Vyāpāra, is a state of being the cause of an effect of something of which it itself is an effect. So the concept of Vyāpāra is not simple at the very face of it. In case Kṛti is admitted as 'ākhyātavācya', on the other hand, 'Kṛtitva' will be a Śakyatāvacchedaka. Compared to Vyāpāratva, Kṛtitva is much easier to be conceived. Hence to avoid 'kalpanāgaurava' ('i.e., cumbrousness in imagination) Vyāpāra is not to be admitted as 'ākhyātavā cya.'[163] But a sentence like 'ratho gacchati' gives us the śābdabodha only in the form 'gamanānukūlavyāparavān rathaḥ'. The Śābdabodha in the form of 'gamaṇānukūlakṛtimān rathaḥ' is not possible as no deliberate effort can ever be thought of as pertaining to an unconscious agent like a Chariot. Vyāpāra is undoubtedly the only possible meaning of the Ākhyāta in 'gacchati' in the expression 'ratho gacchati'. This sense of Vyāpāra comes undoubtedly to be syntactically connected as an attribute of the Kartā in the aforesaid expression. Under such unavoidable circumstances, Naiyāyikas like Viśvanātha are prepared to understand Vyāpāra only through Lakṣaṇa. A further analysis will show that the Vyāpāra in the case of "ratho gacchati" is the saṁyoga of the reins (i.e., ropes) with the 'ratha'. But, such a saṁyoga is present even when there is no 'gamaṇa' i.e., no movement at all. Hence there is less justification even for admitting Vyā pāra as the Lakṣyārtha of the Ākhyāta. Conceding to such an objection, Viśvanātha says that the meaning of the Ākhyāta could better be taken as a Lakṣyārtha in the form of 'āśrayatva', i.e. the state of being a substratum. But Viśvanātha is silent as to whose 'ā śrayatva' he means. It could be the 'āśrayatva' for the Vyāpāra or for the Kṛti or for the 'Phala', i.e., 'gamaṇa'. As pointed out in the DK.,[164] it is the 'āśrayatva' for the 'Phala', i.e., 'gamaṇa'. Hence in the expression, 'ratho gacchati', the Śābdabodha should be in the form of 'gamanāśrayatvavān rathaḥ' and that is quite tenable in so far as the movement, though not a deliberate effort actually, belongs to the 'ratha'.

In 'jānāti', a 'karttṛpada' like Caitra is to be supplied. In 'Caitraḥ jānāti', the Śābdabodha can never take place as 'jñānānukū lakṛtimān caitraḥ', because no kṛti or physical effort can be involved in the matter of knowing. It cannot be placed on a par with 'caitraḥ pacati'. Again it cannot mean 'jñānānukūlavyāpā ravān' as it does not involve a Vyāpāra. It cannot be placed on a par with 'kuthāreṇa kāṣṭhaṁ chinatti' to involve a Vyāpāra. So Lakṣaṇā in respect of Vyāpāra is not possible. But the idea we get is 'caitraḥ jñānāśrayavān' (Caitra is a repository of Knowledge). So there is 'āśrayatve lakṣaṇā' (Caitra = atman of Caitra. The 'jñā na' occurs as a 'guṇa' of 'ātman'.) Similarly, in 'naśyati', a Kartā, say 'ghaṭaḥ' is to be supplied. Here also Śābdabodha cannot be like 'ghaṭaḥ nāśānukūlakṛtimān.' The pitcher does not make any effort for its destruction. It also obviously does not involve a Vyā pāra. In the Nyāya system whatever is subject to a destruction is called Pratiyogī of the destruction. Hence there is the state of being a Pratiyogī (i.e., counter-positive) in the 'ghaṭa' in respect of its own destruction. So the meaning of 'naśyati' is a Lakṣyārtha in respect of 'nāśapratiyogitva'. The Śābdabodha will be 'nāśapratiyogitvavān ghaṭaḥ'.

According to Viśvanātha the Lakṣaṇā in 'caitraḥ jānāti' and 'ghato naśyati' is of 'nirudha' type. We reserve our discussion on it till our examination of Viśvanātha's Lakṣaṇā.

M(13). upamānād yathā śaktigrahastathoktam.

Viśvanātha here refers to his earlier treatment of Upamāna which is accepted as one of the 'śaktigrāhakas'.

The process of Upamāna, as recognised by Viśvanātha, has been already discussed by us in the introduction of the present work. The very definition of Upamāna asserts that its only utility lies in producing the knowledge of Śakti of words. Viśvanātha's idea in admitting Upamāna as śaktigrāhaka' is that the knowledge, 'gosadṛśaḥ gavayaḥ' (the gavaya is like a cow) finally comes to lead to the knowledge, 'gavayaḥ gavayapadavācyaḥ' (the creature 'gavaya' is what is denoted by the word 'gavaya'). Thus we find Viśvanātha accepting Upamāna as 'śaktigrahopāya'. We have already discussed in the introduction the position of Upamā na Pramāṇa vis-a-vis śabdapramāṇa. We have also discussed the reason for Viśvanātha's treatment of Upamāna prior to that of Śabda. It has also been observed that by virute of involving an

Āptavākya in the form of the Atideśavākya, every Upamāna involves the earlier operation of Śabdapramāṇa. Here it will obviously be useful to examine the position of Upamāna in other systems and in the works of other writers also. Of the Mīmāṁsakas, Śabarasvāmin regards Upamāna as a Pramāṇa and defends it as an instrument of knowledge on the basis of similarity.[165] The Vedāntins also hold that Upamāna is based on the knowledge of similarity.[166] Of the Prācīna-Naiyāyikas, Gautama who recognises Upamāna as a Pramāṇa along with Pratyakṣa, Anumāna and Śabda, defines it as the instrument of valid knowledge of an object derived through its similarity with another well-known (prasiddha) object.[167] Vātsyāyana holds that Upamāna conveys the knowledge of the relation of a name with the corresponding object signified by it (saṁjñasaṁjñi-saṁbandha), and it is an instrument for the attainment of the valid knowledge of similarity which is technically called Upamiti.[168]

M(14). koṣādapi śaktigrahaḥ. sati bādhake kvacit tyajyate. yathā nīlādipadānāṁ nīlarūpādau nīlādi-viśiṣṭe ca śaktiḥ kośena vyutpāditā. Tathāpi lāghavād nīlādāveva śaktiḥ, nīlādi-viśiṣṭe tu lakṣaṇeti.

Here Viśvanātha observes that the meaning of an unknown word is obtained through 'Kośa' (Lexicon or Dictionary) also Dictionary gives us the knowledge of the equivalent word-meanings with regard to a particular word. But in the event of there arising any clash with their own principles, the Naiyāyikas are ever prepared to reject the knowledge of Śakti gathered through the Kośa in the context of a particular word. For example, for the word 'nīla' (blue), Dictionary gives both 'nīlavarṇa' (blue colour) and 'nīlavarṇaviśiṣṭa' (blue coloured objects) as the primary meaning. It has been observed in the Dictionary that the words 'śukla' etc. denote 'śuklavarṇa' etc. (white colour etc.) and also the śuklavarṇaviśiṣṭa dravya' etc. (the objects possessed of white colour etc.)[169] The list of words hinted in the Dictionary referred to above obviously includes 'nīla'. Similarly Viśvanātha's list of words in the context beginning with 'nīla' (nīlādipadānām) also surely includes 'śukla', 'pīta' etc. Now the Śakti of the word 'nīla' is recognised by the Naiyāyikas including Viśvanātha only with regard to 'blue colour'. The meaning 'blue coloured object' is said to be conveyed by Lakṣaṇā, the power of secondary signification. They point out to 'simplicity' (Lāghava) as the ground for coming to such a conclusion.

If the Śakti of 'nīlādipada' is admitted even with regard to 'nīlā diviśiṣṭa', 'nīlādiviśiṣṭa' will be Śakyārtha. Of the meaning, namely 'nīlādiviśiṣṭa' (the object possessed of blue colour etc.), the determinent (Śakyatāvacchedaka) will obviously be 'nīlatvaviśiṣṭa-nīlarūpa' (the blue colour characterised by blueness). But in the case of admitting 'nīlavarṇa' or 'nīlarūpa' as a Śakyā rtha, only the 'nīlatva' (blueness) will be the Śakyatāvacchedaka. In the earlier case, even the Śakyatāvacchedaka i.e., the blue colour can also be innumberable and hence for the knowledge of blue colour, innumerable significative powers (anantaśakti) shall have to be admitted. But in the later case, the blueness (nīlatva) being one and one only, the admission of only one Śakti would suffice. So Viśvanātha rejects the 'śaktigraha' of 'nīādipada' with regard to 'nīlādiviśiṣṭa' for avoiding a Kalpanāgaurava. This phenomenon, as we have already observed, occurs in respect of all words which signify colours. We know from Jagadīśa that Kośa allows such two-fold 'śaktigraha' in respect of certain other words also such as 'Śīta' when they come to be used in the sense of quality and qualified. [170] The idea is this : we find in the dictionary that the word 'Śīta' in the masculine gender means the 'cold temperature' and it may also mean any object 'having a cold temperature' with a gender similar to that of the qualified object.[171] Now though Kośa allows both the meanings as Śakyā rthas, from the stand point of Viśvanātha, we can recognise only the first meaning as Śakyārtha and the second only as Lakṣyā rtha.

M(15). evamāptavākyādapi. yathā kokilaḥ Pikapada-vācya ityādi - śabdāt pikādiśabdānāṁ kokile śaktigrahaḥ.

Here Viśvanātha observes that like the already mentioned 'Śaktigrāhakas', Āptavākaya or the statement of a trustworthy person also comes to serve as such. We have already dealt with the notion of an Āpta in the context of our examination of Śabda in the introduction of the present work. Now according to Viśvanātha, we may know the meaning of a word from the statement of a trustworthy person (Āpta). For example, an Āpta may give some ignorant person to learn directly that the word 'pika' means a 'Cuckoo' (Kokila). In the succeeding pages at an appropriate stage, we shall examine the Āptavākya again in comparison with some of the other 'śaktigrāhakas'.

We find Jagadīśa not referring to Āptavākya as a śaktigrāhaka'. It of course, does not speak of any difference in attitude between Jagadīśa and Viśvanātha. It is because the other 'śaktigrāhakas' viz. Vyākaraṇa, Upamāna, Kośa, Vākyaśeṣa Vivaraṇa, and 'Prasiddhapadasannidhi' are also certain specific cases of Āptavākyas. We shall point out later on that the special mention of Āptavākya as a 'śaktigrāhaka' is only to cover the non-specific cases or the cases other than the specific Āptavākyas such as Vyākaraṇa etc.

M(16). evaṁ vyavahārādapi. yathā prayojaka-vṛddhena ghaṭamānayetyuktaṁ. tacca śrutvā prayojyavṛddhena ghaṭa ānītaḥ. Tadavadhārya pārśvastho bālo ghaṭānayanarūpaṁ kāryaṁ ghaṭamānayeti śabdaprayojyamityavadhārayati. tataśca ghaṭaṁ naya gāmānayetyādivākyāvāpodvāpābhyāṁ ghaṭādipadānāṁ kāryānvita - ghaṭādau śaktiṁ gṛhṇāti.

Here Viśvanātha names and illustrates Vyavahāra as a means of determining the Śakti of a word. This Vyāvahāra is popularly known as Vṛddhavyavahāra. Viśvanātha's exposition also confirms that his 'vyāvahāra' is nothing other than the commonly known Vṛddhavyavahāra. In his illustrative statement, Viśvanātha uses the terms 'prayojakavṛddha' 'prayojyavṛddha' and 'bāla' to mean respectively an experienced person who is in command, a less experienced person under Command and an ignorant person who simply observes and learns thereby. His example is this : The experienced person utters 'Bring the jar'. Hearing that (expression), the less experienced person under direction brings the jar. Observing this, as he happens to be nearby, the child, i.e., a person who is ignorant of the Śakti of the uttered words infers that the act of bringing the jar is due to the utterence of the expression 'Bring the jar'. Thereafter, on further hearing of directions 'Take away the jar' 'Bring the cow' etc. by means of the inclusion (Āvāpa) and the exclusion (Udvāpa) of the particular words, he ascertains the Śakti or significative power of the words, 'ghata' etc. with regard to objects, 'jar' etc. as connected with some action like bringing. The idea regarding Vṛddhavyavahāra can be put in the following manner also. The Vṛddha or experienced person utters a sentence in the form of a certain imperative statement. Another Vṛddha or experienced person who is junior to the former acts in a certain manner in response to the direction. The inexperienced person who stands near by, hears the utterances and observes the performance. He then infers vaguely that the meaning of the sentence is a Command and the action done is the result. Observing many other utterances and subsequent performances, he comes to have a general idea about the meanings of individual words through the process of the inclusions and exclusions of words (in and from the directing sentences).

Now it will be relevant on our part to examine the approach by other scholars to this Vṛddhavyavahāra or simply Vyavahāra. As we have already mentioned, Vṛddhavyavahāra seems to be the most important of the 'śaktigrāhakas' as it is invariably recognised in almost all the schools of thought. According to the Prābhākara school of Pūrvamīmāṁsā, this method leads to the knowledge of śakti through three definite stages and involves three Pramāṇas.[172] They are (1) *Pratyakṣa* or direct perception.

The child or the learner in the above instance has direct auditory perception of the uttered sentence and a direct visual perception of the action of the directed person, performed in response to the uttered injunction. (2) *Anumāna* or Inference : The child infers from the listener's activity that he has understood the meaning of the utterence. (3) *Arthāpatti* (Postulation or Assumption): The child postulates that what is performed by the directed person is the meaning of the verbal statement concerned. According to the Prābhākaras, it is the only method of learning a language.[173]

Of the Grammarians, we find Kātyāyana giving preference to the usage of day to day life for learning a language. If anybody is curious to know a language properly, he should observe the usage of words by the experienced persons. That is what he says in the beginning of his Vārtikas on Pāṇini's Sūtras.[174] Nāgeśa considers the Vyavahāra to be the best method of learning.[175]

Of the Naiyāyikas, Jagadīśa claims Vṛddha Vyavahāra to be the foremost of all the eight-methods. But the order of enumeration as we have it in the verse 'śaktigrahaṁ' etc. and in the subsequent illustration of the 'śaktigrāhakas' by Viśvanātha in the *BP* does not tally with this approach of Jagadīśa. Jagadīsa contends that Vṛddhavyavahāra should come first and then the others Viz. Upamāna etc. [176]

M(17). itthañca bhūtale nīlo ghaṭa ityādiśábdānna Śābdabodhaḥ. ghatādipadānāṁ kāryānvita - ghaṭādibodhe sāmarthyāvadhāraṇāt, kāryatābodhaṁ prati ca liṅādīnāṁ sāmarthyāt, tadabhāvānna śābdabodha ityapi kecit. tanna. prathamataḥ kāryānvita - ghaṭādau śaktyavadhāraṇe'pi lāghavena paścāt tasya parityāgaucityāt. ata - eva "Caitra putraste jā taḥ, kaṇyā te garbhiṇī" tyādu mukhaprasāda - mukhamālinyābhyāṁ sukhaduḥkhe anumāya tatkāraṇatvena pariśeṣācchābdabodhaṁ nirṇīya taddhetutayā taṁ śabdamavadhārayati tathā ca vyabhicārānna kāryānvite śaktiḥ. na ca tatra "taṁ paśye" tyādi - śabdāntaramadhyāhāryaṁ; mānābhāvāt. "Caitra ! putraste jāto mṛtaśce" tyādau tadabhāvācca. itthañca lāghavādanvita-ghate'pi śaktiṁ tyaktvā ghaṭapadaṣya ghaṭamātre śaktimavadhārayati.

In "itthaña---------kecit," Viśvanātha records and refutes an opinion which may be traced back to the Prābhākara Mīmāṁsakas. Like Viśvanātha other Naiyāyikas also have taken note of this attitude of the Prābhākaras.[177] According to these Prābhākaras, it is not possible to have Śābdabodha from expressions like 'bhūtale nīlo ghaṭaḥ' (a blue jar on the ground). It is because, in view of ascertaining the Śakti by means of Vṛddhavyavahāra, the Śakti of words 'ghaṭa' etc. is understood with regard to objects 'jar' etc. only as belonging to a state of remaining connected with some actions (Kārya). The Mīmāṁsakas insist that all sentences must convey the idea of some Vidhi, which involves the idea of the state of being enjoined as duty (Kāryatā). The presence of suffixes like 'liṅ' (as in 'gāṁ nayet') 'lot' (as in 'gāṁ naya') and 'tavya' (as in 'gau ānetavyaḥ) serves as the determinant (prayojaka) of the knowledge of the 'Kāryatābodha'. As in the expression 'bhūtale nī lo ghaṭaḥ', there is no suffix like Liṅ, no knowledge of any action being enjoined occurs in this context. Hence the word 'ghaṭa' cannot be understood to mean the object 'jar' as connected with some action. Prābhākaras understand all 'śaktigraha's initially through vṛddhavyavahāra. The Vṛddhavyavahāra involves in its turn the engaging of someone by a Vṛddha (i.e., an elderly person) in some action (Kārya). Only by observing one engaged in an action in accordance with the 'Vṛddhavacana', the child comes to know the meaning of words through an inferential process. The Vṛddha can make one go for some action only by the use of Liṅ and similar suffixes. Under the circumstances, the 'śaktijñāna' from Vṛddhavyavahāra is possible only in the form of some 'Kāryānvitajñāna'. So the Prābhākaras are not prepared to recognise 'śaktigraha' from a statement like 'a blue jar on the earth' which does not involve the knowledge of something as connected with some action. The Prābhākaras are again not prepared to recognise directly any 'Śaktigrāhaka' other than Vṛddhavyavahāra

178 which facilitates only 'Kāryānvitaśaktijñāna' and not otherwise. In 'tanna-------parityāgaucityāt' of the *Muktāvalī* the 'Kārya nvitaśaktivāda' of the Prābhākaras stands opposed. Even if for the first time the Śakti of a Pada like 'ghaṭa' is ascertained with regard to the object 'jar' only as connected with some action like 'bringing', it is proper for the sake of simplicity, Viśvanātha argues, that one would come to understand it with reference to mere 'ghaṭa' (i.e., jar) without any regard to its connection with some action. In advocating such an opinion, Viśvanātha is obviously influenced by his predecessors.[179] In 'ata eva-------śabdamavadhārayati', Viśvanātha proceeds to substantiate his contention with illustrations. Some Caitra is told, 'putraste jātaḥ' (a son is born to you). The child (i.e., one ignorant in the matter) who does not know the Śakti of the words involved in the sentence observes that the cheeks of the person spoken to come to flush. He infers from the brightness of the face that the man is happy. He ascertains the knowledge of the sentence or the clustar of words as the cause for the happiness of the person. Here the word 'Śabda' in the *Muktāvalī* stands for a vākya. Again if that caitra is told, 'kaṇyā te garbhiṇī (your unmarried daughter is pregnant), the child similarly observes that the face of the man darkens. The child infers that the man is wounded and ascertains the knowledge of that sentence or that cluster of words as the cause (kāraṇa) for the plight of the man. In these cases, without the involvement of any action, there is the scope for corresponding Śābdabodha. In 'tathā ca------ kāryānvite śaktiḥ,' Viśvanātha wants to bring home the idea that the occurrence of Śābdabodha in sentences like 'caitra putraste jatāḥ, kaṇyā te garbhiṇī' present cases of deviations to nullify the contention that there can be the knowledge of a word with regard to an object only as connected with some action, i.e., the 'kāryānvitaśaktivāda' of the Prābhākaras. In the *Muktāvalī* text 'na ca tatra -------- tadabhāvācca', Viśvanātha seeks to meet more points of the 'kāryānvitaśaktivādins' in this context. Those who advocate only the 'kāryānvitaśaktigraha' may speak of the necessity of supplying some

action like seeing in 'caitra putraste jātaḥ' etc. Viśvanātha feels that it will be farfetched as we cannot deduce any proof in support of such a necessity. Or to supply some action in certain contexts comes or may come to be void of any sense and properiety. For instance, in connection with the sentence. 'Caitra putraste' jāto mṛtaśca' (Cairta, a son born to you is dead), such a supply is not possible as because it will be cruel on one's part to ask Caitra to see his dead son. In "ithañca -------- śaktimavadhārayati", Viśvanātha concludes that even if the child learns first only the 'kā ryānvitaśakti' of a pada, he thereafter, simplifies the process of his knowledge of Śakti. The child discards his knowledge ofthe 'ghaṭa' Pada with regard to the object 'ghaṭa' as connected with some action and finally understands the mere object 'ghaṭa' as the śakyārtha of the 'ghaṭapada'.

In order to get rid of the Prābhākaras' notion of kāryānvitaśakti, Viśvanātha brings in the argument of simplification. Now a doubt may arise whether a child is competent enough to come to the logic of simplification. It may be said that the child is not necessarily a minor. He may be a mature man with ignorance only in this matter and is, therefore, capable of utilising his own logical sense for simplification. In that case, one who is a child from the view point of age will get obstructed in having Śābdabodha from sentences like 'caitra putraste jātaḥ' etc. The expression 'ata-eva' between 'tanna-------parityāgaucityāt' and 'caitra putraste jāta' etc. in the *Muktāvalī* above confirms that Viśvanātha offers the two sentences 'caitra putraste jātaḥ' and 'kaṇyā te garbhiṇī' as examples of simplification from 'kāryā nitaśktijñāna' to mere 'śaktijñāna' Viśvanātha would have done better by illustrating the process of simplification in the very example of 'kāryānvitaśaktijñāna' from Vṛddhavyavahāra, i.e., in the sentence 'ghaṭamānaya'. He takes up the sentences, 'Caitra putraste jātaḥ' and 'kaṇyā te garbhiṇī' presumably because these are two examples already current in the circle of scholars for showing the non-conformity of the 'kāryānvitaśaktivāda' of the

Prābhākaras.[180] Rather, he could have easily asserted that as virtually Śābdabodha takes place in sentences like 'caitra putraste jā taḥ' etc., the 'kāryānvitaśaktivāda' does not factually hold good. On this argument, he would have better supplied 'parityā ganiyamāt' instead of 'parityāgaucityāt'. In the event of such a modification, the aforesaid 'ata eva' is to be dropped.

Though Viśvanātha concludes that one learns the Śakti of the 'ghaṭapada' with regard to the mere object 'ghaṭa', in his illustration of the process of simplification of 'śaktijñāna', in sentences like 'caitra putraste jātaḥ' etc. he refers to the entire sentence 'caitra putraste jātaḥ' or 'kaṇyā te garbhiṇī' as the cause of the happiness or otherwise of Caitra. His reference to the cause as 'that Śabda' (taṁ Śabdaṁ) is actually a reference to a Vākya. Here he is not free from the influence of the Prābhākaras who hold that as 'śaktigraha' is possible only through Vṛddhavyavahāra, the knowledge of a padārtha from a Pada is possible only where a 'samudāya' (a cluster of words, i.e., a padasamūha) is involved.[181] In such a position, the acceptance as 'śaktigrāhaka' of Vyākaraṇa, Kośa etc., which do not involve a 'samudāya would creat a difficulty.

M(18). evaṁ vākyaśeṣādapi śaktigrahaḥ
yathā yavamayaścarurbhavatītyatra yavapadasya
dīrghaśūkaviśeṣe āryāṇāṁ prayogaḥ. kaṅgau tu
mlecchānāṁ. tatra hi "yatrānyā oṣadhayo mlāyante'
thaite modamānāstiṣṭhanti" tathā -
"vasante sarvaśasyānāṁ jāyate patraśātanaṁ/
modamānāśca tiṣṭhanti yavāḥ kaṇiśaśālinaḥ"//
iti vākyaśeṣād dīrghaśūke śaktirnirṇīyate.
kaṅgau tu śaktibhramāt prayogah; nānāśaktikalpane
gauravāt. haryādipade tu vinigamakābhāvānnānāśaktikalpanam.

Viśvanātha now comes to illustrate śaktigraha on the strength of Vākyaśeṣa. Certain words, as we find, have two or more primary meanings. For avoiding ambiguity, such a word should convey only one meaning with reference to a certain context. Here remaining sentence or sentences uttered in continuity come to our aid. In other words, the meanings of such words as may have more than one primary meaning are ascertained on the strength of Vākyaśeṣa, i.e., the rest of the passage. As for example, in the Vedic passage 'yavamayaścarurbhavati'[182] a doubt arises with regard to the meaning of the word 'yava'. The word 'yava' is used in the sense of 'barley' (lit. long bearded seed) by the 'cultured people' (Āryas) and in the sense of 'kaṅgu' (panic seed by the 'uncultured' (Mlecchas, i.e., the lay men). Here we have to consult the rest of the passage or the supplementary text, if there be any, in the context. The context gives us a statement simulataneously uttered, 'yatrānyā'[183] etc. which describes the 'yava's flourishing with green leaves at a time when other plants are found withering away. Or we may have recourse to another passage read together with 'yavamayaścarurbhavati'. This passage, namely 'vasante sarvaśasyānāṁ'[184] etc. also describes the longawned 'yava's rejoicing (i.e., thriving with new leaves), in the season of spring, when generally all herbs and plants come to be devoid of leaves. On the strength of either of these two passages, we come to be confirmed in the notion that 'yava' in 'yavamayaścarurbhavati' means the Barley. Viśvanātha points out that if some one understands panic seed from the word 'yava' in the context, he will do it only by mistake; because in order to understand 'kaṅgu' also in addition to a particular variety of long-awned grains from the word 'yava' one is to admit more than one Śakti of the word. This is to be avoided as it obviously leads to a complexity (Gaurava) of imagination. In case of words having many meanings such as Hari which means Viṣṇu, Indra, horse, monkey etc. at the same time, we have to admit more than one Śakti for lack of ascertainer (vinigamaka) i.e., grounds for fixing the denotative capacity of a word only with reference to a particular meaning.

Here we have to note that Viśvanātha's recognition of vākyaśeṣa can be traced back to Pūrva Mīmāṁsā of Jaimini. Jaimini first has asserted that in case of a doubt as to which of several meanings should be accepted, the rest of the passage should be taken in to account.[185] Thus in the Vedic sentence 'aktā śarkarā upadadhāti' (the wet pabbles are placed nearby), the meaning of the term 'aktā' is not clear as to whether it is soaked in water or in any other liquid. But fromthe rest of the passage, 'tejo vai ghṛtaṁ' (clarified butter is the brilliance), it is to be understood that the pabbles are to be soaked in ghee. Viśvanātha's example of Śaktigraha from Vākyaśeṣa, i.e., 'yavamayaścarur (bhavati) is also a Vedic passage illustrated by Śabara in his *Bhāṣya* in the same context of ascertaining the meaning of a word from supplementary passages.[186] Viśvanātha's predecessors like Gaṅgeśa and Jagadīśa also have given this very example to illustrate Vākyaśeṣa. They have obviously influenced Viśvanātha in the mode of the treatment of Vākyaśeṣa as a 'śaktigrāhaka'. Like Śabara, Gaṅgeśa illustrates how in the event ofthere being different connotations current in the circles of Aryans and non-aryans, the meanings of words like 'yava', 'varāha' and 'vetasa' have been fixed as barley (yava), boar (śūkara) and cane (vañjula) on the strength of supplementary sentences like 'vasante' etc.[187] In the case of nānārthapadas like Hari, Jagadīśācārya, also made a similar observation with the same illustration in respect of 'yavapada' in the context of vākyaśeṣa as a 'śaktigrāhaka'[188] Gaṅgeśa was more elaborate than his two successors. For the portion 'modamānāstu tiṣṭhanti' there is also an alternative reading 'modamānāḥ pradṛśyante' as evidanced in the text of Gaṅgeśopādhyāya.

M(19). evaṁ vivaraṇādapi śaktigrahaḥ. vivaraṇantu tatsamānā rthaka - padāntareṇa tadarthakathanam. yathā ghato' stītyasya kalaśo'stītyanena vivaraṇād ghaṭapadasya kalaśe śakti-grahah. evaṁ pacatītyasya pākaṁ karotītyanena vivaraṇādākhyātasya yatnārthakatvaṁ kalpyate.

By the term 'vivaraṇa', Viśvanātha means to refer to the term 'vivṛti' of the verse, 'śaktigrahaṁ vyākaraṇopamāna' etc. Here

Viśvanātha observes that even on the strength of Vivaraṇa, one can ascertain the śakti of a word with regard to a particular meaning. Now Vivaraṇa or Vivṛti is the act of putting some synonymous words for the original. Inthe words of Viśvanātha, it is the statement of the meaning of a particular word by means of another synonymous word or a word having a similar meaning. Thus, the sentence 'ghato' sti' is explained by putting the sentence 'kalaśo' sti' and as a result, the meaning of the word 'ghaṭa' is understood as 'kalaśa'. Here we actually come to know the meaning of an unknown word through a commentary describing the meaning. Patañjali also observes that the meaning of a word is to be understood or determined with the help of a commentary in cases of doubt.[189] Viśvanātha gives another instance of śaktigraha through Vivaraṇa in explaining 'pacati' by the expression 'pākaṁ karoti'. By the Paraphrasing of 'pacati' it is ascertained that the 'Ākhyāta' in 'pacati' means an effort[190] (yatna) that facilitates the cooking (pāka). Thus Vivaraṇa's service as a 'śaktigrāhaka' is evident, of course, through an Inference. So, the entire Śābdabodha in the context will be finally 'pākānukūlakṛtimān' (caitraḥ). It has been already stated that Gaṅgeśa does not mention Vivaraṇa as a 'śaktigrāhaka'. Jagadīśá recognises Vivaraṇa as a 'śaktigrāhaka' and gives the same illustration as that given by Viśvanātha, and admits the śakti of 'tiṅ' in 'pacati' with regard to Kṛti which means effort.[191]

Here it becomes necessary to make a comparative examination of Vṛddhavyavahāra, Kośa, Vivaraṇa and Āptavākya. It appears that while the Āptavākya means the statement of a trustworthy person, Kośa and Vivaraṇa or Vivṛti also in fact happen to be statements made by certain trustworthy authorities. It is therefore, necessary to examine the differences amongst them. It requires to be examined if there is any basis for not allowing the term Āptavā kya to cover all these three. It may be pointed out that Āptavākya means a statement made by an authority who is physically present. He gives the statement apparently on the spot as a reply to specific query. In the Kośa, the Āpta presents the meanings in a ready-made form and in a systematic manner. The Kośa presents all the words irrespective of their familiarity and otherwise. In Vivaraṇa, the man of authority furnishes at his own initiative meanings of only such and such words and expessions which are supposed by himself to be unfamiliar.The Kośa in the shape of a book and the Vivaraṇa in the form of a commentary come to serve the purpose of the entire community and the succeeding generations of learners. The Āpta in case of an Āptavākya serves the purpose of only an individual physically close to himself.

Āptavākya, again, is different from Vṛddhavyavahāra, because, the former is a deliberate process of tutoring while in the latter process the learner simply happens to learn without anybody's deliberate effort in that direction, e.g. : The authoritative person (Āpta) deliberately teaches the child regarding the identity of his parents by pointing out the parents and making the statements like 'he is your father', 'she is your mother' etc. The child, through this process learns the Śakti of words like 'pitṛ', 'mātr', etc. But in case of Vṛddhavyavahāra, while the 'prayojaka' or 'uttamavṛddha', the seniormost person commanding, engages the 'prayojya' or 'madhyamavṛddha', the less senior person in some act, say, in bringing a horse or tying a cow, and the latter obliges the former, they may not actually know on the spot and at the time that the Bāla, a person, ignorant in respect of the meanings of certain words, observes them and comes to know thereby the significative power of certain words like 'cow' or 'horse', with reference to certain meanings like 'an individual cow' or 'an individual horse' etc.

Again, there is the need to examine the justification of Āptavākya being named as a 'śaktigrāhaka' at all, in presence of the other ones. As we understand an 'Āpta-vākya' as the statement of a trustworthy person, the Āpta being one who speaks with knowledge (yathārthavaktā), all other 'śaktigrāhaka's like Vyākaraṇa etc. also are to be regarded as Āptavākyas : Hence we are to find out reasons for separately naming Āpta-vākya as one of the 'śaktigrāhaka's. The great treatises pertaining to the domain of Vyākaraṇa are obviously the versions of trustworthy persons like Pāṇini, Kātyāyana and Patañjali.[192]

The Upamāna Pramāṇa, as we have already observed in the introduction in the context of the order of the enlisted Pramāṇas, involves as its basis an Atideśavākya, which is nothing less than an Āptavākya. We cannot maintain that great lexicographers, like Amerasiṁha have made their contributions without adequate knowledge. As such, the Kośas are also the Āptavākyas. (Vṛddha) Vyavahāra involves the statements of some Vṛddhas who are to be regarded as Āptas as their words are warranted by facts. The 'madhyamavṛddha' engages himself in doings only, on the trust of the 'uttamavṛddha. As the 'bāla' observes, there is exact correspondence between the words of 'uttamavṛddha' and objects handled by the 'madhyamavṛddha'. The 'bāla' also finalizes his conclusions only on the strength of the reliability of the two 'vṛddhas', senior and less senior. Thus Vṛddhavyavahāra involves Āptavākyas. In case of Vākyaśeṣa also, we observe that one learns the significative power of a word in relation to a specific meaning on the strength of supplementary statements. The supplementary statements are already established or proved statements, demanding no further scrutiny on their own veracity. As such, they are obviously Āptavākyas. Their acceptability being not questioned, the reliability of the speakers or authors involved therein also stands admitted. A Vivaraṇa, i.e., a commentary comes to be accepted only when the commentator is trusted or reliable. So Vivṛti also is basically an Āptavākya. Learning the meaning of a word because of 'siddhapadasannidhi' presupposes the earlier knowledge of the meanings of certain words uttered side by side with unknown words. Those 'prasiddhapada's or already known words might have been earlier known through one of the aforesaid 'śaktigrāhaka's or directly by an Āptavākya. So the 'siddhapadasannidhi' directly or indirectly involves an earlier

Āptavākya. Now the pertinent question is : All other 'śaktigrāhaka's, being Āptavākyas in this or that way, where is the necessity of naming Āptavākya as a Śaktigrāhaka again ? The most plausible reply is this : The 'śaktigrāhaka's other than Āptavākya mentioned in the list, are specific cases of Āptavākya. Hence Āpta-vākya is separately named as a śaktigrākhaka' to cover the non-specific cases of Āptavākyas. There may be an Āpta or trustworthy person who is not a Grammarian, nor a Lexicographer nor even a commentator. Sometimes an Āpta or reliable person may not speak regarding the simiarity between two things as the forester did in case of the stock example of the Upamāna Pramāṇa, 'gosadṛśo gavayaḥ', or he may not be an 'uttamavṛddha', one commending another to get engaged in some specific action. But yet sometimes from a comparitively reliable person, in ordinary contexts, one happens to be trained in the matter of meanings of unknown words. One may argue thus : In that case, the word Āptavākya should have been uttered in a broader sense to cover all the 'śaktigrāhaka's. But simply naming Āptavākya as the only 'śaktigrāhaka' would not have been a desirable position as it might have led to many misgivings and confusions regarding the services rendered by Grammer etc. in learning the meanings of new words of a language. The Āptavākya, named separately can cover the non-specific cases of Āptavākya and at the same time may be broad enough to stand for all. Such an arrangement in the Shastras even in the Nyāya comes to our notice. After the enumeration and necessary illustration of the five kinds of Anyathāsiddha, Viśvanātha in the *Bhāṣāpariccheda* admits the essentiality ofthe fifth one and opines that it (the fifth Anyathāsiddha) covers also the earlier four.[193]

M(20). evaṁ prasiddhapadasya sānnidhyādapi śaktigrahaḥ yathā - iha sahakāra - tarau madhuraṁ piko rautītyādau pikaśabdasya kokile śaktigraha iti.

Viśvanātha has rightly substituted the word 'siddha' in the verse, 'śaktigrahaṁ' etc. by the word 'prasiddha' in his *Muktāvalī*.

Here Viśvanātha explains that proximity (sānnidhya) to a well-known word (Prasiddhapada) helps in ascertaining the Śakti of a word (so long unfamiliar, i.e., aprasiddha.) For instance, in the expression like "iha sahakāratarau madhuraṁ piko rauti", the Śakti of the word 'pika' is ascertained on such a ground with regard to a Cuckoo (Kokila). Viśvanātha's idea here is this : In this sentence 'iha sahakāratarau' etc., the word 'pika' is unfamiliar, while the words 'sahakārataru', 'madhura' and 'rauti' are already familiar. The familiar words under discussion convey the idea of sweet singing on a mango tree, an activity invariably attributed to the Kokila (Cuckoo). Now, the unfamiliar word 'pika' having physical proximity with the familiar words comes to convey the idea of Kokila as its Śakyārtha. It may be added that the word 'pika' cannot be taken to mean a human singer because such a singer is without any tradition of singing seated on a mango tree. The other birds 'crow' etc. may be, however, found opening their mouths as seated on a mango tree. But yet as the singing happens to be sweet, the said word 'pika' cannot be taken in the sense of crow etc.[194] Hence the word 'pika' comes to stand for a Cuckoo. It is interesting to note that Gaṅgeśopādyāya and Jagadīśācārya did not accept mere proximity (Sānnidhya) of a familiar word as a responsible factor in ascertaining the Śakti of an unfamiliar word uttered with it. The two predecessors of Viśvanātha wanted that both the familiar and unfamiliar words for that account are to be in agreement regarding their case-endings[195] (i.e., in Sāmānā dhikaraṇya). It means that there should be an 'abhedānvaya' between two Padas and then, only one being known, the other would naturally be known. Moreover, they used the expression 'prasiddhārthakaśabda' instead of 'prasiddhaśabda' (i.e., siddhapada). The underlying idea is that one should not have a chance to mistake that the familiarity of a word in its mere external structure or form can come to serve as a Śaktigrahaka of another word even though they are in the same case agreement. The familiarity is to be there with the very meaning of the word. Only the knowledge of the meaning of a word can make us know that of another word which stands syntactically connected with the former by a relation of identity. Jagadīśa objects to this type of Śaktigraha in the setnence "iha sahakāratarau madhuraṁ rauti pikaḥ." which is given by Viśvanātha as an illustration of Śaktigraha from the 'siddhapadasānnidhya'. Jagadīśa points out that it is not possible as there can be no 'abhedānvaya' between 'pika' a 'nāmapada' with 'rauti', 'tiṅanta pada'.[196] It is because Naiyāyikas are already commited to admitting Kṛti as the 'tiṅartha' (i.e., ākhyātārtha). Presumably, being aware of such an objection Viśvanātha avoided the expression 'sāmānādhikaraṇya'. He means to say that only from the proximity of other already known words, 'pika' comes to be understood as signifying a Cuckoo. Jagadīśa however, finds it simpler in this case to have the Śaktigraha otherwise.[197] Such a stand seems to be more plausible. Annaṁbhaṭṭa. as already, seen, accepted only Vṛddhavyavahāra as a 'śaktigrāhaka'. He refers to the Śaktigraha from this 'prasiddhapadasānnidhya' in order to show that even herein is seen the involvement of Vṛddhavyavahāra. The act of ascertaining the Śakti of a Pada from the 'siddhapadasāmānādhikaraṇya', it is admitted, is possible only through an inferential process.

M(21). tatra jātāveva śaktigrahaḥ; na tu vyaktau, vyabhicārād, ānantyācca. vyaktiṁ vinā jātibhānasyā' sambhavād vyakterapi bhānamiti kecit.

Viśvanātha here introduces the problem of the import of a word. It involves the controversial issue of recognising Jāti etc. as the Śakyārtha of a word.

The issue of exact nature of Śakyārtha has arrested the minds of almost all the thinkers of Ancient India working in various fields of Philosophy, Grammar and Rhetorics. The problem is whether a word through Śakti signifies a certain generic meaning (Jāti) or the idea of a particular object (Vyakti) or a form (Ākṛti) or more than one of these entities. In other words, the issue is what does a word like 'go' (cow) convey primarily. Do we understand the Śakti with regard to the form 'cow' constituted by dewlap, tail, horn etc., or, to the object 'cow' or the common property 'cowness' or all the two or three of these meanings together ? The issue has given rise to a great controversy amongst the scholars who can be broadly divided into seven groups in this context : (1) Ākṛtivā dinaḥ, (2) Jātivādinaḥ, (3) Vyaktivādinaḥ, (4) Jātyākṛtivyaktivā dinaḥ, (5) Jātiviśiṣṭavyaktivādinaḥ and Jātyākṛtiviśiṣṭa-vyakti-vādinaḥ, (6) Apohavādinaḥ and (7) Jātyādivādinaḥ.

Before we analyse Viśvanātha's view point on the issue, we feel it necessary to make a brief survey of the views generally prevalent in the various schools of thought in the light of the aforesaid divisions.

(1) Ākṛtivāda is an assertion that the Ākṛti (configuration) is the primary import of a word. The scholars hold this view on the plea that the denoted sense of any particular word is determined by what the speaker wants to convey and what is understood by the listener. It is reasonably only the Ākṛti that can be the denoted sense of a word as, these scholars feel, what is cognised by Perception is nothing but this Ākṛti. It is form or configuration (Ākṛti) that is attested by Perception.[198] We may here note that the Jainas may be identified as Ākṛtivādins. The Jainas believe that the words denote an Ākṛti (form or shape of an object). This Ākṛti is nothing but 'avayava' that every object (Vyakti) must have. Obviously then an Ākṛti gives the idea of a Vyakti. This notion of Jainas is also noticed by Gautama.[199] Dr. Gauri Nath Shastri holds that the different schools of thinkers have not taken any serious notice of the theory of Ākṛtivādins.[200] It is, as Dr. Shastri points out, because of its obvious inherent weakness. The whole problem relating to understanding of Ākṛti as the only import of a word is based on a superficial view of nature. The theory may hold good 'in case of specific kinds of the animal and Botanic kingdom', but with reference to material things which donot possess 'definite structure or morphological characteristics, the view can have no relevance. The view will be of no use especially in the case of abstract ideas.[201] Furthermore, as the Ākṛti is

nothing but the 'organisation of parts', it must differ in each case. Hence it cannot be the import of a word, which must be common to all the members of a class. To check any chance of confusion, here we may note that Jaimini, who as a Mīmāṁsakā is a Jātivādin, uses this word 'Ākṛti' only in the sense of Jati. Jayantabhaṭṭa takes cognizance of this use of Jaimini while he himself understands Akṛti only in the sense of 'saṁsthāna' (organisation of parts) in consonance with Gautama's approach to it in his Sūtra.[202]

(2) As Patañjali informs us, it was some sage, Vājapyāyana by name, who first initiated the view of Kevalajātivāda. The Mīmāṁsakas, both the Bhāṭṭas and Prābhākaras, as well as the Vedāntins can be identified as the Kevalajātivādinaḥ. They hold that only the Jāti (the Universal) is the import or denoted sense (Śakyārtha) of a word. Dr. Gauri Nath Shastri presents the mind of the Jātivādins very transparently in his *Philosophy of word and meaning* in the light of Jayantabhaṭṭa's analysis of the Jātivāda.[203] Let us take the problem of understanding the import of the word 'go' (cow). As there are millions of cows in this world itself, the cows as individuals vary widely amongst themselves in respect of age, configuration, colour and the like. If the word 'go' means an individual cow, say, the cow whom I saw yesterday, it will be of no use in the context of signifying any other individual cow, say, the cow I see just now. It is, indeed, a fact that two individuals are never identical. In the event of admitting 'a particular cow' as the import of the word 'Cow', we must seek a second word 'Cow' to signify another individual cow. But it will be practically incovenient to coin as many different words to signify every individual. Moreover, it may be argued as follows. A child for instance, is told that the creature that stands before him is a horse. The child happens to see another horse later on and without any difficulty he understands the animal as a horse. What is it that enables the child to understand like that ? If we proceed in the light of the Vyaktivādins who believe that an individual horse is the import of the word 'horse', there can be no justification on the

part of the child in the matter of understanding the second animal also as a horse. But it is undeniable that the understanding of the child is correct. The Jātivādins maintain that there is such a 'community' (i.e., identity of character) amongst the numerous horses, which enables one to use the term'horse' suitably with regard to each of the individual horses. This community, which goes by the name Jāti is the import or denoted sense of a word. This is the basic view of the Jātivādins.

It may be pointed out that the Vyaktivādin also believe in understanding the Jāti from a word. But they maintan that the 'jātyartha' (the sense of a Jāti, i.e., the universal) does not enter into the import of a word just as the determinant of the nature of a cause (Kāraṇatāvacchedaka) is not regarded as the cause proper. The 'jatyarth' also is not to be reckoned as the actual denoted sense of a word.[204] In reply to the Vyaktivādins, the Jātivādins contend that if Jāti is to be understood, it must be understood from the very Śabda as the source of knowledge.[205] And between the two cognitions of Jāti and Vyakti, the knowledge of Iāti precedes that of the Vyakti. It is because, in case of a qualified cognition, the knowledge of attribute precedes that of what is possessed of that attribute (i.e., the substantives). Hence, it follows that in the present case, the cognition of the individual cannot be gathered prior to that of the universal itself.[206].

The scholars of this group understand even the proper names like Dittha as signifying a 'Jāti'.[207] The Jātivādins, however, come to be compelled to admit the arguments of the Vyaktivādins that the syntactical construction of cases with Verbs is possible only when words are understood with regard to individuals. They hold that as the Vyakti is inseparably connected (i.e., as it is not possible to understand a Jāti without the Knowledge of the corresponding Vyaktis), the Knowedge of Vyakti automatically comes to us. Yet the Jātivādins maintain a marked difference from the Vyaktivādins. Both the Bhāṭṭas and the Prābhākaras understand a Vyakti only as a Vākyārtha. The Bhāṭṭas recognise Lakṣaṇā function to obtain this Vākyārtha. (i.e., the 'Vyaktyartha', i.e., the sense of particular objects). But in the view of Prābhākaras, Abhidhā itself is competent to convey the Vākyārtha, i.e., the meaning of the Vyaktis. We shall discuss this difference elaborately in the context of our examination of Mīmāṁsakas' approach to the Lakṣaṇā function. This 'kevalajātivāda' of the Mī māṁsakas shall have to be examined again in the context of our exposition of the relevant *Muktāvalī* text. Regarding the Vedāntins, we find them making no difference between a Jāti and a Vyakti. They, however, maintain that if the Jāti is understood through Śakti, the Vyakti comes to be understood through Lakṣaṇā.[208]

(3) The Vyaktivādins, onthe other hand, contend that for all practical purposes, reference is invariably to be made to the individuals (Vyaktis) and never to a universal (Jāti). Individuals alone are possessed of necessary intelligence for getting engaged in or abstaining from an activity. It requires no proof to believe that only the individuals are capable of serving a practical purpose. As for instance, in the Context of the Command, 'Bring a Cow', obviously what is required to be brought is an 'individual cow' and not a universal (Jāti) existing in the entire class of Cows, of all the times. The Vyaktivādins further assert that it is the individuals and not the abstract universal which form, the context of Perceptual Knowledge. There is no difference of opinion that what a word denotes is what is perceived. Hence it is certain that only the individuals being perceived can be the import of a word.[209] The scholars of the Sāṁkhya school as Vyaktivādins hold this view because they think that a word cannot convey a Jāti inasmuch as portability, countability, growth, colour, sensibility, multiplicity etc. are superimposed on the Vyakti. The Vyakti is called so because of these very attributes. The Nyāyasūtrakāra takes cognizance of this view of the Sāṁkhya Philosophers.[210]

MM.P.V. Kane refers to a section[211] of Naiyāyikas who can be described as Vyaktivādins. In this context, he refers for illustration to the author of the *Dīdhiti* commentary, who maintains that

Śakti is to be admitted only in Vyakti and not in Jāti which remains only as the Śakyatāvacchedaka of the former.[212] In view of the criticism of their opponents, some of the Vyaktivādins come to remodel their theory to admit that Jāti is to be understood as the determinant of the denoted sense (Śakyatāvacchedaka) which is not to be understood as entering into the very import of a word (Śakyārtha). The Vyaktivādins maintain that the Vyakti as the import of a word is a substantive in relation to the Universal which is its determinant or attribute.

(4) It is all the more interesting to note that it is Gautama, the founder of the Nyāya school of thought who initiates the Jātyākṛtivyaktivāda. Gautama finds no truth in the views detailed above. He feels that any one of the three entities, namely Ākṛti (Configuration), Vyakti (individual) and Jāti (universal) cannot by itself be the denoted sense of a word. Gautama analyses the process with arguments against the earlier theories and finally concludes that all the three entities, namely, Vyakti, Ākṛti and Jāti get combined to be the import of a word.[213] As Vātsyāyana, the Bhāṣyakāra, points out, the word 'tu' in the sūtra 'vyaktyākṛtijātayastu padārthaḥ' is significant.[214] It is given to mean that Vyakti, Ākṛti and Jāti together come to be the denoted sense of a word without any invariable notion of relative superiority or inferiority. None of these three is to hold a permanent position of importance or otherwise. As Vātsyāyana expounds,[215] when it is desired to convey a sense of differentiation and when the knowledge of a particular is mainly sought to be conveyed, then Vyakti is principally understood; Jāti and Ākṛti remain subordinate in the matter of signification. When a notion of differentiation is not sought and only the idea of a general is desired to be conveyed, Jāti is principally understood; Vyakti and Ākṛti are secondarily expressed. The principal status of an Ākṛti is congnised in such expressions like 'a cow made of clay' (mṛdgovaka) etc.

(5) The Navya Naiyāyikas in the context of the issue under discussion can be divided into two groups and as such be identified

as Jātiviśiṣṭavyaktivādins and Jātyākṛtiviśiṣṭavyaktivādins. The scholars of the first group do not seem to pay any heed to the view that Ākṛti is the import or a part of the import of a word. Regarding Jati and Vyakti, they take a balanced view and thereby make a fresh contribution on the subject. Their view may be explained as follows : A Jāti (the Universal) alone can never be the denoted sense of a word. A word consists of two elements, namely, a base, nominal or Verbal and a suffix. The import of a suffix is case, gender and number. If the Universal be recognised as the only import of the stem, it comes to be impossible to construe the import of the stem with that of the suffix. It is because only the individuals are capable of being qualified by case, number and gender. We can practically ascribe a Kartṛtva (agenthood) or Karmatva (objecthood) only to a Vyakti (individual). Under these circumstances, only individuals can reasonably form the import of a word. But here again there is a limitation. Individuals are innumerable. Hence it is necessary that the particular individuals that can be denoted by a word should be restricted or determined. This restriction or determination can be achieved only through a reference to the Universal which underlies all these individuals : So these Navyanaiyāyikas contend that the individuals as determined by an Universal (Jātiviśiṣṭavyakti) be the import of a word.[216] The Navya Nyāya thinkers of the other group, including Viśvanātha, are 'Jatyākṛtiviśiṣṭavādins' in the sense that they include the concept of Ākṛti also along with Jāti as qualifying the denoted Vykti. We shall know more of the view of these scholars in succeeding pages in course of our examination of the view of Viśvanātha.

(6) Regarding the signification of a word, the Bauddha scholars maintain that anything understood is momentary (Kṣaṇika). A word, according to them, denotes a particular object as belonging to a particular moment only. An object of today being completely different from another of tomorrow, the word

'go' for instance can signify only one cow and that again as belonging to a particular moment. The Buddhists are called 'apohavādinas' as they believe, that the import of all words is 'apoha' or 'atadvyāvṛti' (distinction from all other different objects). As Vyaktis (individuals) are innumerable, we cannot understand the Saṁketa with regard to them. As all things are 'Kṣaṇika', a Jāti is impossible in view of its own nature. Therefore, what the word 'ghaṭa' really signifies is that a certain thing possesses peculiarities which distinguish it from all other things.[217] As MM P.V. Kane explains the position, "we do not exactly know what ghaṭa is, we know what it is not; we know that is not Paṭa or anything else."[218]

(7) The Vaiyākaraṇas and the Ālaṁkārikas may be identified as Jātyādivādins as they hold that the import of a word is either a Jāti or a Guṇa or a Dravya or again a Kriyā. Thus they believe in four sets of words. Grammarians first come to believe in words signifying these four entities and the Rhetoricians simply follow them. Hence, to the Grammarians and the Rhetoricians, there are Jātiśabdas, Guṇaśabdas, Dravyaśabdas and Kriyāśabdas.[219] These four kind of words, Grammarians observe, denote the attributes (Upādhis) belonging to the Vyaktis (individuals). The words do not directly signify the Vyakti. The Ālaṁkārikas admit this fourfold classification of the Vaiyākaraṇas. They follow the Vaiyā karaṇas even in the matter of bringing out the relative difference between the four entities of words. The Ālaṁkārikas do not at least basically differ from the Vaiyākaraṇas in their approach to the problem of the import of words.

Of modern scholars, Dr. Gaurinath Śāstri reviews the entire problem critically and analytically.[220] He sums-up his discussions on the subject with Bhartṛhari's opinion that the meaning of words is largely determined by our subjective attitude and culture and so the denotation of words is held to be different in different systems of thought. Bhartṛhari wants us not to be surprised at the incompatibility or conflict of one theory with another.[221]

Bhartṛhari further thinks that the discussion on the import of words should not be carried to any inordinate length. He is inclined to accept a state of indeterminism and thinks that it is impossible to 'hit upon' a theory which will meet universal approval.

In the *Muktāvalī* text 'tatra jātāveva śaktiḥ--------vyakterapi bhā namiti kecit', quoted above, the author of the *Bhāṣāpariccheda* refers to the Mīmāṁsakas who admit only Jāti as the Śakyārtha of a Pada, and object to recognising Śakti with reference to Vyakti on grounds of involving two irregularities, namely 'violation' and 'endlessness'. They also find the knowledge of the Vyaktis (belonging to a particular Jāti) being inevitable as the knowledge of a Jāti is not possible without that of the Vyakits (concerned)[222]

We have already examined the view ofthe Mīmāṁsakas as Jātivādins. To recapitulate, the Mīmāṁsakas assert that a word denotes a Jāti only and is not further competent to denote a Vyakti or Vyaktis belonging to that Jāti.[223] It is to be understood that a Śā bdabodha in the form of Padārthasaṁsarga (mutual connection of objects signified by individual words) necessarily involves the knowledge of Vyaktis[224] (the particulars, the objects or individuals). The knowledge of Vyaktis also would be meaningful only with that of the community to which they belong. Now between the two cognitions of Jāti and Vyakti, that of Jāti, the Viśeṣaṇa, should precede the other relating to Vyakti, the Viśeṣya.[225] The denotative capacity of a word gets exhausted with the conveying of the Viśeṣaṇa and cannot proceed further to signify the Viśeṣya.[226] But as the Knowledge of Vyaktis is a must to carry any meaning in the sentences like 'gāmānaya', 'aśvaṁ vadhāna' etc., it comes in some other way and not by Abhidhā. Here Mīmāṁsakas differ amongst themselves. Some contend that the knowledge of Vyakti occurs due to postulation and some say that it is because of Inference as both Jāti and Vyakti form the same unit of knowledge. Others hold that the power of secondary signification comes to our aid at this stage.[227]

Again, as Viśvanātha has pointed out above, the Mīmāṁsakas have raised the possibility of the occurrence of two irregularities in case Śakti of a Pada is admitted with regard to Vyakti also. In the context of admitting Śakti, or widely Saṁketa, with reference to Vyaktis belonging to a Jāti, we have to face two problems[228] : (1) Whether Śakti is to be admitted in respect of one or many individuals? If only one Śakti is admitted to mean innumerable individuals, it will give rise to the irregularity known as Vyabhicāra (Violation); (2) If innumerable Śaktis come to be admitted to signify innumerable Vyaktis, it will again lead to the defect of Ānantya (endlessness).

The objections of Mīmāṁsakas may be expressed in other words as follows :

(1) Śābdabodha finally arises from the knowledge of Padārthas brought about by the knowledge of the Padas with specific aid of the knowledge of the Śakti of their own. Now if the Śakti of a word, e.g. 'ghaṭa', gives the idea not only of a particular individual 'ghaṭa' (jar) concerned but also comes to be responsible for conveying the knowledge of all other individual 'ghaṭas' (without the involvement of the knowledge of Śakti of those other ghaṭas), obviously it will be a departure from the accepted regulations concerning Śābdabodha. This is what goes as Vyabhicāra.[229]

(2) If Śakti is to be separately admitted to understand every different individual 'ghaṭa' from every different use of the word 'ghaṭa, then there will be the admission of innumerable Śaktis inasmuch as the individuals (Vyaktis) belonging to a genus (Jāti) also are innumerable. This is what goes as Ānantyadoṣa (the defect involving an endless process) and is not at all desirable.[230] Under these circumstances, Mīmāṁsakas are not prepared to admit Śakti of a Pada with regard to Vyakti. It may be added that these two objections of the Mīmāṁsakas were taken note of for

the sake of refutation also by some of the predecessors of Viśvanātha.[231]

In view of the objections raised, Mīmāṁsakas rule out the recognition of Vyakti as Śakyārtha. They assert that the knowledge of Jāti obtained through the knowledge of the Śakti of a Pada would automatically bringforth the knowledge of Vyakti also as a Jāti can never be known without a reference to the Vyaktis that constitute it. Gaṅgeśopādhyāya and Jagadīśācārya also have elaborately discussed this point of the Mīmāṁsakas. The Mīmāṁsakas referred to by Viśvanātha as some (Kecit), who believe in the knowledge of Vyakti as an automatic result of the knowledge of Jāti through Abhidhā, can be easily identified as the Prābhākaras.[232] As we have already observed, the Bhāṭṭas have maintained a different opinion regarding how the undenoted Vyakti comes to be known from the denoted Jāti.

M(22). tanna. śaktiṁ vinā vyaktibhānānupapatteḥ.

Here Viśvanātha asserts that the Vyakti is to be understood only by means of the Śakti of a Pada. It is an agreed opinion that even with the knowledge of a Jāti already obtained from a Pada, there can be no corresponding Śābdabodha unless and until the Vyakti or Vyaktis belonging to that Jāti come to be known. Now, if a Śābdabodha necessarily involves the knowledge of Vyaktis, the very knowledge must come from the Padas (word) occurring in the context. In the process of Śabda (pramāṇa) in the intermediate stages, there is no legitimate scope for any other Pramāṇa like Arthāpatti and Anumāna. If the 'vyaktijñāna' in a context is not a 'padārthajñāna' brought about by a 'padajñāna' with the assistance of corresponding śaktijñāna, then there exists no propriety in calling that 'vyaktijñāna' as being the subject of a Śā bdabodha.[233] As such, that 'vyaktijñāna' is no 'vyktijnāna' worth the name in the context of a Śābdabodha. Hence we must have recourse to the recognised significative powers of a word in the matter. Viśvanātha as a Naiyāyika admits only two significative powers of a word, namely Śakti and Lakṣaṇā. In the succeeding text of the *Muktāvalī*. Viśvanātha would forward his arguments against admitting Lakṣaṇā for conveying the sense of Vyaktis in a sentence. Granting that the recognition of Lakṣaṇā is ruled out, Viśvanātha here makes his bold assertion of the need of admitting only Śakti for obtaining the knowledge of Vyaktis. Gadādhara also makes a similar observation.[234]

M(23). na ca vyaktau lakṣaṇā, anupapattipratisandhānaṁ vinā pi vyaktibodhāt na ca vyaktiśaktāvānantyaṁ, sakalavyaktā vekasyā eva śakteḥ svīkārāt na cānanugamaḥ gotvāderevānugamakatvāt. kiñca gauḥ śakyeti śaktigraho yadi, tadā vyaktau śaktiḥ yadi tu gotvaṁ śakyamiti śaktigrahastadā gotvaprakāraka-padārthasmaraṇaṁ śābdabodhaśca na syāt, samānaprakārakatvena śaktijñānasya padārthasmaraṇaṁ śābdabodhaṁ. prati ca hetutvā t. kiñca gotve yadi śaktistadā gotvatvaṁ śakyatāvacchedakaṁ vācyaṁ, gotvatvantu govetarasamavetatve sati sakalagosamavetatvam.

tathā ca govyaktīnāṁ śakyatāvacchedake'nupraveśāt tavaiva gauravaṁ. tasmāt tattajjātyākṛtiviśiṣṭatattadvyaktibodhānupapattyā, kalpyamānā śaktirjātyakṛtiviśiṣṭa-vyaktāveva viśrā myatīti.

In the Muktāvalī above, "na ca vyaktau --------- vyaktibodhāt," Viśvanātha opposes the attempt at explaining Vyakti as a 'lakṣyārtha' in a sentence and forwards his own argument. Some Mīmāṁsakas and Vedāntins plead that the Lakṣaṇā function is to be resorted to in lieu of Śakti in the matter of signification of Vyaktis. Of the Mīmāṁsakas, Maṇḍanamiśra specially draws the attention of the Naiyāyikas in this regard.[235] As for Vedāntins, we can refer to Dharmarājādhvarindra, who is of the opinion that the Vyakti and Jāti form one unit of knowledge.[236] So when the Jāti is known through Śakti, Vyakti comes to be automatically known or we can understand Vyakti through Lakṣaṇā also. Just as in the sentence 'nīlo ghaṭaḥ', there is Lakṣaṇā admitted in the word 'nīla' (blue) to mean 'nīlaguṇaviśiṣṭa' (blue-coloured object) also, similarly a word denoting a Jāti comes to signify individuals characterised by that Jāti (i.e., tadviśiṣṭa) only through Lakṣaṇā as that 'vyaktyārtha' cannot be known by any other means. In the context of Maṇḍanamiśra's view also, Jagadīśa refers to the Tātparyānupapatti as being admitted by the Mīmāṁsaka scholar as the ground for recognising Laksana in Vyaktis.[237] But Viśvanātha does not find any scope for 'the knowledge of incompatibility' (i.e. anupapattipratisandhāna) and hence rules out the possibility of recognising Lakṣaṇā in conveying a Vyakti or Vyaktis.

Viśvanātha recognises Tātparyānupapatti (i.e., the incompatibility of the intention of the speaker with reference to the Śakyārtha) as the Lakṣaṇābīja (i.e., the ground for the operation of Lakṣaṇā). Hence, the expression 'annupapattipratisandhāna' in the text of the *Muktāvalī* above is to be understood as the 'tātparyānupapattipratisandhāna'. 'Pratisandhāna' means 'jñāna' (knowledge). Viśvanātha is not convinced of the argument of Vyaktilakṣaṇāvādins that it is the Tātparyānupapatti, which leads to the operation of Lakṣaṇā for conveying the idea of the Vyakti. Pending a discussion on Tātparyānupapatti in the context of the relevant text of the *Bhāṣāpariccheda* on Lakṣaṇā, Viśvanātha's idea is briefly presented as follows. In the expression 'gāmānaya', as for instance, we can somehow admit the operation of a Lakṣaṇā, as, there takes place the failure of the syntactical connection (Anvayānupapatti) between the Śakyārthas of the Padas in the sentence. In the event of only the Jāti being admitted as a Śakyārtha, the word 'gau', primarily signifies 'cowness' which cannot have 'anvaya' with the Śakyārtha of 'ānaya' (bring). The fact that cowness cannot be an object for the act of bringing may be treated as a basis for the Anvayānupapatti which is a ground for Lakṣaṇā for the Prābhākaras and some of the Bhāṭṭas. Or here we can explain this finally as a case of Tātparyānupapatti also, which is the Lakṣaṇābīja for Viśvanātha, the author of the *B.P.* As it is not possible even to imagine the bringing of the cowness, we may understand that the intention of the speaker is not with regard to the generic property 'cowness' but with reference to an individual possessed of that. This knowledge of the lack or incompatibility of speaker's intention may form the ground for resorting to Lakṣaṇā to convey the sense of an individual cow in the sentence 'gāmānaya'. But in sentences like 'gaurasti' (cowness exists), there is no scope for suspecting any Anvayānupapatti which is understood as the Lakṣaṇābīja by the Prābhākaras and some of the Bhāṭṭas also. So we cannot make a rule that there arises or will arise some sort of 'anupapatti' to allow the operation of a Lakṣaṇā for conveying the sense of a Vyakti.[238] Now some thinkers, like the Vedāntins, who categorically accept Tātparyānupapatti as the Lakṣaṇābīja in the matter of Vyaktilakṣaṇā may argue that the cases like 'gaurasti' may be placed on a par with 'kākebhyo dadhi rakṣyatāṁ' where Lakṣaṇā is resorted to only on the ground of Tātparyānupapatti without a prior involvement of Anvayā nupapatti. The reply may be given as follows : 'kākebhyo dadhi rakṣyatām' and 'gaurasti' cannot be placed on a par. Normally the Śakti stands admitted in the 'kākapada' to convey a crow (a particular bird of the name). It is only casual or occasional that we come to suspect the lack of Tātparya in respect of the sense 'crow alone' from the word 'kāka'. In the sentence 'kākebhyo dadhi rakṣyatām' (Protect the curd from the crow), we feel that the speaker intends to mean not only the crow but all the spoilers of curd (dadhyupaghātakas) as creatures other than crow are also found to spoil curd. It is the context (Prakaraṇa) which comes to serve as the pointer to the speaker's intention (tātparyagrāhaka). The context demands that in the expression 'kākebhyo' etc. the word 'kāka' is intended to mean all the 'dadhyupaghātkas'. But there is no such 'tātparyagrāhaka' in case of 'gaurasti' to demand that 'gau' should mean an individual cow possessed of cowness as a Lakṣyārtha. As a matter of fact, here the individual cow possessed of cowness is the direct regular meaning of the word 'go' and this regular and normal meaning is unlike the 'tīra' (bank) recognised as the casual Lakṣyārtha of the word 'gaṅgā' or the 'dadhyupaghātaka' (spoiler of curd) recognised as the casual Lakṣyārtha of the word 'kāka'.

Viśvanātha uses the word 'pratisandhāna' in the text of the *Muktāvalī*. viz.. 'anupapattipratisandhāna' to carry the sense of the process of cognising Anvayānupapatti or Tātparyānupapatti as the Lakṣaṇābīja. In the matter of Śābdabodha from 'gaṅgāyaṁ ghoṣaḥ' or 'kākebhyo dadhi rakṣyatāṁ', the two stock examples of Lakṣaṇā, some transitional stages are undoubtedly involved. We first come to know the Śakyārthas of the words. Then follows our knowledge that the Śakyārthas cannot be syntactically or logically connected. Then we apply our knowledge of Lakṣaṇā to know the Lakṣyārthas. Here again follows our knowledge of the syntactical or logical connections between the Śakyārthas and Lakṣyārthas involved. But as a matter of fact, the experession, 'gā mānaya' or 'gaurasti', at the very first phase, presents to us the idea of an individual cow as being asked to be brought or as existing. Here our knowledge of the mutual connection of the meanings of the words in the sentence takes place once and once only.

In "na ca ------- svikārāt", Viśvanātha shows the propriety in the admission of Śakti of a Pada with regard to a Vyakti. He points out that there is no fear of the flow of endlessness (ānantya) being involved in case the Śakti be admitted with reference to Vyakti. Though there are innumerable Vyaktis belonging to a Jāti, we need not admit innumerable Śaktis to understand them. We can understand them even by admitting one Śakti with reference to all the Vyaktis. Viśvanātha asserts that the word concerned should convey the idea of all the individuals with the help of only one Śakti. This, however, need not necessarily mean that the word should bringforth the idea of all the probable individuals at a time. In fact, the word should convey the idea of only such an individual which may be relevant to the context. Even with reference to many such individuals which may be relevant to various context, only one Śakti will operate. The *Dinakarī commentary* elucidates the idea of Viśvanātha by saying[239] that the Śakti of a certain word, (employed even to convey the idea of various individuals on various occasions) is to be taken to be one because Śakti is nothing but a will of God and that will is undoubtedly one and the same for all the individuals of all the occasions. The idea of Viśvanātha, as elucidated by the commentator appears to be as follows : Śakti is after all a will of God that such and such a word should convey such and such an idea or such and such ideas. Śakti is not a separate Padārtha, requiring to be numerically limitless in respect of the limitless number of individuals. Being the will of God, it is one and uniform for all the individuals that are required to be gathered as the meaning of a specific word.

In the *Muktāvalī* above, 'na cā'nanugamaḥ ------------- anugamakatvāt', Viśvanātha proceeds to arrest further misgivings that may arise in the event of admitting Śakti of a Pada with regard to Vyakti. The problem is like this : The Knowledge of the Śakti of a word is generally gathered from Vyavahāra, i.e., from observing the use of the word in respect of one or a few individuals. In that way the knowledge of the Śakti of the word should be restricted to one or a few individuals. How could then the same word be expected to convey the idea of those individuals which donot belong to the group of the individual or the few individuals recognised at the very first instance to be the primary meaning of the word concerned ? For, example. if the meaning of the word 'go' is learnt for the first time in respect of 'an individual red cow', how could we expect the same word to mean 'another black individual cow' on a later occasion, since the two individuals are different and there is nothing common between them ? In reply to this problem, Viśvanātha says that though the individuals are different yet they have something invariably common, an uniform attribute (anugamaka) which should facilitate the employment of the same word for all the different individuals belonging to a certain class. The uniform attribute in most cases is the Jāti or the generic attribute itself. For example, in case of the word 'go' its employment to mean and understand all the different individual cows is possible on account of recognising 'gotva' or cowhood as the common attribute in all of them.

In 'kiñca gauḥ śakyeti--------- vyaktau śaktiḥ', Viśvanātha opposes the view of the Prābhākaras who understand the Vyaktis as Śakyārtha by virtue of admitting Śakti with reference to the corresponding Jāti only. They understand the Śakti of a Pada only with reference to a Jāti and not with reference to the Vyaktis belonging to that Jāti. But they also donot recognise a Lakṣaṇā in respect of the Vyakti. They deem the Vyakti as the Śakyārtha without however recognising a Śakti in respect of the Vyakti. This is possible, they say, as a Jāti and the Vyaktis pertaining to it, form a single unit. Gaṅgeśopādhyāya analyses the view of the Prābhākaras in this regard.[240] Viśvanātha has already ruled out the scope of Lakṣaṇā for conveying the idea of a Vyakti. The Prābhākaras also are not prepared to see any scope for Lakṣaṇā in this regard. Hence in the matter of conveying the idea of a Vyakti, of the two significative functions accepted by both the Naiyāyikas and the Mīmāṁsakas, only Śakti or Abhidhā remains to be considered. Viśvanātha here argues thus. If the Prābhākaras believe that the 'vākyārthajñāna' is nothing but the 'anvitapadārthajñāna' and that the 'anvayajñāna' in the sentences like 'gāmānaya', is possible only with the 'vyaktibhāna' (i.e., the knowledge of the Vyaktis), then the only natural and rational course of action will be to admit Śakti of Padas with reference to Vyaktis also. A meaning can be Śakyārtha if it comes from the knowledge of the relevant pada by means of its own corresponding Śakti. When an individual 'gau' is finally accepted as understood from the word 'go' and at the sametime, no verabal function other than Śakti is admitted to that effect, then there is no meaning in not admitting Śakti of a Pada with regard to Vyakti.

In consonance with what he has stated above Viśvanātha now proceeds to point out in the text of the *Muktāvalī*, 'yadi gotvaṁ śakyamiti śaktigrahas------ hetutvāt', the serious difficulties in the matter of Śābdabodha in the event of admitting Śakti only with reference to Jāti. It is an universally accepted formula that the 'śaktijñāna' of a Pada is to contribute as a cause (hetu, i.e., a Sahakāri Kāraṇa) in the matter of Śābdabodha only by following a norm. The norm is that it must produce initially a 'padārthajñāna' and thereby finally a Śābdabodha being in the same form or structure. This sameness in its form is to be judged from the sameness of qualification (Prakāra or Viśeṣaṇā). This symmetry is to take place at two stages, between Śaktijñāna and Padārthajñāna and between the 'padārthajñāna' and the Śābdabodha. If after the Mīmāṁsakas who are Jātivādins - 'gotva' is understood as the Śakyārtha, the 'gopadārthajñāna' (the knowledge of the word 'go') will take the form of 'gotvatvaprakārakagotvaviśeṣyakajñāna' (the knowledge of the qualified cowness with cownessness as its qualification). It is needless to add that whenever there is a Śakyārtha, it includes in its fold the knowledge of its determinant also, which serves as a qualifcation to distinguish the Śakyārtha from anything else. So, from the above 'gopadārthajñāna', the corresponding Śābdabodha will involve a similar knowledge viz., 'gotvatvaprakāraka gotvaviśeṣyakajñāṇa'. But it is not warranted by facts. Even the Jātivādins contend that from sentences, 'gāmānaya' etc. by way of observing 'vṛddhavyavahāra', the child comes to understand the significance of 'go' etc. with reference to 'govyaktis' (individual cows etc.). In other words, even the Jātivādins understand the Śābdabodha from a word like 'go' in the form of 'gotvaprakārakagoviśeṣyakajñāna' (the knowledge of the individual cows characterised by the generic property 'cowness'). Now if the Śābdabodha in the context of the word 'go' takes place as 'gotvaprakārakagoviśeṣyakajñāna', the corresponding 'śaktijñāna' and Padārthasmaraṇa also must be admitted as of the same form. In other words, these two also must come as 'gotvaprakārakagoviśeṣyakajñāna'. It is because, as already shown, there must be the admission of the same Prakāra in all three concepts. Hence the reality demands the recognition of Śakti with regard to 'jātiviśiṣṭavyakti'.

The recognition of mere Jātiśakti may again be shown as more cumbrous than that of mere vyaktiśakti. Viśvanātha makes such an attempt in the text of the *Muktāvalī*, 'kiñca gotve yadi śaktistadā------------- tavaiva gauravaṁ.'

As we have already seen, the admission of a Śakyārtha demands along with the admission of a Śakyatāvacchedaka also. In admitting 'gotva' (Jāti) as the Śakyārtha after the Mīmāṁsakas and Vedāntins etc., 'gotvatva' comes to be automatically admitted as its Avacchedaka. Now when one demands to know what this 'gotvatva' means, even the Jātivādins at this stage have no way out but to admit that it (gotvatva) is something which, according to ultimate analysis inherently exists in all the individual cows. Thus the notion of all cows comes to be involved in that of the cownessness (gotvatva), the determinant of the denoted sense 'cowness'. Viśvanatha points out that while the Jātiśaktivādins prefer to recognise Śakti in respect of the Jāti in order to get rid of the flaw of 'ānantya' (endlessness), they get indeed more and more involved in cumbrousness themselves, because the notion of a Jāti like 'gotva', recognised as the Śakyārtha, also includes the notion of 'gotvatva', as the Śakyatāvacchedaka, which can be conceived of only in terms of 'gotva', which again in terms of the innumerable individual cows. Thus the whole process involves a lot of 'kalpanāgaurava' (cumbrousness of ideas) and also the flaw of 'ā nantya' all the same.

In the text of the *Muktāvalī*, 'tasmāt -------- viśrāmyatīti', Viśvanātha gives his own verdict in the context of the problem of recognition of Śakti with regard to Jāti etc. We have seen that the recognition of Śakti with reference to mere Jāti leaves no scope for understanding Vyakti as Śakyārtha. We have also seen the inappropriateness of seeking the aid of Lakṣaṇā in the matter. We also cannot deny that the Śābdabodha necessarily involves the knowledge of the Vyakti. When Jāti alone is taken to be the Śakyārtha it becomes difficult to gather the idea of the individual possessing a relevant Jāti and Ākṛti. But while understanding the

Śakyārtha of a word, we must not fail to understand the individual characterised by its own Jāti and Ākṛti. Hence, Viśvanātha asserts that the Śakti, which is being imagined to be there, must finally be recognised to be in respect of the individuals having the respective Jātis and Ākṛtis. Viśvanātha calls the Śakti a 'kalpyamānā' Śakti (i.e. a Śakti, which is imagined to be there) because while in Mīmāṁsā Śakti is recognised a separate Padārtha in the Nyāya it is only a will of God supposed to be involved in respect of the word and its meaning.

Now here we are to see if and where Viśvanātha differs from the Prācīna Naiyāyikas and from some other Navya Naiyāyikas also.

We have already seen that the Prācīna Naiyāyikas are ofthe view that every pada denotes a Jāti, a Vyakti and an Ākṛti.[241] The singular number of the word 'padārtha' in the relevant Nyāyasūtra is admitted by scholars as significant.[242] It is to signify that by one and the same Śakti all the above three are conveyed. Viśvanātha is convinced of the basic logic of his earlier predecessors that the universals (Jāti), the individuals (Vyakti) and their particular forms (Ākṛtis) cannot be cognised apart from each other. Hence he includes the three concepts in the same unit of knowledge and employs only Śakti and only one Śakti, for conveying those ideas. Yet we find a difference of Viśvanātha from the Prācīna Naiyāyikas. The Prācīna Naiyāyikas have admitted different degrees of prominence in all the three that may be gathered on different occasions.[243] While one of the above three factors comes to be prominent, the other two remain subservient in the meaning of a word. Viśvanātha however, unlike the old Naiyāyikas, gives a stress on the Vyakti.

As observed earlier, some of the Navya Naiyāyikas come to us as the Jātiviśiṣṭavyaktivādin by way of excluding the Ākṛti from the concept of a Śakyārtha.[244] As for instance, we can refer to Jagadīśa and Annaṁbhaṭṭa.[245] Gaṅgeśopādhyāya recognises

Śakti in case of Ākṛti also and admits of the same unit of experience covering all the three.[246] So Viśvanātha might have been influenced by the idea of the author ofthe *Tattvacintāmani* in order to unite all the three factors in the concept of a single denoted sense. There again Viśvanātha concludes with a clear emphasis on Vyakti as the qualified. Thus he maintains his difference somewhat from some Navya Naiyāyikas and somewhat from the Prācīna Naiyāyikas.

M (24). Śaktam padam.

Now Viśvanātha comes to give a general definition of Pada before he shows its division. The assertion of the knowledge of Śakti as a Sahakāri (Kāraṇa) of Śābdabodha in the Kārikā ('padajñānantu' etc.) also demands a clear indication as to what Śakti belongs to. It is all the more necessary as the Grammarians[247] and others are there to recognise Śakti in both pada and Vākya. The admission of Śakti as pertaining to a Vākya would lead one to recognise Vākyalakṣaṇā also which the Naiyā yikas do not. Under the circumstances, Viśvanātha, in the *Muktā valī* above, comes to assert that it is only pada which is 'śakta' in the sense of being 'śaktimat'. In other words, the primary power of signification belongs only to a word and never to a sentence.

Viśvanātha's admission of Śakti only in a Pada is in agreement with the view of his colleagues in the school of Nyāya.[248] But here we can point out that interestingly enough, Nāgeśa refers to the Nyāyabhāṣyakāra Vātsyāyana as admitting Śakti in both Pada and Vākaya.[249] Nāgeśa maintains that by admitting the utility of Grammar for the preservation of the knowledge of Samaya (convention) corresponding to Vāk (speech) in the form of Padas and Vākyas, Vātsyāyana admits Śakti in both Pada and Vākya. It is because in the stage of Vātsyāyana, samaya or saṁketa pertaining to God, i.e., 'Īśvarasaṁketa' itself was accepted as the Śakti.

One may now be inclined to make a reference to the Prābhākaras who also accept Śakti as pertaining to a Pada.[250] But we must bear in mind that the Prābhākaras understand a very prolonged capacity of the Abhidhā or Śakti in order to cover even the relational thought (anvayabodha) i.e., the Vākyārtha. Though they do not speak of Vākya as 'śaktimat', they as 'anvitābhidhānavādins', unhestitatingly utilize the knowledge of Śakti in understanding the Vākyārtha. This is possible because of their peculiar concept of the process of the relational thought. In their concept, as we shall see in succeeding pages, Pada and Vākya and again Padārtha and Vākyārtha come just to be the same. Though the Bhāṭṭas do not admit Śakti as pertaining to a Vākya, they recognise Lakṣaṇā in a Vākya. Vedāntins also believe in understanding Vākyārtha by Śakti, though they recognise Śakti as pertaining to a Pada Only.[251] Under these circumstances, Viśvanātha, very reasonably asserts here that only a Pada is 'śakta'. He would pursue the point and make it clear that the Vā kyārtha would come as neither Śakyārtha nor Lakṣyārtha.

M(25). taccaturvidhaṁ. kvacid yaugikaṁ kvacid rūḍhaṁ kvacid yogarūḍhaṁ kvacid yaugikarūḍhaṁ.

Here is a fourfold classification of the denotative (Śakta) words (Pada). The words are classified into four groups on the basis of nature of the primary meanings singified by them. The groups are, as Viśvanātha puts it, (1) Yaugika (etymological), (2) Rūḍha (conventional), (3) Yogarūḍha (etymologo-conventional and (4) Yaugikarūḍha (etymological cum conventional). This fourfold classification actually holds good only in respect of nāmapadas (Nouns). Prior to Viśvanātha, some eminent Naiyāyikas had already taken up the issue of classification of Padas on the stength of Rūḍhi and Yoga. Gaṅgeśa in his characteristic way has dealt at length with the issues that may crop-up in admission of the classification of words on the strength of the concept of Yoga and Rūḍhi in separation and in combination. As we shall see in succeeding pages, several illustrations of the different kinds of Padas as we find in the *Muktāvalī* can be traced back to the work of Gaṅgeśa.

Here we are to note that Jagadīsā who divides Padas into Nāmapada and Dhātu comes to show Padas classified into five varieties.[252] The five varieties of Jagadīśācārya are (1) Rūḍha, (2) Lakṣaka, (3) Yaugika, (4) Yogarūḍha, (5) Rūḍhayaugika. Of these only the first four varieties are recognised by Jagadīsā as genuine and the fifth variety, namely, Rūḍhayaugika is mentioned only as something recognised by others. Annaṁbhaṭṭa seems not to have accepted Yaugikarudha Padas. It is because he refers to only three kinds of Śaktis as Yogarūḍhi, Yoga and Rūḍhi.[253] Thus he appears not to be in favour of recognising the Yaugikarūḍha variety. Of the Grammarians, we know Nāgeśa classifying Abhidhā into three varieties. His 'vācaka' śabda (the denotative word) accordingly comes to be of three varieties. In Nāgeśa's classification, the Yaugikarūḍha variety of the Naiyākas is leftout. The Yaugikarū ḍha Padas are actually homonymous words. Hence his exclusion of Yaugikarūḍha words may (be said to) have some justification. Some later Mīmāṁsakas have come to admit this entire fourfold classification of padas into Rūḍha, Yaugika, Yogarūḍha and Yaugikarūḍha.[254]

M(26). tathā hi-yatrāvayavārtha eva budhyate, tad yaugikam. yathā pācakādi-padam.

Here in the *Muktāvalī*, the word 'yatra' should be understood in the sense of 'yasmin' (in which) with reference to a Śakta Pada. The expression shall have to be understood thus also in case of other relevant portions of the *Muktāvalī* in the context of the other varieties of Śakta Pada.

It is universally accepted that a word is named 'yaugika' when only the meaning of the 'avayava' or its component parts comes to be realised.[255] By 'avayava' or the component parts of a word, we are to understand the stem or the base, the prefixes and the suffixes. The word 'pācaka' is an example of this variety of words. The word 'pācaka' is derived from the root 'pac' (read in the *Pāṇinīyadhātupāṭha* in the sense 'to cook', cf. (ḍu) pacas pāke and the suffix 'ṇvul'. Of 'pac' + 'ṇvul', 'ṇ' and 'l' are dropped, leaving 'pac' + 'vu'. By the rule 'yuvoranākau'[256] we come to have 'pac' + 'aka'; 'a' in 'pac' comes to be 'ā' by the rule 'taddhiteṣvacāmā deḥ'.[257] Thus we get 'pācaka'. Now the meaning of the word 'pācaka' as determined by its derivatives is 'the person who cooks'. The suffix 'nvul' means the subject, (one who acts) by the rule 'kartari kṛt.[258] Thus a yaugika word, as we find, conveys the meaning of only the 'avayava' or component parts; nothing more or nothing less. Now that the yaugika is a division of Śakta Pada (denotative word), the 'yaugikārtha' or the etymological meaning is also a variety of Śakyārtha (the denotative sense).

We find that the denotative power or Śakti involved in a Yaugika Pada is called Yogaśakti.[259] Jagadīśa, a senior Naiyāyika maintains that the word is Yaugika when it presents as its meaning only as much is conveyed by the Yogaśakti. Yet we do not see any basic difference between Viśvanātha and Jagdīśa with regard to their notion of a Yaugika Pada. Jagdīśa, however, proceeds further to divide the Yaugika word into three varieties, namely, 'samāsānta', 'taddhitānta' and 'kṛdanta'.[260] Samāsa or the 'samasta pada' is etymological, because the meaning is determined by the respective meanings of the component parts. 'Taddhitānta' words are secondary derivatives where the meaning is derived from the nouns and the suffixes involved. 'Kṛdanta' words are the primary derivatives formed by the roots and suffixes.

The word 'pācaka' is almost universally accepted as an example of Yaugikapadas.[261]

M(27), yatrāvayavaśakti - nirapekṣayā samudāyaśaktyā gṛhyate, tad rūḍham. yathā gomaṇḍalādi - padam.

A word is called Rūḍa when its meaning is conveyed by the denotative capacity of the word as a whole (Samudāyaśakti), without any care to the denotative capacity of its component parts (avayavaśaktinirapekṣayā).[262] The Rūḍha word conveys an idea as a whole. The total capacity of the word serves the purpose and the etymology of word is not at all taken into consideration; the word 'go' is an example of this variety of word.[263] The word 'gauḥ' comes to be formed according to the 'uṇādi sūtra' 'gamerḍo' etc. and comprises of the component parts, the root 'gam' and the suffix 'das' which should give the meaning as 'something that goes'. But the primary meaning of the word is 'a cow' in general irrespective of the fact of its moving or sitting idle and this primary meaning is derived irrespective ofthe component parts of the word.

Along with 'go', 'maṇḍala' and sometimes 'maṇḍapa' also appear in the *Muktāvalī* as examples of the Rūḍha variety of words. For instance, the *Bhāṣāpariccheda* (Sanskrit Pustak Bhandar edition) records 'maṇḍala' and the *Nyāyasiddhāntamuktāvalī* (Chowkhamba edition) records both 'maṇḍala' and 'maṇḍapa'. Scholars have raised objections to the inclusion of these two words as examples of Rūḍhapada. Pañcānana Śāstrī objects to naming both the words as examples of Rūḍha variety. It is because both 'maṇḍala and 'maṇḍapa' can obviously be examples of yaugikaruḍha variety of words where both the etymological and conventional senses are separately understood. Etymologically or by significative capacity of component parts, 'maṇḍala' means 'one who takes scum of rice' and conventionally it means a 'circle'. Now both these two meanings are recognised as Śakyārthas of 'maṇḍala'. Similarly the etymological meaning of 'maṇḍapa' is 'one who drinks the scum of rice' and the conventional one is a 'pavilion'. Here also both the meanings are derived as Śakyārthas of the word independently of the either at different occasions. Here Pañcānana Śāstrī points out that the illustration of the Rūḍha variety by these two words goes against Viśvanātha's own definition of the Rūḍha variety.[264] Dinakarabhaṭṭa however, accepts 'maṇḍala' as the right example and observes that the insertion of 'maṇḍapa' in certain texts in place of 'maṇḍala' is actually by mistake.[265] But Rāmarudrabhaṭṭa does not agree.[266] He observes that though 'maṇḍapa' is undoubtedly a Yaugikapada its rūḍhatva' is independent of its 'yaugikatva'. A yaugikapada being Yaugika in one sense may be Rūḍha in another. Hence the inclusion of a Yaugikarūḍhapada like 'maṇḍapa' in the list of Rūḍhapadas, on the strength of its 'rū ḍhatva' is justified. Rāmarudrabhaṭṭa might have been inspired by the fact that the great Navyanaiyāyika Gaṅgeśa also accepts 'maṇḍapa' as an illustration of Rūḍha.[267] Here we may conveniently recall how Jagadīśa has been justifiably unwilling to admit Yaugikarūḍha as a seperate kind of Pada in addition to the Yaugika and Rūḍha varieties. Jagadīsā, however, recognises 'maṇḍapa' only as an illustration of Yaugikarūḍha.[268] It is interesting to note that in the circle of certain Ālaṁkārikas, 'maṇḍapa' is given as an example of a 'lākṣaṇikapada' and not 'śakta' in the sense of a house (gṛhaviśeṣa).[269]

This 'samudāyaśakti' or Rūḍhi is actually the commonly known Saṁketa (Convention). Hence the author of the *Śabdaśaktiprakāśikā* equates this Rūḍhi with Saṁketa, refers to its celibrity as Saṁjñā and divides it into three types, viz., Naimittikī, Pāribhāṣikī and Aupādhikī.[270] According to him, the Naimittikī variety of the Rūḍha word denotes the Jātiviśiṣṭavyakti, while the Pāribhāṣikī and Aupādhikī varieties denote Jāti and Vyakti respectively. As maintained by the Ālaṁkārikas again, Rū ḍhi is the 'akhaṇḍaśakti' (unmutiliated denotative capacity).[271] A word is called Rūḍhaśabda when its meaning comes to be apprehended through its 'akhaṇḍaśakti'. Paṇḍitarāja Jagannātha records a very interesting view referred to as 'of others'. According to this view only the Rūḍha variety of words is to be recognised inasmuch as there is actually no scope for Yaugikapadas. It is because the stems, roots, prefixes and suffixes i.e., so called component parts of words are imaginary divisions of words which are originally indivisible.[272]

M(28). yatra tvavayavaśakti - viṣaye samudāyaśaktirapyasti, tadyogarūḍham. yathā paṅkajādi-padam. tathā hi - paṅkajapadamavayavaśaktyā paṅkajanikartṛrūpamarthaṁ bodhayati. samudāyaśaktyā ca padmatvena rūpeṇa padmaṁ bodhayati. na ca kevalāvayavaśaktyā kumude'pi prayogaḥ syāditi vācyam.

rūḍhijñānasya kevalayaugikārthabuddhau pratibandhakatvāditi prāñcaḥ. vastutastu samudāyaśaktyupasthitapadame' vayavārtha-paṅkajanikartturanvayo bhavati, sānnidhyāt. yatra tu rūḍhyarthasya bādhaḥ pratisandhīyate, tatra lakṣaṇayā kumudāderbodhaḥ. yatra tu kumudatvena rūpeṇa bodhe na tātparyajñānam, padmatvasya ca bādhastatra cā' vayavaśaktimātreṇa nirvāha ityāhuḥ. yatra tu sthalapadmādāvavayavārthabodhastatra samudāyaśaktyā padmatvena rūpeṇa bodhaḥ yadi tu sthalapadmaṁ vijātīyameva, tadā lakṣaṇayaiveti.

Now Viśvanātha comes to expound the concept of the Yogarūḍha variety of a Pada. Of the four, this variety is specially and more elaborately discussed by the scholars as its concept gives rise to certain delicate issues. Gaṅgeśa's discussion of the issues involved in the concept of Yogarūḍhi runs for as many as twenty three pages.

Nāgeśa defines Yogarūḍhi as the denotative capacity which involves a mutual relation between a specially conveyed, i.e., conventional meaning and a meaning allowed by the Śāstra (Grammar) on the basis of the component parts of a Pada.[273] Gāgābhaṭṭa presents a simplified definition which demands of Yogarūḍhi a combination of 'samudāyaśakti' with 'avayavaśakti' in order to convey one meaning only.[274] Or, to put it in a different way, a word is called 'Yogarūḍha' when in the matter of denoting a sense the total capacity of the word is also taken into consideration along with the capacity of its component parts. In case of a Yogarūḍha word, the meaning agrees with the derivation but yet depends on a convention in respect of the scope of its denotation. Here the convention (Rūḍhi) works in such a way that although the meaning is in full agreement with the derivation, it appears to be determined irrespective of its etymology. The word 'paṅkaja' is an example of this variety of words. The etymology of the word 'paṅkaja' is 'paṅke jāyata iti', 'paṅka + jan + ḍa'. Hence the etymological meaning of 'paṅkaja' is an object which grows in the mud. But, on the other hand, the word 'paṅkaja' is restricted by 'samudāyaśakti' i.e., convention to mean lotus only. In other words, the word 'paṅkaja' means a lotus by virtue of its lotusness. So if anybody utters the word 'paṅkaja', the idea and the image of a lotus come to the mind immediately, If the sense would not have been restricted then the word 'paṅkaja' would have denoted also a lily flower which grows in the mud. The word 'ādi' in 'paṅkajādi' in the *Muktāvalī* above is to include in the list of 'yogarūḍhapada' other words like 'kṛṣṇasarpa'. The word 'kṛṣṇasarpa' etymologically means a black snake but is restricted to cobra only. In 'na ca kevalāvayavaśaktyā----------- prāñcaḥ' above, Viśvanātha like his predecessor Gaṅgeśa[275] records a view of the earlier scholars (prāñcaḥ i.e., prāgvartinaḥ). These earlier scholars can be idnetified as Mimāṁsakas on the strength of Jagadīśa's ascribing this view to them.[276] Mīmāṁsakas also recognise 'paṅkaja' as a Yogrūḍha Pada. But their approach comes to be different in the matter of explaining why 'paṅkaja' cannot be taken to denote a lily (kumuda) on the strength of etymology. We know that the etymological or derivative meaning (avayavārtha) of the word is the subject of the action of growing in the mud (paṅkajanikartā, i.e., an object that grows in the mud). As a lily is also found growing in mud, a pertinent question arises as to why a lily is not understood from the word 'paṅkaja. The Mīmāṁsakas hold that it cannot do so inasmuch as the knowledge of the Rūḍhi or convention concerning the word 'paṅkaja' comes to stand in the way of understanding only the etymological sense of a word.[277] Viśvanā tha rejects the view of the Mīmāṁsakas. In 'vastutastu -------- sā nnidhyāt' above, he maintains that on hearing the word 'paṅkaja', the meaning 'lotus' occurs first in one's mind on the strength of the 'samudāyaśakti' or convention. Then the etymological meaning of the word 'paṅkaja', i.e., 'an object that grows on mud' comes to be connected with the already obtained conventional meaning, i.e., the lotus. The conventional meaning occurs first in one's mind because of immediacy of knowledge (sānnidhya) as it already stands determined by the convention concerning the word. In presenting this notion, he might have been influenced by

Gaṅgeśa who also holds a similar view. According to Gaṅgeśa, the knowledge of Rūḍhi is not necessarily to serve as an obstacle or does not serve at all as an obstacle to the knowledge of Yogaśakti of a word.[278] As a matter of fact, the lotus, recollected because of the conventional knowledge (rūḍhijñāna) from the word 'paṅkaja', comes to be known as one that grows on mud (i.e., paṅkajanikartā) because of the knowledge of the component parts. Annaṁbhaṭṭa corroborates the view of Gaṅgeśa.[279] Jagadīśa also, after a lengthy discussion on the views of the Mīmāṁsakas, echoes the opinion of the author of the *Tattvacintāmaṇi*.[280] Now a question may be pertinent here. If as a matter of fact, it is the 'rūḍhijñāna' which immediately fixes the meaning of the word 'paṅkaja' to a lotus and if only for the knowledge of a lotus, the word 'paṅkaja' is normally or ordinarily uttered, then we can do well only with the recognition of the Rūḍhiśakti. What is it that leads to admit here both Yoga and Rūḍhiśakti and to call it a Yogarūḍha Pada ? We find the scholars quite aware of this query. As for instance, Gaṅgeśa, Nāgeśa and Gāgābhaṭṭa have spoken of the utility of both Yogaśakti and Rū ḍhiśakti in the case of words like 'paṅkaja' by way of conveying corresponding meanings in the event of failure of the other.[281] Though we cannot say that there is the agreement of Viśvanātha with the aforesaid scholars in the matter, we can, however, say that Viśvanātha also was aware of certain such misgivings regarding the concept of Yogarūḍhi. It is why he takes up the theme a bit elaborately in the *Muktāvalī* text, 'yatra tu rūḍhyarthasya bādhaḥ --------- tadā lakṣaṇayaiveti.'

In the sentence, 'niśāyāṁ paṅkajaḥ', the word 'paṅkaja' cannot mean a 'lotus'. It is because the lotus thrives only during the day. Here as there is no Tātparya with regard to a lotus, Viśvanātha proceeds to make a Lakṣaṇā on the strength of Tātparyānupapatti. Now a 'kumuda' (Lily) comes to be understood as a Lakṣyārtha of the word 'paṅkaja'. So Viśvanātha makes the rule that when there is a difficulty regarding the understanding of a 'rūḍhyartha', Lakṣaṇā is resorted to. In the sentence 'niśāyāṁ paṅkajaḥ', the Tatparya is finally settled with regard to a lily. But it may happen sometime that while it is difficult to understand a conventional meaning like lotus, it may be that the intention of the speaker is also not with reference to a secondary meaning like 'a lily'. As for instance, we can take the sentence, 'paṅkajo mostaghāsaḥ'. Here the paṅkaja is used as the qualification of a particular kind of grass that grows on mud. In such cases, the business is served only by the Yogaśakti. It does not allow any scope to Rūḍhiśakti or Lakṣaṇā. Sometimes again the Yogaśakti may get obstructed allowing Rūḍhiśakti to function independently. For instance, in the sentence, 'bhūmau paṅkajam" the word 'paṅkaja' cannot mean a water lotus by the combination of Yogarūḍhaśakti. It also cannot go to mean a water lily by Lakṣaṇā as the Tātparya is not felt with regard to that. The Yogaśakti also is of no avail because of the presence of the word 'bhūmau'. In such a case, 'samudāyaśakti' or Rūḍhi will step in to mean a land lotus (sthala-padma). The knowledge of the land lotus occurs as a conventional primary meaning by virtue of understanding it as merely a variety of lotus without any reference to the etymological meaning of the word. If, however, the land lotus is not recognised as a variety of lotus at all to allow the conventional meaning to occur easily, Lakṣaṇā shall have to be resorted to get the desired meaning. In 'yatra tu--------- avayaśaktimātreṇa nirvāha ityāhuḥ', the expression 'mātreṇa' is to be taken to suggest a disregard to Lakṣaṇā. In this context, we may note that the earlier Naiyāyikas recognised only the Lakṣaṇāśakti in understanding the mere 'yogārtha' or 'rūḍhārtha' from a Yogarūḍhapada. Jagadīśa makes a mention of the Nyāyavārttika wherein either a lily or land lotus is shown as understandable from the word 'paṅkaja' by Lakṣaṇā only.[282] But we learn from Gaṅgeśa that the Neologicians are reluctant to take the aid of Lakṣaṇā in this matter. They want to have even the aforesaid meanings by Śakti only.[283]

M(29).. yatra tu yaugikārtha - rūḍhyarthayoḥ svātantryeṇa

bodhastadyaugikarūḍham. yathodbhidādi - padam. tatra hyud-bhedanakarthā taru - gulmādirbudhyate yāgaviseṣo' - pīti.

A word is called 'yaugikarūḍha' or etymological cum conventional when its meaning is determined either by the derivation i.e., its component parts or by a convention concerning the whole word irrespective of any derivation.[284] In other words, in case of a Yaugikarūḍha word the etymological and conventional meanings come to be independently understood. As for instance, the word 'udbhid' etymologically means which grow up perforating the ground (i.e., tree, plant, creeper etc.) and again conventionally it means a sacrifice of this name.[285] By 'ādi' in 'udbhidādi padam' in the *Muktāvalī* text, other similar words like 'maṇḍapa' had been referred to.[286] Now the word 'maṇḍapa' etymologically means one who drinks the scum of rice and Conventionally the open hall. Here from both the examples, we have seen that the Yaugikarūḍha words have two meanings, both being determined parallelly. Again we have the idea that this division of words is applicable only in case of 'anekārthaśabdas' (words having more than one meaning). We find Nāgeśa not recognising this variety of words. He refers to the variety as recognised by others.[287] It is because, according to the Grammarians, an 'anekārthaśabda' is not a single word but it assumes the form of different words varying according to various meanings. The Grammarians' maxim in this context is 'arthabhede śabdabhedaḥ' (i.e., Difference of words results from difference in meanings). According to them, therefore, the words like 'udbhid' and 'maṇḍapa' are Yaugika on the strength of their etymological meanings and Rūḍha on the strength of their Conventional meanings (i.e., when their meanings are determined by the 'samudāyaśakti'). We have also noticed Jagadīśa's reluctance to give recognition to this vaariety of a Pada. Now it behoves us to discuss a question at this stage. Both the so called Yogarūḍha and Yaugikarūḍha words involve the operation of Yogaśakti and Rūḍhiśakti. Hence there is the necessity for drawing a line of demarcation. Naiyāyikas are alive to this necessity. Jagdīśacārya states in this context that a Yaugikarūḍha Pada sometimes comes to convey a 'rūḍhyartha' without any reference to the Yogārtha or sometimes signifies only the 'yogārtha' without any reference to the 'rūḍhyartha'. As for instance, in maṇḍape śete, the etymological meaning of the word 'maṇḍapa' i.e., 'maṇḍapānakartā' does not fit in for necessary connection and is not conveyed. Similarly in 'maṇḍapaṁ bhojaya' the Conventional meaning of the word 'maṇḍapa' i.e., a pavilion fails to be syntactically connected and as such is not understood. But, in the case of the words of the Yogarūḍha variety, like 'paṅkaja' the etymology also conveys what has already attained the status of a conventional meaning, and the Conventional force also operates to convey such a meaning which happens to agree also with the etymology.[288]

K(2). LAKṢANĀ ŚAKYASAMBANDHASTĀTPARYĀNUPAPATTITAḤ 82 a.

In the Kārikā above, Viśvanātha forwards his own definition of Lakṣaṇā. In the works of scholars anterior to Viśvanātha, we meet with a two fold controversy in the very definition of Lakṣaṇā. (1) The Mīmāṁsakas understood Lakṣaṇā as based upon what may be described as 'svabodhyasaṁbandha' (or 'svajñāpyasaṁbandha'). They did not conceive it as 'Śakyārtha Sambandha'; (2) The Prābhākaras, some of the Bhāṭṭa Mīmāṁsakas and even some Naiyāyikas, including their stalwart Gaṅgeśopādhyāya, recognised Anvayānupapatti and not Tātparyānupapatti as the factor leading to the operation of Lakṣaṇā. In the face of such differences of opinion, Viśvanātha's definition of Lakṣaṇā deserves to be carefully studied by way of a comparative examination of the earlier views. Hence, we proceed to discuss first the three terms involved in the aforesaid definition, namely, Lakṣaṇā, Śakyasambandha and Tātparyānupapatti.

The term Lakṣaṇā in the Kārikā above, obviously, is with reference to Viśvanātha's earlier contention that Vṛtti is the relation consisting in either Śakti or Lakṣaṇā. After having discussed the issues connected with Śakti and Śakyārtha, the author now proceeds to divulge the nature of Lakṣaṇā.

LAKṢAṆĀ : Ideas are found to be conveyed or atleast sought to be conveyed metaphorically in all existing literatures of the word. This metaphor, we may say, is the English word popularly used for what we call a Lakṣaṇā.[289] As Gonda has rightly observed,[290] the metaphorical use found place in languages even of the primitive people. Comparison is the basis of all metaphorical expressions. The process of comparision which is easily traced back to primitive writings and which comes to be extensively developed in later literary works is undoubtedly the basis of figures of speech like Rūpaka and Atiśayokti. But these figures of speech clearly exhibit the involvement of Lakṣaṇā in them. Here we may take an example from the Vedic literature itself. The hymn 'dvā suparṇā'[291] wherein the Jīvātman and Paramātman have been described as two birds, is quoted in the Kāvyamīmāṁsā by Rājaśekhara[292] to show the presence of 'alaṁkāra' in the Vedic writings and is taken by Paṇḍitarāja Jagannātha[293] to illustrate 'Atiśayokti'. In either case, we may be sure of the presence of Lakṣaṇā (of Sādhyāvasānā type, if we speak after the Ālaṁkā rikas) in the description. Thus we observe the occurrence of Lakṣaṇā even in Vedic writings.

To make a brief study in retrospect of the treatment of Lakṣaṇā, we are to mention Yaska first. Yaska discusses the various Upamā s (in comparing unknown things with wellknown ones) and in that context, gives examples of Luptopamā in 'Siṁhaḥ' 'vyāghraḥ' etc.[294] These uses of Yāska, came to give expressions like 'siṁho mānavakaḥ' which are some stock examples of Lakṣaṇā in later theoretical works. Durgācārya's commentary also confirms our ideas.[295] This 'luptopamā' is sought in later times to be identified as Rūpaka which, beyond any doubt, involves what we call a Lakṣaṇā. Thus many examples of Lakṣaṇā without being named as such occur in Yāska's work. The concept of the phenomenon, however, emerges out only in later writings. Most of the different schools of Indian thought have accepted Śabda (Verbal testimony) as one of the Pramāṇas. Consequently in their treatment of Śabda, the scholars of these schools have examined the nature of meaning and as such naturally they have dealt with the concept and process as well of the so-called Lakṣaṇā. As a result, the discussion on Lakṣaṇā figures in the writings of Phiolosophers, Grammarians and Rhetoricians of Ancient India.

Of the Mīmāṁsakas, Jaimini, the founder of the school, as a believer in the natural theory of meaning maintains that the words and their corresponding meanings stand in an inherent relation. The words have inherent potentiality to convey their own meanings.[296] Such meanings as are conveyed by the words through their inherent potentiality are understood as soon as the words come to be heard. Hence these meanings are called 'Śrutyartha' and the significative potentiality of words is called 'śruti'.[297] In certain cases, however, these śrutyarthas come to be irrelevant to the context with all chances to mislead the listener. But in certain cases, this irrelevance is removed by means of conveying a secondary significance. This suggestion comes from Jaimini himself when he asserts that if it is taken as a figurative expression, (Guṇa or Gauṇī Prayoga), the expression (found to be irrelevant earlier) is felt to be meaningful.[298] In this manner Jaimini recognises the concept of what in later times comes to be popularly known as Lakṣaṇā. It may be briefly noted that the term Bhakti was used by Jaimini in the sense of secondary signification (Lakṣaṇā) in the sūtra III.2.43.[299] In the said sūtra, the expression 'īndrapītasya' is being taken as a Bahuvrīhi Compound and not as a Tatpuruṣa.[300] Here (i.e. in 'bhaktipānasya') Jaimini uses the term 'bhakti' in the sense of Lakṣaṇā. This interpretation is sought to be ascribed to an earlier authority named Aitiśāyana.[301] If so, the concept of Bhakti may be traced back to a date much earlier than that of Jaimini. Bādarāyaṇa, the author of the *Brahmasūtra* is evidently earlier than Jaimini as Jaimini is found to have referred to Bādarāyaṇa in the sūtra 1.1.5.[302] We find the concept of secondary signification as well as the term 'Bhakti' in Bādarāyaṇa also. But this Aitiśāyana, referred to by Jaimini, may be earlier even than Bādarāyaṇa as the works of Aitisāyana are not yet available. We come across Jaimini's use of the term Bhakti once again in the Ākṣepa sūtra.[304] Though we donot find Jaimini using the familiar term Lakṣaṇā, it may be that he uses the term 'Lakṣaṇā', in the same sense in the sūtra III.1.14.[305] in as much as we find a case of secondary signification as admitted by him therein. This is clear from Śabara's[306] commentary. We may further note that only the later Mīmāṁsakas maintain a distinction between Lakṣaṇā and Guṇavṛtti. Jaimini and his Bhāsyakāra, Śabarasvāmin use the term Guṇavṛtti, Bhakti and Lakṣaṇa or Lakṣaṇā without much discrimination.

We shall have to bear in mind, however, that though Jaimini recognises the scope of secondary signification, he also prefers a direct signification to an indirect one.[307] We shall have to make a special discussion on this attitude of Jaimini in the context of our examination of text of Viśvanātha's *Muktāvalī* on Lakṣaṇā, 'ata eva niṣādasthapatiṁ yājayet' etc.

In the Bhāṣya of Śabarasvāmin, we find the use of the term Lakṣaṇā very often and in many cases side by side with the term Śruti.[308] It may be that Jaimini's 'Lakṣaṇā' itself comes to be converted into Lakṣaṇā by way of making it a word in the feminine gender for the sake of analogy with the term Śruti. Śabara follows his sūtrakāra very faithfully by way of showing partiality to primary signification in case of conflict with a secondary one. In his assessment, Śruti is stronger than Lakṣaṇā.[309] A very interesting example of Śabara's avoiding Lakṣaṇā in preference to Śruti is provided by his treatment of a statement like 'udbhidā yajeta' in 'udbhid adhikaraṇa'. While commenting on the MS III.2.1., Śabara characterises a secondary sense as a 'jaghanyārtha'. His explanation is this: the primary meaning is called 'mukhya' as because it appears primarily like a face (what appears earlier than other parts of the body) and the secondary meaning is called 'jaghanya' as it comes after the primary meaning just like a hinder part (jaghana) appearing after the face (Mukha).[310] It is worth mentioning that Śabara aims at showing a distinction between Guṇavṛtti and Lakṣaṇā.[311] But we feel that a clear cut definition of Lakṣaṇā along with a line of demarcation between the two broad divisions of Lakṣaṇā, namely, Guṇavṛtti and Lakṣaṇā, has not emerged out during the days of Śabara.

Coming to the Bhāṭṭa school of the Mīmāṁsakas, we find that a high status to the secondary signification is given by Kumārila Bhaṭṭa as he accepts Lakṣaṇā in each and every sentence. According to him, the words individually convey their respective meanings in the form of a 'universal' (Jāti). The power of primary signification (Abhidhā or Śakti) is exhausted in accordance with the maxim 'Śabdabuddhikarmaṇāṁ viramya vyāpārābhāvaḥ'.

The meanings primarily conveyed by the words through Abhidhā, therefore, come to give the sentence meaning (Vākyā rtha) through Lakṣaṇā. This view of Kumārila is merely the development of the idea contained in a sūtra of Jaimini.[312] The earlier thinkers also feel that the sentence meaning is not conveyed by Abhidhā but by 'some other function'.[313] But as the so-called 'some other function', was not earlier spelled out, Kumārila is the first scholar to point out that it is the Lakṣaṇā function which operates to convey the sentence meaning in each and every sentence.[314] Kumārila, moreover, finds scope under Jaimini Sūtra 1.4.22[315] to give his own idea of Guṇavṛtti and Lakṣaṇā and as well on their mutual difference.[316] Kumārila is supported by his followers like Pārthasārathi-Miśra[317] and Nārayana Bhaṭṭa.[318] Coming to the Prābhākara school, we find that Prabhākara Miśra uses the terms Upacāra, Guṇa and Bhakti for secondary signification under various contexts.[319] His illustration of Upacāra, 'kuntā n praveśaya' may be said to have been modelled precisely on the example 'yaṣṭīḥ praveśaya' and 'yaṣṭikaṁ bhojaya' given by Vā tsyāyana under NS II.2.62.[320] Prabhākara's illustration of Guṇavṛtti is 'gaurvāhikaḥ',[321] Śālikanātha, the follower of

Prabhākara, presents the view of Kumārila and asserts that Lakṣaṇā cannot be resorted to in each and every sentence. It can be resorted to only when the primary meaning of a word comes to be discarded as in 'gaṅgāyāṁ ghoṣaḥ.[322]

Śālikanātha finally analyses the concept of Lakṣaṇā in the light of Prabhākara and for that purpose adds a 'saṁgraha śloka'[323] as the definition of Lakṣaṇā which we find utilized in the *Tattvacintāmaṇi* by Gaṅgeśa. We find here two indispensable factors admitted by Śālikanātha. (i) Anupapatti which is Anvayā nupapatti and not Tātparyānupapatti in marked difference with Viśvanātha Nyāya Pañcānana; (ii) Saṁbandha (between the primary and secondary concepts). Here we find a new concept evolved in place of 'avinābhāvasaṁbandha' and 'ekavākyatā' of the Bhāṭṭas. Rāmānujācārya, the author of the *Tantra Rahasya*, a work of the Prābhākara school, re-establishes the view already expressed by Śālikanātha.[324]

In the Vedānta school we find that Bādarāyaṇa recognises the secondary signification under discussion either as Gauṇī or as Bhākta prayoga. But we can make some more ideas regarding Bādarāyaṇa's notion of secondary signification only from Śaṅkara's commentary on the *Brahmasūtras*. In addition to the above two terms, Śaṅkara uses the terms Upacāra and Guṇavāda also. Śaṅkara finds an occasion to expound the notion of Lakṣaṇā in connection with BS II. 3.1. & II.3.3.[325] It is held that the scriptural statement on the origin of Ākāśa[326] should be treated as Gauṇī (Figurative expressions). Saṅkara cites parallels.[327] We are to take note of Bādarāyana's mention of the term 'Bhākta' and Saṅkara's comments in that context.[328]

Of the Grammarians, Patañjali is the earliest to recognise the phenomenon of the transference of epithet which is nothing other than what we call a Lakṣaṇā. Though he does not mention the terms Lakṣaṇā or Guṅavṛtti, he comes to refer to the practice of using a certain word for something other than what it usually stands for.[329] His examples of transference of epithets, we may note, are precisely the examples of Lakṣaṇā as have been recognised by later theorists.

Bhartṛhari comes to use the term Guṇa alone for the secondarily signified meaning. He details, however, the different views regarding the nature of 'gauṇa artha' and its difference from 'mukhya artha' as propounded by different authorities. He opines that the sentence conveys its meaning as a whole and in the total meaning of the sentence the individual word-meanings retain very little of their individual identity. While illustrating this point, Bhartṛhari gives some expressions which in later times come to serve as stock-examples of some or other variety of Lakṣaṇā. For example, the example 'Kākebhyo dadhi rakṣyatāṁ' may be said to have originated from Bhartṛhari's 'Kākebhyo rakṣyatām sarpiḥ'.[330] In later works, this has been recognised as an example of 'Upalakṣaṇa' or as a case of Ajahatsvārthā or of an Upādānalakṣaṇā. It is to be noted that nowhere in his work Bhartṛhari has mentioned the term Lakṣaṇā. Of the later Grammarians, Nāgeśa shows origninality in his approach to the concept of Lakṣaṇā as we find him in his *Paramalaghumañjuṣā*. He is found adding 'tādarthya' to the factors recognised by Patañjali and the illustration given in the context by Nāgeśa is 'amī indrāḥ'. He concedes to the position of the Naiyāyikas like Viśvanātha Nyāyapañcānana in respect of the nature of Lakṣaṇā. He discusses as to whether Tātparyānupapatti or Anvayānupapatti is the Lakṣaṇābīja and finally decides in favour of Tātparyānupapatti.[331] We propose to discuss the issue elaborately in the context of our examining the relevant text of the *Muktāvalī*. As we have already pointed out, Nāgeśa, however, observes that Lakṣaṇā is not a secondary function but is also a Śakti, i.e., a denotative potentiality of the word itself in respect of the so-called secondary meaning. There is, however, as he maintains, one difference between the Śakti that conveys the idea of 'the current' and the Śakti which gives the idea of 'the bank'. The earlier Śakti is 'Prasiddhā' and the latter is 'aprasiddhā'. The 'prasiddhā' Śakti is familiar to one and all irrespective of possession or lack of intelligence while the 'aprasiddhā' śakti is familiar only to the connoisseurs.[332] The classification of Śakti into Prasiddhā and Aprasiddhā varieties seems to be modelled on the principle of distinguishing the Mukhya and Gauṅa arthas on the basis of 'siddhi' (Prasiddhi) and 'asiddhi' (Aprasiddhi) as propounded by Bhartṛhari.[333] It may be added that Nāgeśa admits here a role to be played by Tātparya in the matter of a word's conveying a meaning only by means of Śakti.[334] In the circle of Ālaṁkārikas, it is observed, that the phenomenon of secondary function does not come to lime light till Ānandavardhana's time. A fringe of speculation in this regard is, however, noticed in the *Kāvyālaṁkāra* of Bhāmaha, the first systematic writer on the science of poetry.[335] An observation of Abhinavagupta confirms our idea (Vide fn 335) in the matter.[336] Daṇḍin following Bhāmahācārya clearly recognises Guṇavṛtti as the cause of certain Alaṁkāras and recommends its acceptance for the purpose of removing Grāmyatādoṣa in poetry.[337] Vāmana comes to use the term Lakṣaṇā in the sense of secondary signification in general, covering thereby what is called Gauṇī Vṛtti by the Mīmāṁsakas. As classified by Vāmana, Lakṣaṇā is of two varieties, one based on the relation of similarity and the other depending on the relation other than similarity.[338] Notwithsanding his great anxiety to establish Vyañjanā as an independent function, Ānandavardhana deals with the nature and scope of the secondary signification. Ānanda uses the term Guṇavṛtti in a wider sense so as to cover all possible varieties of secondary signification. His use of the term 'amukhyavṛtti' also comes only as a description of this Guṇavṛtti.[339] Thus Ānanda's Guṇavṛtti is not identical with the Gauṇīvṛtti of the Mīmāṁsakas or with the Gauṇī variety of Lakṣaṇā of the later Ālaṁkārikas. It appears to us that he uses the word 'guṇa' in the sense of a subordinate element and not in the sense of qualities. To the contrary, Abhinavagupta understands this word 'guṇa' in the sense of 'dharma' and still covers both the Gauṇī and Śuddhā varieties of Lakṣaṇā by the term Guṇavṛtti. Bhojarāja also in his *Śṛṅgāraprakāśa* still seeks to maintain a line of demarcation between Guṇavṛtti and Lakṣaṇā.[340] Lakṣaṇā, however, comes to receive very elaborate treatment with the later Ālaṁkārikas like Mammaṭa, Hemacandra and Viśvanātha. The definition of Lakṣaṇā as given by Mammaṭa set the standard for all the later Ālaṁkārikas.[341] From Mammaṭa onward Lakṣaṇā came to be a generic name for all the later varieties of secondary signification including the Guṇavṛtti. Later Ālaṁkārikas insist on the fulfilment of three conditions, (1) Mukhyārthabādha or the failure of the primary meaning, (2) Tadyoga or the relation of the primary sense with the secondary one and (3) Ruḍhi or Prayojana, the usage or motive.[342] In the works of the later Ālaṁkārikas Lakṣaṇā received such an elaborate treatment that it has been shown to have as many as eighty sub-varieties.[343]

Now we proceed to examine the history of the concept of Lakṣaṇā in the school of Naiyāyikas. As we are primarily concerned with the treatment of Lakṣaṇā by the Naiyāyika Viśvanā tha, the history of the origin and development of the concept of Lakṣaṇā in the Nyāya school of thought is naturally of special interest to us.

We meet with the terms Bhākta and Upacāra in Gautama's *Nyāyaśutra* itself. These very terms have come to be popularly used in the later times for identifiying the phenomenon of secondary signification. Gautama uses the term Bhākta only once in the sūtra 2.2.15,[344] But there is very little in the sūtra itself to make us understand as to what is technically implied by this term. The sūtra in question is concerned with the probable meanings of the term 'nitya' (tattva) or 'a so-called state of nitya' (i.e., Bhākta). That such a line of demarcation is intended to be drawn by the sūtra may be gathered with the help of the *Bhāṣya*. But the *Bhāṣya* also does not explain the term Bhākta immediately under the sūtra very elaborately. The question in the context is whether 'ghaṭābhā va' can be called 'nitya' or not. The Bhāṣyakāra first explains the 'tattva' (the genuine state of nitya) and then concludes that the word 'nitya' in respect of the 'ghaṭābhāva' is 'Bhākta and as such 'similar to 'nitya' and not 'nitya as it is'.[345]

The Bhāṣyakāra, however, gets an opportunity to speak a little more about the 'Bhākta Prayogas' under the sūtra 4.1.16. The question as posed by Gautama in NS 4.1.14 is whether a 'Sat' may arise from 'asat' or not. In support of the earlier alternative, the Bhāṣyakāra supplies the illustration that the 'aṅkura' (the sprouting) rises after demolishing the 'bīja' (seed) implying thereby that the non-existence of the seed caused by the demolishing is the pre-condition for the origin of the 'aṅkura'. At this stage, an objection is raised by the sūtrakāra (in Sūtra 4.1.15)[346] saying that the 'aṅkura must be already there before the demolishing of the 'bīja' as the very agent of the act of demolishing. If the 'aṅkura' would not have been already present it would not have been described as the agent for the said action as in the expression 'bījamupamṛdya aṅkuraḥ prādurbhavati.' In reply to the objection it is pointed out in the Sūtra 4.1.16[347] that even what has already ceased to be or what is yet to come into existence may be described as agent. Explaining this position the Bhāṣyakāra gives a number of illustrations like 'ajātāḥ putrāḥ pitaraṁ tāpayanti' and concludes that such 'bhākta prayogas' are numerous.[348] Then he questions himself as to what is the guiding factor for such a Bhakti (i.e., a 'bhā ktaprayoga') and replies that an immediacy is the guiding factor for Bhakti in respect of the example of 'bīja and aṅkura'. Because of an immediacy of the origin of the 'aṅkura', it is justified to call the agent of the act of demolishing an instance of 'bhākta prayoga' and though admittedly the 'aṅkura' is not the real agent.[349] It may be noticed that the Bhāṣyakāra uses both the terms Bhākta and Bhakti. But even after all illustrations, a clear picture of Bhakti does not emerge out from his elucidations. The Sūtrakāra himself mentions certain factors or relations which guide the use of words with secondary signification in the Sūtra 2.2.64.[350] But the factor of immediacy (ānantarya) does not occur in the list given by the Sūtrakāra. The Bhāṣyakāra again uses the expressions under Sūtra 1.2.14[351] where it seems to stand for all sorts of secondary significations in general. We find Gautama using the term 'Upacāra' in as many as seven sūtras. The first use of the word is made for naming the third variety of 'chala' as 'upacārachala' in sūtra 1.2.14[352] He repeats it again in the following sūtra. The meaning of the sūtra defining 'upacārachala' is not so much clear. As explained by the Bhāṣyakāra, Upacārachala is the conceit involved in a listener's pretention to have understood the statement in its literal sense, while it is intended by the speaker to convey the idea of a 'dharmavikalpa', i.e., a transference of epithet. The example given here by the Bhāṣyakāra is 'mañcāḥ krośanti'. Where the listeners take the literal sense and raise the objection that it is the people belonging to the platform are crying and not the platforms themselves.[353] Here the Bhāṣyakāra explains the phenomenon of Upacāra as signifying something by a word, which is other than a literal meaning. He points out that the transference of epithet (Upacāra) must be guided by certain definite relations like 'sahacaraṇa' etc.[354] As we have already noted, the relations of 'sahacaraṇa' etc. are given by the Sūtrakāra himself in the Sūtra 2.2.64.

In the context of discussing Śabdaśakti, Gautama at one stage maintains that a word denotes an universal (Jāti). If the idea of an individual (Vyakti) is gathered from such a word it is because of a transference of epithet.[355] This transference of epithet is, in the words of Gautama, 'atadbhāve'pi tadupacāraḥ'.[356] In the Sūtra concerned, he says, such a transference of epithet is guided by any one of the relations of 'sahacaraṇa', 'sthāna' etc. The relations and corresponding examples are as follows - Sahacaraṇam-yaṣṭīkaṁ bhojaya etc. Gautama gives only the token standing either for the secondarily signified meaning as in the case of the word 'brāhmaṇa' or for the original word itself involving such a secondary signification as in the case of the word 'mañca'. These token examples are fully elaborated by the Bhāṣyakāra along with an explanation of the term 'atadbhāve'pi tadupacāraḥ'. The explanation enables us to understand that 'atadbhāve'pi' etc. easily as the transference of epithet.[357] The Naiyāyikas of the old school have invariably accepted the position of the Sūtrakāra and the Bhāṣyakāra. Factually the Naiyāyikas immediately following Gautama and Vātsyāyana do contribute very little towards the development of the concept of Lakṣaṇā. Towards the close of the line of the old Naiyāyikas, Jayantabhaṭṭa, the author of the *Nyāyamañjarī*, speaks about the distinction between the Gauṇīvṛtti and the Lakṣaṇā.[358] While explaining the 'upacārachala' he shows that the speaker might make a statement involving either a Gauṇīvṛtti or a Lakṣaṇā with the intention of conveying a secondary sense so as to be wrongly understood by the listener in the primary sense itself. In this context, he finds it essential to show the distinction between a 'gauṇa' and a 'lākṣaṇika prayoga'. We propose to consider this distinction maintained by Jayantabhaṭṭa in the context of our examining the examples of Lakṣaṇā in the *Muktāvalī*.

Gaṅgeśopādhyāya has discussed the operation of Lakṣaṇā Vṛtti in the Śaktivāda section of the Śabda Khaṇḍa, the fourth part of his work, *Tattvacintāmaṇi*. He defines Lakṣaṇā as a seperate Vṛtti of words to bring forth a secondary meaning for getting involved in a syntactical relation with a primary meaning of other words where the primary meaning of a word fails to do so.[359] Gaṅgeśa seems to follow the view of the Prābhākaras so far as the conception of Lakṣaṇā is concerned. This idea can be gathered from his agreeably quoting a verse[360] which means : When the primary meaning of an individual word fails to get involved in a syntactical relation of the sentence meaning, it brings another meaning having a relation with itself so as to have syntactical relation. This very process is called Lakṣaṇā. This verse can be traced to Śālikanātha who cites it as a definition of Lakṣaṇā .[361]

From the definition of Lakṣaṇā given by Gaṅgeśa, we observe that the operation of Lakṣaṇā is based on two factors. They are (i) Śakyārthasambandha and (ii) Anvayānupapatti. Regarding the first factor, we may bear in mind that the Sambandha, i.e., Śakyārthasambandha for Viśvanātha, is not merely a factor for the operation of Lakṣaṇā, but is the Lakṣaṇā itself. With regard to the second factor maintained by Gaṅgeśa for the operation of Lakṣaṇā, i.e., Anvayānupapatti, there is a series of counter arguments of the opponents which have been discussed at length by the author of the *Tattvacintāmaṇi*. He finally establishes that the Anvayānupapatti and not the Tātparyānupapatti is the Lakṣaṇābīja (the ground for the operation of Lakṣaṇā). Viśvanātha Nyāyapañcānana believes in the Tātparyānupapatti as the Lakṣaṇābīja. Hence we shall get an opportunity again for discussing the position of Gaṅgeśa in this context. We may simply comment here that from the Nyāya point of view, Gaṅgeśa's assertion is a queer one and that his notion of Lakṣaṇābīja comes to be rejected by his successors like Viśvanātha and Jagadīśa.

We shall have to admit however, that it is Gaṅgeśopādhyāya who comes first to detail the process of Lakṣaṇā at length. He covers new issues in his wider and peculiar plan of discussion of the problem. His mode and range of observations have very largely influenced the author of the *Bhāṣāpariccheda*.

ŚAKYASAMBANDHAḤ : As we have observed earlier, with the earlier Naiyāyikas, the concept of Lakṣaṇā was yet to take a full shape. In the circle of the later Naiyāyikas including Viśvanā tha, Lakṣaṇā comes to be described as a Śakyasambandha or Svaśakyasambandha.[362] The term Śakya stands for the Śakyārtha. Hence the expression, 'śakyasambandhaḥ' may be expounded as 'śakyasya śakyārthasya sambandhaḥ'. By virtue of this assertion, the Naiyāyikas have maintained a difference with the Mīmāṁsakas and the Ālaṁkārikas in the context of the concept of Lakṣaṇā. The Lakṣyārtha is universally understood as the secondary meaning or the meaning next only to the primary meaning. All have accepted that the Lakṣyārtha stands in a specific relation with the primary meaning. But the Naiyāyikas have gone to the extreme in this direction in so far as they maintain that the very relation of the primary meaning with a newer meaning, i.e. a secondary meaning is the Lakṣaṇā Vṛtti. The

Prābhākara Mīmāṁsakas were quite categorical in maintaining that Lakṣaṇā is brought into operation by a relation of the primary meaning (the relation being with regard to another meaning which comes to be designated as the Lakṣyārtha.)[363] The Bhāṭṭas also admitted Lakṣaṇā as being based on a relation of the denoted sense of the word that signifies a secondary sense.[364] The Ālaṁkārikas except Paṇḍitarāja Jagannātha have conceived the relation between the primary and the secondary meanings occurring in a case of Lakṣaṇā as one of the pre-requisites for the operation of the Lakṣaṇā concerned.[365] Jagannātha, however, fully corroborates the view of the Naiyāyikas that the very relation of the denoted sense with a secondary one is Lakṣaṇā.[366] In the circle of the Vedāntins also, Lakṣaṇā is described as a Śakyasambandha.[367] But here we must be cautious to avoid a confusion. For the Naiyāyikas, a Śakya (artha) i.e., a meaning conveyed by Śakti is invariably a Padārtha (i.e., the meaning of an individual word). But for the Vedāntins, a Śakya (artha) may be both a Padārtha and a Vākyārtha (i.e., the total meaning of a sentence). Though the Vedāntins do not conceive Śakti as pertaining to a Vākya, they cherish the notion that Śakti brings about the relational thought (in the form of the syntactical connection of the word-meanings)which constitutes a Vākyārtha. So, in the view of the Vedāntins, Lakṣaṇā in the form of a 'śakyasambandha' is possible not only in a Pada but also in a Vākya.[368] As against this, the Naiyāyikas conceive only a Padalakṣaṇā. It is because, as viewed by the Naiyāyikas, only a Pada is denotative or what is possessed of a Śakti. As the Vākyārtha is in no way a Śakyārtha in the sense of being conveyed by a Śakti, Lakṣaṇā as a Śakyārthasambandha is never possible with regard to a Vākya.

In the circle of the Mīmāṁsakas, the primary meaning (the relation of which with a newer meaning, i.e., Lakṣyārtha, is stated to be the basis for a Lakṣaṇā) is described as 'svabodhya', 'svajñāpya' and sometimes 'svaśakya' also. These terms, in the sense of the primary meaning, are applicable not only to a Padārtha but also to a Vākyārtha. While in the Bhāṭṭa school the primary meaning is the meaning of an individual word, in the school of Prābhākaras, it may be the total meaning of a sentence. As we know, the Prābhākaras maintain that Abhidhā does not rest with the conveying of the meanings of the individual words. Abhidhā, in their view, extends itself to bring out the total meaning in a sentence, i.e., a Vākyārtha.

TĀTPARYĀNUPAPATTITAḤ : Viśvanātha defines Tātparya in the succeeding Kārikā as 'Vakturicchā, (the intention of the speaker). Here in the foregoing Kārikā, he wants to maintain that the Tātparyānupapatti (the failure of the speaker's intention) is the Lakṣaṇābīja (the ground for the operation of a Lakṣaṇā).

It is universally accepted that the operation of Lakṣaṇā is possible where there is some incompatibility of the primary meaning (mukhyārthabādha);[369] but a very strong controversy exists as to whether this incompatibility is due to the failure of a syntactical relation among the words in a sentence (Anvayānupapatti) or the failure of the intention of the speaker, i.e., the failure of the denotating word or words to convey the intended sense or senses (Tātparyānupapatti). Mīmāṁsakas, some Naiyāyikas like Gaṅgeśopādhyāya and the Ālaṁkārikas, hold that the operation of Lakṣaṇā is caused by the Anvayānupapatti. The Vedāntins, Grammarians and some of the later Naiyāyikas hold an opposite view as they consider Tātparyānupapatti as the Lakṣaṇābīja. It is to be noted that the earlier Bhāṭṭa Mīmāṁsakas who admit Lakṣaṇā for understanding every sentence-meaning[370] do not subscribe to either of the aforesaid views. But some later Bhāṭṭa-Mīmāṁsakas have come to accept the necessity of a Lakṣaṇābīja. Gāgābhaṭṭa, as for illustration, admits Śakyārthānvayānupapatti (the failure of the denoted sense to stand the required syntactical connection) as the determining factor for the operation of a Lakṣaṇā.[371] Tātparyānupapatti is not obviously accepted by the Bhāṭṭas as it is not possible for them to encourage any free play in the intention of a Speaker in the context of Vedic statements. Even in case of popular statements, it is not possible to accept Tātparyānupapatti as the Lakṣaṇābīja. As for instance, in 'yaṣṭīḥ praveśaya', the primary mening of the word 'pravesaya' in the sense of fetching for the purpose of feeding (bhojanaprayojanaka praveśanaparatva) cannot be logically connected with the primary meaning of the word Yaṣṭī in so far as the sticks are not competent to take food. Hence in order to remove the incompatibility, Lakṣaṇā is resorted to,for conveying a relevant secondary sense of the term 'yaṣṭīḥ', i.e., the persons holding the sticks (Yaṣṭīdhara). Thus Lakṣaṇā arises out of an Anvayānupapatti.[372]

Prabhākara and his followers substantiate that the 'Anvayā nupapatti' of the primary meanings leads to the operation of Lakṣaṇā.[373] They hold that it is Abhidhā that conveys the syntactically related meanings (anvitārtha) of the words in a sentence. But if there arises any inconsistancy in the syntactical connection of the senses, then Lakṣaṇā comes to operate to remove the inconsistency involved. In doing so Lakṣaṇa conveys a different meaning of a word the primary meaning of which fails to secure the desirable syntactical connection. The meaning conveyed by Lakṣaṇā comes to be consistently connected with the primary meaning of the other words which stand already mutually related. Regarding this problem of the basic condition for the operation of Lakṣaṇā, the Ālaṁkārikas appear to have followed the footsteps of the Prābhākaras. In their view also, when the primary meaning of a word is logically incompatible with rest of the sentence, Lakṣaṇā function is resorted to for bringing into comprehension a new meaning connected with the failing primary meaning of the word.[374] As we have already noticed, Gaṅgeśa makes an unusual departure from the trend of thought prevailing in his own circle. Of the Naiyāyikas, he comes forward to rally behind the Prābhā karas in the context of the problem of Lakṣaṇābīja.

We find Gaṅgeśa presenting vast material in the Śaktivāda section of Śabdakhaṇḍa of his work. We meet therein with series of arguments and counter-arguments presented by this erudite Navya Nyāya scholar in search of an answer to the problem of Lakṣaṇābīja. His treatment of the subject is undoubtedly confusing. We present below our impression of Gaṅgeśa only as far as we can understand him.

Lakṣaṇā in the *Tattvacintāmaṇi* is a separate verbal function that comes to operate when the primary meaning of a particular word fails to get duly involved in a syntactical connection with the primary meanings of the other words in the same sentence.[375] Now this relation of that particular incompatible primary meaning (Śakyasambandha) with the relevant secondary meaning is identified as the Lakṣaṇāvṛtti. The Lakṣaṇāvṛtti which is nothing but the aforesaid Śakyasambandha comes to convey the idea of the relevant secondary sense which as a substitute for the abandoned primary meaning duly gets involved in the syntactical relation of the entire sentence. Thus we find that with Gaṇgeśa, the Anvayānupapatti is the Lakṣaṇābīja. After having refuted the arguments of opponents, he finally decides that the incompatibility of a primary meaning of a valid word to get involved in a syntactical relation of meanings of words in a sentence is the fundamental factor for the operation of a Lakṣaṇā. This Anvayānupapatti is what immediately strikes the mind of a listener. Tātparya or the intention of a speaker is obviously a remote factor. If we accept Tātparyānupapatti as the Lakṣaṇābīja, then in a valid case of Lakṣaṇā, the relevant Tātparya will be the intention of the speaker in respect of conveying a particular secondary sense. Under this circumstance, a case of Lakṣaṇā would surely involve the fallacy of a logical gig - saw. It is because for arriving at the idea of the secondary meaning one must already have the idea of the intention of the speaker in respect of the same secondary sense. That is how it 'begs the question' or involves the fallacy of Anyonyāśraya.[376] Gaṅgeśa shows by way of illustrating 'gaṅgāyāṁ ghoṣaḥ' that the knowledge of an Anvayānupapatti comes necessarily before that of Tātparya with regard to what is sought to be conveyed as Lakṣyārtha. Gaṅgeśa does not seem to intend the total rejection of Tātparya. But he seriously contends that only Anvayānupapatti can genuinely prepare the ground for the operation of Lakṣaṇā. It is because of the immediacy of its occurrance to the mind of the listener. Gaṅgeśa asserts the status of Anvayānupapatti as the Lakṣaṇābīja, fully independent of Tā tparya. Even in the examples like 'yaṣṭīḥ praveśaya' and 'chatriṇo yānti' we may accept 'Anvayānupapatti' as the 'Lakṣaṇābīja'. In 'yaṣṭīḥ praveśaya' for instance, the word 'yaṣṭī' is incompatible to get related with the primary meaning of the word 'praveśaya' atleast in the context of a feast. Again in the example, 'chatriṇo yā nti' the primary meaning of the word 'chatriṇaḥ' is incompatible with the primary meaning of the word 'yānti' in the context of movement of a group comprising of carriers and non-carriers of umbrellas.

One may argue that the context determining the Anvayānupapatti also, simultaneously leads to the knowledge of Tātparya with regard to the relevant Lakṣyārtha. It may be argued further that the Tatparyānupapatti in the sense of incompatibility of the primary meaning of the particular word with regard to that very Tātparya should be regarded as Lakṣaṇābīja. Gaṅgeśa forcefully rejects such a logic. In the event of admitting Tatparyānupapatti as the Lakṣaṇābīja, Gaṅgeśa argues, even in the light of above arguments, one shall have to admit the presence of that particular Lakṣyārtha prior to the operation of Lakṣaṇāvṛtti. In case the scope for both Tātparyānupapatti and Anvayānupapatti is to be admitted, Gaṅgeśa maintains, the knowledge of an Anvayānupapatti would necessarily precede that of a Tātparyā nupapatti. Gaṅgeśa in this respect is supported by Jānakīnātha Bhaṭṭācāryya also.[377] Now in the Nyāya school of thought, we come across the other opposite view with regard to the fundamental condition for the operation of a Lakṣaṇā. In the older school of Nyāya, of course, we find no concrete proof to the recognition of Tātparyānupapatti as the Lakṣaṇābīja. Jayantabhaṭṭa, a Prācīna

Naiyāyika accepts Tātparya as a function for conveying a relational thought.[378] According to him, Abhidhā conveys the individual word-meanings which constitute the sentence-meaning is further conveyed by the Tātparyavṛtti. Already we have referred to the Navya Naiyāyikas, generally accepting only the Tātparyānupapatti as the Lakṣaṇābīja. (Of the Navya Naiyā yikas, as we have already mentioned, Gaṅgeśopādhyāya is an extraordinary exception). The Navya Naiyāyikas accepting Tā tparyānupapatti as the Lakṣaṇābīja have actually taken the clue from Jayantabhaṭṭa to prepare the ground for formulating their theory in the context. But they maintain their difference from Jayantabhaṭṭa in the sense that they do not admit Tātparya as a Verbal function but as one of the four factors for a Śabdabodha. They advocate that whenever there is the incompatibility of the primary meaning of a word with reference to Tātparya (Speaker's intention), Lakṣaṇā comes in to remove the incompatibility by way of conveying a secondary but intended meaning. We gather this impression of the Navya Naiyāyikas from later writers like Jagadīśa and Viśvanātha. These scholars have come to discard unhesitatingly the views of their respectable pioneer Gaṅgeśopā dhyāya. Jagadīśa in his *Śabdaśaktiprakāśikā* opposes the Ālaṁkā rikas in their bid to make Anvayānupapatti the fundamental condition for the operation of Lakṣaṇā. He observes that the knowledge of Anvayānupapatti cannot lead to the idea of a Lakṣaṇā as the rule is vitiated in cases like 'yaṣṭīḥ praveśaya.'[379] Viśvanātha's views in this regard will be discussed more elaborately later on. Annaṁbhaṭṭa who succeeded Viśvanātha maintains that the cause of Lakṣaṇā is the non-intelligibility of the intention.[380]

With regard to the Lakṣaṇābīja, the Vedāntins are found holding the same view with the Naiyāyikas. According to them Lakṣaṇā operates only when there arises the inconsistency of primary meanings in respect of the intention of the speaker. Dharmarājādhvarīndra, in this *Vedānta Paribhāṣā*, refutes the views of Prābhākara, and Ālamkārikas and asserts that Lakṣanā is caused by the non-intelligibility of the 'purport' and not that of any 'syntactical relation'. For instance, in 'kākebhyo dadhi rakṣyatām', there is no inconsistency with regard to the syntactical relation in the sentence. Yet there is Lakṣaṇā because of a Tātparyānupapatti.[381] Here, by resorting to Lakṣaṇā' the consistent intended meaning of the word 'kākebhyaḥ' has been restored. The intention of the speaker here is to mean all the creatures that spoil the curd.

Likewise, the Grammarians also hold the same view with the Navya Naiyāyikas. According to them Lakṣaṇā comes for operation because of a Tātparyānupapatti. As for instance, Nāgeśa holds that if Tātparyānupapatti be not accepted as the determining factor for the operation of a Lakṣaṇā, in the expression 'gaṅgā yāṁ ghoṣa' the word 'ghoṣa' may mean an aquatic creature by Lakṣaṇā. Again in the expression, 'nakṣatraṁ dṛṣṭvā vācaṁ visṛjet', Lakṣaṇā comes to be admitted because of a Tātparyānupapatti and not due to any sort of Anvayānupapatti.[382] But here we must be cautious to note that Nāgeśa's very recognition of Lakṣaṇā is provisional. He adds subsequently that Lakṣaṇā is only the 'aprasiddhā' (uncelebrated) type of Śakti.[383] Now to examine Viśvanātha Nyāya-Pañcānana in particular in the context of the fundamental condition for the operation of Lakṣaṇā, we skip over to certain portions of the text of his *Muktāvalī* only for the sake of systematic persuit of the issue:

'Gaṅgāyāṁ ghoṣa-------anvayānupapattistātparyānupapattirvā yatra pratisandhīyate-------- parantu yadyanvayānupapattirlakṣaṇābījaṁ syāt, tadā yaṣṭīḥ praveśayetyādau lakṣaṇā na syāt, yaṣṭīṣu praveśānvayasyā' nupapatterabhāvāt ------- evaṁ kākebhyo dadhi rakṣyatāmityādau -------- tātparyaviṣayatvāt.----- yadi cānvayānupapattirlakṣaṇābījaṁ syāt, tadā kvacit gaṅgāpadasya tīre kvacid ghoṣapadasya matsyādau lakṣaṇeti niyamo na syāt' (Vide BPS 442-43)

From the *Muktāvalī* above, it is clear that Viśvanātha fully shares the opinion of his predecessor Jagadīśa in the matter of Lakṣaṇābīja. In the foregoing Kārikā (K 82a) he precisely defines Lakṣaṇā in the form of a specific relation of the Śakyārtha (with regard to a relevant secondary sense), that comes to operate due to the incompatibility of the primary meaning in respect of the intention of the speaker. (Tātparyānupapatti). Notwithstanding Viśvanātha's reference to both Anvayānupapatti and Tātparyā nupapatti as Lakṣaṇābīja in the context of explaining the ground of his first example of Lakṣaṇā, 'gaṅgāyāṁ ghoṣaḥ', his belief in the Anvayānupapatti seems to be only initial and not final. Only to arrest an impression that he finally believes in the Anvayā nupapatti as the Lakṣaṇābīja, he hastens to add the anomalies that may crop up if the Tātparyānupapatti be not accepted as the Lakṣaṇābīja. Even in case of the example 'gaṅgāyāṁ ghoṣaḥ' where he initially refers to Anvayānupapatti as the Lakṣaṇābīja alternatively with Tātparyānupapatti, he explains in the subsequent text the difficulties involved in the event of recognising Anvayānupapatti as the fundamental condition for the operation of Lakṣaṇā. As we understand him, he wants to cover even this example under Tātparyānupapatti. His decision in respect of Tā tparyānupapatti is confirmed not only by his clear assertion in the relevant Kārikā, but also by his examples, the explanatory notes there on as well as his handling of Lakṣaṇā of words in compounds by his peculiar device of referring to 'Tātparyagrāhakas' in the *Muktāvalī* which we shall have the scope to examine in the succeeding pages.

M(30). lakṣaṇā śakyasambandha iti. gaṅgāyāṁ ghoṣa ityādau gaṅgāpadasya śakyārthe pravāharūpe ghoṣasyā' nvayānupapattistātparyānupapattirvā yatra pratisandhīyate, tatra lakṣaṇayā tīrasya bodhaḥ. sā ca śakyasambandharūpā. tathāhi-pravāharūpaśakyārthasambandhasya tīre gṛhītatvāt tīrasya smaraṇam. tataḥ śābdabodhaḥ.

Viśvanātha now proceeds to amplify his concept of Lakṣaṇā briefly hinted in the Vṛtti, 'lakṣaṇā śakyasambandhaḥ'.

To illustrate Lakṣaṇā from the latest standpoint of the Naiyāyikas, Viśvanātha brings in the example 'gaṅgāyāṁ ghoṣah'. 'Gaṅgāyāṁ ghoṣaḥ' is the foremost of the stock examples of Lakṣaṇā, that catch our notice in different works on Grammar, Philosophy and Rhetorics. We meet with this example even in the *Bhāṣyas* of Śabara and Patañjali[384] at a stage when the concept of Lakṣaṇā was yet to emerge out. We have already shown that the use of the example by Śabara and Patañjali was undoubtedly in the context of a secondary sense which finally got recognised as the Lakṣyārtha. All the later works in different schools illustrate 'gaṅgāyāṁ ghoṣaḥ' whenever the occasion of Lakṣaṇā demands.[385]

As we have already observed, Viśvanātha's admission of both Anvayānupapatti and Tātparyānupapatti as the possible 'lakṣaṇā bīja' in the case of operation of Lakṣaṇā in 'gaṅgāyāṁ ghoṣah' is only initial and not final. He makes a provisional admission of both of the much debated factors and proceeds to eliminate one of the two by way of forwarding arguments with illustrations. Viśvanātha first admits 'gaṅgāyāṁ ghoṣaḥ' as a case of Lakṣaṇā because of the knowledge of the incompatibility (anupapatti) of the word 'gaṅgā' with the word 'ghoṣa' with reference to either the syntactical connection (Anvaya) or the intention of the speaker (Tātparya). An examination of the succeeding *Muktāvalī* text, 'yadi cānvayānupapattirlakṣaṇābījaṁ syāt tadā kvacid gaṅgāpadasya tīre kvacid ghoṣapadasya matsyādau lakṣaṇeti niyamo na syāt', will leave no doubt that Viśvanātha intends to cover the example 'gaṅgāyāṁ ghoṣaḥ' also by the concept of Lakṣaṇā with Tātparyānupapatti as its 'bīja'.

By Lakṣaṇā the word 'gaṅgā' conveys the meaning of 'a bank'. This Lakṣaṇā is nothing but the relation of the denoted meaning with an additional meaning. In the present example of 'gaṅgāyāṁ ghoṣaḥ', the relation of the Śakyārtha of the word 'gaṅgā', i.e., a current is understand with regard to 'a bank'. This is the Lakṣaṇā here. The knowledge of this Lakṣaṇāvṛtti in the form of the relation between the two meanings, 'a current' and 'a bank', leads to the recollection of the bank. The recollection of the bank is the contextual 'Padārthadhī' which serves as the Vyāpāra to be immediately followed by the corresponding Śābdabodha. Just as the Śakti as the relation between a Pada and its Śakyārtha brings about the śakyārthasmaraṇa which leads to the śābdabodha, the lakṣaṇā as the relation between a śakyārtha and a Lakṣyārtha brings forth the idea of the relevant Lakṣyārtha that leads to the corresponding Śābdabodha.

M(31). parantu yadyanvayānupapattirlakṣaṇābījaṁ syāt, tadā yaṣṭīḥ praveśayetyādau lakṣaṇā na syāt, yaṣṭīṣu praveśānvayasyā-'nupapatterabhāvāt. tena yaṣṭī-praveśe bhojanatātparyānupapattyā yaṣṭīdhareṣu lakṣaṇā. evaṁ kākebhyo dadhi rakṣyatāmityādau kākapadasya dadhyupaghātake lakṣaṇā, sarvato dadhirakṣāyāstātparyaviṣayatvāt.

Viśvanātha here initiates his discussion on possible anomalies in the event of not recognising Tātparyānupapatti as the Lakṣaṇā bīja. He wants to clarify his stand by illustrating certain stock exmples of Lakṣaṇā, namely 'yaṣṭīḥ praveśaya', kākebhyo dadhi rakṣyatām' and 'chatriṇo yānti'. We have already referred to how Gaṅgeśa makes an effort to show in the very above quoted expressions that Lakṣaṇā operates owing to Anvayānupapatti and not Tatparyānupatti.[386]

In the text of the *Muktāvalī* above, Viśvanātha tries to show the necessity of admitting Tātparyānupapatti as the Lakṣaṇābīja with regard to the expression 'yaṣṭīḥ praveśaya'. In 'yaṣṭīḥ praveśaya' (Bring in the sticks), there is no failure of the syntactical connection inasmuch as the sticks can be the object of the act of bringing in. In case Anvayānupapatti be admitted as the Lakṣaṇābīja, there can be no admission of Lakṣaṇā in 'yaṣṭīḥ praveśaya'. But when one speaks thus in the context of a feast, there being no meaning in admitting the sticks to a dinning hall, 'yaṣṭīḥ' is to be taken to mean the 'yaṣṭīdharas' (the holders of the stick.) This is a case of Lakṣaṇā because of the incompatibility of the speaker's intention with 'yaṣṭīḥ' in the sense of sticks. This example of Lakṣaṇā may be said to have been modelled on 'yaṣṭīkān bhojaya'.[387] Viśvanātha's example 'yaṣṭīḥ praveśaya' is met with in works of Kumārila, Patañjali, Gaṅgeśa, and many others.[388] Patañjali, while illustrating how a word is used for what it usually does not stand for, gives examples of 'gaṅgāyāṁ ghoṣaḥ' and 'yaṣṭī ḥ praveśaya'. In that context, the words 'gaṅgā' and 'yaṣṭī' are shown to give certain unusual meanings on the basis of their relation of 'tatsāmīpya' and 'tatsāhacarya' respectively with the usual meanings. Nāgeśa also gives 'yaṣṭīḥ praveśaya' based upon the relation of 'sāhacarya' between the Śakyārtha and Lakṣyārtha. Here we can remember that Vātsyāyana also gives the example to illustrate the relation of 'sahacaraṇa'. The relation of 'sāhacarya' or 'sahacaraṇa' (togetherness) exists between the sticks and the persons carrying them.

Viśvanātha gives another example in 'kākebhyo dadhi rakṣyatām' to strengthen his plea for admitting Tātparyānupapatti as the Lakṣaṇābīja. The said sentence literally wants someone to guard against the spoiling of the curd by the crow. But as the intention of any milkowner would naturally be the protection of his curd from all the spoilers of curd, the person directed must not take the word 'kāka' seriously in its literal sense. Though apparently there is no inconsistency in the syntactical connection of the words involved in the sentence, the Tātparya is to be thought as incompatible with only the primary meaning of the word 'kāka'. On the strength of this Tātparyānupapatti, the word 'kāka' is to mean all the 'dadhyupahātakas' as its Lakṣyārtha. This example may be said to have been modelled on Bhartṛhari's 'kā kebhyo rakṣyatāṁ sarpiḥ'.[389] The example is of course, seen in its present form also in earlier works.[390]

M(32) evaṁ chatriṇo yāntītyādau chatripadasyaikasārthavāhitve lakṣaṇā. iyamevājahatsvārthalakṣaṇetyucyate, ekasārthavāhitvena rūpeṇa chatri-tadanyayorbodhāt.

Viśvanātha here adds that 'in the same way' i.e., only because of the admission of Tātparyānupapatti as the Lakṣaṇābīja, 'chatriṇo yānti' comes to be an example of Lakṣaṇā. If we admit Anvayānupapatti as the Lakṣaṇābīja, there is no scope for having a recourse to Lakṣaṇā as the words in the sentence can syntactically be connected even in view of their denoted senses. When by observation, it is felt that the word 'chatriṇaḥ' is used to mean not only the holders of umbrellas but also others in the group even without umbrellas, the Tātparya is felt as incompatible with the mere primary sense of the word 'chatrinaḥ'. This TĀtparyā nupatti is the basis for the operation of a Laksaṇā function in respect of the word 'chatrin' for conveying a secondary sense where the Tātparya practically rests. This new meaning comes to cover all in the group irrespective of holding umbrellas or not. This example also is found in many earlier works including the *Bhā ṣya* of Śabara.[391] Viśvanātha now identifies this sentence 'chatriṇo yanti' as an example of Ajahatsvārthā Lakṣaṇā where the Śakyārtha is also retained in full or part along with the Lakśyā rtha. As the Lakṣyārtha of the word 'chatrin' is 'ekasārthavāhin' (all persons belonging to the group), it obviously covers the Śakyā rtha, i.e., the holders of the umbrellas. Though Viśvanātha refers to only 'chatriṇo yānti' as an illustration of Ajahatsvārthā, at least two of the earlier examples, namely, 'yaṣṭīḥ praveśaya' and 'kā kebhypo dadhi rakṣyatām' also belong to the same group. The Lakṣyārtha of 'yaṣṭī' in 'yaṣṭīḥ etc.' covers the Śakyārtha of the word. Similarly the Śakyārtha of the word 'kāka', i.e., crows stands included in the Lakṣyārtha of the word, i.e., all the spoilers of curd. Gaṅgeśa refers to 'yaṣṭīḥ praveśaya' as an Ajahatsvārthā Lakṣaṇā.[392] According to Dharmarājādhvarīndra, 'kākebhyo dadhi rakṣyatām' is an instance of Jahadajahallakṣaṇā.[393] We shall discuss the issue in the succeeding pages.

M(33). yadi cānvayānupapattirlakṣaṇābījaṁ syāt, tadā kvacid gaṅgāpadasya tīre kvacid ghoṣapadasya matsyādau lakṣaṇeti niyamo na syāt.

Viśvanātha points out above that if Anvayānupapatti be accepted as the Lakṣaṇābīja in stead of a Tātparyānupapatti then there would be no regulation in respect of various probable secondary meanings of a verbal expression. As for example, in the example 'gaṅgāyāṁ ghoṣaḥ' the Anvayānupapatti (which is accepted as the Lakṣaṇābīja in the context by the Ālaṁkārikas and even by the Navya Naiyāyikas like Gaṅgeśopādhyāya and Jānakīnātha-Bhaṭṭācārya) involved therein can be removed either by taking 'bank' as the secondary meaning of the word 'gaṅgā' or by taking 'fish' as the secondary meaning of the word 'ghoṣaḥ'. Under the circumstances, we must be sure of the Tātparya (the intention of the speaker) in order to restrict the Lakṣaṇā to either of the two words. Hence Viśvanātha finds it necessary to accept only the Tātparyānupapatti as the fundamental condition for the operation of Lakṣaṇā. Here we point to a similar argument put forward by the Grammarian Nāgeśa. Nāgeśa also apprehends the possibility of an anomaly in the example, 'gaṅgāyāṁ ghoṣaḥ' in the event of recognising Anvayānupapatti as the Lakṣaṇābīja. As we understand him, he also feels that one can get rid of Anvayānupapatti in Gaṅgāyām ghoṣh' even by understanding an aquatic creature (makara) instead of a 'dairy farm' from the word 'ghoṣa' with the aid of Lakṣaṇā. He also feels the need of Tātparya to restrict the Lakṣaṇā only with regard to the meaning 'dairy farm' of the word 'ghoṣa'. This argument from Viśvanātha Nyāya Pañcānana and Nāgeśabhaṭṭa seems to contain a loophole. By recognising Lakṣaṇā with regard to the word 'gaṅgā', one can find both the primary and secondary senses, 'the current' and 'the bank' respectively in the relation of 'sāmīpya'. But in the event of admitting Lakṣaṇā with regard to the word 'ghoṣa', it is not possible to understand a specific relation between the primary and secondary concepts. How can there be a relation between 'the dairy firm' and 'an aquatic creature' (either 'matsya' or 'makara') ? As we have already observed, the Naiyāyikas including Viśvanātha have accepted Lakṣaṇā as Śakyasambandharūpā'. Nāgeśa also refers to this view point of the Naiyāyikas.[394] Hence in the event of recognising Lakṣaṇā in 'ghoṣa', we do not find any workability of Lakṣaṇā as understood by Viśvanātha and Nāgeśa. Here, of course, we shall have to add that the very recognition of Lakṣaṇā by Nāgeśa is only provisional.

Now before we conclude on the issue of Lakṣaṇābīja, we may desirably take a further note of Viśvanātha's concept of Tātparya.

Like Gaṇgeśopādhyāya, Viśvanātha accepts Tātparya as one of the four factors (the other three being Āsatti, Yogyatā, and Ākaṁkṣā) responsible for bringing about a Śābdabodha. It may be that the clue of this idea of Tātparya is taken from Jayantabhaṭṭa, but unlike Jayanta, Viśvanātha (following Gaṅgeśa) does not accept Tātparya as a Vṛtti on par with Abhidhā and Lakṣaṇā. Again unlike Gaṅgeśa, the author of the *Bhāṣā pariccheda* believes only in an Tātparyānupapatti as the Lakṣaṇā bīja. Now like Gaṅgeśa again, he understands Tātparya as the very intention of a speaker (Vakturicchā). Now in illustrating the involvement of Tātparya in the process of Śābdabodha, Viśvanātha refers to a sentence containing a homonymous word. The sentence in question, which we shall meet with in the relevant *Muktāvalī* text in a succeeding page is 'Saindhavamānaya'.

If we take this illustration seriously, then the scope of Tātparya shall have to be admitted as very limited. Tātparya comes to be hardly acceptable as the indispensable factor for the understanding of the meanings of all sorts of sentences. But the subsequent text of the *BP.* in the context of Tātparya as Śābdabodhakāraṇa does not confirm this impression. By reading between the lines of Viśvanātha, one may rather have the idea that the author of the *Bhāṣāpariccheda* wants Tātparya to be involved in the process of Śābdabodha in all sentences, Vedic and non-Vedic. If we believe in the impression created by the said example regarding Viśvanātha's approach to Tātparya as a Śābdabodhakāraṇa, it will lead to limiting the scope of Lakṣaṇā. If Tātparyānupapatti be admitted as the Lakṣaṇābīja and Tātparya be shown as involved only in sentences like 'saindhavamānaya' the scope of the 'anupapatti' of Tātparya will be restricted only to the homonymous words. But we find Viśvanātha recognising Lakṣaṇā in expressions like 'gaṅgāyaṁ ghoṣaḥ' which donot involve any homonym. As such, we feel that the example chosen by Viśvanātha for showing the involvement of Tātparya in a sentence as the Śābdabodhakāraṇa, i.e., the expression 'saindhavamānaya' is virtually misleading.

Now, again, there is the problem whether Tātparya would operate at the level of a word or at the level of the whole sentence. A Tātparyānupapatti may be known only when Tātparya is known. The idea of Tātparyānupapatti may be had only from the minimum idea of the total import of a sentence because Tātparya (which depends on the Tātparyagrāhakas, i.e., certain determining factors like 'Prakaraṇa') tends to be concerned with a whole sentence and not with any individual word. But the Naiyāyikas including our Viśvanātha are not prepared to recognise a Lakṣaṇā in a whole sentence. Hence it is really confusing as to how they can accept as Lakṣaṇābīja the very Tātparyānupapatti, which is concerned with an entire sentence only.

Though Viśvanātha does not accept Tātparya as a Vṛtti, yet we find it relevant to refer to the fate of Tātparyānupapatti in case of understanding Tātparya as a verbal function as Jayantabhaṭṭa does. Jayantabhaṭṭa, the author of the *Nyāyamañjarī* propounds the theory of Tātparya Vṛtti; but he remains satisfied with Lakṣaṇā as Śakyasambandha as he does not come forward to accept either of the two 'anupapatti's as the Lakṣaṇābīja. But if we now understand Tātparya as a Vṛtti even in the context of Tā tparyānupapatti, the so-called Lakṣaṇābīja, we find that there remains a very thin line of demarcation between a Tātparyā nupapatti and an Anvayānupapatti. Our idea is this : Where the Tātparyavṛtti fails, 'anvaya' also obviously fails, because the Tā tparya as Vṛtti stands admitted only for effecting an 'anvaya' amongst the meanings of individual words. We may talk just the reverse also. If an 'anvaya' fails, it fails due to a failure of the operation of Tātparya Vṛtti. As we understand from Abhinavagupta, the Abhidhā Vṛtti conveys the unrelated meanings of the individual words and gets exhausted. It cannot come into operation again to bring forth the idea of an anvaya in a context. Here comes in the Tātparya Vṛtti to serve the purpose of presenting the 'anvaya'.[395] In case of a Lakṣaṇā, however, where we have as the Lakṣaṇābīja, a Tātparyānupapatti resulting in an Anvayānupatti or an Anvayānupapatti, resulting from a Tātparyā nupapatti, the Tātparya Vṛtti comes to operate twice. There is, however, no explicit reference to such a two fold operation of Tā tparya. Yet we can gather the idea as an implied fact. As for instance, in the expression 'siṁho maṇavakaḥ', Abhidhā conveys the primary meanings of the individual words and then Tātparya in its turn presents the syntactical relation amongst the meanings in the sentence. But Tātparya fails to identify the 'māṇavaka' (boy) with the 'siṁha' (lion). Now Lakṣaṇā comes in to convey 'siṁhasadṛśa' (someone like a lion) as the secondary meaning of the word 'siṁha'. Now again Tātparya operates to bring forth the syntactical relation (anvaya) between the meanings 'māṇavaka' and 'siṁhasadṛśa'.[396] Thus we find that an operation of Lakṣaṇā comes to be preceded by both Tatparyānupapatti and Anvayā nupapatti. Here, of course, one is to understand Tātparya in the sense of a Vṛtti responsible for presenting the syntactical relation in a sentence (Padārthānvayasādhikā). We humbly point out that the Tatparyānupapatti as the Lakṣaṇābīja, wherein Tātparya is taken in the sense of Vakturicchā is not practically tenable. The sentences involving homonyms as in Saindhavamānaya do not generally involve any Lakṣaṇā. It is because the accepted factors such as 'context' (i.e., prakaraṇāditātparyagrāhakas) are found available for restricting the Tātparya to one of the senses of such a homonymous word. But in the event of Tātparyānupapatti not being admitted as the Lakṣaṇābīja, Viśvanātha fears the possibility of anomalies in the sentences like 'gaṅgāyāṁ ghoṣaḥ'. As there will be no Tātparya restricted in favour of a particular secondary meaning, one will be free to use Lakṣaṇā even with regard to the word 'ghosa' instead of the word 'gaṅgā'. As the Anvayānupapatti is understood in such a case as the basic condition for the operation of a Lakṣaṇā, one can remain satisfied by removing either way the 'anupapatti' of the 'anvaya' involved therein. In other words, according to Viśvanātha, in the event of not admitting Tātparyānupapatti as the Lakṣaṇābīja, the word 'ghoṣa' also may be taken to mean 'a fish' secondarily to remove the inconcistency in respect of syntactical relation in the sentence 'gaṅgāyāṁ ghoṣaḥ'. This, we feel, is an argument for argument's sake only. Tātparya itself in the sense of the intention of the speaker is determined on the basis of certain factors like a context. Viśvanātha himself refers to these Tātparyagrāhakas like a 'prakaraṇa' (i.e., context) in course of his explaining Tātparya as a Śābdabodhakāraṇa. Even if there be no Tātparyānupapatti with reference to the primary meaning of a word, because of the lack of restriction of the Tātparya in the context to a particular secondary meaning, it is unlikely for one to use the word 'ghoṣa' in the sense of an aquatic creature like fish in complete violation of convention (Saṁketa). If we accept Viśvanātha's fear of anomalies in sentences like 'gaṅgāyāṁ ghoṣaḥ' in the event of not admitting Tātparyānupapatti (as the Lakṣaṇābīja), we shall automatically admit that because of the ignorance of Tātparya in a context, the listener can arbitarily use a word in any sense he likes even at the utter neglect of Saṁketa. If it be argued that it is Śakti or Abhidhā that is to take care for Saṁketa or Convention it may be said in reply that even the Tātparya as the intention of a speaker is not free from the regulation of the Tātparyagrāhakas. Moreover we reiterate our earlier opinion that Lakṣaṇā as the Śakyasambandha must be understandable through justifiable and specific relations between the Śakyārthas and Lakṣyārthas. While we can reasonably understand a Lakṣaṇā as a relation between 'a current' and 'a bank' respectively as primary and secondary concepts of the word Ganges (i.e. 'gangā) because of 'sāmīpya' (nearness) between the two, we naturally find it inconvenient to understand the same as a relation between 'a dairy farm or cowherds' colony and 'a fish' as primary and secondary senses of the word 'ghoṣa'. We understand that Viśvanātha personally does not believe in the Lakṣaṇā with reference to 'ghoṣa' in the sense of a 'fish' and that he is very much anxious not to allow a scope for such an admission. But our humble submission is that the very definition of Lakṣaṇā as Śakyasambandha is a safeguard against such possibilities.

Gakulanātha Upādhyāya in his *Vivaraṇa*, a commentary on the *Kāvya Prakāsā* seems to offer a solution to the problem of Lakṣaṇābīja. Gakulanātha points out that if there is to be a Śābdabodha in a sentence that involves the operation of a Lakṣaṇā in any one of its words, that Śābdabodha must necessarily be preceded by a Mukhyārthabādha (the untenability of a Verbal judgement involving the primary sense of a particular word). Now the Lakṣaṇābīja we have been so long discussing is actually the factor responsible for such a Mukhyārthabādha. Gakulanātha maintains that this Mukhyārthabādha may occur in three different ways.

(1) Sometimes this Mukhyārthabādha may occur because of the realisation of an incompatibility (ayogyatā) of the primary meaning in the context. As for example, in the expression, 'gaṅgāyāṁ ghoṣaḥ' the untenability of the Śābdabodha at the first instance takes place due to the realisation of the incompatibility (ayogyatā) of the 'current of water of Ganges', the primary meaning of the word 'gaṅgā' to hold 'the dairy farm' or the cowherds' colony (the primary meaning of the other word in the sentence, namely 'ghoṣa').

(2) Sometimes this untenability is due to a lack of expectancy (nirākāṁkṣatva) of the primary meaning concerned. For example, in the compound, 'rājapuruṣa' there are two component parts viz., 'rājan' and 'puruṣa'. Here the primary meaning of the two words may get syntactical relation either through relation of 'abheda' or 'bheda'. The second alternative is not possible since remaining

quite apart and independant two primary meanings do not happen to have any mutual expectancy. On account of lack of this expectancy they fail to bring about a tenable Śābdabodha. In case of the first alternative wherein because of both the words occurring in the same vibhakti (owing to their having Sāmānā dhikaraṇya) two primary meanings can get mutually connected through the relation of abheda, (identity). But here arises the fallacy of Ayogyatā, in so far as a king as a rule cannot come down to be identified with an ordinary person.

(3) Sometimes, this untenability of Śābdabodha may occur because the primary meaning of a word does not conform to the actual intention of the speaker. As for instance, in the sentence, 'kākebhyo dadhi rakṣyatām', if we take only the primary meaning of the word 'kākebhyaḥ' there will be no grammatical irregularity or no occurrence of either incompatibility (ayogyatā or absence of yogyatā) or lack of expectancy (nirākāṁkṣatva or absence of Ākā ṁsā).

Even then the primary meaning requires to be abandoned at least practically as the speaker here intends to mean by the word (kākebhyaḥ) all the creatures including the crow (kāka) that can spoil the curd (dadhyupaghātakas). Hence here is also the scope of Lakṣaṇā to convey the aforesaid idea of 'dadhyupaghātakas' in addition to Kāka. So Gakulanātha wants to assert tnat the factor responsible for the operation of Lakṣaṇā by way of causing an untentability of the primary meaning of a particular word varies from situation to situation. He finds, therefore, no justification in asserting either Tātparyānupapatti or Anvayānupapatti as the sole fundamental condition for the operation of a Lakṣaṇā.

M(34). idantu bodhyam - śakyārthasambandho yadi tīratvena rūpeṇa gṛhītastadā tīratvena tīrabodhaḥ, yadi tu gaṅgātīratvena rūpeṇa gṛhītastadā tenaiva rūpeṇa smaraṇam. ata eva lakṣyatāvacchedake na lakṣaṇā, tatprakārakabodhasya tatra lakṣaṇāṁ vināpyupapatteḥ. parantvevaṁ krameṇaśakyatāvacchedake'pi śaktirna syāt. tatprakāraka - śakyārthasmaraṇaṁ prati tatpadasya sāmarthyamityasya suvacatvāditi vibhāvanīyam.

Here Viśvanātha draws our attention to the fact that in any case of Lakṣaṇā, the knowledge of Lakṣaṇā, the recollection of the Lakṣyārtha and the contextual Śābdabodha correspond to each other. He illustrates the point with the example, 'gaṅgāyāṁ ghoṣaḥ'. As the intention of the Speaker does not tally with the Śakyārtha of the word 'gaṅgā', i.e., because of a Tātparyā nupapatti with reference to the Śakyārtha of 'gaṅgāpada', there arises the scope of the operation of Lakṣaṇā in the word. Now Lakṣaṇā being a 'śakyārthasambandha'. the meaning on which the relation of the denoted sense can be fixed or ascertained is to be treated as Lakṣyārtha. In case of 'gaṅgāyāṁ ghoṣaḥ', the relation of the Śakyārtha of the word 'gangā' may be understood with reference to two meanings, either a bank in general or the bank of the river Ganges. If the 'śakyasambandha' is understood with reference to (a bank as characterised by) the bankness, the recollection of the object 'bank' will also be as characterised by the bankness and the Śābdabodha also will correspondingly be of the bank as characterised by bankness. Similarly if the 'śakyārthasambandha' i.e., Lakṣaṇā is understood with regard to (the bank of Ganges as characterised by) the Gangetic bankness, the, (Lakṣya) Padārthasamaraṇa and the corresponding Śābdabodha will also be of the same form. The idea is that in the case of Lakṣaṇā also as in the case of Abhidhā or Śakti, the Vṛttijñāna, Padārthasamaraṇa and Śābdabodha occur in the same form. This very regulation regarding Śābdabodha involving either Śakti or Lakṣaṇā may be presented in a traditional pattern as follows : 'yaddharmāvacchinnaviśeṣyakavṛttigrahastaddharmā vacchinnaviśeṣyakameva padārthasmaraṇaṁ Śābdabodhaśceti'.

In 'ata eva --------upapatteḥ', Viśvanātha points out a consequence of the admission of the said regulation. It is clear from the exposition above that a Lakṣyatāvacchedaka (i.e., the determinent of a secondary sense, viz., 'tīratva' with regard to the Lakṣyārtha, 'tīra' or 'Gaṅgātīratva' with reference to the Lakṣyārtha 'Gaṅgātīra) comes to be known along with the corresponding Lakṣyārtha. As a Lakṣaṇā can convey a Lakṣyārtha only by virtue of conveying the corresponding Lakṣyatāvacchedaka, there is no necessity of admitting another Śakyārthasambandha with reference to the Avacchedaka of a Lakṣyārtha.

Now a question is very much pertinent. The regulation that Vṛttijñāna, Padārthasmaraṇa and Śābdabodha are to correspond to each other is common to both Śakti and Lakṣaṇā. If as a consequence to the acceptance of the regulation, there is the admission that another Lakṣaṇā is not to be admitted again for the knowledge of Lakṣyatāvacchedaka, the same logic will force the plea that Śakti is also not to be admitted in the case of a Śakyatāvacchedaka. In Parantvevaṁ -------- Vibhāvanīyam, Viśvanātha refers to this problem. The author of the *BP* does not straightway give any solution. He admits the logic in the argument (cf. suvacatvāt) and at the same time urges a consideration of the matter cf. Vibhāvanīyam) in anticipation of the complicacies that may arise in case Śakti is not admitted with regard to the Avacchedaka of a Śakyārtha.

The anticipated complicacy may be like this : In the case of the word 'Pṛthivī (Earth), as for illustration, the Śaktijñāna, Padārthasmaraṇa and the Śābdabodha will be of same form as Pṛthivītvaprakārakapṛthivī - Viśeṣyakajñānam. The Avacchedaka, i.e., Pṛthivītva is a Prakāra or Viśeṣaṇa and the Śakyārtha, i.e., Pṛthivī is a Prakārī or viśeṣya. As there can be no knowledge of the Viśesya without a prior knowledge of corresponding Viśeṣana, the Viśeṣaṇa is understood first. If only one Śakti is admitted with regard to the world 'Pṛthivī' and utilized first to convey the Śakyatāvacchedaka, because of the exhaustion in the matter of conveying the Viśeṣaṇa, the same śakti will not be competent to convey the Viśeṣya. This is not a desirable position. As 'Pṛthivī' is the conventional meaning of the world 'Pṛthivī', we cannot proceed to understand it otherwise. If in the other way, the meaning 'Pṛthivītva' is kept out of the jurisdiction of the Śakti of the world

'Pṛthivī', the recognised need of an Avacchedaka of the Śakyā rtha, i.e., the object Earth will forcefully lead to conveying of any meaning that can serve as a Prakāra to the object Earth. As Earth is something that has smell (gandhavat), the meaning 'gandhavattva' (the state of something having smell) being a relevant prakāra can serve the rule that the knowledge of a qualified is to be preceded by that of the qualification.

In that case, the Śābdabodha of the word 'Pṛthivī' will be as 'gandhavattvaprakārakapṛthivīviśeṣyakajñānam.' This is neither desirable nor is warranted by facts. Hence there is the need of admitting another Śakti for the purpose of conveying a Śakyatā vacchedaka. It may be argued that the fear of the same type of irregularity may demand the admission of another Lakṣaṇā in order to understand a Lakṣyatāvacchedaka. It may be replied in this context thus. In the case of understanding Lakṣayatā vacchedakas, there is no scope of such an irregularity. A Lakṣyā rtha is a Viśeṣya and its Avacchedaka is a Viśeṣaṇa. Here also the Viśeṣaṇa is to be known first. The Lakṣaṇā, that is expected to convey a Lakṣyārtha, cannot be utilized earlier to convey its Avacchedaka as in that case, the very Lakṣaṇā being exhausted will not remain competent to convey the Lakṣyārtha. There is also no necessity of admitting any Vṛtti (function) to get the Lakṣyatā vacchedaka conveyed. The regulation that the knowledge of Viśeṣya is to be preceded by that of Viśeṣaṇa will bring about the knowledge of the Lakṣyatāvacchedaka along with the Lakṣyārtha. There is at the same time no scope for a Lakṣyatāvacchedaka being undesirably conveyed. The very Śakyasambandha will serve as the restriction. The relation of a Śakyārtha with an would be Lakṣyārtha, as Viśvanātha has shown in 'idantu bodhyam' etc., is understood with due regard to the Avacchedaka.

If the Lakṣyatāvacchedaka is thought otherwise, the Lakṣyā rtha also would be quite different. Hence the scope of irregularity does not arise.

M(35). yatra tu śakyārthasya paramparāsambandharūpā

lakṣaṇā, sā lakṣitalakṣaṇetyucyate. yathā dvirephādipade rephadvayasya - sambandho bhramarapade jñāyate, bhramarapadasya ca sambandho bhramare jñāyate, tatra lakṣita-lakṣaṇā.

In the examples of Lakṣaṇā so long cited, the relation between the Śakyārthas and their corresponding Lakṣyārthas is felt as straight or direct. But in certain cases, Lakṣaṇā appears in the form of an indirect relation of a Śakyārtha with a Lakṣyārtha. Such a Lakṣaṇā, as Viśvanātha points out, goes by the name of Lakṣitalakṣaṇā. 'Dvirepha' is an example in hand. The word 'dvirepha' primarily means 'two r-sounds'. But because of obvious absence of Tātparya with regard to this Śakyārtha of the word in a context like 'dvirepho guñjati', Lakṣaṇā comes to convey the word "bhramara" as a Lakṣyārtha. The relation between the word 'Bhramara' and 'two-r-sounds' is easily discernible. But yet the original Tātparyānupapatti does not go away. The necessity of fixing the Tātparya still exists. In such a position, the word 'Bhramara' gives its Śakyārtha, i.e., a bee. With the knowledge of this sense of 'bee' only, the necessary 'anvaya' in 'dvirepho guñjati' becomes possible. Thus the word 'dvirapha' is instrumental in conveying the sense of a bee. But the relation between the 'two-r-sounds', the Śakyārtha of the word 'dvirepha' and 'a bee' is an indirect one.

As we have pointed out earlier, in the circle of the Vedāntins also, Lakṣitalakṣaṇā stands admitted on the same ground and with the same example.[397] The Guṇavṛtti of the Mīmāṁsakas or the Gauṇī Lakṣaṇā of the Ālaṁkārikas and some of the Naiyā yikas reveal such an indirect relation between the Lākṣaṇikapada and the final Lakṣyārtha. As for example, we may consider 'siṁho māṇavakaḥ' or 'gaurvāhīkaḥ'.

So Dharmarājādhvarīndra observes that Gauṇī Lakṣaṇā is no other than Lakṣitalakṣaṇā[398] Dr. N.N. Choudhury also maintains that the Naiyāyikas have admitted the so-called Gauṇīvṛtti in 'siṁho māṇavakaḥ' etc. only as a kind of Lakṣaṇā on par with Lakṣaṇā in 'dvirepha' etc.[399] Here we shall have to point out that the author of the *Bhāṣāpariccheda* is interestingly silent on the Gauṇivṛtti of Mīmāṁsakas or the Gauṇī Lakṣaṇā of some of his own colleagues[400] and the Ālaṁkārikas. The examples of Lakṣaṇā given by Viśvanātha do not show even a single case of such a Gauṇī prayoga where a meaning comes to be conveyed as a 'lakṣyaguṇa'. In discussing the examples of Lakṣaṇā given by the author of the *Bhāṣāpariccheda*, we have seen that he did not make any precise classification of Lakṣaṇā. Before we come to assess Viśvanātha's attitude in the context, we propose to make a historical study in brief of this issue of classification of Lakṣaṇā.

As we have already discussed, the terms Guṇa, Bhakti and Lakṣaṇā have been used by Jaimini in the sense of secondary signification. But Jaimini does not show any discrimination in using the said terms. But from the treatment of the terms in the *Bhāṣya* of Śabarasvāmin, one comes to have a notion of two different types of secondary signification in the form of Lakṣaṇā and Gauṇī. Śabara's idea of Lakṣaṇā may be understood as the popular usage of everyday life wherein there is an arbitrary assumption of a sense by the society. Again in Guṇavṛtti, the generic status of one object is attributed to another on the basis of similarity in qualities. This transference is possible through Guṇavāda. Guṇavāda is the transference of similar attributes metaphorically from one object to another. Thus a difference between Lakṣaṇā and Guṇavṛtti comes out in the *Śābarabhāṣya*. This idea may be gathered from the explanation of the clause 'ū rgudumbara' under the Sūtra 1.2.19.[401] Another division of Lakṣaṇā into Jahatsvārthā and Ajahatsvārthā is revealed in its treatment by Śabarasvāmin. He does not define or discuss Jahatsvārthā Lakṣaṇā. In Śabara's view, Ajahatsvārthā Lakṣaṇā is that where a word while signifying a secondary meaning does not forsake its primary meaning completely, i.e., where a part of its primary meaning is retained along with its secondary sense. In the context of explaining the term 'Liṅgasamavāya', Śabara cites the expressions 'chatriṇo yānti' etc. as the examples of secondary signification. He maintains that the words 'chatrin' etc. do not give up their own primary meanings while signifying the group to which the objects literally meant by the words belong as parts.[402] Here we observe a very much noteworthy similarity between Viśvanātha and Śabara. Like Śabara, Viśvanātha also does not define the Jahatsvārthā Lakṣaṇā. Though he discusses 'gaṅgāyāṁ ghoṣaḥ' as his first example of Lakṣaṇā, he does not name it as an instance of Jahatsvārthā. We know that this expression, 'gaṅgāyāṁ ghoṣaḥ' is a stock example of Lakṣaṇālakṣaṇā or Jahatsvārthā in other circles. Viśvanātha however, comes forward like Śabarasvāmin to name 'chatriṇo yānti' as an example of Ajahatsvārthā. Though Viśvanātha does not define Ajahatsvārthā anywhere in his work, his idea of Ajahatsvārthā Lakṣaṇā is just the same with that of Śabara. We have this impression from his explanation of the expression 'chatriṇo yānti' as an example of Ajahatsvārthā Lakṣaṇā. But we cannot extend too far the area of similarity between the two scholars in the context of the concept of Ajahatsvārthā Lakṣaṇā. The examples of Lakṣaṇā, given by Viśvanātha do not include even a single instance of Guṇavṛtti, as and when understood in the light of Śabara or Kumārila. But Śabara is found to have regarded Guṇavṛtti also as Ajahatsvārtha Lakṣaṇā because when a word is superimposed on another because of similarity of attributes between the objects conveyed, the Guṇaśabdas do not abandon their primary meanings completely. For example in 'siṁho māṇavakaḥ', in the process of identification between the lion and the child, though the animality of the lion is abandoned, many of its attributes like bravery come to be admitted in the child.

We find a clear cut distinction between Lakṣaṇā and Guṇavṛtti maintained only in the writings of Kumārilabhaṭṭa. Here we note that Kumārila finds Lakṣaṇā and Guṇavṛtti as belonging to different planes. But some of the Naiyāyikas, the Ālaṁkārikas and Vaiyākaraṇas regard Guṇavṛtti as a variety of Lakṣaṇā itself. According to Kumārillabhaṭṭa Lakṣaṇā is the invariable association between primary and secondary concepts. Because of this invariable association when a primary meaning leads to the idea of an additional meaning connected invariably with it, what takes place is known as Lakṣaṇā.[403] But when Lakṣaṇā brings the idea of some attribute (Guṇa) invariably connected with the primary meaning, then it is a Guṇavṛtti which operates to convey the idea of yet another object sharing the attributes belonging to the object conveyed primarily by the word. We can gather an idea from Kumārila that every 'nāmapada' would primarily signify a Jāti which in its turn would signify the Vyakti on the strength of an invariable association, i.e., Lakṣaṇā.

Kumārila's example of Guṇavṛtti is 'agnirmāṇavakaḥ' wherein we get the 'vahnitvajāti' as the Śakyārtha of the word 'agni', by Abhidhā. Then from the same expression we get paiṅgalyādiguṇa' (i.e., the qualities like that of possessing a red colour) as the Lakṣyārtha by Lakṣaṇā. Herein again by means of Guṇavāda (on the strength of similarity of attributes 'paiṅgalyādi' of the boy with those of Agni) finally the boy comes to be understood.[404] The Mīmāṁsakas, as a whole, however classify Lakṣaṇā into Jahatsvārthā and Ajahatsvārthā.[405] As we find in the *Bhāṭṭacintāmaṇi*, 'gaṅgāyāṁ ghoṣaḥ' is cited as an example of Jahatsvārtha Lakṣaṇā wherein the primary meaning comes to be Virtually dead, leading to an additional meaning, i.e., the secondary meaning. 'Yaṣṭīḥ praveśaya' is given as an illustration of Ajahatsvārthā wherein the primary sense retains a part of itself as a participant in the desired syntactical relation in a sentence. It will not be out of context to record here that the Mīmāṁsakas include Lakṣita-lakṣaṇā (recognised by the Vedāntins and even by the author of the *Bhāṣāpariccheda)* as a separate category under the Jahatsvārthā group.[406]

The Vedāntins divide Lakṣaṇā into two varieties

(i) Kevalalakṣaṇā and (ii) Lakṣitalakṣaṇā. Kevalalakṣaṇā involves a direct relation between the primary and the secondary meanings of a word whereas Lakṣitalakṣaṇā involves an indirect one. In other words when the secondary sense is directly related with the primary meaning then the function involved is called Kevalalakṣaṇā. When it is otherwise there occurs the scope for Lakṣitalakṣaṇā.[407] 'Gaṅgāyāṁ ghoṣaḥ' is given as an example of Kevalalakṣaṇā while the word 'dvirepha' as the illustration of the other type. Dharmarājādhvarīndra holds that Guṇavṛtti should come under the purview of Lakṣitalakṣaṇā. In the example 'siṁho māṇavakaḥ' (the boy is the lion), which is a typical example of Gauṇi Lakṣaṅā, the word 'siṁha' gives the idea of a lion as its Vācyārtha. The qualities of a lion like 'cruelity' etc. are connected with the lion and hence come to us as a Lakṣyārtha. The idea of the boy now occurs as a scondary sense connected with the expressed sense indirectly through its relation with the earlier secondary sense, 'cruelty' etc.[408] Thus the idea of 'the boy' having 'a chained relation' (paramparitasambandha) with the vācyārtha may be recognised as presenting a case of Lakṣitalakṣaṇā. The Vedāntins divide Lakṣaṇā in a different way also. According to them, Lakṣaṇā is of three types viz., Jahallakṣaṇā, Ajahallakṣaṇā and Jahadajahallakṣaṇā.[409] Jahallakṣaṇā operates in those expressions where primary meanings are not included in the secondary meanings. As for example, in the expression 'viṣaṁ bhuṁkṣva', the primary meaning is not retained. The primary meaning being totally abandoned the sentence comes to indicate the secondary sense 'Do not eat in this house' (na cāsya gṛhe bhakṣaya).[410] In Ajahallakṣaṇā the primary meaning retains its place in the body of the secondary sense. For example, in 'śuklo ghaṭaḥ', the primary meaning of the word 'śukla' is the 'śukla guṇa' (white colour) and the secondary meaning is a 'śuklaguṇavaddravya' (a white coloured object). The idea of a white colour' is invariably involved in the idea of 'a white coloured object'[411] Jahadajahallakṣaṇā comes to operate only when the half of the primary meaning is retained and the other half of it is abandoned in the process of conveying a secondary sense. In the expression 'so'yaṁ devadattaḥ' (this is the very Devadatta), the word 'saḥ' signifies Devadatta belonging to a particular time (tatkālaviśiṣṭo devadattaḥ.) The word 'ayaṁ' signifies Devadatta of the present time (etatkālaviśiṣṭo devadattaḥ). To establish the syntactical relation between these two words, the words should abandon their parts viz., 'tatkālaviśiṣṭa' and 'etatkā laviśiṣṭa' and signify only the common part, i.e., Devadatta through Lakṣaṅā. Similarly in the expression 'tattvamasī' the vedā ntines find a case of Jahadajahallakṣaṇā.[412] We are to add that this Jahadajahallakṣaṇā is known as Bhāgalakṣaṇā also.[413] It is worthmentioning that while recognising Jahadajahallakṣaṇā Dharmarājādhvarīndra does not recognise 'tattvamasi' and 'so'yaṁ Devadattaḥ' as its examples. For him in these expressions there is no incompatibility of the primary meanings for getting syntactically related.[414] He, however, recognises, 'kākebhyo dadhi rakṣyatām'. Where the secondary meaning of the word 'kāka' is 'dadhyupaghātaka' (destroyer of curd) in general. In that secondary sense, the 'crow' also finds a place, but at the cost of discarding its identity as a crow and only by virtue of the state of being a 'destroyer of curd', which is not the primary import of the word.[415]

As we have earlier observed, Lakṣaṇā received so much elaborate treatment in the works of the Ālaṁkārikas that it came to be finally shown as of eighty varieties. Broadly Lakṣaṇā was classified into Rūḍhimūlā and Prayojanamūlā. Each again came to be divided into Upādānalakṣaṇā and Lakṣaṅalakṣaṇā which stand for Ajahatsvārthā and Jahatsvārthā respectively. Again there took place a further classification of Lakṣaṇā in to Sāropā and Sādhyavasānā varieties. Each of the aforesaid kinds of Lakṣaṇā came to be shown either as Śuddhā or as Gauṇī. The Prayojanamūlā lakṣaṇās again came to have another division because of the suggested motive involved therein (i.e., prayojanarū pavyajñya) being sometimes easily discernible and sometimes very much concealed as can be appreciated only by the connoisseurs of poetry. The suggested motive again sometimes pertains to an attribute (dharma) and sometimes to one possessed of some attribute (dharmī). Hence we meet with another classification of the Prayojanamūlalakṣaṇās.[416] All Lakṣaṇās are again shown as pertaining to either a word (Pada) or a sentence (Vākya).

The Naiyāyikas in general, as we find, divide Lakṣaṇā into two broad varieties viz., Gauṇīvṛtti and Lakṣaṇā. The terms Bhakti, Guṇa and Upacāra, as we have already pointed out, have been used in the *Nyāyasūtra* of Gautama to mean the figurative expressions. But no explicit distinction between Lakṣaṇā and Guṇavṛtti is brought about therein. The term Upacāra is used in the sense of superimposition. The superimposition may be qualitative or pure. Unlike the Mīmāṁsakas, the Naiyāyikas, generally speaking, include Guṇavṛtti under the purview of Upacā ra or Lakṣaṇā.

Jayantabhaṭṭa, however, clearly distinguishes Lakṣaṇā from Guṇavṛtti. He defines Lakṣaṇā as follows -- A word is to be recognised as Lākṣaṇika when it conveys a meaning in addition to the primary meaning. The additional meaning may or may not be a quality. In case of Guṇavṛtti we find the superimposition of one idea upon another because of a word being in apposition (sāmānādhikaraṇya) with another word. This is not the case with a Lakṣaṇā. Jayanta gives the expression 'gaṅgāyāṁ ghoṣaḥ' as the example of Lakṣaṇā. Here the word 'gaṅgā' conveys the additional idea of 'the bank of the Ganges' and the operation of Lakṣaṇā is not necessitated by any case of apposition.[417] But in a case of Gauṇīvṛtti as in the expression 'Gaurvāhīkaḥ' the word 'Gau' is required to convey a secondary sense because of being in apposition with the word 'vāhīka'. The word 'gau' conveys first the primary sense in the form of a lump having dewlap etc. Then it conveys the idea of the cows' qualities like dullness and slowness as a secondary sense. Without resting at that stage, the word goes on to convey the idea also of the Vāhīka as its further secondary sense because of the sāmānādhikaraṇya. It may be noted that the Gauṇīvṛtti is so-called because it invariably involves the qualities (Guṇa) belonging to what is conveyed as the primary meaning.[418]

Jagadīśa divides Lakṣaṇā into several types. He classifies it into Jahatsvarthā, Ajahatsvarthā, Nirūḍhā, Ādhunikā and Gauṇī.[419] The term Gauṇī is not present in the Kārikā concerned. He, however, explains the word 'ādi' in the Vṛtti on the Kārikā and maintains that the word 'ādi' signifies the Gauṇīvṛtti also.[420] We find Annaṁbhaṭṭa deviating from other Naiyāyikas in the matter. He divides Lakṣaṇā into three types as Jahallakṣaṇā, Ajahallakṣaṇā and Jahadajahallakṣaṇā. His example of Jahadajahallakṣaṇā, we may note, is Tattvamasī.[421]

Viśvanātha's classification of Lakṣaṅā, as we have already observed, is at least apparently not precise. He does not give the definition of the sub-varieties of Lakṣaṇā save and except the Lakṣitalakṣaṇā which is again understood by the scholars only as included in the Jahatsvārthā type of Lakṣaṅā. But Viśvanātha makes no direct mention of the Jahatsvārthā variety of Lakṣaṅā. He refers to the expression 'chatriṇo yānti' as an example of Ajahatsvārthā Lakṣaṇā and to the expression 'dvirephaḥ' as an example of Lakṣitalakṣaṇā. While illustrating the other expressions as cases of Lakṣaṅā, he makes no mention as to which varieties of Lakṣaṇā they belong to. Though he makes no mention of the Jahatsvārthā type of Lakṣaṅā, his first example of Lakṣaṅā, viz. 'gaṅgāyāṁ ghoṣaḥ' is undoubtedly a stock example of the variety. So the scholars unhesitatingly describe Viśvanātha as classifying Lakṣaṇā into two types, namely Jahatsvārthā and Ajahatsvārthā.[422] Notwithstanding Viśvanātha's reference to Lakṣitalakṣaṇā, he is not recognised to have divided Lakṣaṇā into three types, because of his including Lakṣitalakṣaṇā as a division of Jahatsvārthā. Dinakarabhaṭṭa observes that Viśvanātha's very treatment of Lakṣitalakṣaṇā is only to arrest the notion that

Lakṣitalakṣaṇā is an additional variety.[423] It may be pointed out that in the course of ascertaining the Śakti of an Ākhyāta, Viśvanā tha admits Lakṣaṇā in the Ākhyāta of the expression 'naśyati' (say, in the sentence 'ghaṭo naśyati') with regard to the state of being the counterpositive (i.e., pratiyogitva) (of destruction). He describes the so admitted case of Lakṣaṇā as a Nirūḍhālakṣaṇā. Dinakarabhaṭṭa points out that the Lakṣaṇā admitted by Viśvanātha in the Ākhyāta 'gacchati' in the sentence, 'ratho gacchati' is also a Nirūḍhalakṣaṇā. In support of his assertion he maintains that some manuscripts of the *Bhāṣāparicchеda* show the reading as 'nirūḍhālakṣaṇā'.[424]

Now, the question arises as to whether this so-called Nirūḍhā Lakṣaṇā is same with or different from Rūḍhimūlā Lakṣaṅā. Should we recognise other examples of Lakṣaṇā given in the *Bhā ṣāparicchеda* as those of Prayojanamūlā or some variety of Lakṣaṇā other than Ruḍhimūlā? Thus the context may lead to many queries. In anticipation of these queries, we may assert that Viśvanātha did not envisage any division of Lakṣaṇā like the Prayojanamūlā. As a matter of fact, all the examples of Lakṣaṇā given by Viśvanātha are Rūḍhimūlā or in other words, his illustrations of Lakṣaṇā donot include any one representing the Prayojanamūlā variety. This Nirūḍhā Lakṣaṇā stands for certain special cases of Rūḍhimūlā.

Every case of Lakṣaṇā presupposes the incompatibility of the speaker's intention with regard to a Śakyārtha leading to the fixation of the Tātparya to a newer meaning which comes to be designated as a Lakṣyārtha. Thus the Tātparya that comes to be directed to the Lakṣyrtha is of later origin, i.e., that originates in subsequent times. But in the case of Nirūḍhālakṣaṇās, the Tā tparya is not of immediate origin and cannot be traced back to an immediate past.[425]

Under the circumstances we may explain the term Nirūḍhā Lakṣaṇā as 'niḥśeṣeṇa rūḍhā lakṣaṇā' to give the idea that the

Lakṣaṇā in these cases is as good as Rūḍhi. (In other words, the Lakṣyārtha in these cases is strongly based as a Śakyārtha. But such an explanation should not create an impression that in a Nirūḍhālakṣaṇā, the Tātparya with regard to a Lakṣyārtha is an original one. It also presupposes an earlier 'anupapatti' of the Tātparya as a result of which the Tātparya comes to be fixed to the present meaning.) But in case of a Nirūḍhā Abhidhā as in the word, 'go', the original Tātparya stands and the 'abhidheyārtha' (the conventional meaning) does not suffer any set back by way of making space for a Lakṣyārtha to come in. We may add again that the examples of Lakṣaṇā given by Viśvanātha in the *BP* may be described as belonging only to the Śuddhā variety of the Ālaṁkārikas. Viśvanātha makes no reference to the Guṇavāda or Guṇavṛtti of the Mīmāṁsakas as well as to the Guaiṇi Lakṣaṇā of the Ālaṁkārikas. Here we may point out that some of his colleagues in the school of Nyāya, unhesitatingly accept Gauṇī as only a variety of Lakṣaṅā,[426] like the Ālaṁkārikas.

M(36). kintu lākṣaṇikaṁ padaṁ nānubhāvakam. Lākṣaṅaikārthasya śābdabodhe tu padāntaraṁ kāraṇam, śakti-lakṣaṇānyatara-sambandhenetarapadārthānvitasvaśakyārtha-śābdabodhaṁ prati padānāṁ sāmarthyāvadhāraṇādityāhuḥ. Navīnāstu tadapyanubhāvakameva. Padārthopasthitistu dvāram, anyathā tulyayuktyā śāktasyāpi padasyā 'nanubhāvakatvāpatterityāhuḥ.

Here in these lines Viśvanātha records a view of the Mīmāṁsakas along with a counter view of the Naiyāyikas. A section of the Mīmāṁsakas maintain[427] that a Lākṣaṇika Pada cannot be an Anubhāvaka, i.e., a Śābdabodhajanaka. If a Lākṣaṇika Pada like 'gaṅgā' etc. in case of 'gaṅgāyāṁ ghoṣaḥ' etc. is recognised as the said Anubhāvaka, then the words, 'gaṅgā' etc. shall have to be recognised also as Śakta (denotative) with reference to the senses 'bank' etc. in view of the accepted principle 'tacchābdānubhavajanakatvaṁ tacchaktatvam' (the denotedness of a word amounts to its causeness to the corresponding Śābdabodhas). The aforesaid principle gives us to recognise only those words as

Śakta which are also Śābdānubhavajanaka. In other words, Padas which are instrumental in the matter of producing relevant verbal comprehension are only to be recognised as Śakta (denotative). And if the words like 'gaṅga' etc. being recognised as the cause of the corresponding verbal comprehension consequently come to be recognised as denotative with reference to senses like 'bank' etc., then there ceases the scope for recognising a Lakṣaṇā in these words. Such a development will obviously lead to discarding the very concept of Lakṣaṇā in toto. Hence the Mīmāṁsakas do not recognise a Lākṣaṇika Pada as an Anubhāvaka. They regarded another Śakta Pada which is found related to the contextual Lakṣyārtha due to nearness as the Anubhāvaka in these cases where a Lākṣaṇika Pada occurs. As for instance, in case of 'gaṅgāyāṁ ghoṣaḥ', 'gaṅgā' is a Lākṣaṇika Pada and 'ghoṣa' is a Śakta Pada. Here 'ghoṣa' is the cause of Śābdabodha. Or again if 'ghoṣa' is admitted by any one to be Lākṣaṇika in the sense of a fish, the word 'gaṅgā' being the nearby Śakta word comes to be the relevant Anubhāvaka. Now Viśvanātha records a counter view in 'navīnāstu'[428] etc. According to him, the modern scholars do not accept the view of the Mīmāṁsakas. To the contrary, they believe that even a Lākṣaṇika Pada is an Anubhāvaka. By the word 'navīnāḥ', Viśvanātha means the Naiyāyikas who are much more modern generally speaking, when compared with the Mīmāṁsakas. According to these thinkers, as Viśvanātha records their views, the non-recognition of a Lākṣaṇika Pada as 'ananubhāvaka' would lead to the non-admission of a Śaktapada also as such. The idea of these scholars may be laid bare as follows : Irrespective of the involvement of either Śakti or Lakṣaṇā in the matter of obtaining the meaning from a word, the knowledge of the meaning(s) of word(s) i.e., Padārthadhī is the Vyāpāra as the immediate cause of the effect, the Śābdabodha. Now the status of Karaṇa must be given to that knowledge of words, which gives rise to the aforesaid knowledge of meaning. i.e., Padārthadhī which brings about the Śābdabodha. In 'gaṅgā yāṁ matsyaḥ' where there is no scope for the operation of

Lakṣaṇa in the word 'gaṅgā', the Śābdabodha of the 'gaṅgā-pada' (which is a Khaṇḍa-vākya) follows the knowledge of the Śakyārtha of 'gaṅgā' i.e., a current, and the knowledge of the 'gaṅgāpada' is the contextual Karaṇa. Similarly in 'gaṅgāyāṁ ghoṣaḥ' where there is the scope for Lakṣaṇā to operate in the word 'gaṅgā', the Śābdabodha of the 'gaṅgā-pada' follows only the knowledge of the Lakṣyārtha of 'gaṅgā' i.e., a bank. Just as in 'gaṅgāyāṁ matsyaḥ', the word 'gaṅgā' as a Śaktapada becomes an Anubhāvaka, similarly in 'gaṅgāyāṁ ghoṣaḥ', the word 'gaṅgā' as a lākṣaṇikapada becomes the Anubhāvaka. If a lākṣaṇikapada despite of being Vyāpāravat by way of producing the knowledge of the lakṣyārtha, the immediate cause of the contextual Śābdabodha, is denied the status of an Anubhāvaka, i.e., a Śābdabodhajanaka or Karaṇa, there is no point in admitting as Anubhāvaka even a Śakta pada only for generating the knowledge of a Śakyārtha which brings about a Śābdabodha. Of other Naiyāyikas, Gadādhara makes a distinct reference to this notion of the Mīmāṁsakas[429] and boldly refutes the same on the same logic.[430]

M(37). vākye tu śakterabhāvācchakyasambhandharūpā lakṣaṇā' pi nāsti.

The observation of Viśvanātha, above, 'vākye tu' etc., has obvious reference to the assertion of the Mīmāṁsakas that Lakṣaṇā pertains to a vākya (sentence). The Bhāṭṭa Mīmāṁsakas led by Kumārila maintain that any sentence-meaning must come to us in the form of a Lakṣyārtha.[431] According to this position, the function of Lakṣaṇā belongs also to a sentence. But the Naiyāyikas claim that Lakṣaṇā may belong to a word and word alone.[432] It is to be noted that of the Naiyāyikas Gaṅgeśa was the first theorist to discuss this problem at great length. In the light of that very discussion by Gaṅgeśa the later Naiyāyikas like Jagadīśa and Viśvanātha have come to offer arguments with illustration for not recognising Lakṣaṇā as belonging to a sentence. We propose to discuss the issue with some elaboration in the following pages.

In the *Muktāvalī* above, Viśvanātha asserts his opposition to the view that there can be operation of Lakṣaṇā as pertaining to a whole sentence. According to him, as Śakti (Abhidhā) is a function exclusively belonging to a word only (Padamātra vṛtti), it cannot exist corresponding to a sentence. Consequently there can never be a Lakṣaṇā also of the form of 'Śakyasambandha' as pertaining to a sentence. As because a sentence does not possess Śakti, it cannot possess a Śakyārtha also. As Lakṣaṇā is nothing but the relation of this Śakyārtha understood with regard to another meaning, the existence of Lakṣaṇā as pertaining to a sentence can never be thought of. The presence of the word 'tu' in the aforesaid text of the *Bhāṣāpariccheda* is very much significant as it is used to focus an opinion in sharp contrast to that of other important schools of thought like Mīmāṁsā, Vyākaraṇa and Alaṁkāra.

In the face of the divergent views, we are to take not first of the Mīmāṁsakas and Vaiyākaraṇas. These scholars regard Lakṣaṇā as a Vākyavyāpāra. The Naiyāyikas in contrast understand Lakṣaṇā only as a Padamātravṛtti. The Vedāntins and the Ālaṁkā rikas accept the two extreme positions as they understand Lakṣaṇā both in Pada and Vākya.

The Bhāṭṭa Mīmāṁsakas, as we have already referred to, believe that every Vākyārtha (sentence-meaning) is a Lakṣyārtha (secondary meaning).[433] They hold that the primary meanings conveyed by the words through Śakti or Abhidhā lead up to a sentence-meaning to be conveyed by Lakṣaṇā.[434] Abhidhā ceases to operate after conveying the primary meaning of each word. These primary or expressed meanings conveyed by Śakti constitute a sentence-meaning. This sentence-meaning is conveyed by Lakṣaṇā. Thus with the Bhāṭṭas, every Vākyārtha is a Lakṣyā rtha as because every Vākya invariably requires the operation of a Lakṣaṇā to get its meaning conveyed.

The Prābhākaras, as Anvitābhidhānavādins, believe that words convey their own meanings not in isolation. According to them, the words in a sentence get syntactically related and then come to convey the sentence-meaning.[435] In case there arises any incompatibility in the context of the syntactical relation (anvayā nupapatti), of the primary meanings of the individual words, Lakṣaṇā comes in to remove the inconsistency.[436] Now when a word occurs alone, there is no question of 'anvaya' or syntactical relation. Hence there is no problem of incompatibility in the syntactical relation (Anvayānupapatti) of the primary meanings. As the Prābhākaras believe only in Anvayānupapatti as the Lakṣaṇābīja, they find no scope at all of Lakṣaṇā as pertaining to a single word. The Prābhākaras also, in the light of the above arguments, hold that Lakṣaṇā comes to operate in a sentence only when it reveals some hindrence for individual word-meanings to be involved in a syntactical relation in order to give the sentence-meaning. Under the circumstances, Prābhākaras reject the notion of the Bhāṭṭas.[437]

As interpreters of the Vedic injunctions which appear in the form of sentences, the Mīmāṁsakas accept Lakṣaṇā in a Vākya for obvious reasons. Whenever any difficulty arises in explaining a Vedic text, they have to take the help of Lakṣaṇā. But we shall have to bear in mind that while the Bhāṭṭas accept Lakṣaṇā in all sentences and again not only in Vaidika (scriptural) but also in laukika (popular) ones, the Prābhākaras find the scope of Lakṣaṇā only in sentences which involve Anvayānupapatti. The stock-example of both the schools recognising Vākya Lakṣaṇā or Lakṣaṇā as pertaining in the whole sentence is 'gabhīrāyāṁ nadyā ṁ ghoṣaḥ'.[438] While opposing the recognition of Vākya Lakṣaṇā Viśvanātha explains his position with the help of this very illustration. Hence we need elaboration of the Mīmāṁsakas' view with regard to this illustration of theirs. According to the Mīmāṁsakas, 'gabhīrāyāṁ nadyāṁ ghoṣḥ' is a case of Lakṣaṇā. It is because they admit Lakṣaṇā with reference to a whole sentence. In their view, the intended sense, 'the bank of a deep river' is conveyed neither by the term 'gabhīra' alone nor by the word 'nadī alone. If the word 'gabhīra' conveys the Lakṣyārtha (the bank) and the word 'nadī' retains its primary sense, a syntactical relation between the two words cannot be thought of. It is because of the impossibility of identification between a bank and a river. If the word 'nadī again is taken to convey the secondary sense (the bank) and the word 'gabhīra' is allowed to retain its primary meaning, it is not possible to have the mutual relation between the two words; because the bank of a river cannot be deep. It is again not possible to have both the words conveying the secondary sense. In that case, the same secondary sense will find itself difficult to be syntactically related with two different primary meanings of two different words. Again there can be no justification for getting the same meaning twice from two different words. Hence they suggest that the proper process is as follows. The syntactical relation between the two primary meanings, i.e., 'deep' and 'river' is first effected. Thereafter, the sentence as a whole, conveys the sencondary sense, 'the bank of the deep river' by means of Lakṣaṇā. This secondary sense is related to the two primary meanings. In other words, the Vākyārtha, i.e., what is conveyed by the Vākya is something related to the meaning 'deep-river' and that is no other than 'the bank of a deep river'

But here we must not forget that to the Bhāṭṭas who regard every Vākyārtha as a Lakṣyārtha, the expression 'gabhīrāyāṁ nadyāṁ ghoṣaḥ' is automatically an illustration of Vākyalakṣaṇā without any involvement of 'anupapatti' (incompatibility) as such. The idea of this view of Mīmāṁsakas can be gathered from the *Tattvacintāmaṇi* of Gaṅgeśopādhyāya who records the position of Mīmāṁsakas as his 'pūrvapakṣa'.[439]

The Naiyāyikas in complete opposition to the Mīmāṁsakas, hold that Lakṣaṇā may belong only to a Pada (word) and not to a Vākya (sentence). Lakṣaṇā is, undoubtedly, only a substitute for Śakti. Since Śakti belongs to the word, Lakṣaṇā also necessarily belongs to the word only. Hence there can be no possibility of Lakṣaṇā as belonging to a whole sentence. As Gaṅgeśa puts it,[440]

Lakṣaṇā like Śakti is only a PadaVṛtti. We must note that the Naiyāyikas always discuss the concept of PadaVṛtti (Verbal functions) in respect of isolated words. They define Lakṣaṇā as a relation between the Śakyārtha and the Lakṣyārtha. The Śakyā rtha may be presented only by what possesses a Śakti. Hence Lakṣaṇā also remains associated with what possesses the Śakti. It is already known that only a Pada possesses the Śakti.[441] The accepted position of the Naiyāyikas is that as there is no Śakti in a Vākya, there is no Śakyārtha also in it. And consequently there is no Lakṣaṇā (Śakyasambandha) in a Vākya. We may refer to Gaṅgeśopādhyāya[442] and Viśvanātha in this context. Viśvanātha's text in the *Muktāvalī*, 'vākye tu' etc. confirms his position. Now of all the Naiyāyikas, the author of the *Tattvacintāmaṇi* handles the problem more seriously and elaborately. Gaṅgeśa first presents the views of Prābhākaras, as we have already mentioned, as the 'pūrvapakṣa' in the context. He reproduces the view of the Mīmā ṁsakas and in reply maintains that as a sentence as a whole cannot have a Śakyārtha. It is because the Lakṣyārtha is only a substitute for a Śakyārtha. It may be argued that the Vākyārtha (which is conveyed by the sentence as a whole) is the 'anvaya' (the syntactical relation) of the meanings ofthe individual words in the sentence and the 'anvaya' is conveyed by the words only being in a group and not individually. In such a context, Gangeśa feels otherwise. According to him, the individual word itself conveys the idea of 'anvaya' of its own meaning. The group cannot convey the idea of an 'anvaya' of the meanings of words belonging to it. It is because a group cannot have a definite primary meaning of its own. The Śakyārtha, therefore, belongs only to the individual word and never to a group. Consequently Lakṣaṇā as Śakyasambandha can belong to the word (Pada) and never to a sentence (Vā kya).[443] We have already referred to Gaṅgeśa's recording the arguments of Mīmāṁsakas with regard to their example of Vā kyalakṣaṇā 'gabhīrāyāṁ nadyāṁ ghoṣaḥ'. In his refutation of the Mīmāṁsakas' view, Gaṅgeśa observes thus : The words 'gabhīra' and 'nadī' first get involved in an 'anvaya' and present the idea of 'a deep river'. Then either of the two words comes to convey the idea of 'the bank of a deep river', as a Lakṣyārtha. This Lakṣyārtha is related to the Śakyārtha of the word which is taken to have conveyed the Lakṣyārtha in the context.[444] Thus it is not the sentence but a single word, either 'gabhīra' or 'nadī', which conveys the Lakṣyārtha. It may be pointed out that there being no decisive factor as to which of the two words would convey the Lakṣyārtha, one shall have to admit Lakṣaṇā in both the words. In admitting a Vākyalakṣaṇā, the opponants may argue, only one Lakṣaṇā would suffice. In reply to such arguments, Gaṅgeśa maintains that even in case of admitting Vākya lakṣaṇā, one is required to recognise Lakṣaṇā in both the words for thesame reason, i.e., the lack of a decisive factor. In the event of a Vākya lakṣaṇā one shall have to admit the third Lakṣaṇā in the Vākya in addition to the two Lakṣaṇās already admitted in the two words. Under the circumstances, Gaṅgeśa strongly argues that the admission of Lakṣaṇā in a Pada instead of in a Vākya does not involve the fallacy of Gaurava.[445] Hence the question of admitting Lakṣaṇā in a Vākya in preference to a single Pada does not arise. In the example under discussion, the Lakṣaṇā is to be admitted as belonging to either of the two words 'gabhīra' and 'nadī'. As a matter of fact it is the word 'nadī' to which Lakṣaṇā belongs. It is because the meaning of the word 'nadī' is directly connected with the bank while that of theword 'gabhīra' is only remotely associated with it (the bank).[446] This logic of Gaṅgeśa comes to be accepted by his successors in the school of Nyāya. Sharing the same opinion, we presume, Viśvanātha, as we shall see in succeeding text of the *Muktāvalī*, categorically asserts that in the example, 'gabhīrāyāṁ nadyāṁ ghoṣaḥ', it is the word 'nadī' that conveys the Lakṣyārtha, i.e., the bank of a deep river.

M(37a) yatra tu gabhīrāyāṁ nadyāṁ ghoṣa ityuktam, tatra nadīpadasya nadītīre lakṣaṇā gabhīrapadārthasya nadyā sahābhedenānvayaḥ, kvacidekadeśānvayasyāpi svīkṛtatvāt. yadi tatraikadeśānvayo na svīkriyate, tadā nadīpadasya gabhīranadītīre lakṣaṇa gabhīrapadaṁ tātparyagrāhakam.

In the text of the *Muktāvalī* above, Viśvanātha shows the operation of Padalakṣaṇā in the Mīmāṁsakas' example of Vākyalakṣaṇā. As we have already noted, the sentence 'gabhīrāyāṁ nadyāṁ ghoṣaḥ' is the stock example of Vākyalakṣaṇā in the circle of Mīmāṁsakas. As such, the Naiyāyikas have come to discuss it whenever they find scope for dealing with the problem of recognising Lakṣaṇā in the entire sentence.

We have already pointed out that Gaṅgeśa, the eminent predecessor of Viśvanātha has discussed the Mīmāṁsakas' arguments in the context and has finally asserted[447] that the inconsistency in the syntactical relation involved in the expression could be removed by a Padalakṣaṇā. He does not find any necessity for recognising a Vākyalakṣaṇā in the context of the expression under discussion. Jagadīśa also comes to reject the view of the Mīmāṁsakas and to establish the logic of recognising a Lakṣaṇā in one of the Padas constituting the sentence.[448] Viśvanātha, however, does not directly refer to the opposing school of thought. Without any discussion of the earlier views on the subject, he briefly records the latest position already arrived at in his circle.

Viśvanātha does not go for elaborate discussion, inasmuch as the recognition of a Padalakṣaṇā instead of Vākyalakṣaṇā for adequately explaining the expression 'gabhīrāyāṁ' etc. already has come to be an established fact in his own school of thought. In the event of admitting a Padalakṣaṇā in the expression 'gabhīrāyāṁ' etc., either of both the words 'nadī' and 'gabhīra' stands competent to have a Lakṣaṇā. But the relation between 'the bank' and 'deep' (the meaning of the word 'gabhīra') is obviously very remote in comparison with that between 'the bank' and 'the river' (the meaning of the word 'nadī'). So Gaṅgeśa justifiably prefers the Lakṣaṇā from the word 'nadī' and not the word 'gabhīra'.[449] Unlike Jagadīśa,[450] Viśvanātha follows Gaṅgeśa in this regard. In admitting that in the example "gabhīrāyam nadyām ghoṣaḥ', it is the word 'nadi' that conveys the Lakṣyārtha, i.e., the bank of the deep river, a very pertinent question arises, as to why the word 'gabhīra' should not be supposed to be redundant. In anticipation of such a question, we may presume that Viśvanātha in his *BP* offers two alternative solutions.

(1) The word 'nadī' presents the idea of 'the bank of the river' as the 'lakṣyārtha'. The word 'gabhīra' conveys its primary meaning 'deep' which gets involved in a syntactical relation with the meaning 'river'. The two meanings get related as completely identified. But the meaning 'river' is only a part of the meaning 'the bank of the deep river'. Now the connection between 'deep' and 'river' is possible inasmuch as sometimes such a partial syntactical connection (ekadeśānvaya) is found to be sanctioned (in cases like 'devadattasya gurukulam' and 'devadattasya guruputraḥ'). We may here add that this concept of 'ekadeśānvaya' may be traced back in its origin to Patañjali's discussion under Pāṇiniān rule 'Samarthaḥ padavidhiḥ'.[451]

(2) If the principle of 'ekadeśānvaya' is not accepted, the word 'nadī' alone may be taken to convey a (wider) secondary sense, i.e., 'the bank of a deep river'. In such a case, the word 'gabhīra' with its primary meaning simply will serve as the Tātparyagrāhaka (a pointer or index to the intention of the speaker in the context). We, however, shall have to add that the idea of admitting a word (other than that which presents the Lakṣyārtha) as the Tātparyagrāhaka in the context of explaining 'gabhīrāyāṁ' etc. by way of recognising only a Padalakṣaṇā, has been originally mooted out by Jagadīśa.[452]

M(38). bahuvrīhāvapyevam. tatra hi citragupadādau yadyekadeśānvayaḥ svīkriyate tadā gopadasya gomati lakṣaṇā, gavi citrābhedānvayaḥ. yadi tvekadeśānvayo na svīkriyate, tadā gopadasya citragosvāmini lakṣaṇā. citrapadaṁ tātparya-grā hakam. evamārūḍhavānaro vṛkṣa ityatra vānarapade vānarārohaṇakarmaṇi lakṣaṇā. āruḍhapadañca tātparyagrāhakam. evamanyatrāpi.

Now in the text of the *Muktāvalī* above, Viśvanātha proceeds to the controversial issue of recognising Lakṣaṇā in Samāsas. Before we come to examine the text of Viśvanātha, it is necessary on our part to have a prior knowledge of the problem as is being handled by other scholars in different schools of thought.

The Mīmāṁsakas admit Lakṣaṇā in certain Samāsas. They admit it in the entire samāsa and not merely in a constituent word of it. To the contrary, the Naiyāyikas including Viśvanātha admit Lakṣaṇā not in an entire samāsa but in one of the component parts of it. The Grammarians, on the other hand, do not find any scope of admitting Lakṣaṇā either in the whole or any part of a compounded word. They find the purpose served by the Śakti itself. Hence the issue of recognising Lakṣaṇā in Samāsas deserves a bit elaborate discussion.

As we have already observed, the Mīmāṁsakas recognise the meaning of certain Samāsas as Lakṣyārtha. In the context of the sacrifice called 'Raudreṣṭi', there is the Vedic injunction, 'etayā niṣādasthapatiṁ yājayet', the word 'yājayet' literally means 'should make some one else perform a sacrifice'. But the act of causing others to perform a saerifice is a professional activity of a brahmin. It is obviously concerned with some material gain. It is, therefore, to be admitted that there cannot be any injunction in this literal sense of the word 'yājayet'. Hence the word 'yājayet' is to be taken to bear the mening of 'yajet' (one should perform a sacrifice oneself). Now the question is whether the 'niṣā dasthapati' who is enjoined to perform the sacrifice should be understood as 'niṣādaścāsau sthapatiśca' or as 'niṣādānāṁ sthapatiḥ'. In the former case we understand some one who is a Niṣāda by caste and who is at the same time a leader or chief. In the latter, we understand from the word some one as leader of the Niṣādas, himself not necessarily being a Niṣāda by caste. The former is a case of Karmadhāraya samāsa and in the latter we have a case of Tatpuruṣasamāsa. If we take the compounded word as a Karmadhāraya, on the strength of this Vedic injunction, even a Niṣāda, an outcaste would have the right to perform a sacrifice. Yet Jaimini prefers this alternative only because he finds a Karmadhāraya samāsa without any involvement of Lakṣaṇā. On the plea that the meaning of the word 'niṣādasthapati' as a Karmadhāraya can be had directly by means of Śruti (Śakti), he shows his anxiety to avoid a Tatpuruṣa compound in the very word as it obviously involves a Lakṣaṇā. To show that there is no scope at all for Lakṣaṇā in a Karmadhāraya compound, the author of the *Bhāṣāpariccheda* indirectly refers to this position of the Mīmāṁsakas by way of illustrating their approach with this very example. Now to persue the matter again, in order to solve the conflict between possible direct and secondary meanings arising out of the formation of the word 'niṣādasthapati', Jaimini observes that the 'sthapati' (chief) should be taken to be a Niṣāda by caste as because that is the (direct) meaning of the word.[453] Śabarasvāmin makes the point clear. We come to know from him that Mīmāṁsakas' preference to the former interpretation of the expression 'niṣādasthapati' is because of its not involving a Lakṣaṇā. The later interpretation shows a case of 'ṣaṣthī tatpuruṣasamāsa' that obviously involves the operation of a Lakṣaṇā. Whenever there is a conflict between a direct meaning (conveyed by Abhidhā) and a secondary meaning (conveyed by Lakṣaṇā), it is the principle of the Mīmāṁsakas to accept a direct meaning and to reject the secondary meaning.[454] The later Mīmā ṁsakas also are anxious to discard the meaning of the word 'niṣā dasthapati' when understood as a Tatpuruṣa compound.[455] This very context of interpreting a Vedic injuction bears testimony to the fact that atleast in certain Samāsas like Tatpuruṣa, the Mīmā ṁsakas take the meaning to be a Lakṣyārtha while in some others like Karmadhāraya they take the meaning of the Samāsa only as a Śakyārtha. We shall discuss the reasons for the admission or otherwise of a Lakṣaṇā in different Samāsas in the context of our examination of the relevant *Bhāṣāpariccheda* text.

Already we know that the Mīmāṁsakas do not admit Padalakṣaṇā. Whenever they have to admit the operation of Lakṣaṇā either universally (as by the Bhāṭṭas) or casually (as by the Prābhākaras) they understand the Lakṣyārtha from the entire sentence. In other words, they recognise Vākyalakṣaṇā only. So in case of samāsas also, whenever they have to recognise a Lakṣaṇā, they do it not in any of the component parts. Instead they understand Lakṣyārtha from the Samāsa as a whole. As a Samāsa is nothing but a compressed sentence, their concept of Vākyalakṣaṇā also does not suffer thereby.

Similarly the position of the Naiyāyikas as regards recognising Lakṣaṇā in Samāsas is linked up with their approach to the problem of recognition of Lakṣaṇā in a Vākya. As we already know, the Naiyāyikas do not admit Lakṣaṇā in a Vākya (i.e., a sentence as a whole). In their view, Lakṣaṇā may belong to one of the several individual words comprising a sentence. Because of this position of the Naiyāyikas, with regard to Vākyalakṣaṇā, it is obvious that they do not come to recognise Lakṣaṇā also in a Samāsa as a whole. It is because a Samāsa is for them a Compressed sentence only. They feel that to recognise a Lakṣaṇā in a Samāsa will virtually amount to recognising a Lakṣaṇā in a Vākya (a full sentence). So with all anxiety to avoid recognising Lakṣaṇā in a Samāsa, the Naiyāyikas assert that whenever a Lakṣyārtha is to be conveyed in a Samāsa, the corresponding Lakṣaṇā operates as belonging to any one of the component words of the compound. Amongst the Naiyāyikas, Gaṅgeśa and Viśvanātha have exhaustively examined the operation of Lakṣaṇā in different types of compounds (Samāsas). Particularly Viśvanātha's treatment of the issue is very lucid and clear. We shall come to discuss the position of both the Naiyāyikas in the context of our examination of the relevant *BP* text.

Now to make a mention of the Grammarians, first we are to note their difference in the context from both the Mīmāṁsakas and the Naiyāyikas. It is because the Vaiyākaraṇas have difference with them in respect of the nature of the implication of Śakti itself. To the Mīmāṁsakas and the Naiyāyikas there is no Śakti in a Vākya as well as in a Samāsa which is nothing but a condensed sentence (Vākya). But unlike the thinkers of these two schools the Vaiyākaraṇas understand Śakti as belonging to a Samāsa as a whole. The Grammarians want a Samāsa to be recognised as a single word endowed with Śakti and Śakyārtha. It is because they are anxious to maintain the status of Samāsa as a Prātipadika. Their idea is this : If a Samāsa is supposed to be 'śabdasamudāya' (a cluster of words) and not as an 'ekapada' (a single word), it will not be possible to apply the definition of Prātipadika to it.

Patañjali in his *Mahābhāṣya*, under Pāṇini's sūtra 'Arthavadadhāturapratyaḥ prātipadikam' (p. 1.2.45) maintains that a cluster of words (śabdasamudāya) being meaningless is not entitled to be a Prātipadika. Patañjali's example of samudāya (a cluster of words) as 'aprātipadika' for being 'anarthaka' is 'daśa dā ḍimāni ṣaḍapūpāḥ'. This samudāya, though meaningful, is treated as meaningless. The idea is this : a cluster of words, even though meaningful is to be treated as meaningless only to exclude it from the list of Prātipadikas. Now then a Samāsa must be recognised as a single word and not as a cluster of words. If it be taken as a cluster of words, it will come to be treated as meaningless and will, as a result, be excluded from the list of the Prātipadikas.[456] But such a position is not desirable as because in the rule Kṛttaddhitasamāsāśca,[457] a Samāsa is clearly given the status of a Prātipadika. Thus, accordingly, to the Grammarians, a Samāsa is a single word. It is a Prātipadika and the meaning conveyed by it is a Śakyārtha. Now we find that in a Samāsa like 'citragu', the entire Samāsa comes to convey the meaning, 'the master of spotted cows' (gosvāmin). This meaning is obviously different from what should have been the direct meanings of the component parts of the compound, namely, 'citra' and 'go'. The Grammarians, in that case, understand unhesitatingly this meaning, i.e, 'the master of spotted cows' as the immediate direct meaning (Śakyārtha) of the Samāsa itself without any reference to what could have been the direct meaning of the word 'citra' and 'go'. Thus in the view of the Grammarians, Samāsārtha is a variety of Śakyārtha. If they fail to explain a samāsārtha as Yaugika, they would then do it as either Rūḍha or Yogarūḍha. As a representative of later Grammarians, Nāgeśa endorses the old view that in order to maintain its status as a Prātipadika, a Samāsa is to be admitted as an unitary word and the Samāsārtha is invariably to be recognised as a Śakyā rtha.[458]

As we see in the *Muktāvalī* above, Viśvanātha, first of all, takes up the case of Bahuvrīhi. He gives the example of 'citragu' wherein he shows that the Samāsa has two constituent parts, i.e., the two words 'citra' and 'go'. The word 'citra' means 'spotted' and the word 'go' means a 'cow'. But the compound instead of meaning this 'spotted cow' means 'the owner of spotted cows'. This latter meaning is not a Śakyārtha of either of the two words 'citra' and 'go'. Hence the meaning is undoubtedly a Lakṣyārtha. But this Lakṣyārtha can not belong to the compound as a whole as that will amount to the recognition of Lakṣyārtha in a Vākya. Hence in the view of Viśvanātha, as we understand him, whatever Lakṣyārtha we get here must belong to any one of the two words. For arriving at this position, he offers two solutions as follows:

(i) If the principle of partial syntactical connection is not to be objected to, the word 'go', the second member of the compound may be taken as presenting the Lakṣyārtha as 'gosvāmin' (the master of the cows). The Śakyārtha of 'citra', the first member of the Compound, i.e., 'spotted' comes to have a syntactical relation with the meaning 'cow' which forms a part (ekadeśa) of the whole secondary meanings, i.e., 'master of the cows'. In case of not recognising 'ekadeśānvaya', (the principle of partial syntactical connection), Viśvanātha suggests his second alternative.

(ii) Of the two words 'citra' and 'go', the latter may be taken as presenting the entire Lakṣyārtha, i.e., the idea of 'a master of spotted cows'. In that case, the whole desirable meaning is conveyed by only one of the two words and the other comes to be redundant. Viśvanātha's approach in this context seeks to save the other word from the charge of being redundant. The author of the *Bhāṣāpariccheda* maintains that the other word, i.e., 'citra' in the aforesaid example, serves as the Tātparyagrāhaka (a pointer to the intention of the speaker involved in the presentation of the Lakṣyārtha by a word like 'go' in the expression under discussion). Viśvanātha's idea is this : As is generally the case with the Naiyāyikas, the 'tātparyānupapatti' has been already accepted as the basic condition for the operation of Lakṣaṇā function. When the Śakyārtha obtained in a context does not satisfy or bring out the intention of the speaker there is the scope for Lakṣaṇā. Hence the cognition of a Lakṣyārtha must invariably be preceded by the knowledge of Tātparya which must be made known by some factors like the present one. Hence in the view of Viśvanātha, one will not find scope for treating as redundant the other word, i.e., the word other than the Lakṣaka (the word that conveys the secondary sense). Prior to Viśvanātha, Gaṅgeśa also pointed out that in case Lakṣaṇā be admitted in one of the Padas of the Compound, the remaining one should not be viewed as useless.[459]

Gaṅgeśa discusses the scope of the operation of Lakṣaṇā in Bahuvrīhi Compound so elaborately that his discourse runs to as many as twenty six pages in his *Tattvacintāmaṇi*. He examines the opinion that Lakṣaṇā is to be admitted in the entire compound to convey the meaning (Anyapadārtha) of the compound, which is different from the Śakyārthas of the constituent words.[460] He also pays his attention to the opposite view that a Śakti covering the entire compound, i.e., Samudāyaśakti is to be admitted for the purpose.[461] After a vigorous analysis of the issue, Gaṅgeśa concludes that the best and simplest possible solution lies in admitting Lakṣaṇā in only one of the constituent words.[462] 'Ārūḍhavānaro vṛkṣa' is the other instance of Bahuvrīhi compound given by Viśvanātha for showing that the operation of a Lakṣaṇā in a compound takes places in respect of one of the constituent members (words) and not as belonging to the entire compound. In the case of 'Ārūḍhavānaro vṛkṣa', the latter member of the compound, the word 'vānara' gives 'vānarā rohaṇakarma' (the object of the act of climbing by the monkey) as its Lakṣyārtha with the aid of Lakṣaṇā. The first member of the compound, i.e., the word 'ārūḍha' serves as the 'Tātparyagrāhaka' in the context. We may add that Jagadīśa refers to the Lakṣaṇā involved in a Bahuvrīhi compound as a Nirūḍhā one and gives the expression 'ārūḍhavānaro (vṛkṣa) as the first illustration in the context.[463] Gaṅgeśa who preceded both Viśvanātha and Jagadīśa already asserted that Lakṣaṇā involved in a Bahuvrīhi compound is of the 'nirūḍhā' type.[464] In 'evamanyatrāpi,' Viśvanātha observes that similar is the case also with other expressions involving Bahuvrīhi compounds. To reiterate the position, he is prepared to admit Lakṣaṇā only in respect of one of the component words. Of this compound the other word, according to him, is there to serve as the Tātparyagrāhaka.

M(39). tatpuruṣe tu pūrvapade lakṣaṇā. tathāhi - rājapuruṣa ityādau rājapadārthena puruṣādipadārthasya sākṣānnānvayaḥ, nipātātiriktanāmārthayorbhedenā' nvayabodhasyā'vyutpannatvā t. anyathā rājapuruṣa ityatrāpi tathānvayabodhaḥ syāt. paṭo na ghaṭa ityādau ghaṭapaṭābhyāṁ nañaḥ sākṣādevānvayād - nipātā tirikteti. nīlo ghaṭa ityādau nāmārthayorabhedasambandhenā 'nvayād - bhedeneti. na ca rājapuruṣa ityādau luptavibhakteḥ smaraṇaṁ kalpyamiti vācyam; asmṛtavibhakterapi tato bodhodayāt. tasmād rājapadādau rājasambandhini lakṣaṇā. tasya ca puruṣeṇa sahābhedānvayaḥ.

In case of Tatpuruṣa Samāsa, Viśvanātha like his predecessors, Gaṅgeśa[465] and Jagadīśa,[466] maintains that Lakṣaṇā must invariably belong to the earlier member (pūrvapada) of the compound. For example, in the compound 'rājapuruṣa' the earlier word 'rāja(n)' gives 'some one related to the king' as its Lakṣyārtha, which by virtue of the word's 'sāmānadhikaraṇya' (i.e., the state of remaining in the same case-ending) with the latter word, gets syntactically connected with the Śakyārtha of the word 'puruṣa' through the relation of identity (tādātmya). It so happens as anticipated by the maxim, 'nipātātiriktanāmārthayorbhedenā-'nvayabodhasyāvyutpannatvam,' according to which the meaning of two nāmapadas (i.e., Nouns, Adjectives and Pronouns) which are in the same case-endings (vibhakti) and are not intervened by any indeclinable (Nipāta) must get mutually related through the relation of identity (abheda). That is why the word 'rāja(n)' must give such a meaning as the Lakṣyārtha, if not as the Śakyārtha, which might easily have the relation of identity with the meaning of the word 'puruṣa' so that we could say 'ya eva puruṣaḥ sa eva rājasambandhī'.

If the syntactical connection through the relation of difference be allowed between two Nāmapadas, even when not intervened by some Nipātas, then such a connection shall have to be understood even in the expression 'rājapuruṣa'. This is naturally unsound. There is nothing here to make us understand that what is meant by 'rāja' is other than what is meant by 'puruṣa'. Hence the maxim 'nipātātirikta' etc. which characterises as unnatural any understanding of syntactical connection between two Nāmapadas through the relation of difference unless they are intervened by some 'Nipāta'. Viśvanātha proceeds to explain the maxim with illustrations which are obviously not Tatpuruṣa compounds. If two Nāmapadas come to be, however, intercepted by any Nipāta, the two meanings of these words can be understood as syntactically connected as different objects. For instance, in the expression, 'paṭo na ghaṭaḥ' (a cloth is not a jar), though the two words 'paṭa' and 'ghaṭa' are in the same case-ending, yet they are not understood as identical only on the strength of being intervened by 'na' (nañ). It should be borne in mind that it is the nature for two Nāmapadas to be identically related when not intervened by anything else. For instance, in the expression, 'nīlo ghaṭaḥ', the meaning of the two Nāmapadas, i.e., 'blue' and 'jar' get syntactically connected through the relation of identity. We can examine how such a relation of identity is possible. According to the Lexicon,[467] words like 'śukla' (white) etc. signify as their primary meanings not only the colours but also the corresponding coloured things. If we accept this position, the word 'nīla' gives as its primary meaning both the 'blue colour' and 'thing having the blue colour'. So in the expression, 'nīlo ghaṭaḥ', the meaning of the word 'ghaṭa' i.e., 'a jar' comes to be connected through the relation of identity with the (primary) meaning of the word 'nīla' i.e., some blue-coloured object. Thus two Śakyārthas in the expression come to have the desired relation of identity ('tādātmya') wihtout allowing any operation of Lakṣaṇā. But as we have seen with Viśvanātha in his approach to Śaktigraha from Koṣa, he is not prepared to admit Śakti of 'nīlādipadas' with regard to the nīlādiviśiṣṭa (things having blue colour etc.). He understands 'nīlādiviśiṣṭa' from 'nīlādipadas' only by Lakṣaṇā. In the light of Viśvanātha's approach, we shall have to admit Lakṣaṇā in the word 'nīla' in the expression 'nīlo ghaṭa' in order to obtain the relation of identity between the meanings of the two words. In whichever way possible, the two words in the expression 'nīlo ghaṭaḥ' must have their meanings mutually connected by the relation of identity as they are not intercepted by any 'Nipāta.' One must have from the aforesaid expression only the idea of a blue jar and not of the blue colour and a jar separately. According to Viśvanātha, of the two words 'nīla' and 'ghaṭa', the earlier one demands the operation of Lakṣaṇā in the uncompounded stage itself. Hence, when compounded, the words do not demand any fresh operation of Lakṣaṇā. Thus Viśvanātha's opinion appears to be that a Karmadhāraya compound does not necessarily demand the operation of Lakṣaṇā as a Samāsa.

Coming back to our expression under discussion, namely, 'rājapuruṣa', which is a Tatpuruṣa compound, we find that the Śakyārthas, 'the king' and 'the person' cannot be understood as connected in the desired relation of identity. Hence we are forced to have recourse to Lakṣaṇā in either of the two words. Viśvanātha fixes the operation of Lakṣaṇā to 'rāja(n)', as it happens to be the earlier member ('pūrvapada') of the compound. In the text of the *Muktāvalī*, 'tatpuruṣe tu' etc., 'tu' is significant. It is desired to be conveyed that Lakṣaṇā in a Tatpuruṣa compound can take place only in respect of its earlier member (word). The very definition of a Tatpuruṣa compound demands that the meaning of the latter member of the compound is all the more important implying there by that the meaning of the earlier word is less important. Now it is the accepted notion in different circles of thinkers that Lakṣyārtha is always to be reckoned as inferior to or at least less important than a Śakyārtha. Hence it is resonably held that only the earlier word in a Tatpuruṣa compound should be allowed to give a Lakṣyārtha as a result of which the principle of allowing more importance to the meaning of the latter member of a Tatpuruṣa compound will not be adversely affected.

Viśvanātha now proceeds to meet with an objection in the *M.* 'na ca ---------- bodhodayāt.'

One may opine that there is no operation of Lakṣaṇā in 'rājapuruṣa' as one understands the connection between 'rāja' and 'puruṣa' in the expression through the relation of identity only by remembering the meaning of the 6th case-ending which is applicable to the word 'rājā' before it comes to be compounded with 'puruṣa' and which stands understood at present because of compounding the two words. The idea behind such an opinion is that factually Lakṣaṇā is not resorted to in a compound like 'rā japuruṣa' as the listener as a matter of fact remembers the uncompounded expression 'rājñaḥ puruṣaḥ' in the context of understanding the compound 'rājapuruṣa'. Such a position is not tenable. We find that a person, even though fully ignorant of the structure of the words in their uncompounded stage, i.e., without remembering or having any scope to remember the understood case-endings, comes to have the desired verbal comprehension on simply hearing the expression 'rājapuruṣaḥ'. Hence, the operation of Lakṣaṇā in respect of the expression, 'rājapuruṣa' is undeniable. Here Viśvanātha concludes that the word 'rāja(n)' gives 'rājasambandhī' (one related to the king) as its meaning by Lakṣaṇā to be identically related with the primary meaning of the word 'puruṣa' i.e., the person. From 'ādi' in *M*, 'tasmāt rājapadādau', it is to be understood that Viśvanātha prescribes the same solution in the form of admitting Lakṣaṇā in 'pūrvapada' in case of other examples of Tatpuruṣa compounds. Even in a Tatpuruṣa compound as in a Bahuvrīhi, Viśvanātha like his poredecessors in the Nyāya school, is not prepared to admit Lakṣaṇā in an entire samā sa.

Thus, as pointed out by Jagadīśa also,[468] the need for maintaining a relation of identity ('abhedānvaya') between the meanings of the two constituent words of a Tatpuruṣa compound like 'rājapuruṣaḥ' forces the operation of a Lakṣaṇā in the 'pūrvapada' of the compound.

M(40). dvandve tu dhave-khadirau chindhītyādau dhavaḥ khadiraśca vibhaktyartha-dvitvaprakāreṇa budhyate, tatra na lakṣaṇā. na ca sāhitye lakṣaṇeti vācyam, sāhitya śūnyayorapi dvandva - darśanāt. na caikakriyānvayitvarūpaṁ sāhityamastīti vācyam. kriyābhede'pi dhava-khadirau paśya chindhītyādi - darśanāt, sāhityasyā'nanubhavācca. tasmāt sāhityādikaṁ nā rthaḥ. ata eva 'rājapurohitau sāyujyakāmau yajeyātā' (Mi. Su. 6.6.12) mityatra lakṣaṇābhāvād dvandva āśrīyate.

In the *Muktāvalī* text above, Viśvanātha also rules out any scope for the operation of Lakṣaṇā in the Dvandva compound, even to be admitted in one of its component parts. As he points out, in a Dvandva compound like 'Dhavakhadirau chindhi', we can have the desired Śābdabodha without any recourse to Lakṣaṇā anywhere. Here the meanings of the two words involved viz. Dhava and Khadira remain in tact and nothing in addition to the individual meanings of the words is to be recognised. The idea of the duality associated with the primary meanings of the two words is also conveyed as a Śakyārtha by the sign of the vibhakti itself.

Certain Dvandva compounds like 'bhīmārjunau', 'rāmalakṣmaṇau' etc. may make an impression that the compound under discussion is possible only with the words signifying object that have some mutual association or togetherness. In view of this, it may be argued that this very sense of association or togetherness, i.e., Sāhitya (sahitasya bhāvaḥ, sahita + ṣyañ) is to be atleast secondarily signified, i.e., to be understood by Lakṣaṇā. In reply to such a contention, Viśvanātha asserts that the Dvandva compound is seen even of words signifying thing without such a sāhitya. Viśvanātha, however, does not give any example of such a Dvandva compound to emphasise his point. We for ourselves may take an example like 'Khalasajjanau' as in the sentence 'Khalasajjanau parasparaṁ na sahete'. (The wicked and good donot or cannot stand each other). We cannot read any sense of 'sāhitya' from the compound 'khalasajjanau'. This being admitted, it follows that the togetherness or association is not necessarily to be understood from a Dvandva compound.

It may be argued again that the 'sāhitya' atleast in the sense of 'being connected with the one and the same verb' is to be understood in such cases of Dvandva compound where the objects signified cannot be said to be co-existant. Such an argument is not tenable because, as Viśvanātha points out, the Dvandva compound takes places with words signifying objects which are connected not with a common verb but each with a separate verb. To illustrate the point, we can take up the case of the Dvandva compound 'dhavakhadírau' in the sentence, 'dhavakhadirau paśya chindhi' (Look at and cut Dhava and Khadira plants). Here while 'dhava', one of the compounding words is connected with the 'darśanakriyā', the other member of the compound, i.e., 'khadira' is connected with the 'chedanakriyā'. Even when the component words of a Dvandva compound come to be connected with one and the same verb, as a matter of fact, no Śābdabodha takes place in respect of such a sense of 'sāhitya' i.e., 'ekakriyānvayitva'.[469]

Now in support of his assertion that Lakṣaṇā is in no way admitted in a Dvandva compound, Viśvanātha refers to the admission of Dvandva compound by the Mīmāṁsakas in the expression 'rājpurohitau' in the sentence 'rājapurohitau sāyujyakāmau yajeyātām'. If the expression be expounded as 'rājñaḥ purohitau' by way of admitting a Tatpuruṣa compound in it, only two royal priests would have been expected to perform the sacrificial rituals and the concerned King would have been spared. To perform rituals is desirably a normal duty of priests and not of kings. Hence it would have been better to free the kings from this extra-ordinary duty of performing sacrifices in order to attend more to his administrative works. But the admission of a Tatpuruṣa compound involves the recognition of a Lakṣaṇā in the earlier member of the compound. The Mīmāṁsakas are always reluctant to accept a secondary sense. We have already referred to Mīmāṁsakas' admission of Śakti and Śakyārtha as superior to Lakṣaṇā and Lakṣyārtha. Out of their keen desire to avoid Lakṣaṇā, the Mīmāṁsakas have admitted a Dvandva compound in the expression 'rājapurohitau' in the injunction 'rājapurohitau sāyujyakāmau' etc. As a consequence, both the king and the priest have been enjoined to get-together in the performance of sacrificial rituals. Mīmāṁsakas' admission only of the Dvandva compound in the expression 'rājapurohitau' in the aforesaid injunction confirms Viśvanātha's contention that there is no scope at all for the operation of Lakṣaṇā in the Dvandva compound. So Viśvanātha concludes that in a Dvandva compound no additional sense of 'sāhitya' is to be understood. This lack of scope for the operation of Lakṣaṇā, we may casually note here, gives a position of superiority to the Dvandva compound over the other varieties of compound. This we may gather from the *Gītā X.* 33,[470] wherein Lord Kṛṣṇa describes Himself as the Dvandva compound amongst all varieties of compounds. This superiority is most probably because of its being free from Lakṣaṇā. This notion of superiority due to lack of Lakṣaṇā seems to owe its origin to the Mīmāṁsakas' preference of the Śruti or Abhidhā to

Lakṣaṇā.

M(41). kintu vāstavo bhedo yatra, tatra dvandvaḥ. na ca nīlaghatayorabheda ityādau kathamiti vācyam. tatra nīlapadasya nīlatve ghaṭapadasya ghaṭatve lakṣaṇā. abheda ityasya cāśrayā bheda ityarthāt.

In the preceeding text of the *Muktāvalī* viz. 'tasmāt sāhityā dikaṁ nārthaḥ', Viśvanātha categorically asserts that the association in any form does not come to be a part of the contextual Śābdabodha in a Dvandva compound like 'dhava khadirau' in the expressions like 'dhavakhadirau chindhi'. The sense of association, even if there be any to justify the Grammatical sanction[471] for the dual or plural number of a Dvandva compound, virtually does not enter into the import of an expression in the form of a Dvandva compound. Such a sense of association between the meanings of the words constituting a Dvandva compound does not again come to be understood even before the compound is formed. So, there can be no misgiving that a sense of association is to be conveyed as the factor leading to the constitution of a Dvandva compound. Under the above circumstances, Viśvanātha deems it necessary to point out a basic character of the constituents of Dvandva compound.

The objects signified by the component words of a Dvandva compound are fully different from each other. As for illustration, Bhīma and Arjuna, understood from the Dvandva, 'bhīmārjunau' are two separate individuals who can remain apart from each other. So also is the case with Dhava and Khadira understood from the Dvandva 'dhavakhadirau'. Dhava and Khadira are two separate plants of either of which we can think in isolation. The objects signified by the constituents of a Dvandva compound differ basically, i.e., by the true nature of things. In other words, the notion of difference here is not figurative or superficial. Thus, the notion of basic difference between or among the things denoted by the compounding words comes to be a differentiating element in the context of Dvandva compound.

In the succeeding text of the *Muktāvalī*, Viśvanātha would show the lack of the scope for Lakṣaṇā even in the Karmadhāraya compound. But in the case of a Karmadhāraya compound, we shall not see such difference between the meanings of the component words of that Samāsa. So, some scholars feel that the above *Muktā valī* text, 'kintu vāstavo bhedo yatra' etc. is only to record Viśvanā tha's rejoinder in anticipation of a query as regards the difference between a Dvandva and a Karmadhāraya.[472] But, as a matter of fact, Viśvanātha makes this observation only out of his anxiety to counteract the notion that a sense of association is to be conveyed secondarily atleast to serve as the pre-requisite for the constitution of a Dvandva. But how is it that an identity is said to exist between 'nīla' and 'ghaṭa' even when they form a Dvandva compound in the expression, 'nīlaghaṭayorabhedaḥ'? Viśvanātha seeks to solve the problem by saying that in the expression above, the word 'abheda' means an identity only of the substratum (ā śrayābhedaḥ). But what is that substratum and for what ? The expression 'nīlaghaṭayoḥ' is the form in the genitive case of the compound 'nīlaghaṭau'. Of the two words constituting the compound 'nīlaghaṭau' the word 'nīla', the earlier member of the compound conveys 'the blue colour' (nīla varṇa) as its Śakyārtha and the word 'ghaṭa', the latter member, signifies 'a jar' (the object, 'ghaṭa') as its Śakyārtha. Neither of these two Śakyārthas can be thought of as the substratum (āśraya) of the other. While a jar as it is can never be thought of as pertaining to the blue colour, the blue colour can also pertain only to a blue jar (nīlaghaṭa) but not to a mere jar. Neither the blue colour nor a jar in general can serve as the common substratum hinted in the context. So, in view of the Śābdabodha demanded by the expression, 'nīlaghaṭayorabhedaḥ'. We shall have to admit a Tātparyānupapatti with regard to the Śakyārthas of the two words of the compound, 'nī laghatayoḥ'. Here Lakṣaṇā comes to our rescue and makes us understand 'nīlatva' (blueness) as the Lakṣyārtha from the word 'nīla' and 'ghaṭatva' (jarness) from the word 'ghaṭa'. A 'nīlaghaṭa' (a blue jar) can be thought of without any difficulty as the common substratum of both 'nīlatva' and 'ghaṭatva'.

An objection may be raised by pointing out that the two meanings between which a difference could be shown are only two Lakṣyārthas. But we cannot overlook the fact that the two Lakṣyārthas namely, nīlatva' and 'ghaṭatva' are again the Śakyatā vacchedakas of the two Śakyārthas, namely 'nīla' and 'ghaṭa', respectively. Thus we find no inconsistency in the expression, 'nīla---------- abheda' even when 'nīlaghaṭayoḥ' is taken as a case of Dvandva which presupposes a basic difference between the concepts of its component parts.

But the admission of Lakṣaṇā in the word 'nīla' with regard to 'nīlatva' and in the word 'ghaṭa' with regard to 'ghaṭatva' in the context of the expression, 'nīlaghaṭayorabhedaḥ' should not create an impression that Viśvanātha comes to admit Lakṣaṇā in the component parts of a Dvandva compound and swerves from his original stand that the Dvandva compound does not allow any scope for the operation of Lakṣaṇā. The admission of these two Lakṣaṇās is a must to justify the desired Śābdabodha even if the two words 'nīla' and 'ghaṭa' are in a uncompounded stage. If the said words, 'nila' and 'ghata' are not allowed to compound, the expression, 'nīlaghaṭayorabhedaḥ' would take the form of nī lasya ghaṭasya ca abhedaḥ.' As demanded by the maxim 'nīpātā rikta' etc., the two nāmapadas, namely 'nīla' and 'ghaṭa' would be syntactically related with each other as they are intercepted by the indeclinable 'ca'. But the context demands a notion of identity to be conveyed between the two. Hence, obviously there is Tātparyā nupapatti with regard to the two Śakyārthas. Hence, here is also the operation of Lakṣaṇā to read 'nīlatva' from 'nīla' and 'ghaṭatva' from 'ghaṭa'. Thus it is obvious that the two Lakṣaṇās admitted in the expression 'nīlaghaṭau' are not there because of any basic nature of a Dvandva Compound.

M(42). samāhāradvandve tu yadi samāhāro'pyanubhūyata ityucyate, tadā'hinakulamityādau parapade'hinakulasamāhāre lakṣaṇā. pūrvapadaṁ tātparyagrāhakam. na ca bherīmṛdaṅgaṁ vādayetyatra kathaṁ samāhārasyā'nvayaḥ, apekṣābuddhiviśeṣarūpasya tasya vādanā'sambhavāditi vācyam; paramparāsambandhena tadanvayāt. evaṁ pañcamūlītyādāvapi. pare tvahinakulamityādāvahirnakulaśca budhyate, pratyekamekatvānvayaḥ. samāhārasaṁjñā ca yatraikatvaṁ napuṁsakatvaṁ ca 'prāṇitūrye'tyādisūtreṇoktam, tatraiva. anyatraikavacanamasādhviti vadanti.

In the *Muktāvalī* above, Viśvanātha provides a clarification in the context of admitting Lakṣaṇā in Samāhāra Dvandvas.

Pāṇini prescribes the Dvandva Compounds by his rule 'cārthe dvandvaḥ'.[473] The particle 'ca' is used in four senses.[474] It is stated that the particle 'ca' in the aforesaid Pāṇinian rule carries the sense of Samāhāra also along with the Itaretara and thereby the samāhāra Dvandva Compounds also stand prescribed. Samāhāra means 'sāhitya' (togetherness). This sense of 'sāhitya' takes place in two ways. (1) There may be a Samāhāra when two or more 'agents' come to be syntactically connected with the same action (ekakriyānvayitvāt) as in 'ahinakulam paśya'. (2) There may also be a samāhāra when a sense of interdependence (apekṣā buddhiviṣayatvāt) is conveyed as in 'bherīmṛdaṅgaṁ vādaya' (Here it cannot be said that the bherī and the mṛdaṅga in the context are connected with the same act of playing upon. Wheras a snake and a mongoose can simultaneously be seen by the same person, it is not possible for one again to strike simultaneously at both a bherī and a mṛdaṅga. Yet by saying 'bherīmṛdaṅgaṁ vādaya' instead of 'bherīmṛdaṅgān vādaya' the interdependence of the strikings at both the instruments is intended in order to serve some musical necessity).

In the *Muktāvalī* above, Viśvanātha introduces the problem of recognising Lakṣaṇā in a Samāhāra Dvandva. The Naiyāyikas are not unanimous in admitting Lakṣaṇā to understand the sense of Samāhāra. Pandit Śrīkṛṣṇavallabhācārya reads the mind of Viśvanātha thus. Viśvanātha is aware of the difference of opinion amongst the scholars regarding the admission of Lakṣaṇā with regard to understand the sense of a Samāhāra in a Samāhāra Compound. The Prācīnanaiyāyikas hold that a sense of Samāhāra is understood from a Samāhāra Compound, and that it is understood with the aid of Lakṣaṇā. Viśvanātha alludes to this old view in 'samāhāradvandve tu yadi' etc.[475] The Navyanaiyāyikas contend that no sense of Samāhāra is understood at all from a Samāhāra Compound. Hence the admission of Lakṣaṇā on that account is out of question. Viśvanātha refers to this modern view in 'pare tu' etc.[476] According to Viśvanātha, if it is admitted that a Samāhāra Dvandva conveys a sense of Samāhāra, in that case in the examples 'ahinakulaṁ' etc., Lakṣaṇā is to be admitted in the latter member of the compound to convey the sense of 'ahinakulasamāhāra' (togetherness of a snake and a mongoose) etc. The earlier member of the compound serves as the pointer to the speaker's intention in the context. Viśvanātha also refers to other scholars who argue that sometimes a Samāhāra Dvandva conveys only the Śakyārthas of the members of the compound and does not necessitate the admission of Śakti or Lakṣaṇā to convey the additional meaning of Samāhāra.[477] It may be added that even in the case of admitting the additional sense (i.e., a Samā hāra) of a Samāhāra Dvandva, some later Naiyāyikas admit Lakṣaṇā in both the Padas involved in a Samāhāra Dvandva.[478] In the *Muktāvalī* above, Viśvanātha observes that in case Lakṣaṇā is admitted in a Samāhāra Dvandva, it is to be admitted with regard to the 'uttarapada' and not to the 'pūrvapada'. An explanation is necessary on this point. The sense of Samāhāra is carried by the neuter gender which is affixed only to the latter member of the Compound. Hence as the sense of Samāhāra is to be conveyed, it is appropriate to fix the Lakṣaṇā to the 'uttarapada' only.

In 'na ca ---------------- tadanvayāt', Viśvanātha points out a possible opposition to the admission of Samāhāra as conveyed by a Compound like 'bherīmṛdaṅgaṁ vādaya'. Now the syntactical connection between the sense of Samāhāra conveyed by Lakṣaṇā from the expression 'bherīmṛdaṅgam' and the act of playing upon as conveyed by the word 'vādaya' may be questioned on the plea that one cannot play upon the Samāhāra which in the example means a specific notion of interdependence (apekṣābuddhi-viśeṣa). The idea is this : the act of playing upon (i.e., vādana) takes place in the form of a contact with the instruments by way of striking at them. Such a contact that goes by the name 'abhighāta' is possible only directly with the instruments, 'bherī' and 'mṛdaṅga' and not with the abstract notion of their interdependence (i.e., the sense of Samāhāra here). The rejoinder to this objection may be given thus : The syntactical relation between the Samāhāra, even in the sense of 'apekṣābuddhi', and the 'vādanakriyā' is possible through an indirect relation that may be described as 'svāśrayavṛttisambandha'. The expression 'svāśraya' etc. may be explained thus : 'svaṁ samāhāraḥ tasya āśrayaḥ bherī mṛdaṅgau tayoḥ (tatra vā) (Vādanakarma vartata iti tasya) vṛttitvarūpaḥ sambandhaḥ'. In other words, the Samāhāra in the sense of a notion of interdependence exists between the two instruments. The act of playing upon also pertains to the two instruments. Thus owing to common substratum, i.e., on the strength of a relation through a medium, the Samāhāra of the expression, 'bherīmṛdaṅgam' comes, to be syntactically related with 'the vādanakriyā' conveyed by the word 'vādaya'.

Viśvanātha in "pañcamūlītyādāvapi" refers to Prācīnanaiyāyikas' admission of Lakṣaṇā in a Samāhāra Dvigu Compound. Viśvanātha's example of Samāhāradvigu in the context is 'pañcamūlī'. The Samāsa comes to be a Samāhāra according to the Pāṇinian rule 2.1.50[479] The Samāhāra is of the Dvigu variety as per P 2.1.51.[480] The Compounded word ends with the feminine suffix 'ī'.[481] According to old Naiyāyikas, there is Lakṣaṇā in the latter member of the Compound, i.e., the word 'mūla' in order to convey the sense of Pañca mūlasamāhāra.

The earlier member of the Compound, i.e., the word 'pañca'

serves as the pointer to the intention of the speaker. The word 'ādi' in the *Muktāvalī* "pañcamūlītyādāvapi" is taken to cover other Dvigu Compounds like 'pañcapulī', 'pañcavaṭī', 'pañcapātram' etc.[482] It may be pointed out that almost all the commentators are inclined to believe that Viśvanātha has in his mind the view points of 'navīnanaiyāyikas' when he writes 'pare tu ahinakulamityādau'.[483] But the commentators do not categorically name the later Nyāya scholars whom Viśvanātha meant as others (pare). Pañcānana Śāstri, however, feels that Viśvanātha with the expression 'pare' (others) makes a respectful reference only to the Pandit Jānakīnātha Bhaṭṭācāryya, a later Naiyāyika who preceeded Viśvanātha.[484] But it is to be noted that the examples furnished by Jānakīnātha and Viśvanātha are different. Viśvanātha's example where Samāhārasaṁjña is stated to be not admitted by 'the other scholars' is 'ahinkulaṁ paśya' while Jānakīnātha's example is 'pāṇipādaṁ vādaya'.[485] Even if we admit both the examples to be on a par, we cannot help admitting that like the author of the *Bhāṣāpariccheda*, the author of the *Nyāyasiddhāntamañjarī* also refers to both the views for and against admitting Lakṣaṇā for understanding a samāhāra.[486]

If we take the word 'pare' as used by Viśvanātha strictly in a plural sense to mean the Navya Naiyāyikas in general, we can explain their position as follows. The Navya Naiyāyikas do not see any scope for the operation of Lakṣaṇā in a Samāhāra Dvandva as in their view a sense of what is actually a Samāhāra is not understood at all from a Samāhāra Compound. As for example, in a so-called Samāhāra Dvandva like 'ahinakulam', only the meaning, 'a snake and a mongoose' are obtained separately from the words 'ahi' and 'nakula'[487] without any idea of the aggregation.

If the attention of these scholars is drawn to the singular number of the compounded form, they want to connect the number separately with each sense.[488]

As a matter of fact, they regard the use of the singular number in the expression, 'ahinakulam' as incorrect. Their position is this: There is no difference of opinion in so far as a Samāhāra Compound takes a neuter gender and a singular number. But the gender and the number as such should be used only with due cognizance of the rule that governs a Samāhārasaṁjñā. These scholars refer to that grammatical rule[489] according to which only the words signifying limbs of animals, musical instruments and divisions of army are competent to be so compounded. The use of singular number and neuter gender without regard to this rule is not correct. Commentator Śrīkṛṣṇavallabhācārya, however, understands the rule 'yeṣāṁ ca virodhaḥ śāśvatikaḥ' along with 'dvandaśca prāṇitūrya' etc. in order to justify the singular number in the expression 'ahinakulam' by way of covering it by a Samāhā rasaṁjñā.[490] In any case, it is clear that the Navya Naiyāyikas understand the Samāhārasaṁjñā as a technical term (Pāribhāṣikī Saṁjñā) like Nadī and Vṛddhi and it need not necessarily convey the sense of an unity or aggregate also.[491] The Samāhāra as a technical term is prescribed to justify the use of singular number (and neuter gender) in certain cases of Dvandva Compounds.

M(43). pitarau śvaśurāvityādau pitṛapade janakadampatyoḥ śvaśurapade strījanakadampatyorlakṣaṇā. evamanyatrāpi. ghaṭa ityādau tu na lakṣaṇā ghaṭatvena rūpeṇa nānāghaṭopasthitisambhavāt.

Here Viśvanātha shows the involvement of Padalakṣaṇā in the case of Virūpa-ekaśeṣa-dvandva compound.[492] The Ekaśeṣa compound is presbcribed by the Pāṇinian rule 'sarūpāṇāmekaśeṣa ekavibhaktau'[493] for words of the same form. Thus 'ghaṭásca ghṭaśca' gives 'ghaṭau' or 'ghaṭaśca ghaṭaśca ghaṭaśca' gives 'ghaṭā ḥ'. Here 'ghaṭau' and 'ghaṭāḥ' are two instances of Ekaśeṣa. But Pā ṇini subsequently prescribes the 'ekaśeṣasaṁjñā' even for certain words not of similar forms.[494] Thus Ekaśeṣa is virtually of two types, Sarūpa and Virūpa. In the *Muktāvalī* above, Viśvanātha admits Padalakṣaṇā in the case of the Virūpa-ekaśeṣas. Let us first consider such a Virūpa-ekaśeṣa, namely, 'pitarau.' 'Pitarau' may be a Sarūpa-ekaśeṣa also in the sense of 'pitā ca pitā ca'. It may mean two fathers corresponding to two sons. But in the case of the expression, 'caitrasya pitarau' such a meaning is not possible. Hence in such a context this expression 'pitarau' must be understood as Virūpa-ekaśeṣa and Lakṣaṇā must be resorted to with regard to the Pada 'pitṛ' in order to understand 'parents' (janakadampatī). The expression 'janakadampatī' stands for 'pitā ca mātā ca' which comes to have Ekaśeṣa (the retention of one word amongst many such words).[495] Similarly in the sentences like 'caitrasya śvaśurau', the word 'śvaśura' conveys by Lakṣaṇā 'the parent of the wife' i.e., Śvaśura (father in-law and) 'śvaśvā' (mother in-law).[496] Here the word denoting a female takes the form of the word, meaning the male as sanctioned by a Pāṇinian rule.[497] By 'evamanyatrāpi' of the *Muktāvalī*, Viśvanātha admits the necessity of recognising Padalakṣaṇā in the case of other possible examples of Virūpa-ekaśeṣa. For instance, in the example 'bhrātarau', the word 'bhrātṛ' conveys, by Lakṣaṇā the idea of both a brother and a sister. In the example, 'putrau', the word 'putra' gives the Lakṣyārtha in the form of 'a son and a daughter-in-law'. We may note here that Pāṇini prescribes Virūpa-ekaśeṣa for 'bhrātā ca svasā ca' and for 'putraśca duhitā ca'.[498] Dinakarabhaṭṭa also reads such a mind of Viśvanātha in the matter of admitting Padalakṣaṇā for all the Virūpa-ekaśeṣas.[499]

But in the case of Sarūpa-ekaśeṣas, Viśvanātha finds no necessity of admitting even Padalakṣaṇā. As for illustration, 'ghaṭaśca ghaṭaśca ghaṭaśca' gives us the Ekaśeṣa in 'ghaṭāḥ'. Now without any recourse to Lakṣaṇā, we can have the notion of the plurality of the jars. As Viśvanātha understands Śakti of a Pada with regard to 'jātyākṛtiviśiṣṭavyakti', the Śakti of the word 'ghaṭa' would convey the meaning in the form of individual jars qualified by the generic property 'jarness'. The knowledge of the generic property 'jarness' facilitates the knowledge of many (or more than one) jars possessed of such a property. The desired Śābdabodha of the expression 'ghaṭāḥ' is the knowledge of many individuals possessed of the generic property 'jarness' (ghaṭatvaprakā rakaghaṭaviṣayakaṁ jñanam). Hence there is no scope for Tā tparyānupapatti and consequently there is also no Lakṣaṇā.

M(44). karmadhārayasthale tu nīlotpalamityādāvabhedasambandhena nīlapadārtha utpalapadārthe prakāraḥ. tatra ca na lakṣaṇā. ata eva "niṣādasthapatiṁ yājayedi"tyatra na tatpuruṣo, lakṣaṇāpatteḥ, kintu karmadhārayo, lakṣaṇābhāvāt. na ca niṣādasya saṅkarajātiviśeṣasya vedānadhikārād yajanāsambhava iti vācyam. niṣādasya vidyāprayuktestata eva kalpanāt. lāghavena mukhyārthasyā'nvaye tadanupapattyā kalpanāyāḥ phalamukhagauravatayā' doṣatvāditi.

Viśvanātha here asserts that there is no need to admit any Lakṣaṇā in a Karmadhāraya compound. A Karmadhārya is a compound between a Viśeṣya (qualified) and a Viśeṣaṇa (qualification). The relation between a Viśeṣaṇa and Viśeṣya is naturally not one of difference (bheda). As a result, the component parts of a Karmadhāraya compound can directly sastisfy the requirement of the maxim 'nipātātiriktanāmārthayorbhedenā nvayasyāvyutpannatvam'. The maxim demands that a connection of identity (abhedasambandha) must exist between two Nāmapadas unless they are intervened by some indeclinable (provided that they do not stand in different case-endings). The maxim is obviously applicable in a case of Karmadhāraya compound which consists of two Nāmapadas, a Viśeṣya and a Viśeṣaṇa not intervened by any indeclinable and not standing in different case-endings. The meanings of the two words in a Karmadhāraya compound directly come to be mutually connected by a relation of identity and thus easily satisfy the aforesaid maxim. In doing so the two members of the compound under discussion do not allow any scope for the operation of a Lakṣaṇā. To illustrate the case of a Karmadhāraya compound as being free from Lakṣaṇā, Viśvanātha gives the example of 'nīlotpalam'. Viśvanātha finds the meaning of both the words immediately connected by the relation of abheda as because the meaning of the word 'nīla' is an attribute (prakāra) of the thing understood from the word 'utpala' i.e., a lotus. Here we need a careful examination of Viśvanātha's position.

Now, to be connected with the primary meaning of the latter word (utpalam) by the relation of identity, the word 'nīla' must convey the meaning nīlavarṇaviśiṣṭa (something qualified by or possessed of blue colour). This could have been a Śakyārtha (primary meaning) of the word 'nīla' as per Lexicons. In the event of admitting that, there would have been no problem to us. But as we have already observed in *Muktāvalī*, Kośādapi śaktigrahaḥ- etc. Viśvanātha accepts the word 'nīla' only as conveying 'nīla varṇa' (blue colour) by means of Abhidhā. So, in the compound 'nīlotpalam', the word 'nīla', to obtain the desired relation of identity, must give up its primary sense of 'blue colour' and convey the meaning 'nīlavarṇayukta' (blue coloured) by means of Lakṣaṇā. Under the circumstances Viśvanātha would not be correct to say that there is no scope for Lakṣaṇā in the compound 'nīlotpalam'. As a result his assertion that there can be no Lakṣaṇā in a Karmadhāraya compound comes to suffer a setback atleast at this stage of our discussion. Moreover, as in the aforesaid earlier observation, Viśvanātha himself recognises as Lakṣyartha the meaning in the form of 'nīlā diviśiṣṭa' etc. from the nīlādipada' etc, it is our turn to see if the author of the *BP* is not involved in a self contradiction. Now as Viśvanātha himself recognises 'nīla (varṇa) viśiṣṭa' as the Lakṣyārtha of the word 'nīla', in the context of his discourse on Śaktigraha. We cannot say that he wants to rule out the possibility of the presence of Lakṣaṇā in the word 'nīla' (in the sense of 'nīlavarṇaviśiṣta') in the expression, 'nīlotpalam'. Unless the word 'nīla' is understood in the compound in its sense of 'nīlavarṇaviśiṣṭa', it cannot be thought of being syntactically connected by a relation of identity with the meaning of the word 'utpala' in the said compound. And the meanings of the two words must be understood in the expression 'nīlotpalam' only through the relation of identity as demanded by the maxim 'nipā tātirikta' etc. Hence it may be suggested that Viśvanātha actually wants to mean the following:

The Lakṣaṇā here is not imposed by the very nature of the Samāsa; for even when the two words occur separately as 'nīlam utpalam' the word 'nīla' must have Lakṣaṇā in order to satisfy the same rule 'nipātātirikta' etc. Hence the word 'nīla' comes to be a Lakṣaṇā before it enters into a compound along with the other word, i.e., 'utpalam'. Hence the presence of Lakṣaṇā in 'nīla' of 'nī lotpala' is not necessitated by the nature of the Samāsa. But a case of Tatpuruṣa discussed earlier is just the opposite. There the Lakṣaṇā as in 'rājapuruṣa' is actually demanded by the very nature of the Samāsa. When the words involved occur separately as 'rājñaḥpuruṣaḥ', it is enough to have the denoted meaning of the word 'rājñaḥ'. Only in the compounded form, we are forced to recognise Lakṣaṇā in the word 'rājā'. Possibly observing that, Viśvanātha wants to speak of the absence, in the Karmadhāraya compound, of a Lakṣaṇā necessitated by Samāsa. Pañcānana Shastri makes a similar observation in this context in his commentary.[500] The commentaries *Dinakarī* and *Rāmarudrī* are silent on the point. Pandit Ḍhuṇḍhirāja Shastri, in a foot note on Jagadīśa's definition of Karmadhāraya quotes one Jayarāma Pañcānanabhaṭṭācārya who observes that Karmadhāraya is free from a 'samāsaprayuktalakṣaṇā'.[501] Jagadīśa's definition of Karmadhāraya, as we shall see by and by, does not so much demand for an explanation of the nature of Lakṣaṇā in some cases of Karmadhārayasamāsa. Hence this remark of Jayarāma might have come because of his own knowledge of Viśvanātha's treatment of the Karmadhāraya Samāsa. Hence Viśvanātha's text in this context may be suitably modified as follows: 'tatra ca na samāsaprayuktalakṣaṇā,' supplying the word 'samāsaprayukta' to the existing text. We note that Jagadīśa's treatment of the issue does not lead him to any controversy as he makes no hard and fast rule regarding presence or otherwise of Lakṣaṇā in a

Karmadhāraya Compound. He recognises Lakṣaṇā in a Karmadhāraya Samāsa wherever it is necessary as in the case of 'puruṣasiṁha'.[502] In fact Jagadīśa does not refer to this possibility of the admission of Lakṣaṇā in his definition of Karmadhāraya. As we understand from Jagadīśa, this Karmadhāraya Samāsa can be there only in case of a couple of Nāmapadas occurring in immediate juxtaposition and showing the identity of the meaning of one with that of the other. Besides Jagadiśa has no objection accepting the dictionary meanings of the words like 'śukla' etc. as 'śuklaguṇayukta' etc.[503] Thus for Jagadīśa there is no difficulty to identify the primary meaning of the word 'nīla' with that of 'utpala' in the expression 'nīlotpalam'.[504] Because of admitting this lack of Lakṣaṇā even in constituent words of the Karmadhāraya compound, the Vedic injunction 'niṣādasthapatiṁ yājayet' comes to be accepted as a case of Karmadhāraya instead of Tatpuruṣa which allows the operation of a Lakṣaṇā in its earlier word (pūrvapada). This position recorded by Viśvanātha may be traced back to the Mīmāṁsakas. We have already made an examination of Mīmāṁsakas' approach in the matter of explaining the aforesaid Vedic injunction. Now to follow the point in the context, we simply recapitulate that the Mīmāṁsakas prefer the expression 'niṣādasthapatim' as a case of Karmadhāraya compound as it does not involve the operation of any Lakṣaṇā in it. When the two component parts directly convey the idea of 'niṣāda' and 'sthapati', the expression comes to be a Karmadhāravya compound. When the compound is viewed as a case of 'ṣaṣṭhī tatpuruṣa', the earlier word 'niṣāda' is to mean 'niṣādānām' (of the Niṣādas). As this cannot be a direct meaning, it must unfailingly be admitted as a case of secondary meaning. But the principle of the Mīmāṁsakas to prefer a direct meaning to a secondary meaning in the event of a conflict between the two makes them finally accept the expression 'niṣādasthapati' as a case of Karmadhāraya compound which does not allow any scope for Lakṣaṇā. This particular example of the Mīmāṁsakas preferring a Śakyārtha to Lakṣyārtha bears important socio-cultural implications and throws as well sufficient light on a very important aspect of Vedic society. As the Mīmāṁsakas preferred a direct meaning and were ever anxious to avoid a secondary meaning in the context of Vedic injunction under discussion, they unhesitatingly gave the right of performing a Vedic sacrifice even to a Niṣāda, an out caste. As Viśvanātha has rightly asserted, from this Vedic injunction the right of Niṣāda even to acquire necessary Vedic learning can easily be understood. In admitting the Vedic expression 'niṣā dasthapati' as a case of Karmadhāraya instead of a Tatpuruṣa, there is the gain of the advantage of a simplicity. This is because of there being the scope of avoiding a Lakṣyārtha. A Tatpuruṣa compound basically involves a Lakṣaṇā whereas a Karmadhā raya does not. The Mīmāṁsakas, as we have already noted, deem Śruti or Abhidhā as superior to Lakṣaṇā. Hence they get the advantage of avoiding the admission of a Lakṣyārtha by way of recognising the aforesaid expression viz. 'niṣādasthapatim' as a case of Karmadhāraya. But the gain is not unmixed with a loss. As we have already seen, the admission of a Karmadhāraya compound in the said expression presupposes the recognition of even a Niṣāda as the Sthapati. Vedas donot explicitely enjoin the right of sacrificing to a Niṣāda. But the admission of the said Karmadhāraya compound by the Mīmāṁsakas in their anxiety to avoid a Lakṣaṇā gives one a chance to assume that a Niṣāda also obtains the right to acquire necessary Shastric know-how to be competent to perform a sacrifice. Such an assumption is undoubtedly a complex or cumbrous situation. But yet that complexity or cumbrouness (Gaurava) is to be tolerated or rather welcome in as much as the said Gaurava leads to or produces the desired result (phalamukha etc.) i.e., the desired objective of the Mīmāṁsakas in the form of maintaining a Śakyārtha in lieu of a Lakṣyārtha, if and when possible.

M(45). upakumbhamarddhapippalītyādau parapade tatsambandhini lakṣaṇā, pūrvapadārthapradhānatayā cānvayabodha iti.

Here Viśvanātha proceeds to show the 'parapadalakṣaṇā' in Avyayībhāva compounds and in a special type of Tatpuruṣa compounds. In Avyayībhāva compounds, the meaning of the first member of the compound is to remain prominent[505] and as such deserves to be the Śakyārtha. Under that circumstance Lakṣaṇā is to be admitted with regard to either of the constituents of an Avyayībhāva, it is in all propriety to be admitted with regard to the second member of the compound. As for illustration, in 'upakumbham', the latter word 'kumbha' by Lakṣaṇā means 'kumbhasambandhī' (related to a pitcher). The 'vigrahavākya' of this example of Avyayībhāva is 'kumbhasya samīpa'. Now the Lakṣyārtha of the word kumbha' i.e., kumbhasambandhī' comes to be syntactically related by the relation of identity with the idea of sāmīpya (proximity) conveyed as vācyārtha by the word 'upa'.[506] The last example chosen by Viśvanātha to show the operation of padalakṣaṇā in a compound is 'arddhapippalī' (the half of a pippalī). The compound, when analysed in a sentence will take the form of 'pippalyāḥ arddham'. Thus it is obvious that 'ardhapippalī' is an instance of Tatpuruṣa. But Viśvanātha has already shown that mere Śakti cannot bring about Śābdabodha in the case of Tatpuruṣa compounds. He has further shown that the purpose of conveying desired Śābdabodha in Tatpuruṣa compounds is best served by admitting Lakṣaṇā only to the first member of the compound and not to the whole of it. Here we are to examine if Viśvanātha indulges in repeating the same idea by way of showing Lakṣaṇā in 'arddhapippalī' which is also a Tatpuruṣa compound. On verification, we find that in an earlier case of Tatpuruṣa, i.e., in rājapuruṣa' Viśvanātha shows the admission of Lakṣaṇā in pūrvapada' as the meaning of the 'uttarapada' was to remain prominent in the compound. Here in 'arddhapippalī' he desires to show the operation of Lakṣaṇā in the uttarapada', i.e., in pippalī as in this case, the meaning of the 'pūrva pada' i.e., 'arddha' is to be all the more important. Dinakarabhaṭṭa also corroborates such an idea.[507] A question is pertinent here. The accepted notion with regard to a Tatpuruṣa compound is that in it the meaning of the second member of the compound is to remain prominent. Under the circumstances, how is it that the expression 'arddhapippalī' is admitted as a Tatpuruṣa compound even though it shows the prominence of the pūrvapada'? The answer to this query is that the word 'arddha' the meaning of which is all the more important in the compound is virtually the 'uttarapada' as is evident from the very vigrahavākya viz. 'pippalyāḥ arddham'.

M(46). itthañca samāse na kvāpi śaktiḥ. padaśaktyaiva nirvāhā diti.

Now Viśvanātha declares with all satisfaction that since Lakṣaṇā as belonging to the Samāsa as a whole could be avoided, the possibility of the presence of Śakti in it is also fully ruled out. In the examples of Samāsas, namely Dvandva and Karmadhāraya where the scope of Lakṣaṇā was completely ruled out, the desired Śābdabodha occurred on the strength of the syntactical connection of the Śakyārthas of the constituent words. In cases where Lakṣaṇā operates in the constituent words in order to effect the desired Śābdabodha, Lakṣaṇā pertains only to the individual Padas. The Lakṣyārthas in these cases are additional meanings related to the Śakyārthas. Thus it does not necessitate any recognition of a Śakti of the whole Samāsa. Hence the question of Lakṣaṇā belonging to a Samāsa (as a whole) also does not arise.

K(3). ĀSATTI-YOGYATĀKĀṄKṢĀ-TĀTPARYAJÑĀNAMIṢYATE. 82b

KĀRAṆAM. SANNIDHĀNAM TU PADASYĀSATTIRUCYATE. 83a

In the text of the *Kārikāvalī* above, Viśvanātha names the conditions essential for obtaining the Śābdabodha in the context of a proposition. As we have already observed, a Śābdabodha is virtually a Vākyārthajñāna (the knowledge of the meaning of a sentence).[508] Our fulfledged ideas in a context come to be conveyed only through a sentence or sentences. A sentence again is a collection of words.[509] The words convey their individual meanings either through Śakti, or if and when necessary through Lakṣaṇā. But here the process does not end. The words shall have to fulfill certain conditions in order to give us a relational thought in the form of a Vākyārtha. Mere grouping together of certain words cannot lead to the formation of a sentence worth the name unless the words in the group satisfy some specific conditions. Scholars, are not unanimous in the choice of these conditions. Hence, the number of these requisites varies in different circles.

Pāṇini is known for his insistence on the capacity (sāmarthya) of words.[510] This 'capacity' is the capability of meanings of words to get united. Hence this capacity or Sāmarthya is actually an ekārthībhāva (unification of meanings).[511] Patañjali explains this Sā marthya of Pāṇini in the sense of Vyapekṣā, i.e., the mutual connection pertaining to the meanings of words in a sentence.[512] We may compare this 'ekārthībhāva' to 'arthaikatva' and 'vyapekṣā' to 'ākāṅkṣā' of Jaimini's definition of a sentence.[513] The idea behind the definition is that so long a number of words come to serve a single purpose, they form 'one sentence' (one yajus mantra).[514] This is clear from the impression of Śabarasvāmin also.[515] Śabara explains the context with reference to a 'yajus mantra". But Kumārila observes that it is applicable to ordinary sentences as well.[516] He understands the 'arthaikatva' in the sense of a single purpose. Prabhākara takes it in order to understand from it 'a meaning' and 'a purpose' as well.[517] Of the Grammarians again, Bhartṛhari wants a group of mutually expectant words to give a single idea.[518] Hence, we may hold that the Ākāṅkṣā in the sense of a necessity for interdependence of words to give an unified meaning in a sentence was maintained first by the Grammarians.

In the circle of Mīmāṁsakas, Kumārila himself comes to add two more conditions to his primarily accepted Ākāṅksā, namely 'yogyatā' and Āsatti' (or Sannidhi or Sannidhāna).[519] Later

Mīmāṁsakas, more or less, come to follow Kumārila's position. Though understood in their own way, Prābhākaras also admit the involvement of Sannidhi, Yogyatā and Ākāṁsā in effecting the Anvyaya i.e., in giving a Śābdabodha.[520] The involvement of Tātparya also comes to be later on admitted by both Bhāṭṭas and Prābhākaras. In the course of our examination of the relevent text of the *BP* on Tātparya, we shall see that Tātparya as understood by the Mīmāṁsakas is not the same as that of the Naiyāyikas. Even the Bhāṭṭas and Prābhākaras clash amongst themselves as regards the nature of operation of this Tātparya. The Naiyāyikas are divided on the issue of Tātparya. Some like Jayantabhaṭṭa regard Tātparya as a separate Vṛtti while others like Viśvanātha add the knowledge of Tātparya (in the sense of the speaker's intention) as a fourth condition to the list of conditions for the production of a Śābdabodha. Vedāntins seem to accept all the four conditions as such.[521] With the Ālaṁkārikas, the admission of the earlier three conditions is universal.[522] Some of them like Abhinavagupta regard Tātparya only as a separate vṛtti in order to effect the syntactical connection of words in a sentence.[523] In the concluding part of the Kārikā above, Viśvanātha refers to the usually accepted meaning of the term Āsatti. Āsatti is the juxtaposition or unintervened occurrence of two words. Here we must be cautious to note that any two words, only by the virtue of being uttered without intervention, cannot claim to have had Āsatti. The two words between which an Āsatti is said to exist must be intended for a mutual connection. Viśvanātha refers to this age-old condition in M, 'anvayapratiyogyanuyogipadayoravyavadhānamāsattiḥ'

We shall take up the issue again to bring out the differences of opinion as regards the concept of Āsatti, in the course of our examination of the relevant text of the *Muktāvalī*.

Certain editions of the *BP* (eg. NSM) show the reading 'āsattiḥ' separately, i.e., not as a member of the compound 'āsattiyogyatā -- ----------- tātparyajñānam', in the first half of the Kārikā above. (cf.

āsattiryogyatākāṅkṣātātparyajñānamiṣyate. Vide NSM, p. 30). In the case of accepting this reading, Āsatti and not Āsattijñāna will be admitted as a Śābdabodhakāraṇa, in the view of Viśvanātha. On the strength of the exposition of the Kārikā in the relevant text of the *Muktāvalī* (cf. āsattijñānam ------ śābdabodhakāranam) Dinakarabhaṭṭa observes that Viśvanātha wants to construe the word 'jñāna' with the word 'āsatti' also as he recognises Āsattijñā na and not Āsatti as the said cause. So the commentator prefers the reading 'āsattiyogyatā' etc. which is a compound of words including 'āsatti'.[524] But this is not tenable. In the succeeding M, 'anvayapratiyogyanuyogi --------- iti kecit', he rejects the old view that the knowledge of Āsatti in the sense of juxtaposition of two words is a cause of Śābdabodha. Again in M, 'vastutastu ---------- śābdabodhe kāraṇam'. he asserts that Āsatti in the sense of immediacy of two specific concepts is to be admitted as a Śā bdabodhakāraṇa. The admission of Āsattijñāna in the earlier aforesaid text of the *Muktāvalī* is only provisional.

M(47). āsattirityādi. āsattijñānaṁ yogyatājñānamākāṅkṣājñānam tātparyajñānañca śābdabodhe kāraṇam.

Viśvanātha here proceeds to expound the above *Kārikā* text, 'ā sattiriti' etc. By way of exposition, Viśvanātha makes it clear that the knowledge of each of the four conditions, namely Āsatti, Yogyatā, Ākāṅkṣā and Tātparya is to be obtained prior to the realisation of the Śābdabodha from a proposition. (But we reiterate, in view of the spirit of the succeeding *Muktāvalī* text that the reference to Āsattijñāna in lieu of Āsatti itself in the context is only provisional.) The singular number in the expression 'Kāraṇam' in both *Kārikāvalī* and *Muktāvalī* is significant. The knowledge of all the four conditions is to combine to constitute a single cause. The knowledge of one or two or three cannot serve the purpose (of bringing about a Śābdabodha) at the cost of the rest. In the *Muktāvalī*, Viśvanātha refers to the knowledge of each separately only to pinpoint their indispensability in clear terms. Our reference to each singly and separately as a Śābdabodhakāraṇa in succeeding lines is only for the sake of ease in elucidating our points. It may be noted further that this Kāraṇa (i.e., āsatti ----- jñānām) is also a Sahakāri-Kāraṇa like Śaktijñāna towards the effect viz. Śābdabodha.

M(48). tatrāsattipadārthamāha - sannidhānantviti. anvaya-pratiyogyanuyogi-padayoravyavadhānamāsattiḥ, tajjñānaṁ śā bdabodhe kāraṇam. kvacidvyavahite' pyavyavadhānabhramāc-chābdabodhāditi kecit. vastutastvavyavadhāna jñānasyān apekṣi-tatvād yatpadārthasya yatpadārthenā'nvayo'pekṣitastayoravya-vadhānenopasthitiḥ śābdabodhe kāraṇam. tena girirbhuktama-gnimān devadattenetyādau na śābdabodhaḥ. nīlo ghaṭo dravyaṁ pata ityādāvāsattibhramācchābdabodhaḥ. āsattibhramācchāb-dabhramābhave'pi na kṣatiḥ.

In the text of the *Muktāvalī* above, Viśvanātha proceeds to expound the concept of Āsatti. Before we examine the concept of Āsatti in the *BP*, it will be fruitful on our part to have a note on the issue as being handled by other scholars and in other schools of thought.

We find that in certain circles, Āsatti is known as Sannidhi or Sannidhāna.[525] Now we find that the Bhāṭṭas also admit Sannidhāna or Sannidhi (i.e., Āsatti) as one of the causes of the relation of clauses and words in a sentence.[526] But this Sannidhā-na in the sense of sequence in utterance of words is not something indispensable. It is defined by Kumārila as an association of the ideas of the words related to the previous words. This Sannidhāna takes place where there is immediacy in utterance of the words or even where there is no immediacy of utterance because of the intervention of a mutually related word between the two involved words. It is clear from this that Kumārila accepts this intervention by a mutually related word as a variety of Sannidhāna. There is no insistence by Kumārila on the immediate sequence in uttering the words. This is because he is to justify a need for recapitulating a certain Vedic word for sake of completing the idea intended in a context. As for example, the idea intended in the expression 'yā te agne rajāśayā' can be completed not by the following of any word but by immediate dragging in of the previously uttered expression 'tanūrvarṣiṣṭhā'. It appears, therefore, that Kumārila's Sannidhāna (i.e., Āsatti under discussion) is the proximity of a word or sometimes of the idea of a word.[527]

In the Prābhākara school of Mīmāṁsakas, however, Sannidhi is understood as the immediate association of the idea of the meaning of a related word. The Prābhākaras do not favour the definition of Sannidhi as the proximity of words. In the concept of 'anvitābhidhāna' which they advocate, it is an accepted fact that the denotative function (Śakti or Abhidhā) conveys only the related meanings of the words. Only an 'artha' (meaning of a word) can have a relation with another 'artha'. For one who believes in the concept of 'anvitābhidhāna', 'abhidhāna' succeeds 'anvaya'. As such, one is to accept the position that there is always 'abhidhāna' of an 'anvitārtha'. Hence the school of Prābhākaras contends that if by Sannidhi (Āsatti) we mean the immediate need of something to complete the relation of an expression, then that 'something' is invariably an 'artha' and not merely a 'Śabda'.[528] Here lies the difference between the Bhāṭṭas and the Prābhākaras. While Bhāṭṭas understand 'Sannidhi' as the proximity of a word or of the idea of a word, the Prābhākaras accept it only as the proximity of the idea of the meaning of a word.

Coming to thc text of the *Muktāvalī* above, we find Viśvanātha asserting the qualification of the two Padas that can claim to enjoy an Āsatti between themselves. In the relevant Kārikā portion, the juxtaposition of a word (with another) is stated to be what is known as Āsatti. Such a definition would entitle any two closely placed words to claim an Āsatti. In the utterence 'girirbhuktamagnimān devadatteḥ' one would understand Āsatti even between 'giri' and 'bhuktam'. To arrest such a wrong notion, Viśvanātha in the *Muktāvalī* proceeds to expound the concept of Āsatti. First he refers to an old view that Āsatti as a condition to contribute towards a Śābdabodha is required to exist between two padas, one being Pratiyogī and the other Anuyogī for an Anvaya. In other words, the two Padas between which an Āsatti is required to be there must be suitable for a syntactical connection.

In the light of references above, we come to be clear that in the circle of scholars preceding Viśvanātha, there is no universal insistance on the actual juxtaposition of words in their claim for an Āsatti. Even the Bhāṭṭas casually believe as Āsatti in the lack of intervention between the ideas of Padas. Viśvanātha disapprovingly refers to this earlier opinion in M, 'tajjñānaṁ śābdabodhe kāraṇam --------- kecit.' According to these scholars, to give rise to the corresponding Śābdabodha, two words need not physically be juxtaposed. To illustrate their point, these scholars point out to the utterence 'girirbhuktamagnimāṅ devadattaḥ' and say that not withstanding the intervention of the word 'bhuktam', one comes to have a Śābdabodha in the form of mutual connection between the two words 'giriḥ' and 'agnimān'. This is possible as and when one wrongly understands the words as proximate. On such an account, not the actual proximity but only the knowledge of proximity is to be regarded as a factor leading to a Śābdabodha. By way of disapproving of this position, Viśvanātha comes to present a better concept of Āsatti in M, 'vastutastvavyavadhānajñānasyānapekṣitatvāt ------- devadattenetyādau na śābdabodhah'. As a matter of fact, the knowledge of the lack of an intervention between the words concerned is not a point to be stressed. But what is necessary is the immediacy of the concepts (Padārthas) which stand already intended to be mutually connected. The recollection without a gap of these two meanings between which an Anvaya is already intended comes to be a factor responsible for producing a Śābdabodha. Hence, in the mere utterence of the words 'girirbhuktamagnimān devadattena' (hill, eaten, fiery, by devadatta) how is it possible for a sane person to have anything like a Śābdabodha. Thus Viśvanātha comes to believe that Āsatti in the sense of immediacy of two concepts is a cause for Śābdabodha. Viśvanātha seems to understand

Āsatti only as backed by Tātparya. Unless already intended for a mutual connection, he does not attach any significance even to the successive recollection of two meanings. The reading 'tā tparyagarbhā cā' sattiḥ', occurring in certain editions like NSM, just after M, 'tena girirbhuktam -------- na śābdabodhaḥ' confirms our idea. If some one points out to the fact of one's having a Śā bdabodha (in the form of nīlatvaprakārakaghaṭaviśeṣyakajñāna) from the utterence, 'nīlo ghaṭo dravyaṁ paṭaḥ' (even without a Tā tparya for such a Śābdabodha), Viśvanātha contends, this is owing to only a false notion of Āsatti. Though there is no intention on the part of the speaker to have the meanings of the two words 'nīla' and 'ghaṭa' mutually related, yet it is very likely for the listener to understand the two meanings as so desired by the speaker inasmuch as the meanings are not only quite capable of being mutually connected but also occur in an immediate succession. If it is pointed out that though the notion of Āsatti in this regard is a mistaken one yet actually it leads to a Śābdabodha which is otherwise quite proper, Viśvanātha would give the rejoinder that there is no harm if sometime a wrong notion of Āsatti does not result in a false Śābdabodha.

M(49). nanu yatra chatrī kuṇḍalī vāsasvī devadatta ityuktam, tatrottarapadasmaraṇena pūrvapadasmaraṇasya nāśādavyavadhānena tattatpadasmaraṇāsambhava iti cet na, pratyekapadā nubhavajanya-saṁskāraiścaramaṁ tavatpadaviṣayaka-smaraṇasyā'vyavadhanenotpatteḥ; nānāsannikarṣairekapratyakṣasyeva nānāsaṁskārairekasmaraṇotpatterapi sambhavāt; tāvatpadasaṁskārasahita-caramavarṇajñānasyodbodhakatvāt. kathamanyathā nānāvarṇairekapadasmaraṇam.

In the preceding text of the *Muktāvalī*, it comes to be maintained that the recollection of the meanings of words (intended for a syntactical connection), in an uninterrrupted sequence is necessary to bring about the Śābdabodha from a proposition. It may be argued now that suh an unintervened recollection of meanings is possible only in the case of a sentence comprising of two words like 'devadatto'sti'. But in the case of a sentence involving several words signifying one substantive with many attributes like 'chatrī kuṇḍalī vāsasvī devadattaḥ', such an Āsatti is virtually impossible. It is because the recollection of the meanings of earlier words are obviously intervened by those of the succeeding words before the former meanings come to be syntactically connected with the meaning of the last word (or in other words, before the previously expressed attributes come to qualify the substantive expressed at the end). Scholars arguing thus hold further that the recollection of an earlier meaning comes to be virtually non-existent or lost because of a succeeding recollection. So Śābdabodha cannot be explained with such a view of Āsatti. In reply, it has been pointed out that even when a recollection of a word-meaning comes to be intervened by that of another, an impression corresponding to the earlier recollection lingers unchecked. All such impressions of earlier recollections come to assist the recollection of the last word-meaning in giving rise to a corresponding Śābdabodha. Though the recollection of the meaning of the earlier word 'chatrī' is intervened by that of meanings of the words, 'kuṇḍalī' and 'vāsasvī', before the said meaning comes to be connected with that of 'devadattaḥ', there is nothing to check the impression left by that earliest possible recollection to linger on. Similarly the recollection of the word 'kuṇḍali', despite being interrupted by that of the word 'vāsasvī' comes to be non-existent only as allowing its own impression to continue. Now the recollection of the meaning of the last word, namely, 'devadattaḥ', combined with the uninterrupted impressions left by the recollections of the earlier word-meanings succeeds in bringing about the desired Śābdabodha from the contextual proposition. In 'nānāsannikarṣairekapratyakṣasyeva' etc, Viśvanātha seeks to justify such a possibility by an illustration pertaining to the field of Perception. It is a matter of day to day experience that several sense-contacts (with the objects) come to give rise to a single perceptive knowledge. If a single Perception may result from even numerous contacts of sense-organs with objects, it is quite understandable that several impressions of recollections of the word-meanings can bring about a Śabdabodha. Actually, Viśvanātha further adds, in such a case the last letter of the series of words, only as aided by the accumulated impressions corresponding to the very words, serves as the reviver of the knowledge of the total meaning that amounts to be the Śābdabodha. The capacity of the last letter to serve as such a reviver need not be doubted, otherwise, it will not possible to explain the knowledge of a single word that consists of only several letters. If we assert that we know the word 'ghaṭa', we shall have to admit that the letter 'ṭa' has the capacity of combining with the impression left by the knowledge of the letter 'gha' in order to give us the knowledge of the entire word 'ghaṭa.[529] If such a capacity of a last letter is to be admitted at the level of a Pada, there is no point in refusing to admit it at the level of a Padasamūha.

M(50). parantu tāvatpadārthānāṁ smaraṇādekadaiva khale kapotanyāyāt tāvapadārthānāṁ kriyākarmabhāvenā'nvayabodharūpaḥ śābdabodho bhavatīti kecit.

'vṛddhā yuvānaḥ śiśavaḥ kapotāḥ khale yathāmī yugapatpatanti/
tathaiva sarve yugapatpadārthāḥ paraspareṇā'nvayino bhavanti'//

Apare tu -
'yadyadākāṅkṣitaṁ yogyaṁ sannidhānaṁ prapadyate /
tena tenānvitaḥ svārthaḥ padairevāvagamyate'.//

tathā ca khaṇḍavākyārthabodhānantaraṁ tathaiva padārthasmṛtyā mahāvākyārthabodha ityapyāhuḥ. etena tāvadvarṇā bhivyaaṇgyaḥ padasphoṭo'pi nirastaḥ' tattadvarṇasaṁskārasahita-caramavarṇopalambhena tadvyañjakenaivopapatteriti.

In maintaining so long that there is to be a sequence in the matter of recollecting the word-meaning intended for a syntactical connection, Viśvanātha is actually reproducing the view of the Prābhākaras, the Anvitābhidhānavādins. The Bhāṭṭamīmāṁsakas as Abhihitānvayavādins are fully opposed to such a view. In the text of the *Muktāvalī* above, Viśvanātha refers to the views of both the schools. The two verses, quoted in the said text of the *Muktāvalī*, namely 'vṛddhā yuvānaḥ' etc. and 'yadyadākāṅkṣitaṁ' etc. respectively represent the two divergent views that come to pass as Abhihitānvayavāda and Anvitābhidhānavāda. As it is not possible to add much to the bulk of the present work, we are required, to be concerned with the two views so far as is demanded by the exposition of the text of *BP*.

As we have already seen, the Bhāṭṭamīmāṁsakas also admit that the three well known conditions, namely Ākāṅksā, Yogyatā and Āsatti to help in effecing the mutual relationship among the individual word-meanings. In their view the individual word-meanings come to serve as the karaṇa in the matter of bringing about the corresponding Vākyārtha with the aid of the aforesaid three factors. The Padārthas (individual word-meanings) are independently apprehended (i.e., abhihitā) until all the words are heard; then there is a simultaneous recollection of various meanings so as to form the sentence meaning. Thus, as held by the Bhāṭṭas, the mutual relation (Anvaya) comes to take place simultaneously at a later stage in respect of all the meanings irrespective of the sequence in which the corresponding words appear. To bring home the idea, the Khalekapotanyāya is utilized by the holders of this view. In M, 'Parantu tāvat ----- kecit,' above, Viśvanātha refers exactly to the aforesaid view. The idea of the maxim 'khale kapota' is saught by Viśvanātha to be broughtout in full with its relevance in the context by way of quoting the verse. It is said that the verse can be traced back in its origin to Udayanācārya.[530] According to this maxim, the various word-meanings in a sentence get related to each other as Kriyā, Karma, etc. simultaneously at a time, like all the old, young and little pigeons which fly down on a barn yard simultaneously. In such a view, obviously the 'abhidhāna' (apprehension of individual word-meanings) precedes the 'anvaya' (the syntactical connection of the already denoted meanings). This view, originally initiated by Kumārila stands advocated by his followers also.[531] But we shall have to note that the Abhihitānvayavāda is not the monopoly of the Bhāṭṭamīmāṁsakas. It is generally accepted by the Naiyāyikas and by the Vaiyākaraṇas also. Of the Naiyāyikas, Jayantabhaṭṭa accepts this Abhihitānvaya theory, of course with certain modifications. He criticises the theories held by both the Bhāṭṭas and prābhākaras and taking views from both sides he comes to advocate a new and moderate Abhihitānvayavāda according to which, Tātparya is a Verbal function. According to the Bhāṭṭas, the words convey the unrelated individual meanings by means of Abhidhā and the unrelated word meanings convey the related sentence-meaning by Lakṣaṇā. But according to Jayanta, it is the Tātparyavṛtti and not Lakṣaṇā which brings about the Vākyartha. It may be pointed out in this context that Viśvanātha accepts neither Lakṣaṇā nor Tātparya in order to obtain a Vākyārtha. Like other Navyanaiyāyikas, he also seems to understand it by means of what is known as Saṁsargamaryādā (i.e., the very strength of an Anvaya brought about by the approved conditions, Āsatti etc.).

The verse, yadyadākāṅkṣitam'[532] etc. is obviously in reference to the view of the Anvitābhidhānavādins. The Anvitābhidhānavāda can be traced back to Prabhākaramiśra, the author of Bṛhatī. According to Prabhākara and his followers, the words can denote their respective meanings only when they are syntactically connected. A word conveys a meaning only as is consistent (Yogya) in relation to other word-meanings, proximate to word-meanings with which it is intended to be connected and only as having expectency i.e., which can demand a curiosity to be known in the context of other meanings. It comes to be clear that in the opinion of the holders of this view, Anvaya precedes Abhidhāna. As we can understand, Prabhākara himself mooted out the idea that a word can convey its meaning only when utterences of all the words are complete.[533] As Śālikanātha expounds the view, a word conveys an 'anvitārtha' (a related sense) and the same word conveys also an 'ananvitārtha' (an unrelated sense, i.e., an isolated sense of a word).[534] Śālikanātha as a follower of Prabhākara seeks to meet the points raised against the theory by the opponents. In Particular, he refuses to accept that the Anvitābhidhānavāda suffers from the fallacy of interdependence. (anyonyāśraya or itaretarāśraya).[535] Thus the Anvitābhidhānavādins understand the effecting of Anvaya in a proposition, phase by phase. According to this view, in the expression, 'grāmaṁ gacchati', first there is the understanding of the meaning from the part sentence (Khaṇḍavākya), 'grāmaṁ' in the form of grāmavṛtiikarmatvam (i.e., the objecthood as pertaining to the village). Then follows the understanding from another part-sentence 'gacchati', of gamanā nukūlā kṛti (an effort favourable to the act of going) and then only follows the final comprehension from the whole sentence (mahā vākya) 'grāmaṁ' gacchati' in the form of 'grāmakarmakagamanā nukūlakṛtimān'. Such an idea is sought to brought home by Viśvanātha in the aforesaid text of the *Muktāvalī*, viz. 'tahtā ca khaṇḍavākyārtha ------- -- ityapyāhuḥ'. In the exposition above, we have taken the terms, 'khaṇḍavākya' and 'mahāvākya' as understood from the Nyāya point of view. But the same explanation for the effecting of Anvaya may be given even in the case of a khaṇḍavākya (like 'caitro grāmaṁ gacchati') and a 'mahāvākya' (eg. a treatise like Mahābhārata) even when we understand the terms from the stand point of Grammarians. In 'etena tāvadvarṇā bhivyaṇgyaḥ padasphoṭo'pi nirastaḥ' etc. .... Viśvanātha seeks to show the futility of the theory of 'sphoṭa' of the Grammarians.

As we have discussed in the introduction of the present work, like other Naiyāyikas, Viśvanātha also believes in the momentary character of the letter-sounds. (cf. tasmādanityā eveti varṇāḥ sarve mataṁ hi naḥ K 168b). In the preceding *Muktāvalī* viz. kathamanyathā etc., there is further admission that a word is nothing but an assemblage of such momentary letter-sounds. In other words, a significant word is also not different from the letters that constitute it. This is the view of the Naiyāyikas as regards the signification of a word. As they assert, though the letters are transitory in character in the sense that a letter may last only for a moment, yet a word comprised of such letters comes to be significant. It is because each succeeding letter is united with each preceding letter through the impression left behind by it and this process continues till the cognition of the last letter. The comprehension of the last letter together with the impressions of the preceding ones goes to convey the meaning of the word. Under the above circumstance, there is no meaning in postulating the so-called sphoṭa or the word-essence by the Grammarians in order to explain a meaning from an assemblage of momentary letter-sounds.

In making a brief reference to the controversial theory of Sphoṭa, we may say that Grammarians donot believe in the explanation of a word-unit by the Naiyāyikas as due to the synthesis of memory and intellect. They donot understand the meanings as signified by momentary sounds but by an indivisible and eternal word-essence known as Sphota, revealed by such momentary sounds. This is what has been referred to by Viśvanātha as the 'varṇābhivyaṅgyo..sphoṭaḥ'. This Sphoṭa, as viewed by the Grammarians, is permanent and indivisible. It is free from any idea of sequence. This very word-essence appears as Varṇa-sphoṭa, Pada-sphoṭa or Vākya-sphoṭa as the case may be, when revealed by sounds, taking the shape of letters, words and sentences. Hence, the Sphoṭa that is manifested by certain letters only (i.e., not letters already enjoying the status of words or sentences) is a Padasphoṭa. In M above, 'etena varṇābhivyaṅgo padasphoṭo'pi nirastaḥ' etc., Viśvanātha holds that the letter-sounds that are said to reveal the so called word-essence (Padasphoṭa) can by themselves justify the significance of a word in the aforesaid manner. Hence the assumption of the existence of some inarticulate permanent word-essence called sphoṭa in order to explain the process of conveying the meaning of a word is uncalled for.

M(51) idantu bodhyam-yatra dvāramityuktaṁ, tatra pidhehīti padasya jñānādeva bodhaḥ, na tu pidhānādirūpārthajñānāt, padajanyatattatpadārthopasthitestattacchābdabodhe hetutvāt. kiñca kriyā-karmapadānāṁ tena tenaiva saha sākāṅkṣatvam, tena kriyāpadaṁ vinā kathaṁ śābdabodhaḥ syāt. tathā puṣpebhya ityā dau spṛhayatītyādi-padādhyāhāraṁ vinā caturthyanupapatteḥ padādhyāhāra āvaśyakaḥ.

The admission of the immediacy of two or more concepts in order to get Śābdabodha from a proposition need not creat an impression that the knowledge of the words corresponding to the concepts can in any way be spared or neglected. As for instance, if one utters the word, 'dvāram' (the door), the contextual comprehension is justifiably possible only by the supply (adhyāhāra) of the word 'pidhehi' or 'saṁvriyatām' (shut) and not merely by the supply of the idea of closing. This is in consonance with the earlier assertion that the knowledge of the meanings of words, only as generated by that of the corresponding words, by means of the knowledge of corresponding verbal function can be a cause of Śābdabodha (cf. Padajanyapadārthasamaraṇaṁ vyāpāraḥ anyathā padajñānavataḥ pratyakṣādinā padārthopasthitāvapi śābdabodhaḥ). Here it may be pointed out that Viśvanātha has to reiterate this already asserted view only to oppose an existing tendency in certain circles to bank on the knowledge of mere ideas at the cost of that of corresponding words. In this context we can specifically refer to the Prābhākaras.[536] Moreover, as Viśvanātha further points out, the words signifying verbs and vocables are mutually expectant (sākāṇkṣa) As Viśvanātha will observe in the succeeding *Muktāvalī*, a word is expectant (sākāṅkṣa or possessed of Ākāṅkṣā) with another (word) without which the earlier one fails to give rise to a Verbal Comprehension. Now, without a Verbal form like pidhehi' and 'saṁvṛiyatām' or like 'apāvṛṇu' and 'apāvriyatām', the objecthood (Karmatva) in the expression 'dvāram' is without any meaning. Otherwise the Śābdabodha from the word 'dvāram', involving as it does an idea of the objecthood comes to be totally impossible. The admission of the immediacy of mere concepts will set at defiance even the time-honoured regulations of the Grammarian Pāṇini. The Pāṇinian rule[537] demands that the fourth case ending is to be added to what is craved for when the root 'spṛh' is used. When there is the expression, 'Puṣpebhyaḥ', with the intention of giving the idea that one craves for flowers, the relevant total idea is possible only by the supply of the word 'spṛhayati' and not of the idea of 'spṛhā' (craving). It is because without the verbal form 'spṛhayati' comprising of the root 'sprh', the use of the fourth case-ending in the expression 'puṣpebhyaḥ' will not be justified. Thus, according to Viśvanā tha, in the case of incomplete proposition, the supply of ideas of Padas and not of padārthas can serve the purpose of Śābdabodha.

K(4). PADĀRTHE TATRA TADVATTĀ YOHGYATĀ PARIKĪRTTITĀ. 83b.

In the Kārikā text above, Viśvanātha defines what is known as Yogyatā. In the course of his treatment of the concept of Āsatti, Viśvanātha maintains, the Śābdabodha of Proposition demands as its pre-requisite the unintervened recollection of two word-meanings, which are intended to be syntactically connected. Here is a query. Can each and every word-meaning be intended to be syntactically connected with another? The reply is obviously in the negative. To be so intended, a word-meaning must have the consistency or Compatibility (Yogyatā). Hence Viśvanātha proceeds to ascertain what this Yogyatā (Compatibility) is.

M(52). yogyatāṁ nirvakti-padārtha iti. ekapadārtha'-parapadā rthasambandho yogyatetyarthaḥ. tajjñānābhāvācca vahninā siñcatītyādau na śābdabodhaḥ. nanvetasyā yogyatāyā jñānaṁ śā bdabodhāt prāk sarvatra na sambhavati, vākyārthsyā'pūrvatvā diti cet. na tattatpadārthasmareṇe sati kvacit saṁśayarūpasya kvacinniścayarūpasyāpi yogyatāyā jñānasya sambhavāt. navyāstu yogytāyā jñānaṁ na śābdajñāne kāraṇam vahninā siñcatītyādau seke vahnikaraṇakatvābhavarūpā'yogyatāniścayena pratibandhānna śābdabodhaḥ tadabhāva-niścayasya laukikasannikarṣājanyadoṣaviśeṣājanya-tadbhānamātre pratibandhakatvācchābdabodhaṁ pratyapi pratibandhakatvaṁ siddham. yogyatājñanavilambāccaśābdabodhavilambo'siddha ityāhuḥ.

In the text of the *Muktāvalī* above, Viśvanātha comes to elucidate his concept of Yogyatā in greater details.

Before we come to the exposition of the text of the *Muktāvalī* above, it will be fruitful to have a brief note on Yogyatā as it occurs in the other schools of thought.

Of the Mīmāṁsakas, the Prābhākara school understands Yogyatā as the suitability of words to have syntactical relation with other words of the same sentence. The knowledge of this Yogyatā occurs to the mind of the speaker and the listener in a particular context on the strength of the previous experience of seeing the words to be in such relations.[538] Kumārila Bhaṭṭa and his followers admit Yogyatā as an essential factor for having a Śābdabodha as they hold that there can be no Śābdabodha in sentences like 'Vahninā siñcati' obviously for lack of Yogyatā between the words 'Vahninā' and 'siñcati'.[539] Yogyatā is defined by the Vedāntins as the absence of any intervention in the matter of understanding the syntactical relation as intended by the speaker. Now in the sentence 'vahninā siñcati' the syntactical relation between the words involved cannot be understood as 'vahni' has no instrumentality (Karaṇatva) to 'secanakriyā' and, therefore, there is no Śābdabodha. The words 'vahninā' and 'siñcati' donot have Yogyatā as constituent parts of the sentence.[540]

According to the Ālaṁkārikas like Viśvanātha Kavirāja, Yogyatā is the absence of hindrence of obstruction in respect of mutual relation of the things denoted by the words.[541]

Of the Grammarians, Nāgeśa understands Yogyatā as possession of such attributes by two or more things as make their mutual relation possible.[542]

An analysis of the definitions of Yogyatā in various circles gives the impression that Yogyatā is actually the capacity of two word-meanings to be coordinated. This is the spirit of the author of the *Kārikāvalī* also.

Coming to the *Muktāvalī*, we find that according to Viśvanātha, Yogyatā in the sense of the capacity of a word-meaning to be co-ordinated with another is in actuality owing to a relation between the two meanings. And the knowledge of this relation is a factor leading to the Śābabodha from a proposition involving the words that convey these two meanings. Because of the absence of such a knowledge, Śābdabodha is not possible in the proposition, 'vahninā siñcati' (sprinkles with fire). As it is not possible to conceive even the instrumentality of fire to the act of sprinkling, one does not have the knowledge of the relation between the meanings of the two words as may exist between a Verb and an instrumental case, although the words as presented in the proposition appear to be in possession of such a relation. Some hold that Yogyatā in the sense of such a relation is not possible inasmuch as the knowledge of a relation of this sort is possible only when there is already a Vākyārthajñāna which is no short of a Śābdabodha. Viśvanātha points out this doubt and then gives the solution in M, 'nanvetasyā yogyatāyā jñānaṁ .... yogyatāyājñānasyāsambhavāt.' Such an objection has been referred to and answered by Śālikanātha also.[543] Particularly the Anvitābhidhānavādins are very likely to raise such an objection. The Anvitābhidhānavādins believe in an Anvaya as taking place prior to 'abhidhāna'. The problem of Yogyatā comes at the stage of Anvaya. If Yogyatā is understood in the sense of a capability of meanings to be related, it comes to be totally impossible to have the knowledge of such a Yogyatā. Such a knowledge demands the completion in the Knowledge of the meanings. But according to Anvitābhidhānavādins, a word completes its meaning only when it is already related to all the meanings. In other words, word-meanings are complete only when they reach the stage of a sentence-meaning. So obviously, without such a sentence-meaning, it is not possible to have the knowledge of such a Yogyatā. Śālikanātha contends that the Knowledge of such a Yogyatā is possible in a general way. According to Viśvanātha, even in such a view, it is possible to have the Knowledge of the said Compatibility in the form of sometimes atleast a doubt and sometimes even a certainty.[544] In 'navyāstu' etc., Viśvanātha refers to some later Naiyāyikas who donot believe in the Knowledge of Yogyatā as a necessary condition for a Śābdabodha. As they hold, it is actually the Knowledge of the incompatibility (Ayogyatā) between the two concepts that stands in the way of understanding of a sentence. As for instance, the Śābdabodha does not occur from a proposition like 'vahninā siñcati' only being prevented by the assertainment (Knowledge) of the Ayogyatā (incompatibility) existing in the form of the absence of the instrumentality of fire in respect of sprinkling. Such a Knowledge of incompatibility in the matter of relation between concepts as verbs and vocabules hinders the understanding of concepts as such. The non understanding or the lack of knowledge of the concepts (i.e., the absence of Padārthadhiḥ) is sure to result in the non-realisation or the absence of the Śābdabodha concerned. In other words, when it is not possible to conceive the relation of 'vahninā' and 'siñcati' as one between a Karaṇa and Kriyā, obviously there will be no knowledge of Vahninā in the sense of 'vahnikaraṇatva' and of 'siñcati' in the sense of 'secanānukūlā kṛti'. As a result, there remains no possibility of the participation of the knowledge of these two meanings in the matter of brining about a Śābdabodha. Thus the Knowledge of incompatibility would serve as the cause for non-realisation of Śābdabodha provided that this knowledge is not due to some worldly sense contact or to some other extraneous defect (like the seeing of a white conch as yellow by one suffering from jaundice)

K(5). YATPADENA VINĀ YASYĀNANUBHĀVAKATĀ BHAVET /

SĀKAṀKṢĀ, VAKTURICCHĀ TU TĀTPARYAM PARI-KĪRTTITAM. // 84.

In the Kārikā above, Viśvanātha defines Ākāṁkṣā and Tātparya, which together with Āsatti and Yogyatā come to constitute a Śābdabodhakārṇa. He elucidates the above definitions in the succeeding text of the *Muktāvalī*. We propose to examine the above Kārikā along with corresponding portions of the *Muktāvalī*

M(53). ākāṁkṣāṁ nirvakti - yatpadenetyādi yena padena vinā yat padasyā'nvayānanubhāvakatvaṁ tena padena saha tasyākāṇkṣetyarthaḥ. Kriyapadaṁ vinā kārakapadaṁ nānvayabodhaṁ janayatīti tena tasyākāṅkṣā. vastutastu kriyā-kāraka-padānāṁ sannidhānamāsatyā caritārtham. parantu ghaṭakarmatābodhaṁ prati ghaṭapadottara-dvityāīrūpākāṅkṣājñānaṁ. kāraṇam tena ghaṭaḥ karmatvamānayanaṁ kṛtirityādau na śābdabodhaḥ. ayameti putro rajñaḥ puruṣo'pasāryatāmityādau putreṇa saha rājapadasya tātparyagrahasatvāt tenaivā'nvayabodhaḥ. puruṣeṇa saha tātparyagrahe tu tena sahā'nvayabodhaḥ syādeva.

In the *Muktāvalī* above, Viśvanātha expounds the concept of Ākāṁkṣā which stands briefly hinted in the Kārikā text above. Here Viśvanātha first maintains that a word is expectant to another (word) without which it cannot convey its meaning (in full). In other owrds, Ākāṁkṣā is the capability of a word to imply something by virtue of its association with another.

Before we fully examine Viśvanātha in the context, it is necessary to understand the concept of Ākāṁkṣā occurring as it does in other schools of thought. In our foregoing general note on the conditions for Knowing the meaning of a sentence, we have, of course, already referred to the concept of Ākāṁkṣā in certain circles of Grammar and Mīmāṁā. To add to our earlier observations on the issue, we find Śālikanātha as rejecting the view of the Naiyāyikas on the issue. He defines (Ākāṁkṣā) as the Jijñāsā, restricted, of course, only to the Prtaiyogin, just what is required to be object of curiosity for Completing the idea in a particular context. Unlike the Grammarians Śālikanātha does not believe that Ākāṁkṣā is a curiosity on the part of a listener and that this curiosity is due to a relation of invariable association (avinābhāva)[545] as he feels that there is no end of curiosity of a listener. He wants it to be conceived in view of the very concept of Anvitābhidhāna.[546] Even in an elliptical expression (requiring Adhyāhāra), Ākāṁkṣā is necessary for completing the construction of the sentence that should normally be there to convey the idea now conveyed by the elliptical expression.

Nārāyaṇa Bhaṭṭa a Mimāṁsaka of The Bhāṭṭa school speaks of the necessity of admitting Ākāṁkṣā as an essential factor, otherwise, we shall be required to recognise a syntactical relation even in the bare string of words like cow, horse, man etc.[547] Just the same idea is saught to be conveyed by Viśvanātha, the Ālaṁkā rika also. He holds that Ākāṁkṣā is the absence of completion of an idea (i.e. of understanding a meaning). Viśvanātha, further, observes that if a sentence be admitted even without Ākāṁkṣā amongs words, then even a group of isolated words like cow, horse, man, elephant etc. would have the status of a sentence.[548]

In the school of Nyāya, the predecessors of Viśvanātha have already asserted that along with Āsatti and Yogyatā, Ākāṁkṣā is also to be admitted as a cause for Śābdabodha. As for instance, we can point out to Udayanācārya.[549] Udayana's Ākāṁkṣā is understood as a Jijñāsā (i.e., the desire to know the meanings of words uttered along with after knowing the meaning of a particular word.)[550] Gaṅgeśopādhyāya holds that so long as there is incompleteness of the expressed meaning, there is Ākāṁkṣa. Jagadīśa holds that Ākāṁkṣā is indispensable in as much as the meanings conveyed by only expectant (sākāṅkṣa) words can be syntactically related in a sentence.[551]

Now as we find in the text of the *Muktāvalī* above, Viśvanātha understands Ākāṁkṣā as the failure of a word to convey a complete idea (ananubhāvakatvam) without the utterance or occurrence of another word. As Viśvanātha understands Ākāṁkṣā not as an inquisitiveness (i.e., jijñāsā) on the part of anybody and as because he conceives it as a qualification of words in the form of not being capable to convey a complete idea without the utterance or occurrence of another, he is not wrong as he maintains that the knowledge of such an Ākāṁkṣā is a Śābdabodhakāraṇa.

To elucidate his points, a word cannot by itself convey a complete meaning. The word 'bring' uttered by some one needs some other (word) denoting some object, e.g. 'the jar'. Otherwise the word 'bring' will not be fully meaningful. In the given example, the word, 'bring' represents a 'kriyā' and the word 'jar' stands for a 'karma'. Similarly a Kartṛpada (i.e., a word in the nominative case) will not serve a purpose, even uttered, unless a Kriyāpada also be supplied. Thus it appears that this Expectancy is the relation between the Kriyātva and Karmādikārakatva. Such an idea seems to be brought home by Viśvanātha in the text of the *Muktā valī*, kriyāpadam.............tena ākāṅkṣā'. But in the immediately succeeding text of the *Muktāvalī*, , 'Vastutastu ....na śābdabodhaḥ'. Viśvanātha rejects this notion in preference to another. According to him, the very concept of Āsatti serves the purpose of bringingforth the unavoidable connection between the Verbs and cases. It is unnecessary, therefore, to conceive of something like Ākāṁkṣā to drag them in. During the deliberations on Āsatti, it so transpired that the immediacy of concepts is a pre-requisite for a Śābdabodha. But the concepts concerned must be intended for a syntactical connection. The syntactical connection among meanings in a sentence shall have to take place by way of the relation of Verbs and Cases. Hence the business of conceiving the concepts in view of this relation of Kriyā and Kāraka need not be left to be demanded by so-called Ākāṁkṣā. In stead, Ākāṁkṣā is to be conceived as the relation between the stems and their suffixes. As for illustration, the knowledge of the expectancy that the word 'ghaṭa' with regard to the second case ending (used after the word 'ghaṭa') is obviously to be admitted as a factor responsible for the knowledge of the objecthood of a jar from the expression 'ghaṭam'. Otherwise such a knowledge would have been possible from a string of words like 'ghaṭaḥ karmatvam ānayanaṁ kṛtiḥ'. As this is not warranted by a fact, the stem 'ghaṭa' and the suffix 'am' must be recognised as expectant to each other as they give a full cognition in combination.

It may be pointed out that if simply or singly left to Āsatti, some times one would be in a confusion in deciding on the knowledge of Anvaya as in a sentence like 'ayameti putro rājñaḥ puruṣo'pasāryatām'. If this sentence is simply lieft to Āsatti, then the syntactical connection of 'rājñaḥ' as an adjunct comes to be possible with 'putraḥ' and as well with 'puruṣaḥ' at the same time. Here Viśvanātha makes a tacit reference to his earlier contention that Āsatti has always Tātparya as its basis (cf. M, 'tātparyagarbhā cā"sattiḥ'). As far as it can be guessed, in the aforesaid sentence, the Tātparya is on the Anvaya of the word 'rājñaḥ' with the word 'putraḥ'. If, however, it is with regard to Anvaya (of the word 'rājñaḥ') with the word 'puruṣaḥ', Śābdabodha will take place that way. Thus it is the contextual Tātparya which will determine the working of Āsatti in cases like 'ayameti putro rājñaḥ' etc.

M(54). tātparyaṁ nirvakti - vakturiccheti. yadi tātparyajñānaṁ kāraṇaṁ na syāt, tadā saindhavamānayetyādau kvacidaśvasya kvacillavaṇasya bodha iti niyamo na syāt. na ca tātparyagrāhakāṇāṁ prakaraṇādīnāmeva śābdabodhe kāraṇatvamastviti vācyam. teṣāmananugamāt tātparyajñānajanakatvena teṣāmanugame tu tātparyajñānameva lāghvāt kāraṇamastu. ithañca vedasthale'pi tātparyajñānārthamīśvaraḥ kalpayate. na ca tatrādhyāpaka - tātparyajñānaṁ kāraṇamiti vācyam. sargādāvadhyāpakābhāvāt. na ca pralaya eva nāstīti kutaḥ sargādiriti vācyam. pralayasyāgameṣu pratipādyatvāt. ithañca śukavākye' pīśvarīyatāparyajñānaṁ kāraṇam. visaṁvādi-śukavāvākya tu śikṣayitureva tātparyajñānaṁ kārṇam vācyam. anye nānārthādau tu kvacideva tātparyajñānaṁ kāraṇaṁ. tathā ca śūkavākye vinaiva tātparyajñānaṁ śābdabodhaḥ. vede tvanādi-mīmāṁsā-pariśodhitatarkairarthāvadhāranamityāhuḥ.

In the above text of the *Muktāvalī*, Viśvanātha proceeds to expound the concept of Tātparya as defined in the corresponding Kārikā. As we find here, the term Tātparya has been used by Viśvanātha in the sense of the intention of a Speaker. Generally speaking, this is the Naiyāyikas' meaning of Tātparya. The listener's knowledge of this Tātparya in the sense of speaker's intention is admitted as one of the conditions for knowing the meaning of a sentence (i.e., a Śābdabodhakaraṇa).

We may recapitulate here that the term Tātparya is found to have been used elsewhere in two other senses also : (i) in the sense of the purport of a verbal statement as admitted in the circle of the Mīmāṁsakas and (ii) in the sense of the function of a sentence in order to convey its meaning i.e., a function placed on a par with Abhidhā etc. as advocated by the Naiyāyika Jayantabhaṭṭa and Ālaṁkārika Abhinavagupta.

(i) The concept of Tātparya is not all the same even with all the Mīmāṁsakas. The Prābhākaras as Anvitābhidhānavādins believe that it is Tātparya which makes the power of Abhidhā to convey the (total) meaning of a sentence also in addition to the meanings of the individual words.[552] The Bhāṭṭas come to reject this notion of Tātparya prevailing in the circle of Prābhākaras.[553] As we know, the Bhāṭṭas restrict the Abhidhā function only to convey the meanings of individual words. They assert that the individual word-meanings combine to give additionally the very meaning of the sentence with the aid of Lakṣaṇā, As aids of Lakṣaṇā, Tātparya also comes to be admitted later on along with the alreayd accepted three conditions, namely Ākāṁkṣā, Āsatti and Yogyatā.[554]

The Mīmāṁsakas are never prepared to accept the Nyāya concept of Tātparya. It is because they do not find any necessity of the Knowledge of the Speaker's intention in order to obtain the Śā bdabodha in a sentence. The reason for this difference is obvious. While the Mīmāṁsakas believe in the 'natural' relationship between a word and its meaning, the Naiyāyikas admit only a conventional relation between the two. As has been rightly observed by a modern scholar, [555] the Mīmāṁsakas being all along occupied with the revealed texts, the Vedas, developed a notion in themselves that the Śābdabodha is possible without any reference to the intention of the speaker in a context. So the Mīmāṁsakas are not to be taken to have understood Tātparya in the sense of a speaker's intention. Tātparya as understood by the Mīmāṁsakas is the purport of a passage. (ii) The Naiyāyika Jayantabhaṭṭa and the Ālamkārika Abhinavagupta have come to admit Tātparya as an independent function with the same status as that of Abhidhā. Both Jayantabhaṭṭa and Abhinavagupta hold the view that Tā tparya is a separate Vṛtti that operates in order to convey the syntactical relation of words in a sentence.[556] But Abhinavagupta moves one step ahead of Jayantabhaṭṭa. Abhinava holds that if Tātparya fails to convey the mutual connection of the primary meanings conveyed by the words through Abhidhā, Lakṣaṇā comes to remove the obstruction in the mutual relation of word-meanings in the sentence. Thus Lakṣyārtha is accomodated by Abhinava casually in the place of Vākyārtha. The functions as admitted by Abhinava are in the order of Abhidhā, Tātparya, Lakṣaṇā and Vyañjanā. Abhidhā gives the primary meaning of words and becomes exhausted because of the maxim 'śabdabuddhikarmaṇām viramya vyāpārābhāvaḥ'. As Abhidhā no longer remains in the process to establish the syntactical relation of words in a sentence, it is Tātparya Vṛtti that comes to operate now to perform the business of effecting the desired syntactical connection (Anvaya). If again Tātparya fails to convey the desired syntactical relation in the second stage, as Abhinava further holds, Lakṣaṇā comes to be resorted to.[557] As we can understand Abhinavagupta, he believed in the involvement of two Tātparya Vṛttis in the process of Śābdabodha in the event of admitting a Lakṣaṇā. For example, in the context of the expression, 'siṁho mānavakaḥ' the second function (Tātparya) fails to convey the Anvaya between the primary meanings of the two words, 'siṁha' and 'māṇavaka'. Then Lakṣaṇā comes to be in operation on the third stage. Now this Lakṣaṇā is to be followed by another Tātparya in order to effect the relation between the secondary meaning of the word 'siṁha' and the primary meaning of the word 'māṇavaka'.[558] Though Jayantabhaṭṭa did not proceed so far, it must be admitted, it was Jayantabhaṭṭa who gave the clue to the later Naiyāyikas to utilize a notion of Tātparya in the matter of an operation of Lakṣaṇā. Here we note a similarity of Naiyā yikas (excluding Jayantabhaṭṭa) with Abhinavagupta in their approach to Tātparya in the context of admitting Lakṣaṇā. The Naiyāyikas in general, like Abhinavagupta, come atleast to realise the necessity of the failure of Tātparya to serve as a prerequisite for the operation of a Lakṣaṇā. Though the Naiyāyikas understand Tātparya only in the sense of Vakturicchā, they admit a Tā tparyānupapatti as leading to the operation of Lakṣaṇā. We have earlier observed the natural link between a Tātparyānupapatti and an Anvayānupapatti. Thus the failure of Tātparya (whether as Vṛtti or Vakturicchā) comes to be commonly understood as leading to an Anvayānupapatti to be removed by the operation of a Lakṣaṇā. We can add that in the matter of admitting Tātparya as a Vṛtti and not as 'Vakturicchā' Abhinavagupta did not go without a following. From Mammata and Viśvanātha Kavirāja also we find reference to the recognition of Tātparya by certain scholars as a Śabdavyāpāra in the 'Abhihitānvaya' theory.[559] But we must carefully note that the 'Abhihitānvaya' theory as understood by Maṁmata and Viśvanātha Kavirāja is factually different from the theory as conceived by the Bhāṭṭa Mīmāṁsakas. In the former, Tā tparya is found to be recognised as a Śābdavyāpāra and in the latter, Tātparya is not recognised as a Śabdavyāpāra as is done by Jayantabhaṭṭa. There, in the 'Abhihitānvaya' theory of Bhāṭṭas, there is no tendency to describe Tātparya as capable of conveying a Vākyartha, as is done by Abhinavagupta. Coming to the Ālaṁkā rikas again, we find Ānandavardhana using the word Tātparya several times in the sense of 'the state of being intent on that' (tatparasya bhāvaḥ tātparyam). The Tātparya is found to be substituted by the word 'tatparatva'.[560] Ānanda seems to strongly oppose the attempts to explain away his Dhvani as only a domain of Tātparyaśakti.[561] But Abhinavagupta seeks to assert that Ānanda was not opposed to recognising Tātparya Vṛtti in the matter of conveying the sentence meaning or the idea of a syntactical relation amongst the word-meanings. Of the Ālaṁkārikas, we find Bhojarāja boldly sharing the view of the Naiyāyikas as regards Tātparya in the sense of a speaker's intention. Now coming to the exposition of the text of the *Muktāvalī* above in the context of Tātparya, we shall have to arrest some misgiving that may arise from using the word 'icchā' on several occasions. We find the Naiyāyikas using the word 'icchā' (intention) in three places. (1) In defining Śakti, the primary verbal function, it is said that Śakti is the form of Divine intention as to 'this meaning is to be understood from this word.' (cf M 'asmācchabdādayamartho bodhavya itīśvarecchārūpā.) This is actually the view of the Prācina Nyāya, (2) To remove the difficulty involved therein, the Navya Nyāya asserts that not merely the Divine intention but any intention is the Śakti. (cf M 'navyāstveśvarecchā na śaktiḥ, kintvicchaiva'.) (3) Tātparya as one of the four pre-requisites for a Śābdabodha comes to be defined as the intention of a speaker (cf K 'vakturicchā tu tātparyaṁ parikīrttitam').

Under the above circumstance, one may confusingly think that as 'icchā' in this or that form is a Śakti, and as Tātparya also is an 'icchā' of some speaker, so, virtually, Tātparya and Śakti are identical. But as a matter of fact, as we find on examination, in the earlier two cases, 'icchā' is concerned only with the Śakyārtha or the meanings of the individual words. In the last case, it is actually concerned only with the Vākyārtha, the total meaning of a sentence.

In the light of such an understanding, both the areas being different, Tātparya and Śakti remain independent of each other.

Moreover, the word 'vaktā' (speaker) the knowledge of the intention of whom is termed as Tātparya and is regarded as Śābdabodhakaraṇa must not be taken seriously in the sense of 'a speaker alone'. Otherwise there will be no Śābdabodha in the case of passage mentally receited by a person under a vow of silence. So scholars understand the word 'vaktā' in the sense of 'abhisandhātā'[562] (one with an intention).

In M, 'yadi tātparyajñānaṁ kāraṇaṁ na syāt ----------- na syāt', Viśvanātha shows the necessity of admitting the knowledge of the speaker's intention in bringing about a Śābdabodha. As for illustration, he takes up the proposition, 'saindhavamānaya'. The word 'saindhava' literally means any product of Sindhu which means a sea and also a territory called Sind. Hence two meanings are probable from the word 'saindhava', namely salt and a particular breed of horse. It is the intention of the speaker which determines either of the two meanings as the primary sense in a context. For instance, in the context of a military expedition, the word 'saindhava' is used in the sense of the horse of that particular breed. In the context of a feast; however, the word comes to be used in the sense of salt. Thus Tātparya in the sense of the speaker's intention comes to be a decisive factor in determing the contexual meaning of the word 'saindhava'. Now the listener must have the knowledge of that speaker's intention in order to have Śābdabodha of the proposition 'saindhavamānaya'. Without that knowledge, he would not be in a position to have the desired Śābdabodha of sentences like 'saindhavamānaya' in different contexts.

In the succeeding text of the *Muktāvalī*, 'anye tu' etc. Viśvanātha disapprovingly refers to scholars like Vedāntins who admit the knowledge of Tātparya as a prerequisite of Śābdaboda only of propositions involving 'nānārthakaśabdas' (i.e., words capable of conveying many meanings). But the sentence chosen by Viśvanātha to illustrate the involvement of the knowledge of Tātparya in the matter of Śābdabodha is 'saindhavamānaya' which is obviously a sentence containing homonymous word viz. 'saindhava'. The succeeding text of the *Muktāvalī* on the issue gives the impression that Viśvanātha believes in the necessity of the knowledge of Tātparya to be involved in one and all Śābdabodhas. But he fails to illustrate his idea fully. In this context, we may record an interesting position maintained by the Naiyāyika Annaṁbhaṭṭa. In the *Saṁgraha*, he makes no admission of Tātparya as involved in the matter of Śābdaboda. He recognises only Ākāṁkṣā, Yogyatā and Sannidhi as a cause for the knowledge of a sentence-meaning.[563] But in the *Dīpikā*, he comes to admit the knowledge of Tātparya as a cause of Śābdabodha as demanded by the case of words having multiple meanings. Though actually the knowledge of Tātparya is required to be admitted in the case of Śābdabodha coming from sentences with nānārthakaśabdas, yet, to keep parity or conformity, he comes to admit the same universally, i.e., in all cases of Śābdabodha.[564] The commentary *Nīlakaṇṭhaprakāśikā* confirms our impression.[565] We shal have to add here that some of the Naiyāyikas assert in clear terms that the knowledge of Tātparya is necessary in bringing about a proper Śābdabodha from all words.[566]

It may be argued that it is not possible for a listener to have the knowledge of Tātparya, i.e., of the intention of the speaker. In this context, scholars point out to certain factors that help in ascertaining the said Tātparya.[567] These factors which are commonly known as Tātparyagrāhakas have been enumerated by Bhartṛhari.[568] They are Saṁyoga (conjunction), Viprayoga (disjunction), Sāhacarya (association), virodhitā (antagonism), Artha (purpose), Prakaraṇa (context), Liṅga (special attribute), Sabdasyānyasya Sannidhi (proximity to another word), Sāmarthya (competency), Aucitī (propriety), Deśa (place), Kāla (time), Vyakti (gender), Svara (accent) etc. On the strength of any one or more of these factors, one comes to be aware of the intention of the speaker with regard to a homonym. As a result, the function of Denotation of such a word comes to be restricted to one meaning instead of many.

Now one may argue as follows. If the knowledge of such a decisive factor is invariably required to be present prior to the knowledge of the Tātparya in a context, it is wise to accept straightway the knowledge of these Tātparyagrāhakas as a cause of Śābdabodha. Viśvanātha seeks to meet such a point in M. 'nacatātparyagrāhakānām ---------- lāghavāt kāraṇamastu'. Viśvanātha rejects the plea on the ground that the so-called Tātparyagrāhakas cannot be grouped under a common denomination. It may be held that those Tātparyagrāhakas however different they are from each other, form a community atleast by virtue of their producing the listener's knowledge of Tātparya in different contexts. In anticipation of such an opinion Viśvanātha maintains that even in the event of finding a common denomination to understand the Tātparyagrāhakas under a group, it is wise to admit the knowledge of only Tātparya as a Śābdabodhakaraṇa atleast for the sake of simplicity (Lāghava).

In M 'ithañea vedasthale'pi -------- pratipādyatvāt', Viśvanātha maintains that in the case of vedic writings, the necessity of recognising the knowledge of Tātparya as a Śābdabodhakaraṇa leads to the admission of the existence of Īśvara. It may be argued that the imagination of the existence of Īśvara can easily be avoided inasmuch as the knowledge of intention of the teachers of the Vedic passages can best serve as a cause in porducing Śābdabodha in the said contexts. Viśvanātha rules out the scope for such an argument by pointing out that atleast at the very beginning of a creation, it is idle to think of the existence of any teacher. In reply, it may be argued again that there being no dissolution (Pralaya) of this cosmos at any stage, there is no meaning in imagining 'the beginning of a creation.' Viśvanātha disapproves of such an argument as he upholds the cosmic dissolution by making a reference to Vedic assertions.[569] Like Viśvanātha, many other scholars admit the knowledge of Tātparya in the sense of Divine intention to serve as cause of Śābdaboda of a Vedic passage.[570] In M 'ithañca śukavākye'pīśvarīya ---------- kā raṇnṁ vācyam', Viśvanātha maintains that as in the case of Vedic passages, in the case of utterances of a parrot also, the knowledge of Tātparya only in the sense of the intention of Īśvara shall have to be admitted as a cause of the concerned Śābdabodha. Though the parrots are capable of speaking, they are not endowed with the power of discrimination between what is correct and what is incorrect. Hence in the case of consistent utterences of parrots, the lack of inconsistency is required to be attributed to the Divine intention. Here the expression 'śukavākye' in the portion of *Muktāvalī* under discussion, is to be read as 'saṁvādiśukavākye'. The knowledge of Tātparya in the sense of 'Īśvarecchā' is admitted by many other scholars as a Śābdabodhakāraṇa in the context of consistent utterences of a parrot.[571] As any inconsistency is not to be admitted in the intention of Īśvara, Viśvanātha hastens to add that in the case of inconsistent utterences of a parrot, the Tā tparya involved is to be understood only in the sense of the intention of the trainer of the parrot concerned.

In M 'anye tu -------- tarkairarthāvadhāraṇamityāhuḥ', Viśvanātha refers to the opinions of those scholars who accept the knowledge of Tātparya (i.e., vakturicchā) as a Śābdabodhakāraṇa only in the case of 'nānārthakaśabda's (words having multiple or more than one meanings.) Amongst such scholars, we may first consider the view of the Vedāntins. Vedāntins are not prepared to accept Tātparya in the sense of the speaker's intention to be known for each and every Śābdabodha. They point out that one comes to have proper Śābdabodha in the case of a Vedic passage even when it is mechanically recited or even in the case of a statement uttered by a parrot under a good trainer.[572] These two instances, they observe, donot involve any intention of either the reciter or the parrot. The Vedātains, however, accept, without hesitation, the Nyāya meaning of Tātparya in the case of ambiguous expressions where the same statement involves the possibility of many implications.[573]

Gāgābhaṭṭa makes a reference to such scholars as are prepared to admit Tātparyajñāna in the matter of Śābdabodha only of words possessed of multiple meanings.[574] He refers to the other scholars who are opposed to admit the necessity of Tātparyajñāna even in the case of 'nānārthakaśabdas' and Vedas.[575] In this context we may point out another interesting view. The Grammarian Nāgeśa is not prepared to accept the knowledge of Tātparya in the case of each and every Śābdabodha. But he is prepared to admit it not only in the case of 'nānārthakaśabdas' but also in the case of the Vedas. He understands the Tātparya in the case of 'nānā rthakaśabdas' in the sense of 'prayuktoricchā' and in the context of the Vedas in the sense of 'Īsvaratātparya'.[576]

Here we shall have to add a few lines more. Earlier in the context of maintaining that Nāgeśa does not actually believe in Lakṣaṇā as a Vṛtti separate from Śakti, we have observed that Nāgeśa's view is based upon Patañjali's notion that all words are capable of conveying all meanings. If all words are cabale of conveying all meanings, the doubt arises that the word 'ghaṭa' may mean not only a 'jar' but also a 'cloth'. To arrest such a doubt, Nā geśa contends that despite the basic capability of all words to convey all meanings, it is Tātparya that finally settles the meanings of a word in context. Hence Tātparya prevents the word 'ghaṭa' from conveying the meaning 'cloth'. Here we must take care to note that Nāgeśa believes in two different notions of Tātparya in order to serve two different purposes. The Tātparya, the knowledge of which is necessary universally, i.e., in the case of all words in order to arrest a wrong notion that may arise from the Grammarian's maxim 'sarve sarvārthavācakāḥ' is understood by Nā geśa as the Divine intention. The Tātparya, the knowledge of which is specially necessary in the non-Vedic words of multiple meanings is understood as the intention of the employer or user of those words. In the case of vedic expressions prone to many meanings however, the Divine intention itself is taken to serve the purpose.[577]

REFERENCES (PART -I)

1. Introduction by Dr. G. Sastri to his Kiraṇāvalī, p. XXV.
2. pradīpaḥ sarvavidyānām
   upāyaḥ sarvakarmāṇām
   āśrayaḥ sarvadharmāṇām
   vidyoddeśe prakīrtitā.
   quoted in VB, under NS 1.1.1.
3. IP, p. 29.
4. "The classical studies of the Hindus comprise the five subjects of Kāvya (literature), Nāṭaka (drama) Alaṁkāra (rhetoric), Tarka (logic) and Vyākaraṇa (grammar). Whatever other specialised studies a student may take up later, the preliminary course includes logic, which is the basis of all studies. Every system of Hindu thought accepts the fundamental principles of the Nyāya logic and even in criticising the Nyāya system, uses the Nyāya terminology and logic. The Nyāya serves as an introduction to all systematic philosophy. IP, p. 32.
5. cf. "There are works on Logic that have been written according to the old school, even during later centuries .... the *Nyāyamañjarī* of Jayantabhaṭṭa too is an exposition of the *Nyāyasūtra*. HIL, p. 529.
6. Preface in Bengali to KIR, p. XXXII.
7. loc cit.
8. cf. "The Vaiseṣika system takes its name from ..... relations." IP, Vol. II, p. 176.
9. Another extensive commentary on the sūtras viz. the *Rāvaṇabhāṣya* is known only by name.
10. cf. IP, p. 31.
11. cf. HIL, p. 519.
12. pramāṇaprameyasaṁśaya ---------- sthānānāṁ tattvajñānānniḥśreyasādhigamaḥ. NS 1.1.1;

dharmaviśeṣaprasūtād dravya --------- tattvajñānān-niḥśreyasam. VS 1.1.4.

13. icchādveṣaprayatnasukhaduḥkhajñānānyātmano liṅgam. NS 1.1.10; ātmatvābhisambandhādātmā prasādhako' numīyate. PPB, p. 360.
14. IP, p. 31.
15. NS 1.1.1. & VS 1.1.4
16. cf. ete ca padārthāḥ pradhānatayoddiṣṭāḥ abhāvastu svarūpavānapi noddiṣṭaḥ, pratiyoginirūpaṇādhīnanirūpanatvāt na tu tucchatvāt. KIR, quoted in MUS, p. 18
17. K 2 & M under Ibid.
18. VB under Ns. 1.1.9
19. "The fusion of these two schools began early and seems to have been complete at the time when the Nyāyavārtika was written" (Jacobi quoted in IP, p. 31) This opinion does not appear to be tenable in the face of the existing literature.
20. cf. "A great part of Indian Philosophy since the thirteen century is unintelligible without Navya-Nyāya", Ingells. Introduction to Materials for the study of Navya-Nyāya Logic (Harvard University), p.1.

    (1) A History of Sanskrit Literature - by A.B. Keith, pp. 482-85

    (2) History of Indian Literature - by M. Winternitz.

    (3) Companion to Sanskrit Literature - by S.C. Banerjee

    (4) Preface to Tarkasaṁgraha - by Dr. Dayānanda Bhārgava pp. XXIII to IXL.

    (5) History of Navya-Nyāya in Mithilā.
21. iti mahāmahopādhyāyavidyānivāsa-bhaṭṭācaryasūtaśrīviśvanāthanyāyapañcānanabhaṭṭācāryaviracito bhāṣāparicchedaḥ samāptaḥ. BPS, p. 581
22. nijanirmitakārikāvalīmatisaṁkṣiptacirantanoktibhiḥ. BPS, p. 2.

But the expression 'nijanirmitakārikāvalī' need not necessarily mean that *Kārikāvalī* is the name of the main book consisting of the basic Kārikās. The term Kārikāvalī may mean also the "cluster of Kārikās" (composed by the author himself), in a general way. If Kārikāvalī would have been really intended by the author as the name of the work, he would have mentioned this name more prominently elsewhere also. Only the later tradition appears to have brought the name *Kārikāvalī* into vogue for the sake of the convenience of keeping the distinction of the Kārikās from the Vṛtti in time of reference and probably also for the sake of economy, the term *Kārikāvalī being easier and shorter than the term Bhāṣāpariccheda.*

23. tatra tāvadbhāṣāparicchedavyākhyānaṁ cikīrṣurviśvanāthapañcānano ---- DK, vide NSM, p. 1; siddhāntamuktāvalī vyākhyāñcikīrṣurmahādevaḥ --- RR, Vide NSM, p. 1.
24. The *Bhāṣāpariccheda* together with the author's own gloss called the *Siddhāntamuktāvalī* was written by Viśvanātha Nyāyapañcānana ----- Satkari Mookerjee, introduction to BPM, p. IX.
25. Cf. Apte, p. 319.
26. Cf. Apte, p. 405.
27. Cf. Apte, p. 322.
28. Cf. Apte, p. 319.
29. 'Granthāvataraṇikā', Vide BPS, p. III-IV; *Vaṅge Navya-nyāyacarcā* by late Dinesh Ch. Bhattācāryya referred to by Pañcānana Śāstri in his granthāvataraṇikā (Preface) to his editions of the *Bhāṣāpariccheda* (Abb. BPS)
30. cf. Preface of TS (MB) by Dr. Dayānanda Bhārgava, p. xxxvii.
31. BPS, p. 581.
32. nijanirmitakārikāvalīmatisaṁkṣiptacirantanoktibhiḥ viśadī-

karavāṇi kautukān nanu rājīvadayāvaśaṁvadaḥ. (Prefatory to M, BP) BPS, p. 2.

33. The Preface in Bengali by Sri Gurunātha Vidyānidhi Bhattacharyya, Vide BPB, p(ii).

34. rājīve śiṣye etc, Dīnakarī under M text nijanirmita etc., Vide NSM, p. 3.

35. cf. iti bhāṣāparicchedo granthaḥ sampūrṇatāṁ gataḥ racito viśvanāthena svapautrahitakāmyayā. referred to by G. Vidyā nidhi, Vide BPB, p. (ii)

36. Vide introduction by Dr. Satkari Mookerjee; Vide BPM, p. (XXIV-V).

37. rasavānatithau śakendrakāle bahule kāmatithau śucau sitāhe, NSV, Vide 'Nivedana', BPS (1354 śaka edition).

38. Introduction on BPM, p. XXIV

39. Preface, BPV, p. (iii)

40. Introduction on BPM, p. XXV.

41. Vide Preface, BPV, p. (iii).

42. According to Professor Keith and Professor Winternitz there are only 166 memorial verses (Kārikās). But all the editions available to us contain 168 Kārikās. Even if we donot recognise the 'maṅgala' verse 'nutanajaladhararucaye' etc. as a memorial verse, the number comes to 167 and in no case it should be 166. These two authors are of the opinion that some of the memorial Kārikās must have been borrowed by Viśvanātha from some earlier source. cf. HSL, p. 486; HIL, p. 534.

43. Vide introduction to BPM, p. ix.

44. Vide Preface (bhūmikā) to BPV, p. iii.

45. Vide introduction to BPM, p. IX.

46. Vide ibid, p. IX.

47. Vide introduction to BPM, p. IX.

48. Preface (bhūmikā) in Bengali to BPV, p. xii.
49. ibid.
50. The German translation by Hultzsch published in ZDMG, lxxiv. 145 ff, is also out of reach to the average students of the BP.
51. tāṁ mā devā vyadadhuḥ purutrā bhūriṣṭhātrāṁ bhūryā veśayantīm. RV X.125.3.
52. yāvad brahma viṣṭhītaṁ tāvatī vāk. Ibid. X.114.8.
53. Ṛgveda X.71.2.
54. Ibid. X.71.5.
55. Ibid. X.71.4.
56. ----- tadyānyetāni catvāri padajātāni nāmākhyāte copasarganipātāśca tānīmāni ---- Nirukta 1.1.1.; catvāri padajātāni nāmākhyātopasarganipātāśca. MBH 1.1.1.
57. MBH 1.1.1.
58. nigamanānnighanṭava uccyanta ityaupamanyavo'pi ------gā rgyaḥ. Nirukta 1.1.
59. VP, I.
60. codanālakṣaṇo'rtho dharmaḥ. MS 1.1.2.
61. autpattikastu ...... tatpramāṇam ------ MS 1.1.5.
62. Kastrhi śabdaḥ ..... tasmāddhvaniḥ śabdaḥ. MBH 1.1.1.
63. śrotramātrendriyagrāhyaḥ śabdaḥ ----- kumārilamate mataḥ. .... na vivādaḥ. MM, p. 218.
64. śabdaḥ ----- dravyaṁ ..... tadbhaṭṭapādairupekṣitam. ibid.
65. Varṇātmakānāṁ śabdānāṁ ------- samāhāraṁ padam. MM, p. 226. padaṁ ca varṇasamūhaḥ - Tarkabhāṣā, p. 14, quoted in NTK, p. 324.

    Yathādarśanaṁ vikṛtā varṇā vibhaktyantāḥ padasaṁjñā bhavanti. VB, under NS 2.2.60.
66. K 164-65, Vide BPS.

67. dvividhāścāyaṁ śabdaḥ varṇātmakaḥ, dhvanimātraśca. VB, under ṆS 2.2.40, Vide ND, p. 188.

68. sa punarayaṁ śabdo ...... varṇātmakaḥ. MM, p. 225.

69. śabdaguṇamākāśam. SP, p. 64; ākāśasya tu vijñeyaḥ śabdo vaiśeṣiko guṇaḥ. K 44, BP, Vide BPS, p. 184.

70. śabdasya ca ...... vyabhicārāt etc. TP, BHC, p. 16.

71. āptopadeśaḥ śabdaḥ. NS 1.1.7.

72. upadeśa anuśāsanam. MANU 12.206.

73. āptāḥ khalu ..... iti evamāptopadeśaḥ. VB, under NS 2.1.69;

The implication of the term Upadeśa gave rise to a lengthy discourse as evidenced by Jayanta's treatment of the term in the NM.

cf. upadeśaḥ śabda ityucyamāne -------- tadevaṁ paryāyame -vopadeśaśabdaṁ --------- anye tu brūvate yuktamupadeśapadameva śabdalakṣanaṁ ----- apara āha ------ bhavatyevam upadiśyate iti ko'rthaḥ, abhidhānakriyā kriyate ------ etc. NM, pp. 137-8.

74. āptavākyam śabdaḥ - TS, p. 65.

Viśvanātha is also found giving the status of Śabda to an Āptavākya. Without being vocal like Annaṁbhaṭṭa, he uses the word 'Śabda' indirectly to mean an Āptavākya.

cf. evamāptavākyādapi ...... ityādiśabdāt. M Text Vide BPS, p. 349.

75. "upadeśa ādyuccāraṇam". SIK, under p. 1.3.3. This means the initial instruction of the teacher in respect of certain basic concepts of the science of grammar. cf.

dhātusūtragaṇoṇādivākyaliṅgānuśāsanaṁ

āgamapratyayādeśā upadeśāḥ prakīrttitāḥ.

BM in SIK, under P. 1.3.3.

76. yatrāpekṣitasyārthajātasya ...... iti Mīmāṁsakāḥ. JNV 7.1.1.
77. upadiśyata anena iti.
78. vākyārthajñānaṁ śābdajñānam. TS, p. 68.
79. āptah khalu --------- vyavahāraḥ pravarttanta iti. VB, under NS 1.1.7.
80. atrāptatvaṁ ca --------- *Nyāyabodhinī* of Govardhanamiśra quoted in NK, p. 126.
81. prakṛtavākyārthayathārthajñānavān, NSV, Under NS 1.1.7.
82. āptastu yathārthavaktā. TS, p.65.
83. anubhavena vastutattvasya kārtsnyena niścayavān rāgādivaśādapi nānyathāvādī yaḥ sa āptaḥ iti carake patañjaliḥ. PLM, p. 7.
84. dṛṣṭamanumānamāpatavacanaṁ ca sarvapramāṇasiddhatvāt trividhaṁ pramāṇamiṣṭam---------SK 4
85. āptaśrutirāptavacanaṁ tu. SK 5;
86. sa dvividho dṛṣṭādṛṣṭārthatvāt. NS 1.1.8.
87. vākyaṁ dvividham - vaidikaṁ laukikaṁ ceti. vaidikamīśvaroktatvāt sarvameva pramāṇam laukikaṁ tvāptoktaṁ pramāṇam anyadapramāṇam. TS, p. 68.
88. anityatve hi śabdānāṁ śaśaśṛngaprahāravat śabdātmakānāṁ vedānāṁ nityatvaṁ hāsyatāṁ vrajet. MM, p. 228.
89. IP, p. 389.
90. PMS, p. 150.
91. cf. nityastu syāddarśanasya parārthatvāt. MS 1.1.18 & SB, under above;

    cf "Jaimini sets forth---------the word is ever present, since the utterance of it is only for the purpose of manifesting it to other." IP, p. 391.
92. cf. karmaike tatra darśanāt-----------nādavṛddhiparā. MS 1.1.6-17;

yaccaitadbahubhirbherī-------tena pratipuruṣaṁ śabdāvayavapracaya iti gamyate -------tena nādasyaiṣā vṛddhirna śabdasyeti. SB, under MS 1.1.17; cf. IP, p. 391.

93. śrotramātrendriyagrāhyaḥ śabdaḥ śabdatvajātimān dravyaṁ sarvagato nityaḥ kumārilamate mataḥ MM, p.218.

94. nityatvapakṣameva vayamādriyāmahe. ibid, p. 225; nanu kathaṁ padārthasambandhasya nityatvaṁ, varṇānā manityatvena padānāmapyanityatvāt,---iti ced --- na------ -ato nānityatvam. BHC, pp. 133-4.

95. VR Under MS 1.1.6-17;

ittham varṇānāṁ nityatvāt arthasya ca pravāharūpeṇa nityatvāttatsambandhasyānāditayā apauruṣeyatvam. TR, p.24.

96. Vide IP, p. 390.

97. sa punarayaṁ śabdo vācakāvācakabhedena dvividho bhavati. tatrāvācako bherīpraharaṇādijanyadhvanivyaṅgyaḥ anyastu tālvādivyāpārajanyadhvanivyaṅgyo varṇā tmakaḥ. MM, p. 225.

98. varṇātmakaśabdasyākāśavadvyāpapakatvena dravyatvāṅgī kārāt---------idānīm ghaṭo jñato ghaṭākāśe dhvanirutpanna ityādyanubhavāt ato nānitvatvam. BHC, P. 135.

99. na caivaṁ saiveyaṁ gurjarīti pratyabhijñānād dhvanīnāmapi nityatvaṁ syāditi vācyaṁ---------varṇābhivyañjakadhvanīnāmevānityatvāṅgīkārāt. BHC, p. 135.

100. kiṁ punarnityaḥ śabda āhosvitkāryaḥ saṁgraha etatprādhā nyena parīkṣitaṁ nityo vā syātkāryo veti tatroktā doṣāḥ prayojanānyapyuktāni. tatra tveṣa nirṇayo yadyeva nityo'thāpi kārya ubhayathāpi lakṣaṇaṁ pravartyamiti. MBH 1.1.1; Vide VMB p. 6.

101. cf. pakṣadvayamupanyasya--------pakṣapātadoṣaṁ parihariṣyatā 'pratītapadārthako loke dhvaniḥ śabdaḥ' iti vivādarahitaḥ pakṣa evālambitaḥ KTS, p. 52.

102. kathaṁ-------nityaparyāyavācīsiddhaśabdaḥ. MBH 1.1.1; Vide VMB p.6.

103. tasmādakṣarāṇyeva padam. SB. Under MS 1.1.5 akṣaraṁ na kṣaram vidyāt, na kṣīyata na kṣaratīti vakṣaram. MBH 1.1.1. Vide VMB p. 36.

104. kiṁ nityaḥ, athānitya iti? ------anityaḥ śabda ityuttaram. VB, Under NS 2.2.13-39; in NS referred to above, the Sūtrakāra replies to the anticipated arguments of the opponents and makes his own assertion regarding the non-eternality of Śabda.

105. sarvaḥ śabdo nabhovṛttiḥ, śrototpannastu gṛhyate. K 165, Part of BP, Vide BPS, p. 580.

106. utpannaḥ ko vinaṣṭaḥ ka iti buddheranityatā K, 167, Part of BP;

nanu śabdasya nityatvādutpattikathanamasaṅgatamata āha - utpanneti. śabdānāmutpādavināśapratyayaśālitvād anityatvamityarthaḥ. M on K, 167.

107. so'yam ka iti buddhisty sājātyamavalambate K. 167a;

nanu sa evāyaṁ kakāra ityādipratyabhijñānācchabdānāṁ nityatvaṁ-----tatra pratyabhijñānasya tatsajātīyatvaṁ viṣayo na tu tadvyaktyabhedo viṣayaḥ -----na bhramatvamiti.

M on K. 167a.

108. tadevauṣadhamityādau sajātīye'pi darśanāt. K. 168a;

yadauṣadhaṁ mayā kṛtaṁ tadauṣadhamanyenāpi kṛtamityādidarśanāditi bhāvaḥ.

M on K 168b.

109. For the Mīmāṁsakas' view point, cf.

"Nor can the fact of the Word being actually recognised as the same in all cases be explained on the basis of mere Similarity. Hence, on the ground of this Recognition, Word should be regarded as Eternal. The Recognition is a form of 'Perception', being brought about by the same organ-----for these reasons the word must be regarded as Eternal".

PMS, p. 151.

110. NM, pp. 200-06.

111. tasmādanityā eveti varṇāḥ sarve mataṁ hi naḥ. K. 168b.

112. cf. nanu trailokyanirmāṇanipuṇe parameśvare/ siddhe'pi tatpraṇītatvaṁ na vedasyāvakalpate// pade śabdārthasambandhe vedasya racanāsu vā/ kartṛtvamasyāśaṇkyeta tacca sarvatra durvacam// varṇanāṁ cāvināśitvātkathamīśvarakāryatā/ sambandho'pi na tatkāryaḥ sa hi śaktisvabhāvakaḥ// etc. NM,p.188.

113. Pratyakṣādipramāṇānāṁ tadyathā'stu tathā'stu vā / śabadasya hi pramāṇatvaṁ parato muktasaṁśayam // NM, p. 173.

114. Manvantarayugāntareṣu cātītāgateṣu sampradāyābhyāsaprayogāvicchedo vedānāṁ nityatvam. VB, Under NS 2.1.69

115. cf. Pramāyāḥ paratantratvāt sargapralayasambhavāt. NKU, 2.1;

Pralayottaraṁ pūrvavedanāśāduttaravedasya kathaṁ prāmāṇyam, mahājanaparigrahasyāpi tadā abhāvāt.-------- śabdasyā'nityatvam, cotpanno gakāraḥ iti pratīti siddham. Pravāhā' viccedarūpanityatvamapi pralayasambhavānnāstītibhāvaḥ - *Haridāsavṛtti* on NKU above.

116. evaṁ kṛtakatve varṇānāṁ sādhite sati varṇātmanaḥ padātprabhṛti sarvatra puruṣasya svātantryaṁ siddhaṁ bhavati--------tathā ca vaidikyo racanāḥ kartṛpūrvikāḥ racanātvāllaukikaracanāvat--------kartā ya eva jagatāmakhilātmavṛtti/------tenaiva vedaracanā iti Yuktametat.//

Āptaṁ tameva bhagavantamanādimīśa/

māśritya viśvasiti vedavacaḥsu lokaḥ// NM, pp.213.20

117. cf. pramīyate'nena iti karaṇārthābhidhāno hi pramāṇaśabdaḥ VB, Vide ND, p. 16;

Pramākaraṇamevātra pramāṇaṁ tarkapakṣavat. MM, p.2; Pramāyāḥ karaṇam. NSMR, p. 5

118. idaṁ tāvatpramāṇaṁ-------tatphalam, pramā bodha iti. STK, Under SK5.

119. Pramāṇaṁ pramātā prameyaṁ pramitiriti caturvargeṇaiva vyavahāraḥ sa parisamāpyate. NVTT, 1.1.1.

120. Arthavati ca pramāṇe---------yasyepsājihāsāprayuktasya pravṛttiḥ sa pramātā, sa yenār'thaṁ pramiṇoti tatpramāṇam, yorthaḥ pramīyate tat prameyam, yadarthavijñānaṁ sa pramitiḥ------VB, Vide ND, p. 4.

121. ye tu bodhasyaiva pramāṇatvamācakṣate, na sūkṣmadarśanāste bodhaḥ khalu pramāṇasya phalaṁ na sākṣāt pramā ṇam etc. NM, p. 14.

122. For example, as for Prameyas the Sāṁkhya scholars believed in twenty five entities, the Naiyāyikas believed in sixteen catagories, the Vaiśeṣikas only in seven catagories, of the Mī māṁsakas Kumārila accepted five and Prabhākara eight catagories and the Vedāntins admitted five catagories. The difference between Vedāntins and Bhāṭṭa Mīmāṁsakas is that according to Vedānta, Śakti is a Padārtha and in view of Bhāṭṭa Mīmāṁsa Abhāva is a Padārtha. The cārvākas admitted four entites. The Buddhists also shared the same opinion. Thus with reference to the number and identity of Prameyas, we come across divergent views amongst the Philosophers.

123. duḥkhajanmapravṛttidoṣamithyājñānānāmuttarottarāpāye tadanantarāpāyādapavargaḥ. NS. 1.1.2.

124. pramāṇaprameya---------------tattvajñānānniḥśreyasādhigamaḥ. NS. 1.1.1.

125. asandigdhāviparītānadhigataviṣayā cittavṛttiḥ, bodhaśca

pauruṣeyaḥ phalaṁ pramā. STK, Under SK.4,p.97. saṁśaya-viparyaya-vikalpa-smṛtirūpacittavṛttibhinnā yā cittavṛttiḥ sā pramā. STK, Under SK.4, p. 97.

126. pramaṇato'rthapratipattau pravṛttisāmarthyādarthavat pramāṇam. Pramāṇamantareṇa nārthapratipattiḥ, nārthapratipattimantareṇa pravṛttisāmarthyam. pramāṇena khalvayam jñātārthamupalabhya tamarthamabhīpsatti, jihāsati vā. VB., Preface to NS. 1.1.1.

The relation between a knowledge and resultant effort on the part of the knower is very lucidly analysed by Dr. Radhakrishnan also.

cf. "Prior to frution, our knowledge cannot be ascertained to be valid. So we cannot have that confidence without which no endeavour is possible. A valid knowledge of the objects is the precondition of successful activity." IP, p. 129.

127. arthavati ca pramāṇe pramātā, prameyam, pramitirityarthavanti bhavanti kasmāt ? anyatamāpāye'rthasyānupapatteḥ tatra yasyepsājihāsāprayuktasya pravṛttiḥ sa pramātā ---------catasṛṣu caivaṁvidhāsvārthatattvaṁ parisamāpyati. VB, Vide ND, p. 4.

128. cf. "pramākaraṇamevātra pramāṇaṁ tarkapakṣavat. Pramā cājñātatattvārthajñānamevātra bhidyate. ajñātapadenātra jñātaviṣayaḥ smṛtyanuvādayornirāsaḥ tatrānuvādānāmaprāmāṇyaṁ tārkikādīnāṁ nānumatam. Vayaṁ tu brūmaḥ------- tārkikāstu pramākaraṇaṁ pramāṇam. yathārthanubhavaḥ pramā. Anubhavaśsmṛtivyatiriktaṁ jñānam-------- anubhūtiḥ pramāṇam. smṛtivyatiriktā ca saṁvidanubhūtiḥ iti prābhākarāḥ------- avisaṁvādi vijñānaṁ pramāṇam avisaṁvāditvaṁ ca arthakriyākāritvam iti bauddhāḥ." MM, p. 2-7.

129. cf. pramāṇatvāpramāṇatve svataḥ sāṁkhyāḥ samāśritāḥ/ naiyāyikāste parataḥ, saugatāścaramān svataḥ// prathamaṁ

parataḥ prāhuḥ prāmāṇyaṁ, vedavādinaḥ/ pramāṇatvaṁ svataḥ prāhuḥ parataścāpramānatām// quoted in MUS, vide BPS, p 523.

130. M under K 136.

131. pramātvaṁ na svato grāhyaṁ saṁśayānupapattitaḥ K 136, Part of BP, M text under K 136.

132. M under K 136

133. pratyakṣamekaṁ cārvākāḥ kaṇādasugatau punaḥ anumā nañca taccātha sāṁkhyāḥ śabdañca te api nyāyaikadeśino'pyevamupamānañca kecana arthapattyā sahaitāni bhāṭṭā vedāntinastathā sambhavaitihyayuktāni tāni paurā ṇikā jaguriti *Tārkikaraksā* of Varadarāja, quoted in MS. vide BPS, p. 260;

MM, p. 7; pp. p. 44; SPB, under SS23, Vide SS p. 290; VPB, p. 11; NS. 1.1.3.

134. Y.S. 1.7.

135. cf. IP, p. 181.

136. cf. taccaturvidhaṁ pramāṇaṁ tadāha sūtrakāraḥ,-------- NM, pp.24-59.

137. pratyakṣānumānopamānaśabdāḥ pramāṇāni. NS, 1.1.3.

138. VB, under NS 1.1.3, vide ND, p. 17.

139. VB under NS 1.1.3 Vide ND, p. 17.

140. M, vide BPS, p. 263.

141. pratyakṣasya sākṣātkāritvaṁ lakṣaṇam. TC(2), p. 552.

142. indriyārthasannikarśotpannaṁ jñānam. NS. 1.1.4.

143. na catuṣṭvam, aitihyārthāpattisambhavābhāvaprāmāṇyāt. NS 2.2.1; VB, under above; vide ND, pp. 136-142. NM, p. 26-59.

144. STK, under SK 5, p. 152.

145. pratyakṣamanumānaṁ ca śabdaṁ copamitistathā arthā pattirabhavāśca ṣaṭpramāṇāni mādṛśām. MM, p. 7.

tatra pañcavidhaṁ mānaṁ---------pratyakṣamanumātathā śā straṁ tathopamānārthāpattiriti gurormatam. PP, p. 44.

146. tāni ca pramāṇāni ṣaṭ pratyakṣānumānopamānaśabdā rthapattyanupalabdhibhedāt.

VPB, p. 11;

147. sūcīkaṭāhanyāyena śabdanirūpaṇātprāgupamānanirūpaṇamiti dhyeyam. SM under - 'athopamānaṁ nirūpyate------ upamānam'. VPB(2), p. 197.

148. *loc. cit.*

149. anumānataḥ parastādupamānaṁ .... tu śabdaṁ puraskurmaḥ. MM, p. 91.

150. VPB, p. 78

151. NM, pp. 128-9.

152. grāmīṇasya prathamataḥ paśyato govayādikam/

sādṛśyadhīrgavādīnāṁ yā syāt sā karaṇaṁ matam//79.

vākyārthasyātideśasya smṛtirvyāpāra ucyate/

gavayādi-padānāntu śaktidīrūpamāphalam//80 K, BP.

153. M, Vide BPS, pp. 408-9.

154. The Mīmāṁsakas are primarily concerned with the teaching of Dharma and as such with the text of the Vedas as a Pramā ṇa. This, however, does not amount to the complete denial of the status of Śabdapramāṇa to the non-vedic utterences also.

155. cf. pratyakṣamanumā tathā, śāstram-------PP, p. 44; athāgamo nirūpyate. VPB, p. 80

156. dṛṣṭamanumānamāptavacanaṁ ca. SK., 4.

157. cf āptavākyaṁ śabdaḥ. TS, and

athāgamo nirūpyate yasya vākyasya tātparyaviṣayībhū tasaṁsargo mānāntareṇa na bādhyate tadvākyaṁ pramā ṇam. VPB, p. 80.

158. TP, BHC, p. 47

159. tacca śābdaṁ dvividhaṁ pauruṣeyamapauruseyaṁ ca. tatrā ptavacaḥ pauruṣeyaṁ vedavāco' pauruṣeyam.

MM, p. 103.

160. gurustvāha. vaidikameva śabdamasti. puruṣavacanāni tu vaktrabhiprāyānumapakānyeva na svayameva vākyārtham bodhayati-------anumeya eva naravacassu vākyārthaḥ. ibid, pp. 103-4.

161. āptopadeśaḥ śabdah. sa dvividho, dṛṣṭādṛṣṭārthatvāt. NS. 1.1.7-1.1.8 and VB under above.

162. "pratyakṣādīnyanyāni bhavantu nāma pramāṇāni śabdastu na pramāṇam.kutaḥ ? animittaṁ vidyamānopalambhanatvāt." (MS 6/11) animittamapramāṇaṁ śabdaḥ SB cf BR, pp. 95-6.

163. We have already stated that of the Mīmāṁsakas again the Prābhākaras donot admit the non-Vedic sentences under the Śabda-Pramāṇa: cf. nanvaśāstramapi śābdamasti laukikam. tatkimiti na lakṣitam. ucyate na śāstravyatiriktaṁ śā bdamasti. śabdāddhi yadvijñ ānamasannikṛṣṭe tacchāstraṁ syāt-------tadevaṁ laukikādvacaso liṅgabhūtādvaktṛjñ ānamanumīyate. PP, pp. 94-95.

164. śabdasyāpyanumānaviṣayatvena avinābhāvopajīvakatvena vā anumānatvam. SP, p. 115.

There is no scope to mistake 'Ārṣajñ āna' (one of the Pramāṇas accepted by the Vaiśeṣikas) for the Śabda-Pramā ṇa under discussion. The Vaiśeṣikas clearly described their 'Ārṣajñāna' as the exclusive knowledge of the seers: 'owing to their peculiar calibre' PPB, pp. 621-2.

165. śabdo' numānamarthasyānupalabdheranumeyatvāt ?

NS 2.1.50;

śabdo 'numānam, na pramāṇāntaram------ yathā' nupalabhyamāno liṅgī mitena liṅgena paścānmīyate ...... 'rtho' nupalabhyamāna ityanumānaṁ śabdaḥ.

VB, under NS above.

166. upalabdheradvipravṛttitvāt ? NS 2.1.51.

pramāṇāntarābhāve dvipravṛttirupalabdhiḥ------

śabdānumānayostūpalabdhiradvipravṛttiḥ-------

viśeṣābhāvadanumānaṁ śabda iti ?

VB, under NS above.

167. sambandhācca ? NS 2.1.52;

śabdo 'numānamiti varttate. sambaddhayośca śabdārthayoḥ sambandhaprasiddhau śabdopalabdherarthagrahaṇam, yathā sambaddhayorliṅgaliṅginoḥ sambandhapratītau liṅgopalabdhau liṅgigrahaṇamiti ? VB, under above.

168. āptopadeśasāmarthyācchabdādarthasampratyayaḥ NS 2.1.53.

169. VB, under NS above,

170. yatpunarupalabdheradvipravṛttitvāditi ? ayameva sabdā numānayorupalabdheḥ pravṛttibhedaḥ-tatra viśeṣe satyaheturviśeṣābhāvāditi. Ibid.

171. yatpunaridaṁ sambandhācceti ? asti------pratyakṣatastā vacchabdārthaprāpternopalabdhiḥ atīndriyatvāt etc. ibid.

172. na; sāmayikatvācchabdārthasampratyayasya NS 2.1.56

na sambandhakāritaṁ śabdārthavyavasthānaṁ, kim tarhi ?

samayakāritaṁ yattadavocāma------- VB, under NS above.

173. Ibid.

174. sāmayikaḥ śabdādarthasampratyayaḥ na svābhāvikaḥ. VB, under NS 2.1.57

175. śabdasya khalu paśyāmo nānumānādvibhinnatām---------sā mānyaviṣayatvaṁ ca sambandhāpekṣaṇād dvayoḥ------ tatrābhidhīyate

ataḥ sambandhādhigamamūlapravṛttinā, numānena tasya

kathaṁ sāmyasambhāvanā, padasya tu sambandhā dhigamasāpekṣatve satyapi sāmagrībhedād viṣayabhedāccā numānādbhinnatvam etc. NM, pp. 139-40.

176. śabdopamānayornaiva pṛthakprāmāṇyamiṣyate

anumānagatārthatvāditi vaiśeṣikaṁ matam. K 140-41,

vaiśeṣikāṇāṁ mate prātyakṣa ..... tathā hi - daṇḍena gāmā nayetyādilaukikapadāni------ityanumānena pakṣadharmatā balād gavayatvapravṛttinimittakatvaṁ sidhyati. M under K above.

177. tanna samyak, vinā vyāptibodhaṁ śābdādibodhataḥ. K 141, BP

178. M, vide BPS, p. 542.

179. kā punariyam vyāptiḥ ucyate, svābhāvikaḥ sambandho vyāptiḥ. MM, p. 26.

180. jātiviśeṣe cāniyamāt. NS 2.1.57

na svābhāvikaḥ śabdārthayoḥ sambandhaḥ yadi svābhāvikaḥ śabdārthasambandho 'bhaviṣyanna jātiviśeṣe śabdā rthavyavasthā' bhaviṣyat asti tu yathā kāmaṁprayogo jātiviśeṣe ------jātiviśeṣaśabdena punardeśo' bhidhīyata iti.

NV, under NS above.

181. tadaprāmāṇyamanṛtavyāghātapunaruktadoṣebhyaḥ ? NS 2.1.58.

182. 'putrakāmaḥ putreṣṭyā yajeta' iti neṣṭau saṁsthitāyāṁ putrajanma dṛśyate. dṛṣṭārthasya vākyasyānṛtatvād adṛṣṭā rthamapi vākyaṁ - 'agnihotraṁ juhuyāt svargakāmaḥ ityādyanṛtamiti jñāyate. VB, under NS above.

183. VB, under NS above.

184. punaruktadoṣācca-------'triḥ prathamāmanvāha triruttamā m' iti punaruktadoṣo bhavati. punaruktaṁ ca pramattavā kyamiti tasmādapramāṇaṁ śabdo' nṛtavyāghātapunarukta-

doṣebhya iti. VB, under NS 2.1.58.

185. na, karmakartṛsādhanavaiguṇyāt NS, 2.1.59

186. nānṛtadoṣaḥ putrakāmeṣṭau, kasmāt ?----iṣṭyā pitarau saṁyujyamānau putraṁ janayata iti-----kartṛvaiguṇyamavidvān prayoktā kapūyācaraṇaśca sādhanavaiguṇyamhavirasaṁkṛtamupahatamiti, etc.

VB, under NS above vide ND, p. 128.

187. abhyupetya kālabhede doṣavacanāt - NS 2.1.60.

na vyāghāto-------yo 'bhyupagataṁ havanakālaṁ bhinatti------tatrāyaṁ------doṣa ucyate - syāvo' syāhutiṁ etc. VB, under NS above.

188. anuvādopapatteśca. NS 2.1.61; anarthako'bhyāsaḥ = punaruktam, arthavānabhyāsaḥ = anuvādaḥ.

VB, under NS above, vide ND, p. 129.

189. vākyavibhāgasya cārthagrahaṇāt. NS 2.1.62;

pramāṇaṁ śabdo yathā loke. VB, under NS above. Vide ND, p. 129;

vidhyarthavādānuvādavacanaviniyogāt. NS 2.1.63.

190. mantrāyurvedaprāmāṇyavacca tatprāmāṇyam, āpta prāmā ṇyāt. NS 2.1.69.

191. kiṁ punarāyurvedasya prāmāṇyam ? yattadāyurvedenopadiśyate - idaṁ kṛtveṣṭamadhigacchati, idaṁ varjayitvāniṣṭaṁ jahāti, tasyānuṣṭhīyamānasya tathābhāvaḥ satyārthatā' viparyayaḥ mantrapadānāṁ ca viṣabhūtāsanipratiṣedhārthā nāṁ prayoge' rthasya tathābhāva etatprāmāṇyaṁ kiṁ kṛtametat ?

āptaprāmānyakṛtam.

dṛṣṭārthenāptopadeśenāyurvedenādṛṣṭārtho vedabhāgo' numātavyaḥ pramāṇamiti etc. etc.

VB, under NS above, Vide ND, pp. 133-4.

REFERENCES (PART-II)

1. Varṇātmakameva padam. PP, p. 89

   Varṇāḥ------- padasaṁjñā bhavanti. VB, under NS 2.2.60.

2. suptiṅantaṁ padam. P. 1.4.14.
3. Te vibhaktyantāḥ padam. NS. 2.2.60
4. Varṇā vibhaktyantāḥ padasaṁjñā bhavanti. VB, under ibid.
5. Vibhaktīrdvayī nāmiki ākhyātikī ...... ca. ibid.
6. samayapālanārthaṁ cedaṁ padalakṣaṇāyā vāco' nvākhyānaṁ vyākaraṇaṁ vākyalakṣaṇāyā vāco' rtho lakṣaṇam. VB, under NS 2.1.56.
7. śaktaṁ padam. TS, p. 66; M, vide BPS, p. 438.
8. vākyaṁ tu padasamūhaḥ. TS, pp. 65-66.
9. This again should not create an impression that the Naiyāyikas are prepared to accept as Vākya any collection of 'suvantas' and 'tiṅantas'. We find Jagadīśa quite critical of Amarasiṁha for his defining a Vākya as a mere collection of 'suvantas' and 'tiṅantas'.
10. Here at the earliest opportunity, we may note that with the Naiyāayikas, a Padārtha worth the name must be a meaning as understood from a word by means ofthe knowledge of the very significative power of the word.

    cf. vṛttyā padapratipādya eva padārtha ityabhidhīyate.

    SAK V, p. 5.

11. tatra tāvatpadairjñātaiḥ padārthasmaraṇe kṛte. asannikṛṣtavākyārthajñānaṁ śābdamitīryate. MM, p. 92

    padārthajñāne sthite------svasaṁsargarūpaṁ vākyārthaṁ bodhayati ityayaṁ tāvattārkikādisādhāraṇaḥ pakṣaḥ MM, pp.93-94.

12. It is used to mean a sense organ, bodily activity, effect,

because, handwriting, specific dance or song, a particular tribe, a specific posture of a yogī, a court document etc. Vide Vācaspatyam.

13. NSMR, p. 5.
14. asādhāraṇaṁ kāraṇam karaṇam. TS(MB), p. 87
15. phalayogavyavacchinnaṁ kāraṇam, karaṇam *padārtha-candrikā* (commentary on *Saptapadārthī*), quoted in NK, p. 200.
16. yadvilambātprakṛtakāryānutpādastatkāraṇatvasya etc. *Nīlakaṇṭha*, vide TS, p. 229.
17. Dr. Dayānanda Bhārgava has also brought this undesirable position to our notice. Vide TS (MB), pp. 87-90.
18. vyāpāravattve satīti pūraṇīyam.

    anyathā kapālatantusaṁyogayorativyāptiḥ

    Nyāyabodhinī, vide TS, p. 41.
19. (vyāpāravat) asādhāraṇakāranaṁ karaṇam. TS, p. 36.
20. sādhakatamaṁ karaṇam. p. 1.4.42.
21. kriyānvayi kārakam.

    It is the traditional notion of the Pāṇinian system of Grammar as presented in a Convenient way by late Iswar Chandra Vidyasagar in his *Vyākaraṇ Kaumudī*.
22. kriyāsiddhau prakṛṣṭopakārakam kārakaṁ karaṇasañjñāṁ syāt. SK, under P. 1.4.42.

    yadvyāpārānantaraṁ kriyāniṣpattiḥ tat prakṛṣṭam. kartṛvyāpārādhinayadvyāpāravyavahitā kriyāniṣpattiḥ tattasyāṁ karaṇamiti yāvat. *Bālamanoramā*, under above.
23. kriyāyāḥ pariniṣpattiryadvyāpādradanantaram. vivakṣyate yadā tatra karaṇatvaṁ tadā smṛtam.

    VP. 3.7.90, p. 86.
24. nanu ca pramīyate yena tatpramāṇamiti karaṇasādhano'ya-

ṁ pramāṇaśabdaḥ, karaṇaṁ ca sādhakatamaṁ------sāmagrī-sampannameva phalamiti saivātiśayavatī. NM, pp. 12-13.

25. ibid.

26. vyāpāravadasyārthonusaṁdheyaḥ NK, p. 374.

27. cf. upāye nirgame dvāram. *Trikāṇḍaśeṣam* quoted in the *Nānārthasaṁgraha*, p. 161.

28. cf. vyāpāratvaṁ ca .... tajjanyatve ca sati tajjanyajanakatvam, NSMR, p.2, as quoted in NK, p. 830.

karaṇajanyatve sati karaṇajanyaphalajanakatvam ityarthaḥ *Nyāyasiddhāntamañjarī Prakāśa* of Laugākṣibhā skara, p.5, as quoted in NK, p. 830.

29. K. 16.

30. K. 17.

31. K. 18.

32. phalasāmānyalakṣaṇaṁ tu janyatvam.

NSV, under NS 1.1.20.

33. idaṁ tāvad pramāṇam--------tatphalam,

pramā bodha iti. STK, under SK 5.

34. K. 51-52.

35. M, vide BP, p.260-66

36. pramāṇaṁ tvapi śabdo vā tajñānaṁ vā nirūpyate/ padārthastanmatirvā syādvākyārthādhigamo'pi vā// pūrveṣāntu pramāṇatve phalatvaṁ tasya gamyate/ SV, 9 & 10, under MS 1.1.2.

37. vākyamekaṁ na nirbhāgaṁ vākyāntyo' vayavo'pi vā/ padavṛndaṁ smṛtisthaṁ vā prathamaṁ padameva vā// ā khyātapadamātraṁ vā padārtha vāpyananvitāḥ//sāmānyānvayabdohe yo heturvākyārthabodhane//. VM, p. 24, vide PP.

38. padebhya eva vākyārthapratyayo jāyate yathā tathā vayaṁ nibadhnīmaḥ prabhākaragurormatam. padebhya eva,

na vākyād, nāpyantyavarṇād, nāpi padārthebhya ityarthaḥ VM, p.1, vide PP. and VR, under MS 1.1.24. VM, p.14, vide PP.

39. padārthānāṁ hi vākyārthe spaṣṭoktā'tra nimittatā. 32b padairabhihitāḥ svārthā vākyārthasyāvabodhakāḥ 34a NRM, p. 98.

40. āptopadeśaḥ śabdaḥ NS 1.1.7; āptopadeśasāmarthyāccabdā darthasaṁpratyayaḥ. NS 2.1.53.

41. āptavākyaṁ śabdaḥ-------vākyārthajñānaṁ śābdajñānam tatkaraṇaṁ śabdaḥ. TS, p. 65-68.

42. āptopadeśaḥ śabdaḥ atra śabda iti lakṣyapadam.-------hānādibuddhiḥ phalam. NVTT, p. 201.

43. ataḥ padābhidheya evānvitarūpo vākyārthaḥ na tu padā rthagamyaḥ-------na sāsau dṛśyate.

MM, pp.96-97.

44. nanu kiṁ kevalapadārthabodhaḥ padebhyo nāstyeva. ..... ataḥ padābhidheya evānvitarūpo vākyārthaḥ, na tu padārthagamyaḥ. MM, p. 96.

45. cf. tadidaṁ gurumatam gauravādeva heyam. asmanmate hi padārthānāṁ smṛtisiddhatvāt vākyārthasyāpi lakṣaṇāsiddhatvāt ..... tasmādasmadukta evānvaya prakāro laghīyān iti--------atrākāṁkṣā ca yogyatvaṁ sannidhiśceti tattrāyam vākyārthāvagame sarvaiḥ kāraṇatvena kalpyate. MM, pp. 97-99.

46. mithaḥ sākāṁkṣaśabdasya vyūho vākyaṁ caturvidham. SSP, p. 63

subantaṁ ca tiṅantaṁ ca subantaikasamanvitam/.
suptiṅantadvayīgarbhaṁ vākyametaccaturvidham//.

Kṛṣṇakāntiṭīkā under above.

---------na vā ghaṭaḥ pacatītyetayoḥ pratyekaṁ na vākyam. kriyarahitanna vākyamastītyādikastu prācām pravādo niryuktikatvādaśradheyaḥ. SSP, p. 66.

47. Jātyākhyāyāmekasmin bhuvacanamanyatarasyām. P. 1.2.58.
48. cf. āptopadeśaḥ śabda ..... ityabhihitam. MUS, vide BPS, p. 411.
49. atra śabda iti lakṣyapadam. āptopadeśa iti lakṣaṇam..... NVTT, p. 201.
50. K, 44.
51. K, 164.
52. evakārārthakasya mūlastha-'tu'-śabdasya vyavacchedyaṁ spaṣṭayati muktāvalyāṁ na tu jñāyamānamiti. DK, vide NSM, pp. 263-64.
53. mauniślokādau ityādinā dvitvādibodhakavijātīyahastaceṣṭā deḥ saṅgrahaḥ. DK, vide NSM, p. 264. ādinā dvitvādibodhaka-hastaceṣṭādeḥ parigrahaḥ. MUS, vide BPS, p. p. 411.
54. padābhāve jñāyamānapadābhave, padoccāraṇābhāve iti yāvat. MUS, vide BPS, p. 411.
55. vide NKU, pp. 158-161.
56. vākyārthajñānaṁ śābdajñānam. tatkaraṇaṁ śabdaḥ. TS, p. 164.
57. padajanyeti. padajñānajanyetyarthaḥ, MUS, vide BPS, p. 411.
58. K, Vide BPS, p. 194.
59. vṛttiśca śābdabodhahetupadārthopasthityanukūlapadapadā rthayoḥ sambandhaḥ. TC, p. 627.
60. vācyo'rtho'bhidhayā bodhyo lakṣyo lakṣaṇayā mataḥ/ vyaṅgyo vyañjanayā tāḥ. syustiśṛaḥ śabdasya śaktayaḥ// SD 2.3, p. 31;

    viratāsvabhidhādyāsu yayā'rtho bodhyate paraḥ/ sā vṛttirvyañjanā nāma śabdasyārthādikaśya ca// SD 2.12-13, p. 53;

    sa mukhyo'rthastatra mukhyo vyāpāro'syābhidhocyate. KP, Sūtra 11, p. 39.

81. syāccedārthena sambandhaḥ ...... syātām --- ucyate. saṁjñā saṁjñilakṣaṇa iti. SB, under MS 1.1.5.

82. pratyāyakatvaṁ hi vācakatvaṁ tacca svabhāvaśaktyā 'pyupapannaṁ cakṣurādīnāmiva. NRM p. 86.

83. sāmayikatvācchabdārthasaṁpratyayasya. NS 11.1.56; VB, on NS 11.1.56 vide ND, p. 125.

84. VB, under NS 11.1.56 vide ND p. 125.

85. purāṇapradāhapātanānupalabdheśca sambandhābhāvāḥ NS 11.1.54, vide ND, p. 124.

86. na, sāmayikatvācchabdārthasampratyayasya. NS 11.1.56; jātiviśeṣe cāniyamāt. NS 11.1.57, vide ND, pp. 125-26.

87. VB, on NS 2.1.57, vide ND, p. 126.

88. tasminnupayukte śabdādarthasaṁpratyayo bhavati. viparyaye hi śabdaśravaṇe'pi pratyayābhāvaḥ. VB, under NS 2.1.56, vide ND, p. 125.

89. jātiviśeṣe cāniyamāt. NS 2.1.57; VB under above, vide ND, p. 126, NVTT, p. 420.

90. jātiviśeṣaśabdena punardeśo'bhidhīyata iti. NV, p. 265.

91. TRK, quoted in MUS, vide BPS, 260; śrotragrahaṇo śabdaḥ. VSS II. 2.22.

92. śabdādīnāmapyanumāne'ntarbhāvaḥ samānaviddhitvāt. PPB, p. 576.

93. nityāḥ śabdārthasambandhāḥ. VP 1.23, p. 3.

94. indriyānāṁ svaviṣayesvanādiryogyatā yathā/ anādirarthaiḥ śabdānāṁ sambandho yogyatā tathā// VP III. 3.29, p. 70.

95. PLM, pp. 15-16.

96. tasmātpadapadārthayoḥ sambandhāntarameva śaktiḥ, vācyavācakabhāvāparaparyāyā. PLM, p. 15.

97. tasmāt padapadārthayoḥ ..... PLM, pp. 15-16.

98. taduktaṁ pātañjalabhāṣye ..... sa śabdaḥ iti. PLM, p. 18.

99. sākṣātsaṁketitam yo'rthamabhidhatte sa vācakaḥ. KP 9, p. 31.

100. śaktyākhyo'rthasya ---- sambandhaviśeṣo 'bhidhā. RG II, p. 134.

101. PLM, p. 21.

102. tasmādīśvarasaṅketa ...... iti h i nāgeśasiddhāntaḥ. TPr, Vide PLM, p.22.

103. Vide I.P., p. 416.

104. Śaktistridhā. sahajā"dheyā padaśaktiśceti. TP, Vide BHC, p. 17.

105. NS 2.1.56.

106. kaḥ punarayaṁ samayaḥ? ..... abhidhānābhidheyaniyamaniyogaḥ. VB, under NS above.

107. NVTT, p. 418.

108. samayapālanārthaṁ ..... vyākaraṇam. VB, under NS 2.1.56.

109. NVTT, p. 419.

110. From the manner of argument it appears that the expression 'ekādaśe'hani pitā nāma kuryāt' is claimed as a Vedic injunction. The Naiyāyikas take Īśvara to be the author of the Vedas and as such all Vedic expressions are supposed to involve the will of Īśvara as the speaker. But it could not be possible to trace out the expression 'ekādaśe'hani' etc. as it is in the whole of the extant corpus of the Vedic literature. In the *Pāraskaragṛhyasūtra*, however, we find the injunction that the father should name the son on the 10th day. cf. 'daśamyāmutthāpya brāhmaṇānbhojayitvā pitā nāma karoti' '*Pāraskaragṛhyasūtra* 1.22. In the *Manusaṁhitā* it is enjoined that the child should be named on the 10th or the 12th day. cf. nāmadheyaṁ daśamyāṁ tu dvādaśyām vāsya kārayet. Manu 2.30. While commenting on Manu, Kullūka

suggests that the 10th day of Manu should be interpreted as the 11th day in the light of the Saṅkhacuḍasmṛti which opines that the naming should take place only after the period of 'aśauca' is over. cf. aśàuce ca vyatikrānte nā makarma vidhīyate (saṁ. smr. 2.2) iti saṁkhavacanā ddaśame'hanyatīte ekādaśaḥ iti vyākhyeyam. under Manu 2.30.

111. TC, p. 650.

112. SSP, pp. 124-25.

113. tatrādhunikasaṁketaḥ---- mukhyārtha ityucyate. Sak V, pp. 5-6.

114. parameśvareṇa saṇketagrahopāyaḥ ---- NVTT, pp.418-19.

115. TC, pp. 651-57.

116. yatrārthe ..... SSP, pp. 122-24.

117. asmāt ..... Śaktiḥ. TS, p. 66.

118. arthasmṛtyanukūlapadapadārthasambandhaḥ śaktiḥ TD, Vide TS, pp. 313-15.

119. Notes on above *Dīpikā* text by Dayānanda Bhārgava, vide TS (MB), p. 155.

120. mīmāṁsakamatanirāsakatvena --- śaktirityarthaḥ. *Nī lakantha Prakāśikā* on TD, vide TS, pp. 314-15.

121. PLM, p. 15.

122. cf. yathā"tmaguṇatā hīcchādveṣāderupapatsyate/ śabdo nayena tenaiva bhaviṣyati nabhoguṇaḥ.// NM, p. 211.

123. atra tārkikāḥ - 'asmācchabdādayamartho boddhavyaḥ' --- saiva saṅketaḥ sambandhaḥ. PLM, p. 13.

124. TP, vide BHC, p. 56; PLM, p. 216; KK, SSP, p. 103.

125. SSP, pp. 103-10; TC, p. 649.

126. tribhiḥ sambandhasiddhiḥ. SS - 38.

127. abhidhānakoṣataḥ padārthaniścayaḥ. KLSV 1.3.5.

128. SD, p. 32-33.

129. śaktigrahaśca ..... madhukarādivyutpattidarśanācca. TD,

vide TS, pp.319-23.

130. sā ca śaktissādhuṣvivāpabhraṁseṣvapi, śaktigrāhakaśiromaṇervyavahārasya tulyatvāt. PLM, p. 27

131. vṛddhavyavahārādautpattikatvamuktaṁ śabdārthajñānasya ------- na Cā'tra vṛddhavyavahāraṁ muktvā"nyat kāraṇamupalabhāmahe. VR, pp. 254-258 vṛdhavyavahārapūrvikaiva sarvā vyutpattiḥ VM p.2, vide PP; TP, vide BHC, pp.56-57.

132. vṛdhavyavahārādeva ..... śabdavyutpattyadhīnatvāt. TC, pp. 460-63.

133. saṅketasya grahaḥ pūrvaṁ vṛddhasya/ vyavahārātaḥ paścādevopamānādyaiḥ śaktidhīpūrvakairasau// SSP, pp. 103-04.

134. nanu gośabdaḥ ...... tacchaktatvenājñānāditi cet -- TC, p. 646.

135. prayujyamānagrahaṇācca ..... VB under N.S. 2.1.56.

136. sādhvasādhuvibhāgapareṇa vyākaraṇena, -- tathā ca ..... siddham. NVTT, p. 419.

137. vṛddhavyavahārāvadhṛtasamayo..... ityarthaḥ. ibid, p. 420.

138. niruktā prakṛtirdvedhā nāma-dhātuprabhedataḥ/ yatprātipadikaṁ proktaṁ tannāmmo nātiricyate. //SSP, p. 68.

139. RR, Vide NSM, p. 267.

140. gavādipradhānaprātipadikānāṁ kośādeva śaktigraha iti mantavyam. RR, Vide NSM, p. 266.

In fact, if Grammar itself is recognised as Śaktigrāhaka for the nāmapadas also, then there would be no job for the other Śaktigrāhakas at all. But the other Śaktigrāhakas would find enough field of operation, when the nāmapadas are not assigned to the jurisdiction of Grammar.

141. bhūvādayo dhātavaḥ. P 1.3.1.

kriyāvācino bhvādayo dhātusañjñā syuḥ. SIK, under above.

142. ādinā samāsādiparigrahaḥ samāsādāvapi vaiyākaraṇaiḥ śaktyaṅgīkārāt. RR, Vide. NSM, p. 266.

143. pratyayaḥ. P 3.1.1.
paraśca. P 3.1.2.
nyāntādābantātprātipadikācca pare svādayaḥ pratyayāḥ syuḥ. SIK, under P 4.1.2.
vibhaktiśca. P 1.4.103
suptiṅau vibhaktisaṁjñau staḥ SIK, under above. kṛdatiṅ. P 3.1.93.
sannihite dhātvadhikāre tiṅbhinnaḥ pratyayaḥ kṛtsaṁjñaḥ syāt. SIK, under above.
taddhitāḥ. P 4.1.76
vakṣyamāṇāḥ pratyayāḥ taddhitasaṁjñakāḥ pratyetavyā ityarthaḥ. *Balamanoramā* under above Vide SIK, p. 404.

144. bhū sattāyām. *Pāṇinīyadhātupāthaḥ* --- Vartata iti śeṣaḥ. *Mādhavīyadhātuvṛtti* by Sāyaṇa.

145. vartamāne laṭ. P 3.2.23.

146. supaḥ P 3.4.103; supastrīni trīni vacanānyeka -deśaekavacanadvivacanabahuvacanasaṁjñāni syuḥ. SIK, under above.

147. The word Ākhyāta comes to be used in different senses in different systems. But we feel that Naiyāyikas accepted the sense of Ākhyāta as the suffixes 'tiṅādi'.

cf. dhātvarthena viśiṣṭasya vidheyatvena bodhane/ samarthaḥ svārthayatnasya śabdo vā"khyātamucyate// SSP, p. 395;

But the Grammarians come to understand it not as tiṅ but as tiṅanata. cf. taṅna. ākhyātamākhyātena kriyāsātatye'iti sūtre ākhyātapadena tiṅantasyaiva grahaṇāt ---- ākhyātapadena tiṅantasyaiva grahaṇamityalam. PLM, p. 111.

148. laḥ karmaṇi ca bhāve cākarmakebhyaḥ p. 3.4.69; On the strength of the Sūtra above, Nāgeśa comes to oppose Mīmāṁsakas' understanding Ākhyāta in the sense of Vyāpāra.

cf. yattu mīmāṁsakāḥ phalaṁ dhātvartho, vyāpāraḥ pratyayārtha iti vadanti. tanna. 'laḥ karmaṇi' ityādisūtravirodhāpatteḥ. na hi tena vyāpārasya pratyayārthatā labhyate. PLM, p. 89.

149. kṛtā'kṛtavibhāgena kartṛrūpavyavasthayā / yatna eva kṛtiḥ ----- NKU 9, p. 230.

150. --- mīmāṁsakāḥ phalaṁ dhātvartho, vyāpāraḥ pratyayārthaḥ iti vadanti. PLM, p. 89; nanu --- ākhyātāntaraṁ ca na yatnavācakam, anukūla - vyāpāramātre eva ākhyātaśakteḥ, ratho gacchatītyādau tathākalpanāt. vṛtti --- ākṣepādeva ca yatnalābhaḥ, *vṛtti*. NKU, pp. 229-33.

151. bhāvanaiva hi yatnātmā sarvākhyātasya gocaraḥ/ tayā vivaraṇadhrauvyāt ākṣepānupapattitaḥ// NKU, 10, p. 233.

152. caitraḥ pacatītyādau dhātvarthāvacchinnasya yatnasya vidheyatayā --- yatnatvameva tiṅaḥ śakyatāvacchedakam --- nanu kṛtyādikaṁ nākhyātasyārthaḥ --- iti prābhākarāḥ. tadasat --- śābdikāstu ---- kartāpi tiṇarthaḥ --- SSP, pp. 395 - 402.

153. kartṛkarmārthakatattatpratyayasamabhivyāhāraśca tattadbodhe niyāmaka ityāhuḥ. PLM, p. 87.

154. yattu tārkikāḥ ..... kṛtāveva śaktirlāghavāt, natu kartari, kṛtimataḥ kartṛtvena tatra śaktau gauravāt. ibid, p. 104.

155. Ibid, p. 105.

156. ākṣepa-labhye saṁkhyeye nā 'bhidhānasya kalpanā/ saṁkheya-mātralābhe tu sākāṁkṣeṇa vyavasthitiḥ// NKU, p. 238.

ākhyāta-vācyayā saṁkhyayā āśrayasya ākṣepādeva lābhāt na karttari śakti-kalpanā. *Vṛtti,* under above.

157. prathamāntapadenaiva tallābhācca. ---- prathamāntārthe ākhyātārtho viśeṣaṇam. --- tathā ca caitraḥ pacatītyādau viklittyanukūlavyāpārānukūlakṛtimāṁścaitra iti bodhaḥ. PLM, pp. 104-05.

158. viśrāma-viśramaśabdayośca sādhutve ..... sādhu. TC, p. 650.

159. kvacicca vyākaraṇāt, yathā 'karmaṇi dvitīyā' 'karttari parasamaipadami' tyādyanuśāsanāt karmatvādau dvitīyādeḥ. SSP, p. 106.

160. cf. abhidhābhidhāno vyāpāraḥ samasti linādīnāṁ tvasau vyāpāraḥ puruṣapravṛttibhāvanāphalatvād bhāvaneti pravartaneti ca gīyate. NRM, p. 48.

The Liṅs or Pratyayas which are given to denote Vyāpāra are nothing but (i.e., no other than) Tiṅs which only get the status of Ākhyāta in the school of Naiyāyikas.

161. cf. kathaṁ tarhi śabdasyābhidhānalakṣaṇo vyāpara āśriyate tathehāpi kriyāprayatnamākṣipati mā bhūttasyā liṅvācyateti. PP, pp. 174-77.

162. yattu mīmāṁsakāḥ phalam ------- labhyate. PLM, p. 89.

163. janyatādighaṭitasya vyāpāratvasya kṛtitvajātyapekṣayā gurutvāditi bhāvaḥ. DK, vide NSM, p. 271.

164. ratho gacchatītyatra gamanānukūlavyāpārasya na bodhaḥ kintu gamanāśrayatvasyaiveti navīnamatamāśritya"ha āśrayatve veti. DK, vide NSM, p. 271.

165. Upamānamapi sādṛśyamasannikṛṣte'rthe buddhimutpādayati, yathā - gavayadarśanaṁ gosmaraṇasya.

SB, vide BR., p. 82.

166. tatra sādṛśyapramākaraṇamupamānam.

VPB, p. 78

167. prasiddhasādharmyātsādhyasādhanamupamānam.

NS 1.1.6.

168. VB, under NS 1.1.6.

169. guṇe śuklādayaḥ puṁsi guṇiliṅgastu tadvati.

AK 311.

170. kvacit koṣādapi, yathā

guṇe śuklādayaḥ puṁsi guṇiliṅgāstu tadvati
śītaṁ guṇe tadvadarthāḥ suśīmaḥ śiśiro jaḍaḥ.
SS, p. 106;

171. cf. śītaṁ guṇe tadvadarthāḥ suṣīmaḥ śiśiro jaḍaḥ
tuṣāraḥ śītalaḥ śīto himaḥ saptānyaliṅgakāḥ.
AK 182-83.

172. KP V, pp. 219-21.

173. VR, p. 258.

174. V 1.

175. Śaktigrāhakaśiromaṇervyavahārasya tulyatvāt.
PLM, p. 27.

176. SSP, p. 103-04.

177. kāryānvitasvārthe padānāṁ śaktiriti vādīnāṁ gurūṇām etc. SAKV, p. 18.

178. VM, p. 2, vide PP

179. kāryatvasyānvayajñāne prāggṛhītāpi hetutā/ padānāmarthavādebhyaḥ paścādbodhādupekṣyate// SSP, p. 115.

180. yatpunarabhāṇi nākhyātaśūnyaṁ vākyaṁ prayogārhaṁ ..... NM, p. 268.

181. VR, p. 258.

182. SBR 4.2.12; JNV 1.3.4.

183. SBR 3.6.1; JNV 1.3.5.

184. ibid.

185. saṁdigdheṣu vākyaśeṣāt. MS 1.4.24.

186. yavamayaścaruḥ, vārāhī upānahau, --------- iti yavavarāhavetasaśabdān samāmananti. tatra keciddīrghaśūkeṣu yavaśabdaṁ prayuñjate kecit priyaṅguṣu. SB, under MS 1.3.8.

187. kvacicca vākyaśeṣācchaktigrahaḥ, yathā yavamayaścarurbhavati ------- nirastāyāṁ mlecchprasiddhau niṣpra-

tipakṣāyavyaṁhārācchaktigrahaḥ TC, p. 526-29.

188. kvacidvākyaśeṣādapi, yathā yavapadasya kaṅguprabhṛtau ..... vākyaśeṣāddīrghaśūke eva yavapadasya śaktigrahaḥ. SSP, p. 109-10.

189. vyākhyānato viśeṣapratipattirna hi saṁdehādalakṣaṇamiti. MBH 1.1.1., vide VMP, p. 6.

190. na ca vivaraṇasya kathaṁ śaktigrāhakatvam, pratipādakatvā dityanumānavidhayā tasya śaktigrāhakatvāt. DK, vide NSM, p. 276.

191. kvacidvivaraṇādapi, yathā 'pacati, pākaṁ karotī'ti tulyārthakavākyāt kṛtyādau tiṅādeh.

SSP, p. 107.

192. cf. munitrayaṁ namaskṛtya taduktīḥ paribhāvya ca, vaiyākaraṇasiddhāntakaumudīyaṁ viracyate.

SIK, p. 1.

193. ete pañcā'nyathāsiddhā--------------------

pañcamo rāsabhādiḥ syādeteṣvāvaśyakastvasau.

K, BP, 22, vide BPS, p. 117;

M, under ibid.

194. puruṣaviśeṣakarttṛkagānasya .... dhātvarthaviśeṣaṇam.

MUS, vide BPS, p. 433.

195. īśvarasaṅketajñānañca vyavahārāt--------prasiddhārthapadasāmānādhikaraṇyāt--------TC, p. 649

kvacit prasiddhārthakaśabdasāmānādhikaraṇyādapi.

SSP, p. 107.

196. SSP, p. 108.

197. pratyakṣasiddhakokilatvajātyavacchinna eva lāghavena pikaśabdasya śaktyavacchedācca.

SSP, p. 108-09 &

cf. K.K. under above.

198. Tatrākṛtivādinastāvadāhuḥ .... pravarttamānamakṛtāveva

vartitumarhati.

NM, pp. 290-91;

PWM, pp. 136-37.

199. ākṛtiḥ, tadapekṣatvātsattvavyavasthānasiddheḥ ?
NS 2.2.65

200. PWM, p. 137.

201. Anākṛtivyaṅgyāyāṁ jātau mṛt, suvarṇam, rajatamityevamādiṣvākṛtirnivartate, jahāti padārthatvamiti.
VB, under NS 2.2.70.

202. tatrākṛtipadeneha saṁsthāmabhidhīyate/ sūtre pṛthagupādānna jātirjaiminīyavat// NM, p. 290

203. PWM, p. 138.

204. PWM, p. 139.

205. NM, p. 292.

206. śabdaccettarhi śabdaḥ prathamataraṁ gotve varttitumarhati nāgṛhītaviśeṣaṇā viśiṣṭe buddhiriti nyāyāt.
NM, p. 292; PWM, p. 140.

207. cf. Jātireva śabdena pratipadyate vyaktināmānantyāt------- kaiyaṭa. Vol. I, p. 17, Nirnay ed., quoted by M.M. Kane, vide SDK, p. 42.

208. kathaṁ tarhi gavādipadāt vyaktibhānamiti-------- athavā vyakterlakṣaṇayāvagamaḥ VPB, pp. 88-89.

209. NM, p. 292; PWM; p. 137-38.

210. NS 2.2.57 and VB, under above.

211. Vide SDK, pp. 41-43.

212. Dīdhitikṛtastu gotvādīnāṁ śakyatāvacchedakatve'pitatra na śaktiḥ kintu vyaktāvevetyāhuḥ.
MUS, Vide BPS, p. 438.

213. vyaktyākṛtijātayastu padārthaḥ. NS 2.2.68.

214. tuśabdo viśeṣaṇārthaḥ. kiṁ viśiṣyate ? pradhānāṅgabhāvasyā niyamena padārthatvamiti. VB, under NS 2.2.68.

215. yadā hi bhedavivakṣā viśeṣagatiśca,.... tadā Jātiḥ pradhānam aṅgaṁ tu Vyaktyākṛti ---------Ākṛteṣtu pradhānabhāva utprekṣivyaḥ. ibid.

216. PWM, p. 142;

gavādipadānāṁ jātāveva śaktiḥ------ iti kecit, tanna-----Jātiviśiṣṭavyaktāveva śaktikalpanāt.

TD, vide TS, pp. 317-18.

217. saugatāstu vyaktāvānantyādidoṣādbhāvasya ca deśakālānugamābhāvāttadanugatāyamatadvyāvṛttau saṁketaḥ Pradīpa, quoted in SDK, p. 42.

218. SDK, p. 42.

219. K 18, SSP, p. 77;

(Here Jagadīśa refers to Vaiyākaraṇas as 'pare' (others). That his 'spanda' means 'kriyā' here can be gathered from the commentary *kṛṣṇakāntī*, vide SSP, p. 77fn)

yaduktaṁ daṇḍyācāryaiḥ "śabdaireva pratīyante jātidravyaguṇakriyāḥ. cāturvidhyādamīṣāntu śabda uktaścaturvidhaḥ------- iti. SSP, p. 78;

saṅketo gṛhyate jātau guṇadravyakriyāsu ca. SD II.4.

220. PWM, pp. 136-71

221. cf. PWM, p. 170;

asamākhyeyatattvānāmarthānāṁ laukikair yathā/
vyavahāre samakhyānaṁ tat prājño na vikalpayet//
VP 2.142.

222. k 38;

jātyabhīdhāyī hi śabdaḥ tāmeva bodhayati na vyaktiṁ tatrāsamarthatvāt--------- vṛtti. NRM, p. 99.

223. prābhākarāstu jātiśaktijñānādeva jātiprakāreṇa vyakteḥ smaraṇam---------udbodhakasya phalabalakalpyatvāt. SAKV, 190.

ākṛtyā śabdenābhidhīyamānayā saha pratīyamānā

vyaktiḥ--------ākṛtipratyayo hi vyaktipratyayasya nimittamiti---------kevalāyā jāteḥ pratyetumaśakyatvāt. tasmātsaha vyaktyaiva jātiḥ pratīyate---------, vṛtti,

NRM, p. 97;

(In the school of Mīmāṁsā, we are to note here, the word Ākṛti is used to mean the Jāti and not the 'avayavasaṁsthāna');

mīmāṁsakāstu gavādipadānāṁ jātireva vācyā, na tu vyaktirākṛtirvā. SAK, p. 173.

224. SAKV, p. 176.

225. pūrvāvagatirjāteraṅgīkartavyā NRM, p. 99; nāgṛhītaviśeṣaṇā viśiṣṭe buddhiriti nyāyāt. NM, p. 292.

226. viśeṣyaṁ nā'bhidhā gacchet kṣīṇaśaktirviśeṣaṇe

227. jātireva ..... ākṣepācca vyaktilābhaḥ athāpattiḥ samā navittivedyatvaṁ vā"kṣepaḥ nirūḍhalakṣaṇā

vā-------BHC. p. 90; vyakterapi ..... maṇḍanācāryamatam. ibid, p. 187;

prābhākarāstu - jātiśaktijñānādeva jātiprakāreṇa vyakteḥ smaraṇaṁ sābdabodhaśca ------- ibid, p. 190

228. vyaktisaṅketapakṣe sarvāsu vyaktiṣu saṅketa eko nānā vā nā dyaḥ ānantyāt, nāntyo, vyabhicārāpatteḥ.

TP, vide BHC, p. 90.

229. tathā ca yatkiñcidekaghaṭavyaktau ghaṭapadaśaktisvīkāre ...... vyatirekavyabhicāra iti bhāvaḥ MUS, vide BPS, p. 434.

230. sakalavyaktiṣu śaktisvīkāre vyaktīnāmānantyācchaktīnāmā nantyam. tathā cānantaśaktikalpanāyāṁ gauravāt vyaktau śaktirna svīkāryeti bhāvaḥ. ibid.

231. cf. tatra prābhākarāḥ yadyapyānayanādivyavahārāt vyaktāveva śaktirucitā ..... śakyatve'nadhyavasāyaḥ etc. TC, p. 556.

232. cf. kutastarhi vyaktidhīḥ, jātiśaktādeva--------jātiviśiṣṭasya smārakamanubhāvakañca.

TC, pp. 562-66;

prābhākarāstu gotvaśaktatvena jñātaṁ padaṁ tādrūpyena gośabdatvāvacchinnaṁ pratyeva hetuḥ; ato gotvaśaktigrahānna gotvena gavayādeḥ------------- na caivaṁ jāteriva vyakterapi śakyatvamāvaśyakam,-------etc.

SSP, pp. 90-91.

233. padajanyapadārthopasthiteḥ śābdabodhaṁ prati hetutayā vyaktiśaktiṁ vinā tadbhānānirvāhāditi bhāvaḥ.

DK, vide NSM, p. 277.

234. jātimātravācakatvenābhyupagatapadasyāpi vyaktibodhajanakatāyāmavivādād vyaktiśaktirdhruvaiva śaktibhramājanyalakṣaṇāgrahājanyatadbodhakajanakatayā eva --------- SAK V, p. 177.

235. na vyaktirākṣepaḥ ..... nityatvāllakṣymānāyā vyakteste hi viśeṣaṇe" iti. T.C., p. 587.

yadāhurmaṇḍanācāryyāḥ - jāternāstitva----------viśeṣaṇe. iti. SSP, p. 87.

236. tādṛśaśaktiviṣayatvaṁ śakyatvam. tacca jātereva na vyakteḥ ..... śabdārtha iti VPB, pp. 88-89.

237. yattu gaurjjāyate gaurnaśyati ityādau----------lakṣaṇāyā gotvā diviśiṣṭa vyaktirbodhyate,------tāparyyānupapatterapi lakṣaṇāyāṁ bījatvāt.

SSP, p. 87.

238. gāmānayetyādau---------gotvajāterastitvādyanvayānupapatterlakṣaṇābījasyā'bhāvena lakṣaṇāyāḥ svīkartumaśakyatvāditi bhāvaḥ.

DK, Vide NSM, p. 277.

239. -----------īśvarecchārūpāyāstasyā ekatvādityarthaḥ DK, Vide NSM, p. 277-78.

240. cf. tatra prābhākarāḥ yadyapyānayanādivyavahārāt vyaktāveva śaktirucitā ...... stamavabodhayati------------TC, pp. 556-64.

241. vyaktyākṛtijātayastu padārthaḥ. NS 2.2.68.

242. parasparaparityāgena parasparasya bodhābhāvāt triṣvekaiva śaktiḥ ..... sampradāyaḥ. DK, vide NSM, pp. 128-29.

243. yadā tu---------vyaktiḥ pradhānam, aṅgaṁ tu jātyākṛtī---------jātiḥ pradhānam aṅgaṁ tu vyaktyākṛtī----------ākṛtesu pradhānabhāva utprekṣitavyaḥ. VB, under NS 2.2.68.

244. navyāstu saṁsthānānupasthitāvapi gotvādinā ..... śaktiḥ. DK vide NSM, p. 280;

navyāstu jātivyaktyorekaśaktiprāptyarthaṁ prakāreṇa ..... vyakteravagamaḥ SSP, pp. 129-30.

245. jātyavacchinnasaṅketavati----------SSP, p. 19;

avaśyaṁ gotvādiviśiṣṭo gavādirgavādipadasyārthaḥ SSP, p. 103;

246. ---------jātimātranirvikalpakād vyaktimanādāya, ... jātyā kṛtiviśiṣṭasyaivānubhāvāt. TC, p. 590.

247. sa sambandhaḥ pade vākye ca. PLM, p. 18

248. padasyaiva śaktiḥ kalpyate prathamatastasyaiva kāraṇatvāvadhāraṇāt. TC, p. 552; saṁketo lakṣaṇā cārthe padavṛttiḥ SAK V, p. 1. śaktaṁ padam. TS, p. 66.

249. tadāha nyāyabhāṣyakāraḥ samayajñānārthaṁ cedaṁ padalakṣaṇāyā vāco'nvākhyānaṁ vyākaraṇam, vākyalakṣaṇāyā vāco'rtha lakṣaṇam' iti anena padeṣviva vākyeṣvapī śvarasamaya iti spaṣṭamevoktam. PLM, p. 18.

250. prāthamyādabhidhātṛtvāt tātparyāvagamādapi/

padānāmeva sā śaktirvarambhyupagamyatām//

VM, p. 14, vide pp.

na vimuñcanti sāmarthyam

vākyārthe'pi padāni naḥ. ibid.

251. śaktirnāma padānāmartheṣu mukhyā vṛttiḥ-----------śaktijñāpyaśca yathā padārthastathā vākyārtho'pīti na kācidanupapattiḥ. VPB, pp. 87-95.

252. rūḍhañca lakṣakañcaiva yogarūḍhañca yaugikam taccaturddha, parai rūḍhayaugikaṁ manyate' dhikam. SSP, p. 72.

253. paṅkajādipadeṣu yogarūḍhiḥ avayavaśaktiryogaḥ samudāyaśakti rūḍhiḥ. niyatapadmatvādijñānārthaṁ samudāyaśaktiḥ TD, vide TS pp. 334-36.

254. tacca padaṁ caturvidham. rūḍhaṁ, yaugikaṁ yogarūḍhaṁ yaugikarūḍham, ca ---------- etc. TP. vide BHC, p. 59.

255. śāstrakalpitāvayavārthanirūpitā śaktiryogaḥ yathā pācakādau, PLM, p. 30;

avayavaśaktyārthapratyāyakatvam (yaugikatvam). TP, Vide BHC, p. 59.

256. P 7.1.7; cf. p 7.2.113.

257. P 7.2.117.

258. P 3.4.67.

259. śāstrakalpitāvayavārthanirūpitā śaktiryogaḥ, yathā pācakādau. PLM, p. 30.

260. yogalabhyārthamātrasya bodhakaṁ nāma yaugikaṁ/ samāsastaddhitāntaṁ ca kṛdantañceti tattridhā// SSP, p. 187.

261. SSP, p. 275; PLM, p. 30.

262. śāstrakalpitāvayavārthabhānābhave samudāyārthanirūpitaśaktī rūḍhiḥ, yathā maṇinūpurādau. PLM, p. 30.

samudāyaśaktyā' rthapratyāyakatvaṁ rūḍhatvam. TP, BHC, p. 59.

263. tena kiñcinnāma kvacidarthe rūḍhameva, yathā goprabhṛtau gavādi---------SSP, pp. 72-73.

264. maṇḍapamaṇḍalayoryaugikarūḍhatvāt rūḍhodāharaṇatvaṁ na yuktamiti vibhāvanīyam, MUS, Vide BPS, p. 439.

265. 'maṇḍalādi'ityatra bahupustakeṣu 'maṇḍapādi' iti pāṭhaḥ, sa prāmādikaḥ. DK, Vide NSM, p. 283.

266. tanna cārutaram. yaugikarūḍhasyāpi yaugikarūḍhatvayorar-

thaviśeṣe sambhavena maṇḍapapadasya gṛhaviśeṣe rū ḍhatayā rūḍhamadhye parigaṇanasambhavāt. RR, Vide ṄSM, p. 283.

267. Rūḍheḥ prayogapratibandhakatvaṁ maṇḍapādau dṛṣṭameva. TC, p. 613.

268. Rūḍhayaugikamapyadhikaṁ nāma, yathā manḍapamahārajatādi, SSP, p. 74.

269. maṇḍapādipadasyāpi gṛhādau---------- nirūḍhalakṣaṇāṅ-----gīkārāt--------Jhalakikar, Vide KP. p. 42

270. rūḍhaṁ saṅketavannāma. saiva sañjñeti kīrttyate/naimittikī pāribhāṣikyaupādhīkyapi tadbhidā// SSP 17, p. 76.

271. tatra akhaṇḍaśaktimātreṇaikārthapratipādakatvaṁ rūḍhiḥ. VV, p. 1.

272. akhaṇḍa eva hi śabdaḥ tatra samāseṣu padānāṁ ..... ityapi vadanti. R G, II, p. 141.

273. śāstrakalpitāvayavārthānvitaviśeṣyabhūtārthanirupitā śaktiryogarūḍhiḥ, PLM, p. 30.

274. samudāyaśaktyā avayavaśaktyā caikārthapratyāyakatvaṁ yogarūḍhatvam. TP, Vide BHC, p. 59.

275. evaṁ padmaṁ paṅkajapadaśakyaṁ tato niyamataḥ ...... rū ḍhyā pratibandhāditi prāñcaḥ. TC, p. 591-92.

276. mīmāṁsakānāṁ matamupanyasyati -

rūḍhyarthabhinne yogārthabuddau rūḍhervirodhitām vadanti kecidekaikabuddhistaiḥ kvacidiṣyate. etc. SSP, p. 173.

277. parantu rūḍhyarthabhinne yogārthasya bodhaṁ prati rūḍhidhiyaḥ pratibandhakatvam---------- mīmāṁsakānāṁ matam. SSP, p. 172-73.

278. kiñca rūḍhiyogayorvirodha ..... paṅkajanikarttṛtvenānubhāvyate -------- TC, p. 629-30.

279. niyatapadmatvādijñānārthaṁ samudāyaśaktiḥ anyathā kumude'pi prayogaprasaṅgāt. TD, Vide TS, p. 335-36.

280. Maṇikṛnmataṁ darśayati -

rūḍhyarthe'nyatra vā yatra yadā"kāṁkṣādiniścayaḥ tadaiva tatra yogārthasyānvayo maṇikṛnmataḥ. ..... iti cintā maṇikṛtāṁ matam. SSP, p. 185-86.

281. nanvevaṁ rūḍhirevāstu tata evobhayalābhāt kiṁ yogarūḍhyā, na, avayavaśakteḥ kḷptatvāt yaugikārthānubhāvācca. TC, p. 593. na. ... ato yogarūḍhirāvaśyaki. TP, Vide BHC, p. 59.

282. ata eva paṅkajaṁ kumudaṁ ityatra. paṅkajanikartṛtvena 'bhūmau paṅkaja mutpanna mityādau ca padmatvena paṅkajapadasya lakṣaṇayaiva kumudasthala-padmayorbodhaḥ iti vārttikam. SSP, p. 163-64.

283. navyāstu niyamataḥ ..... yogādeva kumudadhīrna lakṣaṇayeti. TC, p. 601.

284. taddhi kadācidavayavavṛttyā yogārthameva, kadācicca samudāyaśaktyā rūḍhyarthamevābhidhatta (ityapareṣāṁ matam) SSP, p. 75;

tathaiva bhinnārthapratyāyakatvam.(yaugikarūḍhatvam). TP, BHC, p. 59.

285. udbhidā yajeta paśukāma. TBR 19.7.3, JNV 1.4.1.

286. ādinā maṇḍapādiparigrahaḥ. MUS, Vide BPS, p. 441; cf. SSP, p. 74; PLM, p. 32; TP, vide BHC, p. 59.

287. aśvagandhādipadamoṣadhiviśeṣe rūḍham .... PLM, p. 32.

288. iyāṁstu viśeṣo - yadrūḍhamapi ..... samudāyaśaktyā cāvayalabhyārthamevānubhāvayati. SSP, p. 162-63.

289. For example, an authority like Dr. K.K. Raja has used the term Metaphor for Lakṣaṇā.

Vide (title page for the chapter on Lakṣaṇā in) ITM.

290. "Similes are not late phenomena in the history of human language,we learn from the fact that we are accustomed to look upon abstract ideas as similar to things we perceive with our sense-organs and that it is in the first place people who have no trained way of thinking that are accustomed to

do so. Naive and primitive men who are scarcely able to abstract, are inclined to name new things after the familiar and to compare things unknown to the well-known. By means of a 'Simile' they bring the unknown within the sphere of the known". RSL, p. 11.

291. RV 1.164.20.

292. 'upakārakatvādalaṅkāraḥ saptamamaṅgam iti yāyāvarīyaḥ. ṛte ca tatsvarūpaparijñānādvedarthānavagatiḥ. yathā - dvā--- -------------abhicākaśīti'. KM, p. 16.

293. iyaṁ cātiśayoktirvede'pi dṛśyate. yathā - dvāsuparṇā---------- -abhicākaśīti -------- RG, p. 34.

294. atha ..... kutsāyāṁ kāka iti-------NIR 3.18.

295. siṁho vyāghra ..... kaścidasti śauryādiḥ ---------Durgācārya under ibid.

296. autpattikastu śabdasyārthena saṁbandhaḥ---------MS 1.1.5. autpattika iti ..... pascātsaṁbandhaḥ. SB, under MS above.

297. śrutiliṅgavākyaprakaraṇa------- viprakarṣāt. MS, 3.3.14. yadarthasyābhidhānaṁ ..... śravaṇaṁ śrutih. SB, under MS above.

298. guṇādavipratiṣedhaḥ syāt. MS 1.2.39.

299. sarveṣāṁ vaikamantryamaitiśāyanasya bhaktipānatvāt savanādhikyato hi. ibid 3.2.43.

300. na īndrapītaḥ - iti ..... mantreṇa vaditum. SB under ibid.

301. syādvāsya .... śāyanaḥ. MS 3.4.24.

302. autpattikastu .... bādarāyaṇasyānapekṣatvāt. ibid 1.1.5.

303. carācaravyapāśrayastu ..... tadbhāvabhāvitvāt. BS II.3.16. vide BSB, p. 224.

304. bhaktirasaṁnidhāvanyāyyeti cet. MS. 3.8.43

305. sarveṣāṁ vā lakṣaṇatvādaviśiṣṭaṁ hi Lakṣaṇaṁ. ibid 3.1.14.

306. tadetat grahādilakṣayitvā ..... sammārgādisambandhaḥ - iti, etc. SB, under ibid.

307. guṇamukhyavyatikrame tadarthatvānmukhyena vedasaṁyogaḥ. MS 3.3.9.

308. api ca vidhitve lakṣaṇā, SB, under MS 1.4.22;

Śrutilakṣaṇāviśaye ca śrutirnyāya, na lakṣaṇā. ibid, under MS 6.1.51;

Śrutilakṣaṇaviśaye ----------------nyāyā syāt. ibid, under MS 9.1.21 & 10.4.33.

309. śrutiśca lakṣaṇāyā jyāyasī ibid, under MS 1.4.24 & 9.3.3;

śrutiśca jyāyasī lakṣanāyāḥ ibid, under MS 9.1.33;

śrutiśca lakṣaṇāyā garīyasī ibid, under MS 10.8.35

mukhyārthatā ca nyāyā na lakṣyārthatā. ibid, under MS 3.2.25.

310. kaḥ punarmukhyaḥ ..... gauṇaḥ iti. ibid, under MS, 3.2.1.

311. iha ye bidhivannigadā------- audumbara ..... stutiriti. ibid, under MS 1.2.19.

312. tadbhūtānāṁ kriyārthena samāmnāyo'rthasya tannimittatvāt. MS 1.1.25.

313. teṣveva padārtheṣu ...... vākyārtha. SB, under ibid.

314. vākyārtho lakṣayamāṇo hi sarvatraiva naḥ sthitiḥ. SV, Vākya, p. 229.

315. ānarthakyādakāraṇāṁ karturhi kāraṇāni guṇārtho hi vidhīyate. MS 1.4.22.

316. arthavādaprasaṅgāttadupakāriguṇavādāvidhitallakṣaṇaṁ -- -nanu ca ...... bāḍhamasti kutaḥ ..... sādṛśyādupajāyate. TV, under ibid, Vide MD pp. 313-14.

317. itareṣāṁ tu ..... Mīmāṁsakāḥ NRM, pp. 101-02. nanvavinā bhāvanimittā ...... tatra nimittaṁ. ibid, p. 102.

318. vayaṁ tu ..... bodhayantīti brūmaḥ. ..... lakṣaṇā bhavati. MM, p. 94.

319. nanu ca ..... śakyate vaktuṁ VR, p. 41-42.

320. sahacaraṇāt ..... tādarthyāt - kaṭārtheṣu ..... karotīti bhavati. VB, under NS 2.2.64.

321. nanu-------gaurvāhīka iti. VR, p. 147.

322. vākyārtho lakṣamāṇo hi sarvatraiva hi lakṣyate, iti; VM, p. 13, Vide PP.

323. vācyasyārthasya vākyārthe sambandhānupapattitaḥ/ tatsaṁbandhavaśaprāptasyānvayāllkṣaṇocyate ityuttaraślokaḥ. ibid.

324. tadāhurvārttikakārapādāḥ - vākyārtho lakṣyamāṇo hi sarvatraiva hi lakṣyate iti.---------------tadayuktamityanye. ..... taddvevidhyaṁ parairaṅgīkṛtam. TR, p. 28:

ato'nyathā ...... pratīteḥ - ibid.

325. 'na viyadaśruteḥ' and 'gauṇyasambhavāt'.

BS II.3.1 & 3, SBH under above, vide BSB, pp. 211-12.

326. tasmādvā etasmādātmana ākāśaḥ saṁbhūtaḥ. ākāśādvāyu. vāyuragniḥ agnerāpaḥ--------TU. II.1.1.

327. tasmādyathā ...... gauṇī draṣṭavyā. SBH under BS II.3.3, vide BSB, p. 212-13.

328. carācaravyapāśrayastu syāttadvyapadeśo bhāktastadbhāvabhāvitvāt. BS II.3.16.

ucyate - carācaravyapāśrayaḥ ...... bhavato, nāsatoḥ.

SBH under BS above, Vide BSB, p. 224.

329. nāvaśyamayamevābhisambandho ...... jaṭinaṁ ...... brahmadatta ityāha. Brahmadatte yāni kāryāṇi......tāni kriyanta ityeto jaṭī 'brahmadatta' ityucyate -------- Tatsāmīpyād ...... yaṣṭiḥ praveśayati

MBH, under Vārtika 3, 'Siddhaṁ tu striyāḥ puṁśabdenā bhidhānāt. on 'Puṁyogādākhyāyāṁ' P. 4.1.48.

330. kākebhyo rakyatāṁ sarpiriti bālo'pi coditaḥ/ upaghātapare vākye na śvādibhyo na rakṣati.// VP. 2.312.

331. vastutastu tātparyānupapattisandhānameva tadbījaṁ. PLM, p. 45.

332. tathāhi - śaktirdvividhā ...... kimanupapannaṁ. ibid, p. 51.

333. śuddhasyoccāraṇe svārthaḥ prasiddho yasya gamyate/ sa mukhya iti vijñeyo rūpamātranibandhanaḥ// yastvanyasya prayogená yatnādiva niyujyate/ tamaprasiddhaṁ manyante gauṇārthābhiniveśināṁ. //VP 2.265-66.

334. nanu 'sarve sarvārthavācakā' ...... surūḍhaṁ. PLM, p. 51.

335. Bhāmaha recommends the knowledge of Śabda and its Artha as one of the important factors in composing a poetry. cf. śabdaśchando'bhidhānārtha ------ mantavyāḥ kāvyagaihyamī (KL 1.9.). Udbhaṭa, the commentator maintains that the expression 'abhidhāna' of Bhāmaha means Abhidhā which includes both the Mukhyā and Gauṇī Vṛttis. If the explanation be accepted, Bhāmaha shall have to be admitted as the first Ālaṁkārika to have recognised the transferance of epithet, i.e., Gauṇīvṛtti.

336. bhāmahenoktaṁ - śabdaśchando ...... guṇavṛttiśca iti. *Locana*, vide DL, p. 34.

337. niṣṭhyūtodgīrṇavāntādi guṇavṛttivyāśrayaṁ/ atisundaramanyatra grāmyakakṣāṁ vigāhate.// KD, 1.95.

338. Bahūni hi nivandhāni ...... 'jarathakamalakandacchedagaurairmayūkhaiḥ KLSV, under' KLS 8.

339. cf. mukhyāṁ vṛttiṁ parityajya guṇavṛttyā ' rthadarśanaṁ. K 17a, DL

and, mukhyāṁ vṛttimabhidhāvyāpāraṁ parityajya parisamāpya guṇavṛttyā lakṣaṇārūpayārthasyāmukhyasya darśanaṁ pratyāyanā,--------- *Locana*, under above, vide DL, p. 157.

340. ------- śabdo vṛttitrayeṇa vartate, taśca mukhyā gauṇī lakṣaṇeti trayaḥ and cf. tatra sākṣādavyavahitārthābhidhāyikā mukhyā. SR.P, p. 223.

341. mukhyārthabādhe tadyoge rūḍhito'tha prayojanāt/ anyo'rtho lakṣyate yatsā lakṣaṇā ropitā kriyā.// 12 KP. p. 40

342. SD II.5.

343. evamaśītiprakārā Lakṣaṇā. Vṛtti, vide SD II, p. 53.

344. tattvabhāktayornānātvavibhāgādavyabhicāraḥ. NS, 2.2.15.

345. nityamityatra kiṁ tāvattattvaṁ?------------- padārtha iti. VB, under ibid.

346. vyāghātādaprayogaḥ. NS 4.1.15.

347. nātītānāgatayoḥ kārakaśabdaprayogāt ?
ibid, 4.1.16.

348. atīte cānāgate cāvidyamāne kārakaśabdāḥ prayujyante........ ajātāḥ putrāḥ pitaraṁ tāpayanti - iti bahulaṁ bhāktaḥ prayoga dṛśyante. VB, under ibid.

349. kā punariyaṁ bhaktiḥ? ānantaryaṁ bhaktiḥ,...... asāmarthyā dupamṛdya ...... upamṛdnātīti bhāktaṁ kartṛtvamiti. ibid.

350. sahacaraṇasthāna ...... tadupacāraḥ. NS, 2.2.64.

351. bhaktyā prayoge prādhānyena kalpanamupacāraviṣayaṁ chalamupacāracchalam. upacāro nītarathaḥ sahacaraṇādinimittena atadbhāve tadvadabhidhānam = upacāra iti. VB under NS 1.2.14.

352. dharmavikalpanirdeśe'rthasadbhāvapratiṣedha upacārac-chalam. NS, 1.2.14.

353. dharmavikalpa = anyatra ...... mañcāḥ krośanti,' VB, under ibid.

354. bhaktyā prayoge ...... upacāra iti. ibid.

355. yāśabdasamūhatyāgaparigrahasaṅkhyāvṛddhyapacayavarṇ
asamāsānubandhānā vyaktāvupacārād vyaktiḥ ?
NS. 2.2.62.

356. sahacaraṇasthānatādarthya--------------------- gaṅgāśāṭakānnapuruṣeṣvatadbhāve'pi tadupacāraḥ. ibid 2.2.64.

357. atadbhāve'pi ...... sahacaraṇāt - 'yaṣtikāṁ bhojaya' ....

bhavati --------- etc. VB, under ibid.

358. satyaṁ gośabdaḥ ...... ghoṣaḥ prativasatīti. NM, Part II, p. 171.

359. lakṣaṇā ca ...... vākyārthānvayaḥ. TC, p. 660.

360. TC, p. 660.

361. cf. VM, P. 13. Vide PP.

362. svārthasambandha ...... śakyasambandho vā ...... lakṣaṇā. TC, pp. 665-66.

śakyasambandho lakṣaṇā. TD, Vide TS, p. 323.

svaśakyasambandho lakṣaṇā. NSMR, p. 173.

363. VM, p. 13, Vide PP.

364. svaśakyasambandhavattvaṁ lakṣaṇā. TP, Vide BHC, p. 57.

365. mukhyārthabādhe tadyoge ------- lakṣaṇāropitā kriyā, 9, KP, p. 40. cf. nātra - ālaṁkārikapakṣasya bhedaḥ. KTS, under KP above, p. 72; SD.II,5, p. 35.

366. śakyasamandho lakṣaṇā. RG.2. KTS, p. 72.

367. tatra śakyasākṣātsambandhaḥ kevalalakṣaṇā etc. VPB, p. 90.

368. nanu vākyaśaktatayā ...... tatsambandho lakṣaṇā. the commentary *Arthabodhinī*, under above, Vide VPB, p. 95.

369. vācyārthānupapattyā hi lakṣaṇā bhavati. MM, p. 94.

370. vayaṁ tu padārthā lakṣaṇayaiva vākyārthaṁ bodhayantīti brūmaḥ. MM, p. 94.

371. lakṣaṇābījaṁ śakyārthānvayānupapattiḥ TP, Vide BHC, p. 58.

372. lakṣaṇābījaṁ ...... bhojanaprayojanakapraveśanaparatvagrahādanvayānupapattireva. ibid.

373. VM, p. 13;

vācyasya gaṅgāśabdārthasya vākyārthe 'nanvayātkhalu

lakṣaṇā gāmānayetyādau tu gopadārthasyānvayādayuktaiva sā. kiṁ ca vākyārthamātrasya lakṣayatvamanupapannaṁ sambandhānupapattiparāmarśamantareṇa padārthavadeva jhaṭiti pratīteḥ. TR, p. 28.

374. SD, II-5, p. 35.

375. lakṣaṇā ca vṛtyantaraṁ yatra vācyārthānvayānupapattyā vācyasambandhopasthāpite vākyārthānvayaḥ TC, p. 660.

376. cf. sambandhadhīḥ smṛtihetuḥ kḷptā na tu tātparyadhīriti api tasyā lakṣyasmṛtijanyatvenānyonyāśrayaprasaṅgāt. TC, p. 687.

vastuto'nvayaparapramāṇaśabdasya ...... mukhyārthānupapatteḥ kḷptatvāt. ibid, pp. 691-93.

377. lakṣaṇāyāṁ mukhyārthe itarānvayānupapattibījaṁ. NSMR, p. 242.

378. abhidhātrī matā śaktiḥ padānāṁ svārthaniṣṭhatā/...... NM, p. 372.

379. upasthitārthānvayānupapattidhīrūpasya ...... pramāṇābhā vācca. SSP, p. 146-47

380. tātparyānupapattirlakṣaṇābījam. TD, Vide TS, p.330

381. lakṣaṇābījantu ...... sambhavāt. VPB, p. 95.

382. vastutastu tātparyānupapattisandhānameva ...... lakṣaṇāsvīkārāt - PLM, p. 45.

383. tanna. sati .... tatra ...... kimanupapannaṁ. ibid. p. 51.

384. cf. MBH, Vide VMB, Vol. IV p. 503.

385. VM, p. 13; NVTT, p. 477; VPB, p. 90;
PLM, p. 43; SAKV, p. 23; TC, pp. 660-78;
SSP, pp. 133-39; TD, Vide TS, p. 323; KP, p. 42.

386. vastuto'nvayaparapramāṇaśabdasya ...... tathāpyanvayānupapattireva lakṣanābījam. TC, pp. 691-93.

387. yaṣṭikān bhojaya iti yaṣṭikasahacarito brāhmaṇo'bhidhīyate. VB, under NS 2.2.64.

388. Vide MB, VMB, Vol. IV, p. 503; TC, p. 689; SSP, p. 147; PLM, p. 43.

389. VP, 2.312.

390. TC, p. 689; VPB, p. 94.

391. Vide SB, under MS 1.4.23 (with the reading 'gacchanti' in place of 'yānti'); TC, p. 689; PLM, p. 39.

392. TC, p. 691.

393. VPB, p. 94.

394. atra tārkikāḥ - svaśakyasambandho lakṣaṇā. PLM, p. 39.

395. trayo hyatra ...... mukhyārthabādhādisahakāryapekṣārthapratibhāsanaśaktirlakṣaṇāśaktiḥ. *Locana*, Vide DL, p. 60.

396. ibid, pp. 55-56.

397. yatra śakyaparasparāsambandhenārthāntarapratītistatra lakṣitalakṣaṇā. dvirephapadasya rephadvayaśaktasya bhramarapadaghaṭitaparasparāsambandhena madhukare vṛttiḥ. VPB, p. 90.

398. gauṇyapi lakṣitalakṣaṇaiva. yathā siṁho māṇavaka iti. atra siṁhaśabda vācyasambandhi-krauryādisambandhena māṇavakasya pratīteḥ. ibid.

399. iyaṁ gauṇī vṛttirlakṣaṇāto bhidyate iti kumārilabhaṭṭamatasya. niṣkarṣaḥ naiyāyikādayastu dvirephādivadatra lakṣaṇāmaṅgīkurvanti. KTS, p. 90.

400. cf. gauṇyapi lakṣaṇaiva lakṣyamānaguṇasambandharūpa. yathā - agnirmāṇavaka iti. TC, Vide TS, p. 327.

401. vidhirvā syādapūrvatvādvādamātraṁ hyanarthakam. M.S. 1.2.19 and nanūktvamasaṁvādo vede, na hyūrgudumbara iti. guṇavādena prarocanārthatāṁ brūmahe. gauṇatvātsaṁvādaḥ. SB, under MS 1.2.22.

402. na cāyaṁ prāṇabhṛcchabdaḥ sṛṣṭiśabdasca ...... yathā chatriśabdena sārthalakṣaṇārthena so'pi cchatrī gṛhyata iti.

SB, under MS 1.4.23.

403. abhidheyāvinābhūte pravṛttirlakṣaṇeṣyate/ lakṣyamāṇaguṇairyogād vṛtteriṣṭā tu gauṇatā.// TV, Vide MD. p. 313.

404. vahnitvalakṣitādarthādyatpaiṅgālyādi gamyate/ tena māṇavake buddhiḥ sādṛśyādupajāyate// TV, Vide MD, p. 314.

405. sā ca lakṣaṇā dvedhā'jahatsvārthā, jahatsvārthā ca.. jahatsvā rthā gaṅgāyāṁ ghoṣa ityādau. BHC, p. 57.

406. lakṣitalakṣaṇāyā apyatraivāntarbhāvaḥ....... dvirephādipade lakṣitalakṣaṇatvāt. eten dvirephapadena bhramarapadaṁ lakṣyate. tena śaktyā bhramarabodha ityapāstaṁ dvirepha padottaravibhaktyarthasyānvayāpatteḥ. ibid. p. 57-58.

407. lakṣaṇā dvividhā kevalalakṣaṇā lakṣitalakṣaṇā ca. tatra śakyasākṣātsambandhaḥ kevalalakṣaṇā....... lakṣitalakṣaṇā. VPB, p. 90.

408. gauṇyapi lakṣitalakṣaṇaiva. yathā siṁho māṇavaka iti. atra siṁhaśabda vācyasambandhi krauryādisambandhena māṇavakasya pratīteḥ. VPB, p. 90.

409. prakārāntareṇa lakṣaṇā trividhā. Jahallakṣaṇā, Ajahallakṣaṇā Jahadajahallakṣaṇā ceti. VPB, p. 91.

410. śakyamanantarbhāvya yatrārthāntarasya ...... atra hi svā rthaṁ vihāya śatrugṛhe bhojananivṛttirlakṣitā. ibid.

411. yatra śakyārthamantarbhāvyaivārthāntara - pratītistatrājahallakṣaṇā. yathā śuklo ghaṭa iti. atra hi śuklaśabdah svā rthaṁ śuklaguṇamantarbhāvyaiva tadvati lakṣaṇayā varttate. ibid, p. 91-92.

412. tasmādyathā 'so' yaṁ devadatta iti vākyaṁ ...... parityajyāviruddhamakhaṇḍacaitanyamātraṁ lakṣayatīti. VS, p. 80-81.

413. itthañca 'tattvamasī'ti vākye bhāgalaksaṇayaivākhaṇḍārthapratītiḥ. *Bhāvabodhini* (commentary), Vide ibid. p. 81.

414. evameva tattvamasīti vākye'pi na lakṣaṇā. śaktyā svātantryeṇopasthitayostattvampadārthayorabhedānvaye bā-

dhakābhāvāt. VPB, p. 93-94.

415. jahadajahallakṣaṇodāharaṇaṁ tu kākebhyo dadhi rakṣyatamityādikameva. tatra śakya-kākātvaparityāgenāśakyadadhyupaghātakatvapuraskāreṇākāke'pi kākaśabdasya pravṛtteḥ. ibid. p. 94-95.

416. cf. SD, Ch. II, K 5-12a and the Vṛtti under it.

417. yastu svārthābhidhānānantaraṁ taditaramarthaṁ guṇamaguṇaṁ vā lakṣayatyeva na sāmānādhikaraṇyena paratra prayujyate śabdaḥ sa lākṣaṇiko bhavati gaṅgāyāṁ ghoṣaḥ prativasatīti. NM, Part II, p. 171.

418. satyaṁ gośabdaḥ svārthamabhidhāya sāsnādimantaṁ tadīyān guṇāneva ...... gaurvāhika ityevaṁ prayujyamānaḥ sa gauṇo bhavati. ibid.

419. Jahatsvārthājahatsvārthanirūḍhādhunikādikāḥ/ Lakṣaṇā vividhastābhirlakṣakaṁ syādanekadhā.//

SSP, K25, p. 154.

420. Ādinā śakyasādṛśatvaprakāreṇa bodhakatayā gauṇyupagṛhyate. Prose Vrtti on K25, Ibid.

421. Lakṣaṇā trividhā Jahallakṣaṇā, Ajahallakṣaṇā. ...... tatra Jahadajahaditi. yathā tattvamasīti.

TD, Vide TS, p. 325-26.

422. lakṣaṇā dvividhā-jahatsvārthā' jahatsvārthā ca. tatrādyāṁ pradarśayati gaṅgāyāmiti. DK, Vide NSM, p. 285.

423. lakṣitalakṣaṇāyā ādhikyamāśaṅkya jahatsvārthāyāmantarbhāvamāha yatra tviti. ibid. p. 288.

424. āśrayatve veti lakṣaṇā-niruḍhālakṣaṇā. kvacittathaiva pāṭhaḥ. ibid. p. 271.

425. nirūḍhālakṣaṇeti. anāditātparyaviṣayalakṣaṇetyarthaḥ. RR, Vide NSM, p. 271;

anāditātparyaviṣayībhūtārthaniṣṭhā lakṣaṇā.

Tarkaprakāsá of Śrīkaṇṭha, CH, I, quoted in NK, p. 430.

426. gauṇyapi laksaṇaiva lakṣyamāṇaguṇasambandhasvarūpā yathā agnirmāṇavaka iti. TD, Vide TS, p. 327.

427. kiñca yadyabhidhānata evānvitapratītiḥ tarhi ...... bhidhatte gaṅgāśabdastu tīrasmaraṇamātro' payogīti. NRM, p. 87-88.

padajñānasya ghaṭaśabde kena rūpeṇa hetutvamna tāvatpadajñāntvena, vyabhicārāt. nāpi ghaṭapadajñānatvena ---. kintu ghaṭaśaktapadajñānatvena na tu vṛttimat padajñānatvena, vṛttitvasya śaktilakṣaṇānyataragarbhatayā gauravāt. tena lākṣaṇikasyānanubhāvakatvam. TP, BHC, p. 55-56.

428. A certain edition of the *Bhāṣāpariccheda*, namely NSM, does not contain the *Muktāvalī* text, 'navīnāstu ----- ananubhāvakatvāpatterityāhuḥ'.

429. cf. na cānubhāvakatā'vacchedakaśaktyabhāvāllākṣaṇikasya nānubhāvakatvasambhavaḥ...... tathā ca nānupapattiḥ. SAK V, p. 23.

430. vastutastu śaktyā lakṣaṇayā copasthitasya tattadarthasya śābdabodhe bhānādubhayavidhā tattadarthopasthitereva tattadviṣayakaśābdabodhahetutā vācyā. ibid. p. 38.

431. vākyārtho lakṣyamāṇo hi sarvatraiva naḥ sthitiḥ Sv, Vākya, p. 229.

vayantu padārthā lakṣaṇaiva vākyārthaṁ bodhayantīti brūmaḥ. MM, p. 94.

432. nanu vākyamapi lakṣakaṁ bhavatyeva ------kathaṁ vā gabhīrāyāṁ nadyāṁ ghoṣa ityādau gabhīranadītīrasya? -----tasmā dvākyameva tatra gabhīranadītīralakṣaakamiti mīmāṁsakāḥ. ...... siddhāntavidaḥ. SSP, p. 140-43.

433. SV, Vākya, 229; MM, p. 94; ata eva vākyārtho lāksaṇika iti Mīmāṁsakāḥ. NRM, pp. 101-120

434. 42, Vide ibid, p. 102.

435. padebhya eva vākyārthapratyayo jāyate yathā /

tathā vayaṁ nibadhnīmaḥ prabhākaraguromatam //
--- yadyadākāṅkṣitaṁ yogyaṁ saniidhānaṁ prapadyate/
tadanvitaḥ padenārthaḥ svakīyaḥ pratipādyate //
VM, pp. 1-5, Vide pp.

436. ibid, p. 1-13.

437. vārtikakārapādāstu lākṣaṇikān sarvavākyārthānicchantaḥ ------ vākyārtho lakṣyamāṇo hi sarvatraiva hi lakṣyate, iti atrāpare brūvate-neyaṁ lakṣaṇā. svārthāparityāgyāt --- anupapattyā sambandhena ca laksaṇā bhavati. ibid, pp. 12-13.

438. nanu vākyamapi lakṣakaṁ bhavatyeva, -------- tasmādvākyameva tatra gabhīranadītīralakṣakamiti mīmāṁsakāḥ. SSP, p. 140.

439. nanu gabhīrāyāṁ nadyāṁ ghoṣa ityatra naikapade lakṣaṇā -------- tasmād gabhīra-nadyoranvayabodhānantaraṁ vākyena svajñāpyagabhīra-nadyā ...... vākyārthagabhīranadīsambandhinastīratvena pratīteḥ TC, pp. 718-19.

440. lakṣaṇā ca padavṛttirvṛttivāt śaktivat. TC,p. 718.

441. śaktaṁ padam. TS, p. 66; M, under K 81.

442. vākyasya jñāpyābhāvena jñāpyasambandhābhāvānna lakṣaṇā. TC, p. 72.

443. athānvayabodhakam vākyaṃ padāni hi sambhūyārthānvayaṁ bodhayanti na pratyekamātramiti cet. na padaṁ hi svārthānvayaṁ bodhayati na tu samūhaḥ samūhe svārthābhāvāt. ibid, p. 721.

444. tathā hi gabhīranadyoranvayabodhottaraṁ nadīpadaṁ gabhīrapadaṁ vā svajñāpyagabhīranadyāstīraṁ lakṣyati na vākyam. ibid, p. 722.

445. na ca vinigamakābhāvāt ------pade ekā vākye cāparā lakṣaṇeti gauravaṁ syāt. ibid, p. 722-23.

446. vastutastu gabhīrapadāt svārthaparamparāsambandhena lakṣyopasthitau vilambānnadīpadāt svārthasākṣāt sambandhena śīghraṁ tīropasthitisambhavāttatraiva lakṣaṇā. ibid. p. 723-24.

447. vastutaḥ padalakṣaṇayaivopapattau na vākyalakṣaṇā, tathā hi gabhīranadyoranvayabodhottaraṁ nadīpadaṁ gabhīrapadaṁ vā svajñāpyagabhīranadyāstīraṁ lakṣayati na vākyam. ibid. p. 722.

448. nanu vākyamapi lakṣakam ------- mīmāṁsakāḥ tanna-------- SSP, p. 140-41.

449. vastutastu gabhīrapadāt svārthaparamparāsambandhena lakṣyopasthitau vilambānnadīpadāt. svārthasākṣāt sambandhena śīghraṁ tīropasthitisambhavāttatraiva lakṣaṇā. TC, p. 723-24.

450. tasmādgabhīrapadaṁ nadīpadaṁ vā tatra gabhīranadītīralakṣakam. SSP, p. 143.

451. devadattasya gurukulaṁ devadattasya guruputraḥ devadattasya dāsabhāryeti. MBH, under P.2.1.1, vide VBM, p. 360.

452. padāntarantu tatra tātparyyagrāhakamiti siddhāntavidaḥ. SSP, p. 143.

453. sthapatirniṣādaḥ syācchabdasāmarthyāt. MS 6.1.51.

454. niṣāda eva sthapatirbhavitumarhati. kasmāt śabdasāmarthyāt. niṣādaṁ hi niṣādaśabdaḥ śaknoti vadituṁ śravaṇenaiva. niṣādānāṁ tu sthapatiṁ lakṣaṇayā brūyāt. śrutilakṣaṇāviśaye ca śrutirnyāyā, na lakṣaṇā. SB, under ibid.

455. dvijaḥ sthapatiranyo vā dvijaḥ ṣaṣṭhisamāsataḥ. karmadhārayamukhyatvānniṣādo raudrayāgakṛd........ JNV 5.4.18.

456. arthavati prātipadikasaṁjñāyāmanekasyāpi padasya prātipadikasaṁjñā prāpnoti. 'daśa dāḍimāni ṣaḍapūpāḥ kuṇḍamajājinaṁ palalapiṇḍaḥ adharorukmetatkumāryaḥ

sphaiyakṛtasya pitā pratiśīna' iti samudāyo'trānarthakaḥ MBH, under P 1.2.45, vide VMB, p. 217.

457. P 1.2.46.

458. atrocyate - samāse śaktyasvīkāre viśiṣṭasyārthavattvābhāvena prātipadikatvaṁ na syāt. ata evārthavatsūtre bhāṣye 'arthavaditi kim, arthavatāṁ samudāyonarthakaḥ - daśadāḍimādivad ...... anarthakatvātprātipadikatvāpatteḥ. PLM, p. 234.

459. na caivamekapade lakṣaṇayā itarapadavaiyarthyaṁ itarapadamahimnaiva viśeṣasya lakṣaṇīyatvāt. TC, p. 737.

460. nanu bahuvrīhau citragumānayetyatra vākyārthacitragosvāminaḥ sambandhitayā anyapadārthasya pratītervākya evānyapadārthe lakṣaṇā etc. TC, p. 727.

461. atrāhuḥ - anastamitapadapadārthavibhāgasya citragusamudāyasyānyonyānvitāvayavārthasambandhinyapada¯rthe śaktiḥ kalpyeta --------- anyapadārtha eva śakya iti. ibid, pp. 738-45.

462. atra brūmaḥ bahuvrīhau na vākye lakṣaṇā kintu pade ------ tarhi lāghavāllakṣaṇaivāstu. TC, pp. 745-46;

Gaṅgeśa rules out the suspicion that as the padalakṣaṇā virtually comes to signify the total meaning of the sentence in the form of the compound, it may be viewed as the very vākyalakṣaṇā. cf. na caivaṁ vākyārthabodhakapadalakṣaṇā hyayameva vākyalakṣaṇā, padavākyayorbhinnatvāt. TC, p. 736.

463. cf. bahuvrīhiḥ svagarbhārthasambandhitvena bodhakaḥ. ...... nirūḍhayā lakṣaṇayā svāṁśajñāpakaśabdavān ...... vṛkṣa. SSP, pp. 244-45.

464. bahuvrīhisthapadadvaye nirūḍhā lakṣaṇā. TC, p. 746.

465. tatpuruṣe'pi rājapuruṣa ityādau pūrvapadasya ṣaṣṭhyarthasambandhe nirūḍhalakṣaṇayaiva ...... śabdārthatvāt. TC, p. 753.

466. ata eva 'rājapuruṣa ityādau pūrvapade ṣaṣṭhyarthasambandhe lakṣaṇe'ti maṇikṛduktamapi' saṁgacchate. SSP, p.204

467. guṇe śuklādayaḥ puṁsi tadvati. AK, p. 16.

468. rājapuruṣa ityādikastu tatpuruṣo na puruṣe ----ata eva rā japuruṣa ityādau pūrvapade ṣaṣṭhyarthasambandhe lakṣaṇeti-------- saṁgacchate. SSP, p. 204.

469. cf. vastugatyaikakriyānvayitvasya dhavakhadirayoḥ sattve'pyekakriyānvayitvasya śābdabodhābhāvādityarthaḥ idamupalakṣaṇam. DK, Vide NSM, p. 296.

470. akṣarāṇāmakāro'smi dvandvaḥ sāmāsikasya ca/

ahamevākṣayaḥ kālo dhātāhaṁ viśvatomukhaḥ//

Gītā X. 33.

471. cf. nanu dhavakhadirāvityādau dvandve sāhityābhāve---------- 'sāhitye dvivacanabahuvacane dvandvasamāso vetyanuśāsanāt------ MUS, Vide BPS, pp. 452-53.

472. nanu yadi dvandve na lakṣaṇā tadā karmadhārayāt dvandvasya ko viśeṣa ityata āha kintviti. DK, Vide NSM, p. 296.

karmadhāraye padadvaye lakṣaṇāvirahena lakṣaṇāvirahitasamāsatvasya dvandvakarmadhārayobhayasādhāraṇatvāditi bhāvaḥ. RR, under DK above.

473. P 2.2.29.

474. cānvācayasamāhāretarasamuccaye. AK, p. 126.

475. atha samāhāradvande prācīnamate samāhārasyā' nubhavasiddhatvāt samāhāre lakṣaṇā' ṅgīkriyate,--------- samāhāradvandve tviti. KI, Vide NSM(K), p. 334.

476. pare tviti atha navīnamatena samāhāre lakṣaṇā' bhāvaṁ vyutpādayati. samāhāradvandvasthale samāhārasya anubhavā' viṣayatvavādinavīnāstu etc. ibid.

477. pāṇipādaṁ vādayetyatra pāṇipādamātrapratīterna samāhāre lakṣaṇā śaktir vā. NSMR, p. 187.

478. ṇavyaikadeśināṁ mate tūbhayapadasyaiva lakṣaṇā---------lakṣayatīti. MUS Vide BPS, p. 454.

pāṇipādamityādau pāṇipādaṁ pāṇipratiyogikaṁ----------- samāhāraṁ lakṣayati. NSMR, p. 187.

479. taddhitārthottarapadasamāhāre ca P 2.1.50

480. saṁkhyāpūrvo dviguḥ ibid. 2.1.51

481. akārāntarottarapado dviguaḥ striyāmiṣṭaḥ. V 2.4.17.

482. ādinā pañcapulī pañcavaṭī pañcapātram, ityādigrahaṇam. KI, Vide NSM (K), p. 334.

483. navyamatamāha pare tviti. DK, Vide NSM, p. 298; atha navīnamatena samāhāre lakṣaṇā'bhāvaṁ vyutpādayati. KI, Vide NSM (K), p. 334.

484. pare tu - nyāyasiddhāntamañjarīkṛtastu, MUS, Vide BPS, p. 455.

485. pāṇipādaṁ vādayetyatrapāṇipādamātra pratītena samāhāre lakṣaṇā śaktirvā. NSMR, p. 187.

486. cf. nanvevaṁ pāṇipādaṁ vādaya ityatrānanvayaḥ samāhāre--------- tyanye. ibid.

487. ahinakulaṁ bherīmṛdaṅgamityādau ...... ataḥ samāhāre na lakṣaṇetyāśayaḥ. KI, Vide NSM(K), p. 334f.

488. nanu tarhi ekavacanarthaikatvasya kvānvayaḥ, ahinakulayorekatvābhāvāt, --------- navīnasya mate ahinakulātmakaprakṛtyarthapratyekavyaktau ekatvasyā'nvayoniravādhaḥ. ibid.

489. dvandvaśca prāṇitūryasenāṅgānām. P. 2.4.2.

490. yatra 'prāṇitūryasenāṅgānāmiti' sūtreṇa 'yeṣāṁ ca virodhaḥ śāśvatikaḥ' iti sūtreṇa ca dvandvaḥ ekavatsyādityarthakena ekatvamuktam = ekavadbhāvaḥ vihitaḥ. -------- tatraiva = tādṛśadvandve eva samāhārasaṁjñā bhavatītyarthaḥ. Kir, Vide NSM(K), p. 335.

491. tathā ca navīnamate samāhārasaṁjñā nānvarthā kintu

nadīvṛddhyādisaṁjñāvat pāribhāṣikyeveti bhāvaḥ. Ibid.; nanu pāṇipādamityādisamudāyasya---------tathā ca pāribhā ṣikyeva sā, anvarthatve' nyatrā'tiprasangāditi bhāvaḥ. DK, Vide NSM, pp. 298-99.

492. The admission of Ekaśeṣa as a Samāsa is itself a controversial issue. Even if it be not admitted as a Samāsa, it cannot be denied that it is a Vākya or at least a 'padasamūha'. So Viśvanātha deems it necessary to show that here also Lakṣaṇā works if and when necessary only as pertaining to a single Pada and not to the 'Samūha'.

493. P 1.2.64.

494. ibid. 1.2.65.

495. Pumān striyā and pitā mātrā. ibid 1.2.67 and 1.2.70.

496. pumān striyā and śvaśraḥ śvaśrvā. ibid 1.2.67 and 1.2.71

497. strī puṁvacca. ibid 1.2.66.

498. bhrātṛputrau svasṛduhitṛbhyām. ibid. 1.2.68.

499. bhrātarau putravityatrā'pi pramāṇāntareṇa ... putraduhitrorlakṣaṇetyarthaḥ. DK, Vide NSM, p. 299.

500. karmadhāraye samāsaprayuktalakṣaṇāyā anaṅgīkārādeva MUS, Vide BPS, p. 455.

501. samāsaprayuktalakṣaṇāśūnyatulyādhikaraṇakanāmadvaya -ghaṭitasamāsatvaṁ karmadhārayatvam, 'citragu 'rājapuruṣa'ityādau samāsaprayuktalakṣaṇāsattvāt. .... Jayarā mapañcānanabhaṭṭācāryāḥ Vide SSP, fn(1), p. 201.

502. kramikaṁ yannāmayugamekārthe'nyārthabodhakaṁ tādātmyena bhavedeṣa samāsaḥ karmadhārayaḥ. ...... siṁhā disadṛśasya, --------- SSP, p. 201.

Jagadīśa incorporates the notion of the relation of identity (between the meanings of two nāmapadas) in the definition of a karmadhāraya compound, and illustrates 'nīlotpalam' to show the relation of identity between two nā mārthas.

503. kvacit kośādapi, yathā-

guṇe śuklādayaḥ puṁsi guṇiliṅgāstu tadvati/

śītaṁ guṇe tadvadarthāḥ suśīmaḥ śiśiro jaḍaḥ//

cūrṇe kṣodaḥ samutpiñjapiñjalau bhṛśaṁākule ityādi-

koṣebhyaḥ śvaityādau śuklādiśabdasya. SSP, pp. 106-07.

504. nīlotpalamityādāvutpalādipadasyārthe nīlādipadārthasya tādātmyenānvayaḥ. ibid, p. 201.

505. pūrvapadārthapradhāno'vyayībhāvaḥ ----- ityapi prācāṁvādaḥ ------ SIK, p. 627.

506. Dinakarabhaṭṭa points out that some scholars understand the word 'upa' in the sense of 'sāmīpya' and not 'samīpa'. cf kecittu upapadārthaḥ sāmīpyam, na tu samīpam, samīpe ...... kumbhasamīpamiti cā 'nvayabodha ityāhuḥ. DK, Vide, NSM, p. 301.

507. atra yadyapyarddhapipalīti tatpuruṣe śaktinirākaraṇaṁ ...... bhedādapaunaruktyamiti dhyeyam. ibid.

508. vākyārthajñānam śābdajñānam. TS, p. 68.

509. vākyaṁ tu padasamūhaḥ. ibid, pp. 65-66.

510. samarthaḥ padavidhiḥ. p. 2.2.1.

511. pṛthagarthānāmekārthībhāvaḥ samarthavacanam. V.I.

512. pṛthagarthānāṁ padānāmekārthībhāvaḥ samartha'mitucyate kva punaḥ pṛthagarthāni kvaikārthāni? vākye pṛthagarthāni - 'rājñaḥ puruṣa' iti. ...... - 'anyasyānayanaṁ bhavatīti. kastarhyekārthabhāvakṛto viśeṣaḥ? MBH on V. above, under P 2.1.1

513. arthaikatvādekaṁ vākyaṁ sākāṅkṣaṁ cedvibhāge syāt. MS 2.1.46.

514. "Therefore it comes to this that a group of words serving a single purpose, forms one sentence". PMS, p. 189.

515. yāvatā padasamūhenejyate tāvān padasamūha ekaṁ yajuḥ.

kiyatā cejyate. yāvatā ----- ekaprayojanatvādupapannam. SB, Under MS 2.1.46.

516. laukikānāṁ hi vākyānaṁ pramāṇāntareṇārthastadekatvaṁ cāvadhāryate tatra prasiddhena hetunā śakyamekavākyatvagantum. TV, Vide MD, p. 432.

517. We find Kumārila declaring - "The Bhāṣya explains, ------------ the word 'Artha' is taken in the sense of purpose (and not in that of Idea or Meaning)." Thus we find Kumārila accepting the explanation of the Bhāṣya ------ The Bṛhatī says ---------- the term 'Artha' in the Sūtra stands for meaning as well as purpose; both being inter-related but of the two; purpose is the predominant factor; that is why it has been emphasised by the author of the Bhāṣya" PMS, pp. 190-95.

518. VP 2.351. p. 45.

519. ākāṅṣā saṁnidhānaṁ ca yogyatā ceti ca trayam/ saṁbandhakāraṇatvena kḷptaṁ nānantaraśrutiḥ........ // TV, Vide MD, p. 445.

520. yadyadākānkṣitaṁ yogyaṁ sannidhānaṁ prapadyate / tadanvitaḥ padenārthaḥ svakīyaḥ pratipādyate. // VM, p. 5, Vide pp.

521. vākyajanyajñāne ākāṁksāyogyatāsattayastātparyajñānañceti catvāri kāraṇāni. VPB, p. 80.

522. vākyaṁ syādyogyatākāṁkṣāsattiyuktaḥ padoccayaḥ. SD II. 1, p.27.

ākāṁkṣāyogyatāsaṁnidhivaśādvakṣyamāṇasvarūpāṇāṁ padārthānāṁ samanvaye ------- KP, p. 26.

523. SD II. 20. p. 67.

524. āsattiryogyatākāṅkṣā' iti mūlādāsatteḥ svarūpasattyā eva kāraṇatvaṁ labhyate, ... 'āsattiyogyatā' tivisargaśūnyapāthastvṛjureva. DK, Vide NSM, p. 302.

525. ākāṁkṣā sannidhānaṁ ca -------- TV, Vide MD, 448.

atha yathā sannidhikathanam ----- VM, p. 8, Vide pp.

ākāṁkṣā yogyatā sannidhiśca --------, TS, p. 66.

526. ------- sannidhānaṁ ----------

saṁbandhakāraṇatvena kḷptam nānantaraśrutiḥ. TV, Vide MD, p. 448.

527. sarvārtho'yamāmnāyamānaḥ ......

anantareṇa saṁbaddhaḥ syātparasyāpyanantaraḥ ......

yā te agne rajāśayā' ityanenapekṣitaḥ śeṣaḥ parastādalabhyamānaḥ purastātparāvṛttyā'locyamāno labhyate tanūrvarṣiṣṭheti. etc. ibid.

528. atha yathā sannidhikathanaṁ tathā buddhau viparivṛttiḥ. sā ca na śabdanibandhanaiva, kevalā'nvitābhidhānavyutpattau upalakṣaṇam. adhyāhṛtenāpi loke'nvitābhidhānadarśanāt. VM, p. 8, Vide PP.

529. cf. ekaikavarṇoccāraṇe'rthānavabodhāt kramoccāritānāṁ ca yugapacchravaṇāsambhavāt pūrvavarṇajanitasaṁskārasahito'ntyo varṇaḥ pratyāyakaḥ. ibid.

530. The verse explaining the 'khalekapotanyāyaḥ' is assigned to Udayanācārya by the writer of Prabhāṭīkā in the following way : Khalekapotanyāyamudayanācāryasammatyā darśśayati; but the Commentator is conspicuously silent regarding the source of the verse ------ almost all the Commentators agree upon the view that the verse should be ascribed to Udayanācārya (quoted with due defference from a Communication from Dr. Vācaspati Upādhyāya of the University of Delhi.)

531. cf. itareṣāṁ tu śabdānāṁ svārtharūpamevābhidheyamanvitarūpastu vākyārthaḥ padārthagamya iti. ataeva ---- abhihitārthasambandhādabhigamyamānatvāt. NRM. pp. 101-02;

tenātra padāvagatāḥ punaḥ padārthā mitho'nvayaṁyā nt/

ityevambhihitānvayasiddhānto darśto' smadādīnām.//

MM, pp. 94-95.

532. The verse can be traced to Śālikanātha's *Vākyārthamātṛkā*. The verse occurs in that work with some varient readings in the second half. VM, p. 5, Vide PP.

533. tasmādyatra samudāyaḥ prayuktaḥ tatraiva padaṁ padārthamavagamayati, BR, p. 258.

534. anvitasyābhidhāne'pi svarūpaṁ vidyate sadā / tena svarūpamātre'pi śabdo janayati smṛtim. // evaṁ sambandhagrahaṇāntargataṁ svarūpasmaraṇamuktam. VM, p. 18. Vide pp.

535. itaretarāśrayamidānīṁ pariharati -

smṛtisannihitairevamarthairanvitamātmanā/

arthamāha padaṁ sarvamiti nānyonyasaṁśrayam.// ibid.

536. atha yathā sannidhikathanaṁ tathā buddhau viparivṛttiḥ. sā ca na śabdanibandhanaiva, ... tathāpi śabdakalpanamanupapannaṁ etc. VM, p. 8, Vide pp.

537. Spṛherīpsitaḥ p. 1.4.36.

538. kiṁ punaridaṁ yogyatvaṁ nāma yat sambandhārhatvaṁ sambandhārhamiti kathamavagamyate. sambandhitvena dṛṣṭatvāt. VM, p. 9, Vide pp.

539. agninā siñcatītyādāvayogyānāmananvayāt yogyatāpi parigrāhyā. MM, p. 99.

540. yogyatā ca tātparyyaviṣayibhūtasaṁsargābādhaḥ......... bādhā bhāvād yogyatā. VPB, pp. 84-86.

541. yogyatā padārthānāṁ parasparasaṁbandhe bādhābhāvaḥ. padoccayasyaitadabhāve'pi vākyatve 'Vahninā siñcati' ityādyapi vakyaṁ syāt. SD. p. 27.

542. yogyatā ca ..... sekānvayaprayojakadravadravyatvābhāvāt. PLM, p. 75.

543. sambandhārhamiti kathamavagamyate --------- nanvevaṁ tarhi kathamapūrve kārye'nvitābhidhānaṁ vede ------ ucyate sāmānyato yogyatāvadhāraṇaṁ etc. VM, p. 9, Vide PP.

544. cf. In reply to the point that, as this Yogyatā, which consists in the relation which one concept bears to another is incapable of being known before deriving Verbal Knowledge, it is not proper to regard Yogyatājñāna as a causal factor of conceptual cognition, Viśvanātha says, when recollection of different concepts ensues from cognition of their corresponding denotative words, it is possible to have knowledge of the relation existing between these concepts, as well. In some cases, this Knowledge being confirmed by Perceptual Experience takes the form of a right notion and in others, having no experience to confirm it, assumes the form of a doubtful cognition."

LCAI, p. 209.

545. kā punariyamākāṅkṣā ? pratipatturijñāsā. kinnibandhanā punarasau. avinābhāvanibanddhaneti kecit. kriyā hi kārakā vinābhāvinīti tāṁ pratītya kārakam jijñāsate ------------ tadayuktamiti manyante. VM, p. 5, Vide PP.

546. anvitasyābhidhānārthamuktārthaghaṭanāya vā / pratiyogini jijñāsā yā sākāṅkṣeti gīyate // ..... ibid, p. 7.

547. gauraśvaḥ puruṣo hastītyākāṅkṣārahitesviha/ anvayādarśanāttāvadākāṅkṣā parigṛhyate. // MM, p. 99.

548. nirākāṅkṣasya vākyatve 'gauraśvaḥ puruṣo hastī' ityādīnāmapi vākyatvaṁ syāt. vṛtti, under SD II.1.

549. anaikāntaḥ paricchede sambhave ca na nirṇayaḥ / ākāṁkṣā sattayā heturyogyā"sattirabandhanā. // NKU, p. 151.

550. cf. ākāṁṣā ca samabhivyāhṛtapadasmāritapadārthajijñāsā ...... the Commentary *Prabhā* under above.

551. sākāṅkṣāśabdairyo bodhastadarthānvayagocaraḥ. SSP, p. 6.

552. prāthamyādabhidhātṛtvāt tātparyāvagamādapi / padānāmeva sā śaktirvaramabhyupagamyatām// VM, p. 14. Vide PP.

553. dṛṣṭānuguṇyādapi padārthanimittaka eva vākyārtho na padanimittaḥ dṛṣṭavādhaprasaṅgāt. ------ tātparyañcāvā ntaravyāparadvāreṇāpi sādhayatāmaviruddhamityucyate tadatrāpi samānam. NRM, p. 85.

554. tatra vākyenānvayānubhavajanane ākāṅkṣāyogyatāsattijñānaṁ sahakāri -------tātparyaṁ tu tatpratītīcchayā vaktrānusaṁhitatvam. -------- kecittu tātparyajñānaṁ lākṣaṇikanānārthasthalīyaśābde heturnatu śābdabodhamātre ------- pare tu tātparyajñānasya na hetutvaṁ sambhavati. TP, BHC, pp. 50-52.

555. 'The Mīmāṁsakas' habit of attending too exclusively to the 'revealed' texts of the Vedas probably encouraged them to formulate a theory of Verbal Comprehension without any reference to the speaker at all. Even a sentence which is unintelligible to the speaker has an inherent capacity to convey its meaning. Thus the phrase, 'the pot in the room' conveys the relation of the pot and the room without the help of the Speaker's intention." ITM, p. 179.

556. abhidhātrī matā śaktiḥ padānāṁ svārthaniṣṭhatā / teṣāṁ tātparyaśaktistu saṁsargāvagamāvadhīḥ. NM, p. 372.

samayāpekṣā vācyāvagamanaśaktirabhidhāśaktīḥ.

tadanyathānupapattisahāyārthāvabodhanaśaktistātparyaśaktiḥ *Locana*, Vide DL, p. 60.

557. cf. samayāpekṣā ---------- mukhyārthabādhādisahakāryapekṣārthapratibhāsanaśaktirlakṣaṇāśaktiḥ. *Locana*, Vide DL, p.60

558. 'siṁho māṇavakaḥ' ityatra dvitīyakakṣyāniviṣṭatātparyaśaktisamarpitānvayabādhakollāsānantaramabhidhātātparyaśaktidvayavyatiriktā tāvat tṛtīyaiva śaktistadbādhakavidhurīkaraṇanipunā lakṣaṇābhidhānā samullasati. *Locana*, Vide DL, p. 56.

559. SD. II. 20.

ākāṅkṣāyogyatāsaṁnidhivaśād ------- padārthānāṁ samanvaye tātparyārtho -------- vākyārthaḥ samullasatītyabhihitānvayavādināṁ matam. KP, p. 26.

560. tatparāveva śabdārthau yatra vyaṅgyaṁpratisthitau/-dhvaneḥ sa eva viṣayo mantavyaḥ saṅkarojjhitaḥ/ DL, I.13, p. 136.

561. na ca padārthavākyārthānyāyo vācyavyaṅgyayoḥ etc. Vṛtti, under DL.I. 37; p. 460;

nanvevaṁ mā bhūdvācakaśaktistathāpi tātparvaśaktirbhaviṣyatītyāśaṅkyāha na ceti etc. *Locana*, under above.

562. tātparyaṁ cedaṁ ------- prayokturicchā. prayoktā cābhisandhāpayitṛmātraṁ, natu vaktaiva. mauniślokāvyāpteḥ. NSMR, p. 242;

vaktā cātrābhisandhātā, na tu vaktaiva, mauniślokāvyāpteḥ. MUS, Vide BPS, p. 466.

563. ākāṅkṣā yogyatā sannidhiśca vākyārthajñānahetuḥ. TS, p. 66.

564. tātparyajñānañca vākyārthajñāne hetuḥ nānārthānurodhāt. TD, Vide ibid, p. 331.

565. 'saindhavamānaya' ityādinānārthakasthale saindhavapadasya aśve lavaṇe ca śakteḥ...... tadanurodhena sarvatra tadāvaśyakateti bhāvaḥ. *Nīlakaṇṭhaprakāśikā*, Vide ibid.

566. pare tu ghaṭādiśabdasthalepi ghaṭapadaṁ kumbhaparam lakṣaṇayā paṭaparaṁ vā iti saṁśaye ghaṭaśābdabodhābhāvāt sarvatra tātparyaniścayaḥ kāraṇam ityāhuḥ. *Nyāyasiddhāntamañjarī*prakāśa of Laugākṣibhāsakara, quoted in NK, p. 327.

567. prakaraṇādikaṁ tātparyagrāhakam. TD, Vide TS, p. 331-33 tātparyaniyāmakaṁ ca loke prakaraṇādikameva. PLM, p. 80.

568. saṁyogo viprayogaśca sāhacaryaṁ virodhitā / arthaḥ

prakaraṇaṁ liṅgaṁ śabdasyānyasya saṅnidhiḥ // sā marthya-
mauciti deṣaḥ kālo vyaktiḥ svarādayaḥ/ śabdārthasyānava-
cchede viśeṣasmṛtihetavaḥ// VP 2.315-16.

569. nāsadīya-sūkta (RV X. 11.129).

570. vedavākye caiśvaratātparyādarthabodhaḥ. PLM, p. 80; śukavākye vedavākye ceśvaratātparyagraheṇa śābdabodho --------- TP, Vide BHC, p. 52.

571. śukavākye ------- ceśvaratātparyagraheṇa śābdabodho------- TP, Vide BHC, p. 52.

śukavākye ca bhagavadicchaiva gatiḥ NSMR, p. 242.

572. kramaprāptaṁ tātparyaṁ nirūpyate. .... tadanyapratīticchayoccaritatvābhāvena etc. VPB, pp. 98-99.

573. Though this is not explicitely stated, we can form this opinion when we examine the observations of Vedāntins in this context.

cf. nanu saindhvamānayetyādivākyaṁ yadā lavaṇānayanapratīticchayā proyuktaṁ ------ cenna taditarapratīticchayānuccaritatvasyāpi tātparyaṁ prati viśeṣaṇatvāt. VPB, p. 99;

cf. The Vedāntins admit, however, that the knowledge of the speaker's intention plays an important role in the comprehension of meaning in the case of ambiguous expressions. ITM, p. 179.

574. kecittu tātparyajñānaṁ lākṣaṇikanānārthasthalīya------ TP, Vide BHC, p. 52.

575. pare tu tātparyajñānasya na hetutvaṁ saṁbhavati........ na tātparyajñānaṁ heturityāhuḥ. ibid.

576. nānārthasthale loke tātparyantu -------- prayokturicchārūpam. ----- ato bhojanaprakaraṇe saindhavamānayetyukte saindhavapadena lavaṇapratyayaḥ, yuddhāvasare'śvapratyayaḥ. vedavākye caiśvaratātparyādarthabodhaḥ. PLM, p. 80.

577. etatvākyaṁ padaṁ vā etadarthabodhāyoccāraṇiyamitīśvarecchā tātparyam. ata eva sati tātparyye 'sarve sarvārthavācakāḥ' iti śābdikanaye ghaṭaśabdātpaṭapratyayo netyādyuktam. nānārthasthale loke tātparyantu etatpadaṁ vākyaṁ vā etadarthapratyayāya mayoccāryate iti prayokturicchārūpam. ------- vedavākya-caiśvaratātparyādarthabodhaḥ. ibid.

BIBLIOGRAPHY

A. ORIGINAL WORKS

Amarakoṣa of Amarasiṁha, Nirnayasagar Press (NSP), Bombay, 1950

Aṣṭādhyayī-sūtrapātha edited (ed) by Brahmadattajijñāsu, Ramlal Kapur Trust Press, Amritsar, 1955.

Bālabodhinī, Comm. by Jhalakikāra on *Kāvyaprakāśa* see *Kāvyaprakāśa.*

Bālamanoramā, Comm. on *Siddhāntakaumudī* see *Siddhāntakaumudī*

Bhāsāpariccheda (Kārikāvalī and *Muktāvalī*) of Viśvanātha Nyāyapañcānana with the comm. *Muktāvalīsaṁgraha* of Pañcānana Śāstri, Sanskrit Pustak Bhandar (SPB), Calcutta, 1374 (Bangabda).

...............ed by Śrīmadgurunātha Vidyānidhibhaṭṭācāryya,

SPB, Calcutta, 1832 (Sakabada).

Bhāṭṭacintāmaṇi of MM Gāgābhaṭṭa, ed by Sūryanārāyaṇa Sukla, Chowkhamba Sanskrit Series (CSS), Banaras, 1933.

Brahmasūtra of Bādarāyaṇa, with *Śāṅkarabhāṣya*, Motilal Banarsidass (MB), Delhi, 1964.

Brahmasūtraśaṅkarabhāsya with commentary (Comm) *Bhāmatī*, ed by MM Anantakṛṣna Śāstrī, NSP, Bombay, 1938.

Bṛhatī of Prabhākaramiśra, ed by C.S. Śāstrī, CSS, Benaras, 1929.

Dhvanyāloka of Ānandavardhana, with *Locana* of Abhinavagupta, Chowkhamba Vidya Bhawan (CVB), Benaras, 1965.

Dhātupātha of Pāṇini, CSS, Benaras, 1969.

Dinakarī, Comm. by Dinakarabhaṭṭa on *Siddhāntamuktāvalī*, see *Nyāyasiddhāntamuktāvalī*.

Iśādyaṣṭottaraśatopaniṣad, published by Shivprasad Raghoram, Ramghat, Benaras, 1938.

Jaiminīyanyāyamālāvistara of Mādhavācārya, Viśvabhāratī Granthālaya, Calcutta, 1358 (Sal).

.... CSS, Benaras.

Kāvyamīmāṁsā of Rājaśekhara, ed by Pandit M. Misra, CSS, Benaras, 1934.

Kāvyaprakāśa of Mammaṭa, with the *Bālabodhinī* of V. Jhalakikar, ed by R.D. Karmakar, Bhandarkar Oriental Research Institute (BOR), Poona, 1969.

Kāvyādarśa of Daṇḍin with Sanskrit and Hindi Comm. *Prakāśa*, ed by Ramchandra Misra, CVB, Benaras, 1958.

Kāvyālaṁkāra of Bhāmaha, CSS,Benaras, 1928.

Kāvyālaṅkārasūtravṛtti of Vāmana, ed by N.N. Kulkarni, Poona, Oriental Book Agency, 1927.

Kiraṇāvalī of Udayanācārya, ed by Dr. G. Śāstrī, Published by Prof. S.N. Bhanja, Calcutta, 1363 (Bangabda).

Kiraṇāvalī, Comm. on *Siddhāntamuktāvalī*, see *Nyāyasiddhāntamuktāvalī*. (2)

Kṛṣṇakāntī, Comm. by Kṛṣṇakānta on *Śabdaśaktiprakāśikā*.

Locana, Comm. by Abhinavagupta on *Dhvanyāloka*, see *Dhvanyāloka*

Mādhavīyadhātuvṛtti of Sāyaṇācārya, ed by Dwarikadas Shastri, Prācya Bhāratī, Benaras, 1964.

Mānameyodaya of Nārāyaṇa, ed by C.K. Raja and S.S. Sūryanārāyaṇa Śāstrī, Theosophical Publishing House (TPH), Adyar, Madras, 1933.

Manusmṛti with the Comm. of Kullūka, MB, Delhi, 1975.

Mīmāṁsādarśana, the *Mīmāṁsasūtras* of Jaimini, with the *Śābarabhāṣya* and the comms *Prabhā*, *Tantravārtika* and *Tupikā*, Anandasram Sanskrit Series (ASS), Poona, 1930.

Nānārthasaṁgraha, ed by Anundoram Barooah, Assam Publication Board, Gauhati, 1969.

Nīlakaṇṭhaprakāsikā, Comm. by Nīlakaṇṭhaśāstrī on *Tarkasaṁgraha*, see *Tatkasaṁgraha* (Chowkhamba)

Nirukta of Yāska with the Comm. of Durgācārya, Published by V.G. Apte, ASS, Poona, 1926.

Nyāyabodhinī, Comm. by Govardhanamiśra on *Tarkasaṁgraha*, see *Tarkasaṁgraha* (Chowkhamba)

Nyāyadarśana of Gautama with the *Bhāṣya* of Vātsyāyana, ed by Svāmī Dvārikā dāsa Śāstrī, BVP, Varanasi, 1966.

Nyāyakoṣa of Bhīmācārya Jhalakikar, ed by Vasudev Shastri Abhyankar, BOR, Poona, 1928.

Nyāyakusumāñjali of Udayanācārya with the Comm. *Prabhā*, ed by Nārāyaṇamiśra, BVP, Benaras, 1968.

Nyāyamañjarī of Jayantabhaṭṭa, ed by Sūryanārāyaṇa Sukla, CSS, Benaras, 1936.

Nyāyaratnamālā of Pārthasārathi Miśra, ed by Pandit Gangadhar Shastri, CSS, Benaras, 1900.

Nyāyasiddhāntamuktāvalī (also called *Bhāṣāpariccheda*) of Viśvanātha, with the Comm. *Dinakarī* and *Rāmarudrī* ed by Harirāmaśuklaśāstrī, CSS, Benaras, 1972.

.... With the Comm. *Kiranāvalī* by Pandit Sri Kṛṣṇavallabhācārya, ed by Shri N.C. Shastri and Shri S.K. Shastri, CSS, Benaras, 1972.

Nyāyasiddhāntamañjarī of Jānakinātha Bhaṭṭācārya, ed by Pandit Jivanath Misra, Benaras, 1916.

Nyāyavārtika of Uddyotakara, Comm. on Vātsyayana's *Bhāṣya* on Nyāyasūtra, ed by Vindhyesvariprasad Dvivedi, KSS, Benaras, 1916.

Nyāyavārtikatātparyaṭīkā of Vācaspati Miśra, ed by Pandit Śrī Rājeswara Śāstrī Dravid, CSS, Benaras, 1985.

Paramalaghumañjuṣā of Nāgeśabhaṭṭa with the Comm.

Tattvaprakāśikā ed by Alakhadeva Sharma. CSS. Benaras, 1974.

Pāraskaragṛahyasūtra, CSS, Benaras.

Prabhā, Comm. by Haridāsa on Nyāyakusumāñjali, see *Vākyārthamātṛkā*, ed by Mukunda Śāstrī, CSS, Benaras, 1904.

Praśastapādabhāṣya of Praśastadeva, ed by Gopinātha Kavirāja and Dhuṇḍhiraj Shastri, CSS, 1924.

Rāmarudrī, - Comm. by Rāmarudrabhaṭṭa on *Siddhāntamuktāvalī* and *Dinakarī*, See, *Nyāvasiddhāntamuktāvalī*.

Rasagaṁgādhara of Paṇḍitarāja Jagannātha, ed by Madanmohan Jha, CSS, Benaras, 1969.

Ṛgvedasaṁhitā with the comm. of Sāyaṇācārya, ed by N.S. Sontakke and C.G. Koshikar, Vedic Research Institute, Poona, 1946.

Śabdaśaktiprakāśikā of Jagadīśa, with the comm. *Kṛṣṇakāntī*, ed by Dhundhiraj Śāstrī, CSS, Benaras, 1934.

Sāhityadarpaṇa of Viśvanātha Kavirāja, ed by Kṛṣṇamohana Śāstrī, CSS, Benaras, 1955.

Śaktivāda of Gadādhara Bhaṭṭācārya, ed by Goswami Damodar Shastri, CSS, Benaras, 1929.

Sāṁkhyasūtra of Kapila with the Comm. *Sāṁkhyapravacanabhāsya* by Vijñānabhikṣu, ed by Dr. Ramaśaṅkara Bhattācārya; BVP, Benaras, 2022 (Samvat).

Sāṁkhyakārikā of Īśvarakṛṣna with *Sāṁkhyatattvakāumudī* of Vacaspatimisra, NSP, 1940.

Sāṁkhyatattvakaumudī Comm. on Sāṁkhyakārikā see *Sāṁkhyakārikā*.

Saptapadārthī of Śivāditya, ed by Amarendra Mohan Tarkatīrtha and Narendra Chandra Vedāntatīrtha, Metropolitan Printing and Publishing House, Calcutta, 1934.

.... ed by D. Gurumurti, TPH, Adyar, Madras, 1932.

Sārabodhinī, Comm. on *Sāṁkhyatattvakaumudī*, see *Sāṁkhyakārikā*.

Śatapathabrāhmaṇa ed by Gaṅgāviṣṇuśrikṛṣṇa Das, Lakshmi Venkateswar Steam Press, Bombay, 1940.

Siddhāntakaumudī of Bhaṭṭojidīkṣita, with the Comm. *Bālamanoramā*, CSS, Benaras,

Śikhāmaṇi, Comm. on *Vedāntaparibhāṣā*, see *Vedāntaparibhāṣā* (2) *(Mīmāṁsā)Ślokavārtika* of Kumārila, CSS, Benaras,

Srīgautamamunipraṇītanyāyasūtraṇī with the *(Nyāyasūtra) Vṛtti* of Viśvanātha ASS, No. 91, Poona, 1922.

Śrīmadbhagavadgītā with *Śāṅkarabhāṣya*, Geeta Press, Gorakhpur, 1988 (Samvat).

Śṛṅgāraprakāśa of Bhojarāja, ed by G.R. Josyer, Vol. I, Mysore, 1955.

Taittirīyopaniṣad, See *Iśādyaṣṭottaropanipsad*

Tāṇḍyabrāhmaṇa with the comm. of Sāyaṇācārya, ed by Cinnasvāmī Shastri, Kashi Sanskrit Series, Benaras, 1936.

Tantrarahasya of Rāmānujācārya, ed by Late R. Sharma Shastri, Oriental Institute, Baroda, 1956.

Tantravārtika of Kumārila, See *Mīmāṁsādarśana*.

Tarkasaṁgraha of Annaṁbhaṭṭa, with the comm. *Nīlakaṇṭhaprakāśikā* and *Nyāyabodhinī*, ed by Śri Satkari Śarmā Vangīya, CSS, Benaras, 1969.

.... ed by Dr. Dayānanda Bhargav, MB, Benaras, 1971.

Tattvacintāmaṇi of Gaṅgeśopādhyāya, ed by MM Kāmākhyānātha Tarkavāgīśa, Asiatic Society of Bengal, Calcutta, 1822 (Sakabda).

...............-Do- Vol. I (Pratyakṣakhaṇḍa) (Re-print) MB, Delhi 1974.

Tattvapradīpikā (Citsukhī) of Citsukhācārya, Udāsīnasaṁskṛtavidyālaya, Kasi, 1956.

Tattvaprakāśikā, Comm. on. *Paramalaghumañjuṣā*, See *Paramalaghumañjuṣā*.

Vaiśesikadarśana of Kaṇāda, ed by Prof. Anantalal Thakur, Mithila Institute of P.G. Studies and Research in Sanskrit Learning (MISL) Darbhanga, 1957.

Vākyapadīya of Bhartṛhari, ed by Prof. K.V. Abhyankar and Acharya V.P. Limaye, University of Poona, 1965.

Vākyārthamātṛka, comm. by Śālikanātha, see *Prakaraṇapañcikā*.

Vārtikas of Kātyāyana, along with the *Mahābhāṣya* of Patañjali, ed, under the auspices of Govt. of India, MB, 1967.

Vedāntaparibhāsā of Dharmarājādhvarīndra, ed by Sri Sri Mohan Tarkavedāntatīrtha, published by A. Choudhury, Calcutta - 10, 1377 (Bangabda).

.... published by K. Śrīkṛṣṇadāsaśreṣṭhī, Bombay, 1850 (Saka).

Vedāntasāra of Sadānanda, with comm. Bhāvabodhinī, CVB, Benaras, 1962.

Vyākaraṇa-Mahābhāṣya of Patañjali, ed by F. Kielhorn, BOR. 1962.

Vyaktiviveka of Mahimabhaṭṭa, ed by T. Gaṇapati Śāstrī, Trivandrum, 1909.

Yogasūtras of Patañjali, with *Yogasūtrabhāṣya* of Vyāsa, Madras Government Oriental Series Madras, 1952.

B. MODERN WORKS

Apte, V.S. : *Students Sanskrit English Dictionary*, MB, Delhi, 1970.

Banerjee, S.C. : *Companion to Sanskrit Literature*, M.B., Varanasi, 1971.

Bhattacharya, D.C.: *History of Navya Nyaya in Mithila*, MISL, Darbhanga, 1958.

Bhattacharya, D.C. & Bhattacharya, M. : *Bhāratīya Darśan Koṣ* (Pratham Khaṇḍa), Calcutta Sanskrit College, 1970*

Bhattacharya, T.V. : *Vācaspatyam*, CSS, Benaras. 1962.

Chatterjee, S.C. : *Nyāya theory of Knowledge*, University of Calcutta, 1965.

Chatterjee, S.C. & Datta, D.M. : *An Introduction of Indian Philosophy*, University of Calcutta 1954 *

Chowdhury, N.N. : *Philosophy of Poetry (Kāvyatattvasamīkṣā)* MB, Delhi, 1959.

Dasgupta, S.N. : *History of Indian Philosophy*, Cambridge (University Press) 1955 *

Gogoi Chutia, (Mrs) L.H. : *The Treatment of Laksaṇā in Sanskrit Poetics and Philosophical Literature*. (P.H.D. Thesis prepared under the guidance of Professor Dr. M.M. Sharma, seen through courtesy), G.U. 1976 *

Gonda, J. : *Remarks on Similes in Sanskrit Literature* Leiden, Holland, 1949.

Guha, D.C. : *Navya Nyāya system of Logic*, BVP, Benaras, 1968.

Hariyanna, M. : *Outlines of Indian Philosophy*, George Allen & Unwin (India) Private Limited, Bombay, 1973 *

Jha, G.N. : *Pūrvamīmāṁsā in its Sources*, Benaras Hindu University, Benaras, 1942.

Kane, P.V. : *The Sāhityadarpaṇa*, with translation and notes on Ch. I, II & X, MB, Delhi, 1965.

Kaviraj, G. : *Gleanings from the History and Bibliography of the Nyāya Vaiśeṣika Literature*, ed by D. Chaṭṭopādhyāya, Indian Studies, past & Present, Calcutta, 1961.

Keith, A.B. : *A History of Sanskrit Literature*, Oxford University press, London, 1961.

Maxmuller : *Six Systems of Indian Philosophy*, CSS, Benaras, 1971 *

Mukherjee, R. : *Literary Criticism in Ancient India*, SPB, Calcutta, 1966.

Pandey, R.C. : *Problem of Meaning in Indian Philosophy MB, Delhi, 1963* *

Radhakrishan : *Indian Philosophy*, Vol. II, George Allen & Unwin Ltd., London, 1971.

Raja, K.K. : *Indian Theories of Meaning*, University of Madras, The Adyar Library, Adyar, 1963.

Shastri, G.N. : *The Philosophy of Word and Meaning*, Sanskrit College, Calcutta, 1959.

Sharma, M.M. : *The Dhvani Theory in Sanskrit Poetics*, CSS, Benaras, 1968. *

.... : 'On Some Discrepencies in the Śabdakhaṇḍa of Bhāṣāpariccheda', *The Journal of the Assam Research Society*, Gauhati, 1960 *

Sinha, Baldev. Dr. : *Padapadārthasamīkṣā*, Kurukshetra Viśvavidyālaya, Kurukshetra, 1969.

Winternitz, M. : *A History of Indian Literature*, Munshiram Monoharlal, New Delhi, 1972.

Swami Mādhavānanda : *Bhāṣāpariccheda with Siddhāntamuktāvalī*, Translation into English, with Introduction by Dr. Satkari Mookerjee. Advaita Ashrama, Calcutta, 1977.

* books consulted but not mentioned in the body of the work.

Mukherjee, R. : *Literary Criticism in Ancient India*, SPB, Calcutta, 1966

Pandey, K.C. : *Freedom of Meaning in Indian Philosophy*, MB, Delhi, 1963 *

Radhakrishnan : *Indian Philosophy*, Vol. II, George Allen & Unwin Ltd, London, 1971.

Raja, K.K. : *Indian Theories of Meaning*, University of Madras, The Adyar Library, Adyar, 1963.

Shastri, G.N. : *The Philosophy of Word and Meaning*, Sanskrit College, Calcutta, 1959

Sharma, M.M. : *The Dhvani Theory in Sanskrit Poetics*, CSS, Benares, 1968 *

.... : On Some Discrepancies in the Sanskrit works of Bhattanarasimha, *The Journal of the Assam Research Society*, Gauhati, 1968 *

Sinha, Baldev Dr. : *Padarthatattvasamiksa*, Kuruksetra Visvavidyalaya Kuruksetra, 1969

Winternitz, M. : *A History of Indian Literature*, Munshiram Manoharlal, New Delhi 1972

Swami Madhavananda : *Bhasaparicheda with Siddhantamuktavali*, translated into English with Introduction by Dr. Satkari Mookerjee, Advaita Ashrama, Calcutta, 1977 *

* books consulted but not mentioned in the body of the work.

INDEX